NEW DIRECTIONS

Spring 2008

CORAL BRACHO

FIREFLY UNDER THE TONGUE. Sel. Poems. Tr. Gander. "Her work has altered the landscape of Mexican poetry" —*Poetry.* $16.95 pbk. original

HORACIO CASTELLANOS MOYA

SENSELESSNESS. Tr. Silver. A powerful thriller set in Latin America. "[He] makes the reader tremble" —Bolaño. $15.95 pbk. orig.

LAWRENCE FERLINGHETTI

A CONEY ISLAND OF THE MIND. Special 50th Anniversary Edition with a newly recorded CD of the author reading from his work. $23.95 cl.

TAKASHI HIRAIDE

FOR THE FIGHTING SPIRIT OF THE WALNUT. Tr. Nakayasu. A dizzying supercharged collection of lyrical poetry. *Bilingual.* $17.95 pbk. orig.

B.S. JOHNSON

THE UNFORTUNATES. Intro. J. Coe. An experimental unbound novel to read in any order. "Brilliant" —*New Statesman.* $24.95 boxed

VLADIMIR NABOKOV

THE REAL LIFE OF SEBASTIAN KNIGHT. *NEW* intro. by Pulitzer Prize winner Michael Dirda. "Brilliantly real" —*NYTimes Bk. Rev.* $12.95 pbk.

MICHAEL PALMER

ACTIVE BOUNDARIES. Sel. Essays and Talks. A poet's prosebook that spans forty years of the award-winning poet's life. $17.95 pbk. orig.

KENNETH PATCHEN

Two editions of Patchen's outlandish, fabulous, hip picture-poems. WE MEET. Preface Devendra Banhart. $17.95 pbk. orig. THE WALKING AWAY WORLD. Preface Jim Woodring. Picture-poems. $19.95 pbk. orig.

TENNESSEE WILLIAMS

A HOUSE NOT MEANT TO STAND. A Gothic Comedy. Foreword Mosher. Intro. Keith. $14.95 pbk. orig. THE TRAVELING COMPANION & OTHER PLAYS. Short & experimental. Intro. Saddik. $17.95pbk. orig.

Titles *NEW* in Paperback

Roberto Bolaño, AMULET. Tr. Andrews. Novel. "Extraordinarily beautiful" —*Francine Prose, NYT Bk. Rev.* $14.95 pbk. • **José Camilo Cela (NOBEL PRIZE WINNER), BOXWOOD.** Tr. Haugaard. Novel. "Unforgettable" — *Washington Post.* $14.95 pbk. • **Julio Cortázar, FINAL EXAM.** Novel. Tr. MacAdam."Anyone who doesn't read Cortázar is doomed" —Neruda. $14.95 pbk. • **Robert Creeley, IF I WERE WRITING THIS.** Poetry. "Powerful"—*Philadelphia Inquirer* $14.95 pbk. • **Felisberto Hernández, LANDS OF MEMORY.** Tr. Allen. "Wonderful" —*NYT Bk. Rev.* $14.95 pbk.• **Javier Marías, YOUR FACE TOMORROW.** *Vol. Two: Dance and Dream.* Literary spy novel. "A maelstrom of literary pleasure" —Lytal, *NY Sun.* $15.95 pbk. • **Octavio Paz & Marie José Paz, FIGURES & FIGURA-TIONS.** Poetry & 12 full color illus. $17.95 pbk. • **René Philoctète, MAS-SACRE RIVER.** Preface Edwidge Danticat. Intro. Lyonel Trouillot. Haitian novel. $13.95 pbk. • **Luis Fernando Verissimo, THE CLUB OF ANGELS.** Tr. Costa. Mystery. "Wickedly satirical" —*Texas Observer.* $12.95 pbk.

NEW DIRECTIONS, 80 8th Ave., NYC 10011
Send for free complete catalog or visit: **www.ndpublishing.com**

COMING UP IN THE FALL

Conjunctions:51
THE DEATH ISSUE
Guest-edited by David Shields

As Cormac McCarthy wrote, "Death is the major issue in the world. For you, for me, for all of us. It just is. To not be able to talk about it is very odd." Death, indeed, is the one aspect of life everyone faces, so in many ways it is the single most important shared fate of being alive.

For our fall issue, *Conjunctions* editor Bradford Morrow invites award-winning writer David Shields to gather work from a diverse cross section of contemporary authors to address the theme of death in its many aspects—from philosophy to consciousness to fear, doom, irony, and even humor. *The Death Issue* will feature innovative essays and meditations ranging from the profound to the jocular by many important writers including Dave Eggers, Tom Robbins, Joyce Carol Oates, Dr. Pauline W. Chen, David Gates, Robin Hemley, Albert Goldbarth, Joe Wenderoth, Daphne Merkin, Dr. Lauren Slater, Greg Bottoms, Mark Doty, Susan Daitch, John D'Agata, Richard Stern, Mary Ruefle, and Christopher Sorrentino, among many others. Guggenheim Fellow David Shields's books include *Dead Languages*, *Black Planet*, and, most recently, *The New York Times* best seller *The Thing About Life Is That One Day You'll Be Dead.*

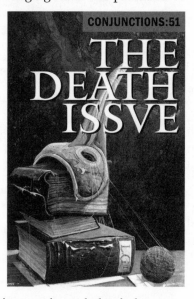

Subscriptions to *Conjunctions* are only $18 for more than eight hundred pages per year of contemporary and historical literature and art. Please send your check to *Conjunctions*, Bard College, Annandale-on-Hudson, NY 12504. Subscriptions can also be ordered by calling (845) 758-1539, or by sending an e-mail to Michael Bergstein at Conjunctions@bard.edu. For more information about current and past issues, please visit our Web site at www.Conjunctions.com.

CONJUNCTIONS

Bi-Annual Volumes of New Writing

Edited by
Bradford Morrow

Contributing Editors
Walter Abish
Chinua Achebe
John Ashbery
Martine Bellen
Mei-mei Berssenbrugge
Mary Caponegro
William H. Gass
Peter Gizzi
Jorie Graham
Robert Kelly
Ann Lauterbach
Norman Manea
Rick Moody
Howard Norman
Joan Retallack
Joanna Scott
Peter Straub
William Weaver
John Edgar Wideman

published by Bard College

CONJUNCTIONS is published in the Spring and Fall of each year by Bard College, Annandale-on-Hudson, NY 12504. This issue is made possible in part with the generous funding of the National Endowment for the Arts, and with public funds from the New York State Council on the Arts, a State Agency.

SUBSCRIPTIONS: Send subscription orders to CONJUNCTIONS, Bard College, Annandale-on-Hudson, NY 12504. Single year (two volumes): $18.00 for individuals; $40.00 for institutions and overseas. Two years (four volumes): $32.00 for individuals; $80.00 for institutions and overseas. Patron subscription (lifetime): $500.00. Overseas subscribers please make payment by International Money Order. For information about subscriptions, back issues, and advertising, call Michael Bergstein at (845) 758-1539 or fax (845) 758-2660.

Editorial communications should be sent to Bradford Morrow, *Conjunctions*, 21 East 10th Street, New York, NY 10003. Unsolicited manuscripts cannot be returned unless accompanied by a stamped, self-addressed envelope. Electronic and simultaneous submissions will not be considered.

Conjunctions is listed and indexed in the American Humanities Index.

Visit the *Conjunctions* Web site at www.conjunctions.com.

Cover design by Jerry Kelly, New York. Cover paintings by Richard Lethem. Front: *The Ring*, 1991, oil on linen, 60 x 50 inches; rear: *Hairpiece*, 2005, acrylic on canvas, 52 x 48 inches. Reproduced by kind permission of the artist.

Available through D.A.P./Distributed Art Publishers, Inc., 155 Sixth Avenue, New York, NY 10013. Telephone: (212) 627-1999. Fax: (212) 627-9484.

Printers: Edwards Brothers

Typesetter: Bill White, Typeworks

ISSN 0278-2324
ISBN 978-0-941964-66-1

Manufactured in the United States of America.

TABLE OF CONTENTS

FIFTY CONTEMPORARY WRITERS
Edited by Bradford Morrow

EDITOR'S NOTE

THE FIFTY WRITERS IN this fiftieth issue include those who go back to the very first volumes of *Conjunctions,* together with startlingly imaginative writers new to our pages. This is what we have tried to do over the course of the last quarter century—gather new voices together with those we have believed in over the years. When I founded *Conjunctions,* it was my hope to publish a few issues before folding. On days when naive hubris surfaced, I thought maybe we could even make it to ten. The history of the literary journal in this country and abroad, now and in the past, is one marked by idealism and, so often, the disappointment of good intentions flying headlong into the chasm of commerce and cynicism. Our project has been one of the fortunate survivors. We have done so in large measure because of several publishers, idealists themselves, who have taken a chance on supporting *Conjunctions.* I'll always be grateful to David Godine and Collier Books, who were our earliest proponents. But it is to Bard College that my deepest gratitude goes. Bard has stood by *Conjunctions* since our fifteenth issue in 1990, and continues to shine as a paragon of what a literary journal publisher should be. We have thrived under Bard's aegis, and many of us in the literary community are indebted to the college for its steadfast belief. Colleagues to whom I'm also grateful are legion, from our editorial assistants to our contributing editors, but without the help of Michael Bergstein, Pat Sims, Bill White, Brian Evenson, Micaela Morrissette, and J. W. McCormack, it wouldn't be possible to conceive, construct, and circulate *Conjunctions* every spring and fall. All of us who are devoted to this project celebrate our fiftieth foray as a milestone, yes, marking a moment in which to look back. As important, it is a fresh threshold, a beginning anew.

—Bradford Morrow
April 2008
New York City

Tradition & the Indivisible Talent
Peter Gizzi

If all the world says something
we think then we know something
don't we and then the blank screen
or memory again. You crazy.
No, you crazy. It's like this
but almost always
when time-lapsed words
and weather-swept flowering trees
move in empathetic wind.
I am rooted but alive.
I am flowering and dying
I am you, the wind says, the wind.

The embiggened afternoon
was just getting started
and to be adrift and stuck
can be a pleasant sensation
like loving abstraction
or a particular object's nimbus.
Pick one and look at it,
human or digital, vegetable,
mineral, alive or dying,
it's all atomic anyhow
much closer to the electron
part of yr being. Being,

it's a small word.
After all absence makes
the particles move faster.
The path tilted up to the right
and the angled view
so dramatic in boisterous sun.

When a thought's thingness begins
to move, to become unmoored,
and you ride the current
with your head and feel yourself
lift off like birdsong caught in the inner ear
even the curios seem animated
in their dusty shelves.
When the inanimate gestures back
with an imperceptible howdy
then the known sets in—
the song *is* alive. A scale
rendered invisibly opening onto once.
That part of tradition.

Birdsong and daybreak,
are they not the same at the root?
Twigs torn from brambles
nest and house this cooing thing.
Close your eyes. The notes
imprint their solar magic homing
a musical refrain built out
in a sculptural vortex and time
is this sculptural vortex—
the applause of rushes

sung into a larger sequence.
The sky. And now the word is fire,
fire in the heart, fire in the head.
Fire above and fire in bed—
seemingly the only element
to get gilded up in song.

How about dirt? I love you
like dirt. I miss you dirty mouth,
dirty smile, oh, and my dirt
is your dirt is nice also.
Closer to the ground, perhaps,
on the ground, that's real enough
and those goddamn spuggies
are fledged and it's spring
and the books in my shelves
in my head have all turned, nothing
but earth and peat and mold
and rich soft living manna
you can breathe, the must.

The must at the root of it all,
desire and wanting, must know.

The Port-au-Prince Marriage Special
Edwidge Danticat

"THEY TOLD ME, MADAME, that I am going to die."

I don't know if it was a dreadful gut feeling that had sent Méli-sande to an AIDS clinic, but she had gone to the one down near the bicentennial park downtown and had gotten her arms pricked and her blood drawn, only to receive a death sentence. She'd been cough-ing for some time, soft and discreet at first, then more and more thunderously, which had led to my removing my young son from her care. But only this morning when she got a fever and developed a level of sluggishness, which I instantly recognized from my own dead parents' battles with various types of respiratory illnesses, as pneumonia; only then did she finally decide to seek medical care.

She was sobbing now as she stood in the doorway of my bedroom, her body as flat and lean as one of the sides of the mahogany door frame. Leaning against the somber wood, she hiked up a flowered silk skirt to wipe the tears from her face. I immediately recognized that skirt as one I'd formerly owned. I had paid about seventy dollars for it at a sale at a fancy boutique in Miami—that is, when I was in college—before I married a classmate, a fellow Haitian, whose fam-ily owned a hotel in Port-au-Prince.

"Have you told your mother?" I asked her.

She was a child really, a girl, fifteen or sixteen at most. Her mother worked as a cook at our hotel. They had lied about her age so that Mélisande could get the job as one of our son's nannies, but given the fact that the mother had six younger children in the provinces, in Léogâne, I figured that Mélisande had plenty of experience for the job. I don't know why I trusted Mélisande. Perhaps it was because she was from my parents' hometown. Some of her relatives might have known some of mine. I didn't trust that many people with my son, but it was obvious as soon as I placed him in Mélisande's arms and she probed out of him the loudest laugh he'd ever tried that he loved her. Perhaps what drew him to her were the same things I found appealing about her: her elfin face, her reedy voice, her slightly hesitant walk, as though she was never really sure it was safe to

11

touch the ground.

Roland, my husband, had thought that Mélisande should be in school, but we hadn't forced it or insisted, as we could have, that she go. Or at least that she attend some type of vocational class in cooking or sewing when she wasn't looking after our son. Sometimes, during her free time, we saw her helping her mother cook or I saw her joke with one of the maids as she cleaned the guests' rooms with them. The deal she had with the maids was that whenever she helped them out whatever was left behind in the rooms would be split with her. Sometimes, aside from the tips, they'd find small pieces of gold or silver jewelry—mostly earrings and bracelets—that my husband would hold on to for a while and then after no one had called or come back to claim them would allow them to sell to the jeweler down the street, who'd pay them a few dollars just so he'd melt them again into other pieces to sell back to other hotel guests. This was a bit of extra money that she might not be making if she were in school, I sometimes told myself. But school might have helped with the future. And now she might not even have a future.

Shame on me, I think now. I'd kept hoping that she'd find a good night school or an adult literacy class, but I never did more than hope. I never even talked to her about it, never offered her the evenings off to do it. I was prepared, however, to let her go if she asked, but she never did. Now I would right this wrong. Somewhere between when she came to work for us (or maybe it was before) and now, she had contracted this disease. Perhaps if she had been in class, and had had homework and exams and yearly promotions, it wouldn't have happened.

"Come in and sit down."

I got up from my bed and walked over to the doorway. I was still in my pajamas, blue pajamas that she was supposed to inherit from me one day. My son was downstairs with my husband in his office. Guiding Mélisande toward my favorite rocking chair—carved for me by a local artisan—she felt extremely light to my touch, almost like paper, cloth, or air. Even though her feet were gliding across the wooden floor, I still felt as though I were carrying her. Her body slid down into the chair, where I immediately piled up a few cushions around her. I pulled an ottoman from a corner and pushed it against the back of her knees. Resting my arms on her shoulders, I felt some of the warmth of her lingering fever through her plain white T-shirt.

"What did the doctor say exactly?" I asked.

"He said," she replied, with her head and face buried in her hands, "that I have AIDS."

I was expecting anything but AIDS. Perhaps pneumonia or some bronchial infection for sure, but not AIDS. When she came home from the doctor, I was prepared to tell her not to wait so long the next time to get herself checked out. There were things that could kill people in the countryside that could easily be treated in Port-au-Prince. This is what I had prepared myself to tell her. I thought at most she would need antibiotics.

"Even with the AIDS," I was telling her, "now they have all these drugs. People live for years on them."

This provoked a new flurry of sobs from her. Her shoulders were bobbing up and down even as a sudden panic set in for me. My son. My Gabriel. My boy. She had touched every part of his body, had washed, had wiped, had kissed and cuddled him. Had they accidentally exchanged saliva, blood? I suddenly wanted to leave her there and run through the hotel and find my son. As usual, he had woken up earlier than all of us and Roland had taken him to his office. He was probably even now crawling under his father's desk, giggling, singing with delight.

Mélisande was still sobbing, her face soaking in the pool of tears gathering in her hands. We'd have to have Gabriel tested. And how would we deal with it? How would I live with myself—how would I live—if he had been infected?

I decided that I would simply let Mélisande cry. Let her get it all out of her system before we tried to come up with some type of solution. There were plenty of clinics, though of course not enough, which offered retroviral treatments. Some offered them for free. Others expected you to be a guinea pig in some questionable experiments. The clinic where Mélisande had been tested, however, offered counseling but no treatment.

Why hadn't I suspected all this sooner? I stepped away from her and staggered to the edge of the bed. I should have urged her to go to the doctor when she first began to lose weight. I should have stopped her flirtations with many of the hotel's male guests. The concierge, a former brothel bouncer, had told Roland that Mélisande liked to seek out some particular guests—the fat white ones—who she thought, because they seemed to have never missed a meal in their lives, were rich. It didn't seem to matter to her that most of the time she had no idea, until they grabbed some part of her body, what they were saying. The exchanges of "What?" and "Who?" were delightful games to her. By repeating some of the sometimes obscene things they said to her, she thought she was learning English or Spanish or whatever language they spoke. She would disappear for a few minutes with them into their rooms, but it never seemed to me long enough for her to have had sex with them, only to make a date, perhaps, for a later encounter, during her free time. Again, I didn't want to cause trouble for her. There were six young children counting on her and her mother for food, clothes, and school fees back in Léogâne. I thought she was protecting herself, *aux moins.*

She stopped crying for a few minutes because she seemed to run out of tears. And now she had the hiccups, which forced her head to jerk back and forth toward and away from me.

"We have to find you another place where you can get a second test performed," I told her.

She raised her head and glared at me, then she opened her eyes really wide as though a beehive or a bird's nest had suddenly appeared on top of my head.

"They told me there was no cure," she said.

Her eyes were extremely red, the bulging capillaries having taken over her eyeballs.

"Let me talk to Roland," I said. "We'll find you some care."

I had no idea where to find the best treatment in town, but I knew that Roland would. He knew something about nearly everything, especially things that involved worst-case-scenario types of problems. This was a hotelier's job, he sometimes reminded me. If someone shows up hungry, you feed them. If they want drink, you ply them. If they want to be left alone, you make yourself scarce. If they want company, you entertain. If they are lovelorn, you find them love. And if someone shows up sick, you find treatment quickly before that person expires on your watch.

My sigh of relief was as loud as hundred-mile winds. My son was negative. The same Canadian doctor who performed his HIV test was the one who'd help us get the retroviral drugs that Mélisande needed. The best thing, he told us, was a new one-pill treatment that many of his patients were opting for because it made compliance easier. Someone like Mélisande, he could already tell, was not going to be compliant. First of all, she was claiming that she'd never had sex and since she'd never injected herself with a needle or had a blood transfusion, all he could conclude was that she was in terrible denial.

"If you won't even own up to the possible ways that the disease might have entered your body," he'd told Mélisande as she sat across a desk from him, her eyelids fluttering between open and closed as she gazed past him at a back wall full of framed diplomas, "how can you hope to treat this disease aggressively?"

Once the doctor provided us with a month's worth of pills from his own private stash—at two American dollars a pill—Mélisande was a lot more compliant than any of us expected. I had told her to come and find me every morning so I could watch her take the pill as we ate breakfast together and she had done it for over two weeks now. Most of the time we ate something quickly on the patio outside my room. Other times we ate in the hotel dining room, with my son at our side. Mélisande was gaining weight, my old clothes fitting her a little better. She cried less and less too at breakfast, in part I think because she knew the staff was watching us. But what she never did again was touch my son, who reached his tubby little arms out to her, contorting his face into a grimace that would turn into wails, then tears, when she would simply ignore him or turn away.

I stopped bringing my son to breakfast with her after a while. It was too much for both of them. By the time Mélisande had to return to the doctor for another month's supply, I cancelled the breakfasts altogether and passed on the job of monitoring her compliance to her mother, who from the day she learned that Mélisande was sick never stopped calling her a *bouzen,* a whore, even as she stopped whatever she was doing every morning to make sure that her oldest child swallowed the pill and chased it down with at least a piece of bread. Some mornings I would watch this exchange between them from the side of the pool, where I took a daily swim with my son, or from the hibiscus garden where we sometimes played. The mother was no taller than Mélisande herself, but was a strapping, muscular woman. I could almost see the veins popping out from the rolls on her dark neck as she continuously berated Mélisande, who'd try to put an end to their transaction by swallowing the pill quickly and rushing off.

"What are you going to do when Monsieur and Madame stop paying for your two-dollar pills?" the mother was shouting like a drill sergeant hazing a recruit. Her fear was palpable. Her daughter's survival now completely depended on Roland and me. If we suddenly decided to sell the hotel and move elsewhere, her child could die. What if the drug companies, who provided the doctor with the free supply that he unethically resold to us, suddenly stopped making the drug or no longer sent it to Haiti? What if that doctor took off as well? Suddenly in the chain that ran from the creation of the drug to our ability to afford it, if any part of it broke down, she could lose her daughter.

One morning, I heard her asking Mélisande as Mélisande was taking the pill, what if the white man starts keeping all of the pills for himself? What if Monsieur and Madame are killed in a horrible car accident?

"You will never have a healthy child," she told her another day. "You will never have a husband."

"You should talk to her," Roland said to me one morning after overhearing this too. "All illness involves state of mind as well as state of body. It can't be helpful for the poor girl to be treated that way."

I felt like a coward for not interfering sooner.

"Where do you want to be buried?" the mother said soon after. "You better start saving now if you want a fancy coffin."

In the Haiti of my time and place, death was always around some corner. In car accidents. Disease. Kidnappings. Unlike the rest of us, Mélisande's mother could not afford the conditional optimism this tiny little pill allowed. I could easily imagine myself in the mother's place. I'd probably have many of the same concerns and fears.

That morning, after Mélisande had gone off to breakfast, I asked to have a word with her mother, who, as soon as I closed my husband's office door behind us, began to cry.

"*Mèsi, mèsi,*" she sobbed, grabbing my hand. "Thank you for not throwing her out. Thank you for not letting her die."

"There are millions of people all over the world being kept alive in this way," I said, gently tugging my hands out of her grasp. "Besides, you're wasting precious time with your daughter, time that you could be spending with her just as you had before. You can help her the most by not cursing but loving her."

"Love her?" She frowned and her eyebrows nearly became one.

"Yes, love her," I said. "This is a precise concrete act that calls for more effort than you think you possess, but you must love her."

I knew what she was thinking. These silly half-assed outsiders, these diasporas with their mushy thinking, why does it all come back to love with them? Love the world. Love life. Love yourself. Love your children. Don't yell at them. Don't hit them. Don't give them away. Don't these diasporas know that there are many other ways to show love than to be constantly talking about it?

"Of course I love her," she said, spreading both her arms wide as if to prove it. "That's why I am so tough on her."

Now sitting on a cushioned bench near the office door, she looked unconvinced, but also ashamed, ashamed that I, on top of everything, now had reason to scold her, ashamed that she had no choice but to sit there and take it.

I too felt ashamed for having made her feel that way. Pressing both her hands down on her knees as if she'd suddenly realized how much they protruded from her body, of the things I'd said, what she responded to was what I did not say.

"I saw you," she said, "I saw you the day your mother drowned herself."

I moved from behind the desk and closer to her. Both our faces were soaked now the way Mélisande's had been the day she'd made her announcement to me. Sitting across from her, our protruding knees nearly touching, I said, "You did?"

"*Wi*," she said, "I was in the kitchen cooking when I heard your scream. I rushed out and saw her floating facedown in the pool. It was awful of her to come all the way from Miami to kill herself in your new husband's pool."

I'm still not sure, I wanted to tell her, that this was what happened. My mother had never been a good swimmer, neither in Miami nor Léogâne. She had only gone near streams and oceans and pools when my father was with her. When he died, she had no one to protect her near water.

"I saw you with her body in your arms," she continued, her eyes fixed rather than on my face or eyes but on her own worn-out sandals, on her own feet, on the floor. "When I heard you scream I thought the sky would open up and it would start to rain because I thought even God would have no choice but to cry with you."

It did rain that evening, I reminded her, a torrential rain that caused mudslides that pulled dozens of houses from the hillside shantytowns into trash-strewn ravines all over the capital. God had shown, I reminded her, that his tears only brought further losses. Still I hadn't been able to feel sad for the others. I felt no solidarity with the mudslide victims, the mothers and fathers and babies whose bodies were engorged by the red earth like my mother's had been by the meticulously maintained pool water. Why should I be the only one grieving, I had thought. Why should my mother be the only one to die? I had not felt bad for even one other person's loss since, I realized. Until I'd learned about her daughter. I didn't want Mélisande to die, I told her. I didn't want her to cry to the heavens for her daughter the way I had for my mother. I didn't want the sky to open and carry others away.

I knew that even after our talk there would be no mawkish mother and daughter embrace between her and Mélisande. There would be no apologies.

The next morning, I watched from my patio where my son was bobbing up and down on a playpen next to me and saw her silently hand Mélisande a glass of water.

"Whatever did you tell her?" Roland asked as we had breakfast at the same table that Mélisande and I had occupied for a few weeks.

"You know . . . ," I said, which he knew meant that I didn't want to talk about it.

At the end of the month, just when Mélisande needed another refill of the drugs, her doctor mysteriously left Haiti and moved back to Montreal. As Mélisande's supply dwindled to nearly nothing, Roland called everyone he knew but couldn't track the doctor down. Mélisande had no choice but to start seeing another doctor, a Haitian female one this time, who ordered a new series of tests, dredging up the distressing diagnosis, the counting of T cells, which I could tell, when Mélisande came back with now several bottles of pills, had taken away whatever illusion she might have harbored that she was getting well. The new regimen did not agree with her. She had stomachaches, diarrhea, and nausea, and began spending her days in bed. It would take time for her body to get used to the new drugs, the new doctor said. Roland made a few more calls and we found Mélisande yet another doctor to confirm that she was indeed getting the right treatment.

She wanted the one-pill treatment back, Mélisande told the third doctor as he examined her on the small cot in the bedroom of one of the hotel's workers' bungalows, a small wallpapered room that she shared with her mother. Fishing out one of the old prescription bottles from one of my old purses, she handed it to the doctor, a tall Cuban man who spoke Creole with only a slight Spanish accent.

"Ay!" the Cuban said when he noticed the Canadian doctor's name.

"What's wrong?" I asked from where I was standing by the door.

It turned out, the Cuban explained, that what Mélisande had first gotten was a placebo. It was more or less an aspirin. It had not been doing anything for her at all. The doctor who had prescribed and sold the first pills to us had suddenly fled Haiti because he'd been dis-covered selling those useless pills to unsuspecting patients all over town.

"Your treatment really begins now," the Cuban told Mélisande as her tiny body sank deeper under the thin cotton sheets on the bed.

"You must be vigilant about it," he added.

I saw Mélisande's eyes sink along with her body. She had lost pre-cious time, the Cuban was telling her. The disease, which was al-ready advanced in her, had probably progressed further.

"She could have actually died," he told me as I walked out of Mélisande's room. She turned her face away from us, burying it in her pillow while I pulled the door behind me.

What would it have cost me to have actually trusted less? This was what I would have done for my son. I would have questioned, made deals, insisted, yelled.

"We've gone way beyond the call of duty," Roland said when I met him for lunch under a sun umbrella by the pool.

"How? By getting her a quack?"

"We tried to give her a chance," he said. "We tried to do everything we could have done for our own child."

Our own child could have left the country. If a quack had inten-tionally fed our child a placebo instead of treating her, Roland him-self would have hired the hit man.

That afternoon, Mélisande's mother served us a late lunch on one of the terraces while our son napped. She was sweating in her tight gray cotton uniform and dirty white cooking apron. Her head was wrapped in a black scarf and though this was something she wore every day, it looked like mourning garb.

"We're sorry," Roland told her. "But she was probably sick before she came to work with us. Maybe someone was with her when she was young, touched her, abused her."

The horrible possibilities were endless.

She laid the food down quickly—grilled lobster and rice with pigeon peas—turned her back to us without saying anything, and walked away. In her mind, we were possibly just as bad as the quack. Had we not fed Mélisande the hope of that pill, perhaps she might have taken her home to a *bòkò* or a leaf doctor, someone who might have really tried to help her. If intention counted, her peo-ple might have better intentions than ours. They might have really wanted her cured.

Perhaps I should apologize to her too, I thought. Tell her that we tried, were doing the best we could.

I got up from my seat and tried to follow her, but Roland grabbed my hand and pulled me down again.

"Leave it alone," he said, sounding now truly angry, but not at me or at her, but rather for us, for her.

After lunch, I went back to the bungalow to see Mélisande again. She was lying in bed in a deep, sound sleep and had not even stirred when I walked in the room. Her thin body, now stripped of both the thin sheet and the nightgown she'd been wearing, naked except for a matching set of polka-dotted bra and panties, would eventually adjust to the new cocktail, the Cuban doctor had told me. And slowly she would once again rejoin our lives at the hotel.

Watching her sleep so quietly, without even the hint of a snore, I thought what will she possessed. Her symptoms had completely disappeared while she was taking that ineffectual pill. It had seemed to help her once she'd believed it could.

There was something different about her face now, though. She no longer seemed young. Perhaps it was because of her sudden weight gains and losses, but she now appeared to have wrinkles, some between her eyebrows, some around her mouth, a few under her eyes.

A few days later, her body did finally adjust to the cocktail and Mélisande got out of bed again. I noticed her one morning sitting by the pool staring into the water, then up at the sky while my son and I ate breakfast on my patio. She reached into her pocket and pulled out something that she traced against the lifelines in her palm, then made a fist around it before placing it in her pocket again. She did this a couple of times, pulled the thing out of her pocket, then looked down at it, then put it back. At some point, I noticed it was something shiny, a small ring, with some kind of stone that, though minute, was catching the light more than the rest of the ring.

I took my son and walked down to the pool to go see her. She was startled to see us. Her eyes had been closed and I had to call out her name to let her know we were there.

"How are you?" I asked, while Gabriel and I slid into the lounge chair next to hers.

Sitting there, I couldn't help but think of my mother, so lost after my father died. They'd married when she was nineteen and, aside from me, he had been, whatever that meant now, her whole life. When I finished school, and retraced my steps back to our beginning, to Haiti, she had dutifully followed, then at the first opportunity had killed herself. Her death had been the last in a series of goodbyes. In many ways, she and I had been like Mélisande and her mother, without the friction, without the harsh words, without any words at all. For so long, before she died, we had already been separated by water.

My son reached out for her, but she pulled her hand away from him and shoved it back into her pocket.

"What's that you have there?" I asked.

She must have been wondering how long I had been looking at her, watching her pull this thing in and out of her pocket. Slowly she reached in deeper into her pocket and out came the tiny ring once more. The gold was as thin as a rope of angel hair pasta, but it had, just as I'd suspected, a small glass stone that was still capturing most of the light.

Drawn by the glint of the stone, my son reached for the ring, but Mélisande yanked her hand away once more to protect it.

"Did one of the guests leave that behind?" I asked her.

She shook her head no.

"Did someone give it to you? A man?"

She nodded.

"Did he give it to you before you were sick?"

Another nod.

"Do you think this is the person who made you sick?"

"Maybe," she answered softly, two lines of tears running down her face.

"He said he was going to marry you?"

He did, then he left and never came back.

The ring was worthless, of course, one of the *krizokal,* hollowed fake gold ones made by the corner jeweler down the street. I had seen a bunch of them on the hands of young girls who came to the hotel for drinks and sexual exploits with many of the foreign male guests. That type of ring even had a name. It was called the Port-au-Prince marriage special.

"Mélisande," I began, trying to think of the best way to tell her something everyone already knew. That ring was like the pills she'd been taking at first. There was no romance or magic in it.

"*Mwen konnen,*" she said. "I know," signaling with a wave of one bony ringless hand that she no longer wanted to talk about it.

21

On Not Growing Up
Ben Marcus

—HOW LONG HAVE YOU been a child?

—Seventy-one years.

—Who did you work with?

—Meyerowitz for the first phase: colic, teething, walking, talking. He taught me how to produce false prodigy markers and developmental reversals, to test the power in the room without speaking. I was encouraged to look beyond the tantrum and drastic mood migrations that depended on the environment, and if you know my work you have an idea what resulted. The rest is a hodgepodge, but I don't advocate linear apprenticeships. A stint in the Bonn Residency. Fellowships at the Cleveland Place, then later a *stage* at Quebec Center. I entered that Appalachian Trail retreat in 1974, before Krenov revised it, but had to get helicoptered out. Probably my first infant crisis, before I knew to deliberately court interference. The debt to Meyerowitz is huge, obviously, if just for the innocence training. Probably I should have laid off after that, because now it's all about unlearning.

—Unlearning as Kugler practices it? That radical?

—I skip the hostility to animals. I skip the forced submersion and the chelation flush. That's proven to be a dead end. But Kugler is a walking contradiction in that respect, isn't he? He keeps a horse barn. He does twilight childishness, and now he's suddenly opposing the Phoenix baby-talk crowd, who I think are not as threatening as he makes out.

—They're not registered.

—True, but they're pro-family, and I still believe, when I'm out in the field, in a pro-parent regimen, in supporting those with maturity fixations.

—Which is admittedly contradictory, isn't it, given how many adult families you've worked with, and how many of them have ultimately disbanded?

—The term "adult" is problematic, I think, and it's too easy to say that my childwork is directly divisive to Matures, particularly Rigid or Bolted Matures. I may help accelerate a latent behavior, I may enable conflict vectors along the lines of the Michiganers, who fasted as a form of warfare, and I feign indifference to familial tension, but I think that success itself has been fetishized, and a certain nostalgia for growth has spoiled our thinking. I can be pro-family without coddling actual families. I can support familial fear-based clustering even if it involves admitting that we are most likely associated with the wrong cluster. There is that famous German phrase, which I can't remember exactly, that describes a certain way to hold a gun to someone's head. The literal meaning of the phrase is that you love that person deeply, just not at the moment. I argue for a love that functions perfectly in theory.

—But you have destroyed an unprecedented number of families.

—I don't destroy anything. I do question the term limits of parents, and I'm not the first to promote child-driven power reversals. We have to remember just how much thinking Benner-Louis did on this subject, and how resonant her geological metaphors were. If prodding an object for flaws causes a momentarily resolved family to unravel, or, as Benner-Louis would have it, dissolve, then what you're saying is that we should stay silent and paralyzed, the classic demand placed upon children. It is not my problem that families are hurt when we notice how they have hardened into stone, how they stoke each other's failure instinct, and if Matures are not powerful enough to admit a stagnation, they are welcome to blame me, but that's fairly evasive. I give choices to children, and I supply functional tunnels to those who have yet to become children. This is mapping as Parsons envisioned it: you don't map a route that has been spoiled by the progress of others. Adulthood looks like an exhaustion farm. Who would knowingly purchase a ticket to that? In my work, I re-child certain people who have presumed a premature adulthood, and, most importantly, I question adulthood as a retreat from the power of infancy. I'm a supplier.

—Which brings us to Maryland.

—My tantrum work is still being fine-tuned, but you could reference an entire series of Chesapeake catastrophes that might seem now like open wounds, even as our daily perspective, as time passes and fewer of us can recall the perished, will refresh itself to show just how essential, for instance, something like the Lake Maneuver was. Assertive Submersion may not be pleasant, in the lived sense, but if the values of a social group are being collectively ignored, forcing Matures, through panic, to relocate their child-state, is an adequate way to broadcast a set of perspectives and beliefs that have been conveniently forgotten. Behaviors are advertised and promoted all the time. Why should we be penalized for making our case so powerfully that people nearly die from the overwhelming logic of it?

—But can you sketch for me a picture of your ethics?

—I think that fixed moral boundaries are harmful, even if they provide momentary comfort and save lives. I think our ethical duty is to eliminate the behavioral corsets that are cinched over children just as their explosive energy is at its most threatening. Is a tantrum disruptive or does it point to an emotional tunnel we're afraid of entering? The doctrines of the tantras involve meditation, mantras, ritual, and explosive behavior. We're talking about ancient ideas that are elementary and obvious to high schoolers. My ethics? I'd like to shed the strictures of adulthood and make maturity an optional result of a freely lived human life, not the necessary path to power and success, lorded over by depressed, overweight, unimaginative corpses. The twenty most central mantras have their roots in baby talk. No one is even disputing this anymore. A syntax comprising these mantras, which should not be confused with NASA's failed language, can marshal the force of an entire infant society, but—and this is key—this syntax is not capable of instructional phrasings, so nothing can be taught, which keeps maturity and its death mask perfectly at bay.

—Has it been necessary to denounce such important figures in child development as Dr. Spock? Where has that adversarial approach benefited your child program?

—Dr. Spock reviewed existing children, but he didn't promote new ones. His art was to survey the past and insure a predictable persona outcome. He devised solutions for the escape of childhood, very good ones, I might add. I think that some of his approaches are worth modifying, if only in service of a kind of dark science. We can bottle that kind of curatorial approach to behavior, but it won't save anyone. These were tonics for escape, and they should have been marketed that way all along. I've simply asked for honesty. Spock's entire approach presents infancy as a problem to be managed, to be grown out of, and I'm not alone in finding this condescending. Physical growth is (mostly) a necessity (although we'll soon see about that), but emotional growth is something Matures crave strictly for others. Rarely is it satisfying to the person who accomplishes it. There's a missionary zeal around this dirty word, development, and it's exerted on otherwise defenseless people. A spell has been cast on all of us, and it leads to a spectacularly depressing failure we have come to call "adulthood." The artwork of children is so often discarded because Matures cannot accept, let alone decipher, the chaos and disorder children depict after only briefly gazing at the crushed and gargantuan figures that supposedly serve them. Children's art perfectly captures the sloppy, disordered, ugly world that awaits them if they choose the path of maturity.

—Many people would disagree with that.

—And I bet they're old and "adult" and reasonable, accumulating comprehension as if it were food. It's a laughable mistake, this certainty compulsion. Your entire line of questioning revolves around the notion that if not everyone agrees with me there must be something wrong with my ideas. This is a classic rhetorical tactic—I think it's called the Consensus Chalice—for a Mature. *The Fear of the Infant* wasn't just a successful film; it depicted a real aversion to kinds of discoveries that might be possible if Matures didn't operate with such staggering fear. Baby talk has tremendous potential, despite its obvious dangers and its near total incomprehensibility. The only reason you don't embrace it is your abject terror.

—What's next for you?

—Meyerowitz, for all of his accomplishments, died as an adult, and it has shamed his entire family. His legacy, in the end, means nothing, because he left this world knowing and thinking too much, headed down the wrong road, with a body that weighed as much as six children. He attacked his own theories, in fear of the complexities and richness of innocence, and now he's dead. I want to die as I am, as a child, looking out at a world that I can admit is too complex to know and far too terrible to join. I want to die. And I want to do it as a child: barely able to walk, careening through the fog of objects and people I can never know, wearing nothing at all but the tattered onesie my first mother bought me. This is my goal.

The Beating
Joyce Carol Oates

STILL ALIVE! FROM THE doorway of the intensive care unit I can see my father in his bed swaddled in white like a comatose infant, and he is still alive.

So long I've been away. So long I've traveled, and so far.

Yet nothing seems to have changed in my absence. My mother and two other visitors are standing beside my father's bed, their backs to me. From their demeanor you can deduce that my father is still "unresponsive" after the morning's surgery to reduce swelling in his brain; he is unmoving except in random twitches and shudders; he is breathing—arduously, noisily—by way of a machine; his every heartbeat is being monitored on a screen above his bed; on this screen as on a TV screen an erratic scribble is being written, accompanied by an electronic beeping that reminds me of the cheeping of baby chicks. Grotesquely my father's wounded head has been swathed in white gauze exposing a single bruised eye like a peephole someone has cruelly defaced so you can't see in.

Earlier that day my mother had asked me to leave, there wasn't room for me at my father's bedside. Descending then three floors to the first floor of Sparta Memorial Hospital where there was a small visitors' lounge adjacent to a small cafeteria beneath dim-flickering fluorescent lights. Such a depressing place! Such chill, such smells! This was July 1959. That long ago, you have to smile—I don't blame you, I would smile in your place—to think that people like us took ourselves so seriously. You think *But you're all going to die, why does it matter exactly when?* Yet this was the time, and this was the place, when my father was still alive.

Madelyn! heard the news about your father, what a terrible thing, what a shock how is he?

Madelyn! tell us all you can remember, all that you must have seen?

Hadn't changed my clothes since my father had been brought to the hospital two and a half days before. Slept in the clothes I'd been wearing at the time of the beating, Rangers T-shirt, khaki shorts,

27

sneakers without socks, we'd been visiting my grandmother earlier that afternoon and we'd dropped by the Sparta Blues Festival on the river on our way home, and after that, a detour, as my father called it, to his office on East Capitol Street, and now my clothes were rumpled and smelly for I'd slept in them sprawled on top of my bed without the energy to undress and anxious to be prepared should someone from the hospital call in the night, if my mother came to wake me *Hurry! get up! they want us at the hospital, your father may be dying.* This terrible call had not yet come and yet every breath I drew was a preparation for it, I was fourteen years old and found myself in one of those cruel fairy tales in which a daughter must perform certain rituals and tests without question, that her father will be allowed to live. And when we were at my father's bedside in the chill of the ICU where your fingernails turned blue without your noticing, and you could fall asleep on your feet like a zombie, and begin to crumple to the floor without your noticing, it could not happen that the terrible call would come waking us from our exhausted sleep for already we were awake and we were at the hospital. Softly my mother spoke my father's name: *Harvey? Harvey? I love you.* And in an urgent undertone I said: *Daddy? Daddy? It's Madelyn.* For to say *I love you* was not possible. For so desperately I loved my father, to have spoken such words *I love you* was not possible. I could not have explained why, there were no words to explain why. Seeing me you'd have thought *A sulky girl, when she should be a good girl.* My mother who was ordinarily very alert to my moods and to my "personal appearance" hadn't seemed to notice that I'd been sleeping in my clothes and smelled of my body for having washed only my sticky hands and rubbed a washcloth over my feverish face, my red-rimmed pig eyes. (Those pig eyes in the mirror, I could not bear to see. Brimming with hot-guilt tears that spilled and burned like acid.) In the past two and a half days I hadn't been able to sit down at any table to eat and had not been able to eat much as a consequence but I made certain that I brushed my teeth until my gums bled for I could not bear the sensation of anything between my teeth.

Who was it? they'd asked. *Who did this to your father?*

Try to remember if you saw. Must've seen.

Hospital rules for ICU differed from rules for the rest of the hospital: no more than three visitors at a time were allowed at a patient's bedside. And so when my father's older brother and his wife came to see my father, my mother asked me to leave. Of course this was a reasonable request. Of course I was not angry at my mother, or my relatives. Yet quickly I walked away, avoiding the friendly smiles of the ICU nurses who'd come to recognize me and my family *Don't look at me! Please don't smile at me! You don't know me! Leave me alone.* I took the stairs down to the foyer, not the elevator. I dreaded being trapped inside an elevator with strangers, still more I dreaded encountering someone who recognized me as Harvey Fleet's daughter who would take my hand in sympathy or hug me, and I would push rudely away, my face would break and turn ugly with tears glistening like snot.

How small the Sparta Hospital was, in 1959! Yet no one then seemed to have known.

Such silly people. It's easy to laugh at us.

The very air exuded a spent, sepia cast as if faded by time like an old Polaroid photograph. Though the hospital was air-conditioned, cold as a refrigerator, yet there was a just-perceptible odor of stale urine, fecal matter, rot beneath the sharper odor of disinfectant. Visitors to the hospital and hospital staff appeared stiff and clumsy as mannequin figures in a painting by Edward Hopper. Voices were overly shrill and emphatic as TV voices and if there was laughter it was not convincing laughter but reminded me of canned TV laughter. Of course I was one of those figures myself, a solitary girl of fourteen in rumpled clothes sitting at a table, at the edge of the cafeteria. My eyes stung with fatigue, my head ached, and there was a sour, dark taste at the back of my mouth. Badly I did not want to be in this place but had nowhere else to go, for if I left the hospital, and went home, my father might die, and I would not be at his bedside. I'd brought a library book with me but couldn't concentrate, how insubstantial were printed words, passages of type in a book of dog-eared pages, I could think only of my father trapped in his hospital bed in the intensive care unit, unconscious, made to breathe in anguished gasps by a machine, his ravaged head and face swathed in white gauze and a single bruised and bloodshot eye exposed. . . . And I thought of how I had found him lying on the floor of his office on East Capitol Street. Thinking at first that he had lost his balance somehow and fallen, struck his head on the sharp edge of the desk, for he was bleeding from a head wound, and he was bleeding from injuries to his face. He was whimpering and moaning through clenched teeth. The door to my father's office had been left open and so I stood in the doorway for an astonished moment uncertain what it was I was seeing. Before I had time to be frightened the thought came to me *Daddy would not want me to see him like this. He would not want anyone to see him like this.*

I began to see how memory pools might accumulate in such places as this cafeteria and in waiting rooms through the hospital. In corners, in the shadows. Beneath tables like mine. These memory pools made the worn tile floor damp, sticky, discolored as by mildew. And maybe there were actual tears, soaked into the floor. I felt a shiver of dread: you could not walk anywhere in such a place without the anguished memories of strangers sticking to your shoes. Their dread of what was to come in their lives, what ruptures, what unspeakable losses. Early that morning my father had undergone emergency surgery to reduce pressure on his brain, into which burst blood vessels had been bleeding since he'd suffered "blunt force trauma" to the head. Yet my father was but one of how many thousands of patients who'd been hospitalized at Sparta Memorial Hospital over the years. . . . One day with precise scientific instruments certain of these memories might be exhumed, I thought. Like organic matter identified from the stains of long ago. And so there might be a future time when these thoughts that so tormented me now would be calmly recalled; when all this, in which I was trapped—the hospital, the visitors' lounge, the slow-ticking afternoon in July 1959—would be past.

He lived! He did live, he survived.

He died. "Passed away." There was nothing to be done.

Yet at this time, I was safe from such knowledge. At this time, my father, Harvey Fleet, was still alive.

"Madelyn?"

Vaguely I had been aware of someone approaching my table, coming up behind me, as frequently individuals were making their way past in this crowded space, and I had been aware of someone pausing, looming over me. I looked up in expectation of seeing one of my male relatives but instead I saw a man whom I didn't recognize at first, with a two days' growth of beard on his jaws, amber-tinted sunglasses, and thick disheveled graying hair that seemed to rise like a geyser at the crown of his head. "Madelyn Fleet. It is you." The surprise was that this man was my seventh-grade math teacher, Mr. Carmichael, whom I had not seen in more than two years and then only in our school building. The way in which Mr. Carmichael had intoned *Madelyn Fleet* was his teacherly teasing way, which I

30

remembered. I had to remember too, with a quick stab of emotion, that I'd been in love with Mr. Carmichael, in secret, when I was twelve years old.

Now I was fourteen, and much changed. In my former teacher's eyes this change was being registered.

Smiling down at me, Mr. Carmichael was smoking a cigarette for in 1959 it was not forbidden to smoke cigarettes in a hospital, even in most hospital rooms. How strange it was to see my seventh-grade math teacher unshaven as none of his students had ever seen him, and his hair that had always been trimmed short now grown long, curling languidly behind his ears, and threaded with silvery gray wires. It was a warmly humid midsummer and so Mr. Carmichael had rolled up his shirtsleeves to his elbows; the cuffs hung free, at a rakish angle. The front of Mr. Carmichael's shirt was damp with perspiration and looked as if it hadn't been changed in days. From such signs I understood that Mr. Carmichael too was an anxious visitor to Sparta Memorial Hospital, yet even in his state of distraction and dread he was smiling at me, and his eyes behind the tinted lenses of his glasses were alert and intense in a way I did not remember from when I'd been his student. When he inquired what I was reading I had no choice but to show him the cover of the book, which was a novel by H. G. Wells that elicited from Mr. Carmichael a remark meant to be clever and knowing, for at our school Mr. Carmichael—whose first name we giggled to see was Luther—had a reputation for being clever and knowing if also, at times, sarcastic, sardonic, and inscrutable; a teacher who graded harshly, at times; for which reason, while some girl students admired Mr. Carmichael and strove to please him, most of our classmates were uncomfortable in his classes, and disliked him. Even boys who laughed at Mr. Carmichael's jokes did not wholly trust him, for he could turn on you, if you were not cautious. There were rumors about Mr. Carmichael being complained of by the parents of certain students and perhaps by certain of his fellow teachers and vaguely last year I'd heard that Mr. Carmichael no longer taught at the school. . . . As if he could hear my thoughts and wished to commandeer them, Mr. Carmichael leaned over me, saying, in a lowered voice, that he thought he'd recognized me as I crossed the lobby and came here to sit, he'd thought it might be me—"Or some older sister of little Madelyn Fleet"—but he wasn't sure that he could trust his eyes—"You've gotten taller, Madelyn. And you carry yourself—differently." In embarrassed confusion I laughed, leaning away from him; my face throbbed with

31

blood; I was overwhelmed by such attention, and did not know how to reply. There was nowhere to look except at Mr. Carmichael's flushed and roughened face, and his eyes so warmly intent upon me beyond the smudged lenses of his sunglasses. Mr. Carmichael's breath smelled of—was it whiskey?—a sweetish-sour odor with which I was long familiar, for all my male relatives drank whiskey at times, and certainly my father drank whiskey. It had not been the case during my year of seventh-grade math that Mr. Carmichael had singled me out for any particular attention, or praise; I could not have claimed that Mr. Carmichael had ever really looked at me as an individual; though I'd been one of five or six reliable students who'd usually received high grades, I hadn't been an outstanding math student, only a doggedly diligent good-girl student. Nor had I been one of the popular and flirtatious girls in our class who'd had no trouble attracting Mr. Carmichael's attention. Yet now he was asking, "Why are you here in this depressing place, Madelyn? I hope it isn't a family emergency. . . ." He did not seem to be teasing but spoke sincerely, with sympathy; lightly his hand rested on my shoulder, to comfort. I was frightened now for such sympathy left me weak, defenseless; I did not want to cry; in my bedroom I'd cried until my eyes were reddened and swollen like blisters but I had not cried in front of anyone except my mother. It would be held against Harvey Fleet's daughter that she was "cold"—"snotty"—stiffening in her relatives' embraces and shrinking from their kisses with a look of disdain. Yet how could I bring myself to say to Mr. Carmichael, *My father is upstairs in the intensive care unit, he had surgery this morning to reduce swelling in his brain, he has not regained consciousness after a terrible beating. . . .* Quickly I told Mr. Carmichael that my mother had come to see a friend in the hospital who'd had minor surgery and I'd been with them for a while then became restless, couldn't breathe, came downstairs to read my novel but couldn't concentrate, and now I was thinking of going home. (For suddenly it came to me; I could leave this hateful place, I could go home without my mother.) Mr. Carmichael said he'd had enough of the hospital too. More than enough. He'd drive me home, Mr. Carmichael said now, nudging my ponytail, and I laughed, saying thank you but I could take a city bus, or I could walk. (In the heat, the three-mile walk would be punishing. My mother would be astonished and would not know if she should be apologetic or disgusted with me.) Mr. Carmichael squinted down at me through his sunglasses, saying in his brisk-bemused-teacher voice that his car was out back: "C'mon, Madelyn. I'll drive you home."

How was it possible to say *no?*

"This is a little detour, kid. Our secret."

It was dusk. We were late returning home. Yet we were driving east along the river, back toward Sparta. If we'd been headed home, as we were expected, my father would have been driving us west. The air at dusk was humid and porous as gauze and through the Cadillac's lowered windows warm air rushed that smelled of something overripe like rotted fruit and beneath, a fainter, sour smell of rotted fish.

It was a festive time of evening! I was very happy. On the river there were ghostly white sailboats and power-driven boats that glittered with lights against the darkening, choppy water and on shore, in the park where the blues festival was being held, there were steadier lights like flames.

A detour. Our secret. These mysterious pronouncements of my father's were usually made in a playful voice that carried an unmistakable warning: do as I say, without acknowledging that I have said it.

By these words I was given to understand that my father didn't want my mother to know we'd gone back into the city. I liked it that there were such understandings between my father and me, which excluded my mother.

On the evening of the beating that was never to be explained, for which no "assailant" or "assailants" would ever be charged, my father was distracted and appeared to be in a hurry. We'd left the blues festival abruptly for he'd said that we had to get home and now, not ten minutes later, he was headed for downtown Sparta and his office on East Capitol Street. Gripped between his legs was a bottle of ale he'd brought with him from the festival. The dashboard of the car gleamed and glittered with so many dials, switches, controls you'd have thought you were in the cockpit of a fighter plane.

The car was my father's newest: a showy 1959 cream-colored Cadillac Eldorado with Spanish red leather interior, a chrome grille like shark's teeth, swooping tail fins and flaring taillights. A massive vehicle twenty feet in length, like a yacht it glided past ordinary traffic seemingly without effort. Within the family it was believed that Harvey Fleet had acquired this car from one of his gambler friends in Sparta in need of quick cash but my father typically offered no explanations, he'd only just driven the Cadillac home: "Look out in the driveway. Anybody want a ride?"

My father was like that: impulsive, unpredictable. He was a man of secrets and he was generous when he wanted to be generous and not so generous when he didn't want to be. He owned properties in Sparta and vicinity, mostly rentals, and recently he'd become a developer, with partners, of a new shopping center north of the city. Business was the center of my father's life. Yet you could not gain entry into that life by asking him about his work, for when relatives asked him such questions he would say, with a disarming smile, "Can't complain." Or, "Holding my own." He would not elaborate. He had as little interest in boasting of successes as he had in acknowledging failures. If a question was too personal or pointed he would say, "Hell, that's business"—as if his business affairs were too trivial to speak of. Yet you knew that what Harvey Fleet meant was *None of your damned business.*

We had stayed at the blues festival for less than an hour and during that time I'd seen how my father, in his trademark white cotton shirt (no tie, open at the collar) and seersucker trousers (melon colored, for summer), and canvas shoes (white), moved easily among the crowd shaking hands with people who were strangers to me; being greeted by the musicians, most of whom were black men (young, middle-aged, elderly) eager to shake Harvey Fleet's hand for Harvey Fleet was one of the sponsors of the festival—"A friend to blues and jazz music." (Was this so? At home, my father never listened to music of any kind, never even watched television.) In Sparta, my father had many friends: local politicians, the chief of police, the district attorney, county officials. On a wall of his office were framed caricatures of Sparta personalities, including Harvey Fleet, crude but clever line drawings by a cartoonist for the *Sparta Herald* who'd exaggerated my father's vulpine good looks, his thick dark hair springing from a low forehead, his fistlike jaw and his trademark smile so wide and emphatic it looked riveted in place. Years later I would see on TV the 1946 film *The Postman Always Rings Twice* with flawlessly blond Lana Turner and darkly handsome John Garfield and it would be a shock to me, how closely my father had resembled Garfield when he'd been young. At the blues festival, to the sexy-seductive strains of "Stormy Weather"—"Mood Indigo"—"Sleepy Time Gal"—I'd seen how my father was acquainted with women who were strangers to me, some of them very attractive, and I thought, *My father has his secret life, which none of us can know.*

I wondered if it was better that way, our not knowing.

Though you couldn't question him about his past, my father some-times spoke of his youthful nomadic adventures: he'd quit school at fifteen and gone to work on a Great Lakes freighter bearing iron ore from Duluth to Buffalo; he'd hitchhiked out west, worked in Washington State, and in Alaska, where he'd worked on salmon fish-ing boats. His own father, Jonas Fleet, who'd died before I was born, had been exhausted and broken by the age of fifty, having worked in a Lackawanna steel mill; my father was determined not to emu-late him; he said, "There's better use for a man's lungs than to be coated with steel filings." In the army, in World War II, he'd been stationed in Italy, and the names of Italian regions and towns—*Tuscany, Brescia, Vicenza, Parma*—rolled off his tongue like an ex-otic sort of music, which meant little to his listeners. Of these long-ago adventures he'd had before he returned home to Sparta he spoke in a tone of wistfulness and pride; he'd made it through the war with-out being seriously wounded or "drove crazy" and of ugly memories he did not speak, at least not to us.

He laughed often. He liked to laugh. There were some in our fam-ily who distrusted my father's laughter, which made them uneasy. Why is Harv laughing? Is Harv laughing at us? You understood that there was a prevailing joke to which my father's joking alluded, but it was a private joke not accessible to others. "The only laugh that matters is the last laugh," my father said. "And that isn't guaranteed."

"Wait here in the car. Read your book. I'll be a few minutes. Don't come looking for me."

My father had parked at the rear of the Brewer Building, on a back street not far from the river. Buildings on the other side of this street had been razed and lay in heaps of rubble behind a ten-foot fence posted NO TRESPASSING: DANGER and a half block beyond was a wharf at which battered-looking fishing boats were docked. This was not the Sparta Yacht Club marina several miles to the east on the Black River, where my father kept his Chris-Craft powerboat; this was the old Sparta waterfront downtown. On Sundays the area was nearly deserted except for a few taverns and riverside restaurants; except for East Capitol, there was little traffic. Seagulls flew over-head and the air was pierced by their sharp cries; river smells—briny water, rotted pilings, dead fish—made my nostrils pinch. These were mostly pleasurable smells, and I liked being here. From time to time my father brought me with him to his office where his secretary Charlotte smiled to see me: "Madelyn, he*ll*o. Come to help us out today?"

The Brewer Building, owned by a real estate broker friend of my father, was the tallest building in the neighborhood and impressive with a smooth-shiny facade like polished marble. Inside was a foyer with a barbershop, a smoke shop, and a newsstand, all of which would be closed on Sunday. Only dimly could you see the stately mosaic figures on the foyer ceiling meant to suggest Egyptian pyramids, ancient hieroglyphics. There was an elevator with an elaborate grillwork door. Yet at the rear and sides of the Brewer Building you saw only weatherworn dark brick; the facade was what a "facade" meant—just a showy front. Especially from the rear, the building looked shabby. On each floor were ugly fire escapes. Some of the windows were cracked and opaque with grime. My father's office on the eighth floor overlooking East Capitol Street and in the near distance the gleaming spire of St. Mary's Roman Catholic Church was nothing like these. Years ago when my father had told me to wait in the car for him I'd disobeyed him, gone inside, and dared to take the elevator to the tenth, top floor of the building; on the tenth floor, I'd dared to climb a brief flight of steps and pushed open a door marked NO ADMITTANCE: ROOF and stepped outside on a shimmering-hot tar roof. So high! A sensation of vertigo overcame me, a sense of being physically drawn to the edge of the roof where the parapet was no more than two feet high; in halting steps I made my way to the edge; my eyes blinked in amazement, at this height I could see the S-curve of the Black River, boats on the river, more tall buildings than I would have imagined in Sparta, rooftops, church spires, chimneys. Airplanes droning high overhead, pigeons and seagulls. Everywhere were bird droppings, white crusted like concrete. How exhausting the wind, and hypnotizing. It was both exhilarating to me and frightening that no one knew where I was. If someone were to glimpse me from a window in another tall building, he would not know who I was; he would not care. When I turned back to the heavy door a chilling thought struck me—*Now the door will be shut and locked against you.*

The door wasn't locked. I'd been eleven at the time. I did not tell my father that I'd dared to walk on the roof of the Brewer Building that day and I never walked on the roof again.

Don't come looking for me, my father had said. I would wait for him in the car, reading my book. I'd opened the passenger's door so that I could sit sideways, with my legs dangling. Close by the river where there were no buildings obscuring the setting sun it was still light enough for me to read and I had only the vaguest awareness of my surroundings. In the near distance waves lapped against the wharf and from farther away came muffled sounds of music. At the periphery of my vision I might have been aware of another car turning onto the street behind the Brewer Building and parking a short distance away but this awareness was scarcely conscious and failed to register. *Did you see—anyone? Must've seen! Try to remember.* I was captivated by H. G. Wells's *The Time Machine,* which was the first of Wells's *Seven Scientific Romances* that I'd discovered in the public library. I was captivated by the brashness of the Time Traveller—flinging himself onto the "saddle" of his home-made time machine into not the near future but the distant future, with none of the provisions you would take on an overnight camp-ing trip. You could foresee that the unnamed Time Traveller would return from his journey to the year 802,701, since he was telling his own story, but the way would not be easy for he'd discovered that humankind had evolved into two distinct subspecies: the "graceful children" of the Upper World and the "obscene, nocturnal Things" that dwelled like humanoid spiders underground. In much of my reading at this time in my early adolescence there was a terrible logic: something virulent and vengeful prepared to rise up in the night, beneath us as we slept, like an animated earthquake, to pun-ish us. Why we were to be punished was not explained. Punishment was something that happened, and could not be averted. Punishment suggests a crime: but what is the crime? *Born bad,* it was said of some people. *Born bad,* it was said even of some individuals in Sparta. Yet I could not understand how an infant could be *born bad,* for no infant in my experience could plausibly be described in such a way.

Out on the river, men's voices lifted in shouts of laughter, muffled by a motor's roar. The sun was starting to set; I was losing the light at last. I left the car and took up a position nearer the river, leaning against a great cracked slab of concrete. If at this time the vehicle that might—or might not—have been parked behind the Brewer Building was driven away—if someone had hurriedly exited the building, gone to the car, and driven away—I had no awareness of it. I was in no position to see. *Didn't see. Don't know. Leave me alone!*

Another powerboat passed by, trailing drunken laughter. Vaguely it seemed to me that my name had been called—*Madelyn! Madelyn!*

37

At the blues festival there had been several boys whom I knew from school, older boys at the high school, they'd called to me, *Madelyn! Madelyn Fleet!* But I'd only just waved to them, I'd been standing with my father listening to a black jazz quartet playing "I Can't Give You Anything But Love, Baby." Now I seemed to hear my name in a faint, failing voice, my father's voice, but unlike my father's voice as I had ever heard it. Quickly I closed *The Time Machine,* and returned to the car.

My father had been inside the building for more than a half hour, I thought. A ripple of pain pulsed in my eyes. How garish the Cadillac Eldorado looked, the cream-colored luxury car with Spanish red leather interior, parked amid rubble. I tossed *The Time Machine* onto the passenger's seat and entered the building, into dim, humid heat and despite the heat I began to shiver. There was the elevator in the foyer: I could not bring myself to take it up to the eighth floor. What if the power failed, what if I was stuck between floors? Instead I took the stairs. Only dimly was the stairwell lighted by naked light-bulbs at each landing. The heat in the stairwell was stifling and by the time I reached the eighth floor I was painting and sweating. My Rangers T-shirt clung to my sticky skin. My hair stuck to the nape of my neck. On the eighth floor I struggled with the heavy door and another time the cruel taunt came to me *Now the door will be locked against you, this is your punishment.* But another time the door wasn't locked against me, I ran down the corridor to my father's office where the door was open. . . .

At first I thought that my father had fallen somehow, struck his head against the sharp edge of a desk. He was bleeding from a head wound and from cuts to his face. His white cotton shirt was dappled with blood, and torn. His melon-colored seersucker trousers were dappled with blood, and torn. One of his sporty white shoes had been wrenched off. He was conscious, trying to sit up. I could hear his ter-rible labored breathing and his grunting with the effort of maneu-vering himself into a sitting position. "Daddy—," I called, and ran to him, and his glassy eyes fixed on me without seeming to recognize me: "Get away, get out of here"—"Don't touch me." Drawers had been yanked out of his desk and out of the green filing cabinet against the wall. There was a sharp, rank animal sweat of panic, male sweat. And a prevailing smell of cigarette smoke. By the time my father managed to stand shakily, he was calling me "Madelyn"—"honey." He assured me he was all right—"Nothing to worry about, honey." He was wiping at his dazed and bloody face with the front of his ruined shirt. When I asked him what had happened, had someone hurt him, he seemed not to hear. I asked if I should call an ambulance or the police and quickly he said *no*. In his stricken and disheveled state my father hovered over me. I could feel the heat of his skin. He was trying to explain through swollen lips that someone whose face he hadn't seen had forced his way into the office and tried to rob him, he had not seen who it was because he'd been attacked from behind. Yet then my father said whoever it was had been waiting for him in his office when he'd unlocked the door, surprised him with a blow to the head. And maybe there was more than one of them, he hadn't seen. I asked him what had been taken from the office and he said nothing had been taken because he'd surprised the thieves. I asked him if I should call the police and he said, with an angry laugh: "Didn't I say no police?"

Now he would wash up, he said. As if his injuries could be washed away! Like a drunken man he leaned heavily on me, making his way to the men's restroom outside in the corridor. "Stay out here. I'll be all right. Don't look so scared, your old man isn't going to die." My father spoke disdainfully, dripping blood. And in the restroom he remained for what seemed like a long time. I could hear water rushing from faucets, a groaning of aged pipes. I heard a toilet flush several times. I stood at the door calling, *Daddy? Daddy?* in a plaintive voice until he staggered back out. His face was washed, his hair dampened though not combed; he'd removed the torn and blood-stained shirt, and was in his sleeveless undershirt of ribbed cotton, which was also bloodstained. Fistfuls of wiry dark hair bristled on his chest, covering his forearms like pelt. He was walking lopsided because he'd left his left shoe back in his office, where I fetched it for him. I also shut the door, and locked it. Afterward I would realize that my father hadn't seemed to be afraid that his assailant or assailants would return, and do more injury to him. He'd seemed to know that his daughter wasn't endangered. The beating was finished, and would not be repeated.

To my amazement my father insisted upon returning to the car and driving home. "I can handle this. My head is clear." Though he was obviously weak, dazed, swaying on his feet. Though his eyes seemed to be swerving out of focus even as he spoke to me in such emphatic terms. So we took the elevator down the foyer, and returned to the cream-colored Cadillac Eldorado parked so conspicuously behind the building. In the west the sun resembled a lurid red egg yolk bleeding into banks of dark thunderhead clouds. I was reminded of the "huge red-hot dome of the sun" the Time Traveller had encountered hundreds of millions of years in the future, swollen to one-tenth of the sky. Once in the car, my father tried to behave as if nothing had happened. He was muttering to himself, giving himself instructions. The fingers of his right hand were strangely swollen; I had to insert the ignition key and turn it for him. By this time I'd begun to cry. I was trembling badly, my bladder pinched with a panicked need to pee. Another time I asked my father if we shouldn't call an ambulance or the police and another time he said *no*—"No police." This seemed strange to me, for my father was friendly with the chief of police and with other men on the Sparta police force. Yet it seemed to infuriate him, the prospect of summoning police. Another time I asked him if he'd seen who had beaten him and another time he said Goddamn no, he hadn't seen. Strange it seemed to me that my father's anger was directed at me, not at whoever had hurt him.

"They jumped me from behind. They were waiting inside. I never saw their faces. It was over before it began."

And, "Might've been just one person. All I know is, he was white."

On Route 31 headed east, the cream-colored Cadillac drifted out of its lane. My father had forgotten to switch on the headlights. He winced with pain, his injured head and face had to be throbbing with pain. At the hospital it would be revealed that he'd suffered a concussion, several of his ribs were cracked, his right wrist and fingers sprained. Teeth had loosened in his jaws, deep cuts would leave scars in both his eyebrows. He'd been beaten with something like a tire iron, and he'd been kicked when he'd fallen. In our wake on the river road the horns of other vehicles sounded in reproach. I begged my father to pull over to the side before we had an accident and at last he did, after a mile or two. He was too dazed and exhausted to keep going. On the littered shoulder of the highway the cream-colored Caddie limped to an ignoble stop. Traffic passed us by. My father slumped over the steering wheel like an avalanche suddenly released, a stream of bright blood trickling down his neck. I scrambled out of the car to stand at the edge of the highway waving frantically until at last a Sparta police cruiser appeared. "Help us! Help my father! Don't let him die."

The cry that came from me was brute, animal. I had never heard such a cry before and would not have believed that it had issued from me.

Madelyn, tell us what you know.

Anything you can remember, Madelyn. If you saw a car any-where near. If you saw someone. In the street behind the building. Entering the building. If your father mentioned someone. Before your father passed out, all that he said to you. Whatever he said to you. Tell us.

In July 1959. That wild ride into the countryside, when my father was still alive.

Mr. Carmichael asked me where I lived and I told him. Then he said we were taking the long way round, a little ride out into the country, how'd I like that; and I said yes, I loved the country, loved riding in a car with the windows rolled down and the radio on loud. *Love love love you, Mr. Carmichael,* shutting my eyes to be kissed. Giggling to think if he sniffed at my armpits—! But Mr. Carmichael looked as if he'd been sleeping in his clothes too.

He hadn't forced me to drink, I would say afterward. None of what happened he'd forced me to do.

Exiting the hospital by the rear revolving door. Inside, the sickish refrigerated air and outside, hot-humid-sticky midsummer sunshine. "Know what a hospital is, Madelyn?—a petri dish breeding germs. Have to get the hell out, sometimes. Save your own life."

I think it was then—on our way to the parking lot—I asked Mr. Carmichael if someone in his family was in the hospital, and Mr. Carmichael, rummaging for his car keys in his trouser pocket, took no more notice of my question than in our seventh-grade class he'd taken notice of certain students who were not his favorites, waving their hands in the air to ask silly questions.

Repeating in a brisk staccato voice tugging at my ponytail:

"Save—your—own—goddamn—*life.*"

Mr. Carmichael's 1955 Dodge station wagon had faded to a dull tin color and was stippled with rust like crude lace. The front bumper was secured by ingenious twists of wire. I might have thought that it was strange, my former math teacher Mr. Carmichael was driving such a vehicle, very different from any vehicle my father, Harvey Fleet, would have driven. Mr. Carmichael was clapping his hands as you'd clap your hands to hurry a clumsy child, or a dog: "Got to keep moving. Like the shark, perpetual motion or it drowns. Chop-chop,

41

Maddie!" Exuberantly Mr. Carmichael gathered up clothes, empty beer bottles, a single shoe out of the front passenger's seat of the station wagon, to toss out into the already messy rear.

Out of Sparta we drove west along the Black River. On the radio, pop music blared, interrupted by loud jocular advertisements from a local radio station. Though I had told Mr. Carmichael where I lived, it did not seem that Mr. Carmichael had heard, or he'd forgotten. He was in very good spirits. It is unusual to see a man, an adult man, in such good spirits. The front windows of the station wagon were rolled down and wind in crazed gusts whipped at our heads. In the gauzy-humid sunshine the wide choppy river glittered like a snake's scales. In Sparta you are always driving along the river, for the river intersects the city: you are driving on Route 31 East, or you are driving on Route 31 West; you are driving on Route 31A West, or you are driving on Route 31A East. Yet the river seemed always different, and sometimes it did not look familiar. That day there was a massive freighter on the river, ugly and ungainly as a dinosaur. Far away downtown were high-rise buildings and one of these was the Brewer Building but it was lost in haze. At Sentry Street beside the railroad trestle bridge a train was passing thunderous and deafening. Mr. Carmichael shouted to be heard over the noise but his words were blown away. It did not seem to matter if I replied to Mr. Carmichael or not. From the side, Mr. Carmichael did not resemble anyone I had ever seen. A faint doubt came to me, *was* this Luther Carmichael? My seventh-grade math teacher? This man's face was flushed as if he'd been running in the heat. His skin looked as if it had been scraped by sandpaper. His silvery brown beard was poking through like tiny quills. The thought came to me *If he brushes his face against my face . . .* I laughed, and squirmed as if I were being tickled. By now the train had passed, Mr. Carmichael glanced sidelong at me, smiling. "Something funny, Maddie?" His smile was quick and loose and crinkled his face like a soft rag. More clearly I could see how the tinted lenses of Mr. Carmichael's glasses were smudged, and his eyes beyond, staring. My hair was streaming in the wind, I had to blink tears from my eyes. How reckless I felt, and how happy: I was sitting as I'd never have dared to sit in my father's cream-colored Cadillac Eldorado with the Spanish red-leather seats, my left leg lifted, the heel of my sneaker on the seat nudging the base of my left buttock. I saw how Mr. Carmichael's gaze moved over my leg—the tanned smooth skin with fine brown hairs, the muscled calf and sudden milky white of my upper thigh.

"Open the glove compartment, Maddie. See what's inside."

Fumbling to remove from the glove compartment a quart bottle of amber liquid: whiskey. Mr. Carmichael instructed me to unscrew the top and take a drink and quickly I shook my head no, shyly I shook my head no, and Mr. Carmichael nudged me in the ribs with his elbow, winking: "Yes, you'd better, Maddie. Kills germs on contact and where we came from—" Mr. Carmichael shuddered, as if suddenly cold.

It is death he is taking me from, I thought. I had never loved anyone so much.

With a gesture of impatience Mr. Carmichael took the bottle from me, and drank. Fascinated, I watched, the greedy movements of his mouth, his throat. Mr. Carmichael handed the bottle back to me with another nudge in the ribs and so—must've been, I lifted the bottle to my mouth, and drank cautiously. Searing-hot liquid flooded my mouth, down my throat like flames. My eyes leaked tears as I tried not to succumb to a spasm of coughing.

Here is a secret Mr. Carmichael was never to know: I knew where he lived, on Old Mill Road beyond the Sparta city limits. I knew for, with the cunning of a twelve-year-old girl in love with her seventh-grade math teacher, I had looked up "Carmichael"—"Luther Carmichael"—in the Sparta telephone directory. More than once I had bicycled past Mr. Carmichael's house, which was approximately four miles from my house, a considerable distance. But I had done this, in secret. And I'd forgotten more or less, until now. On a mailbox at the end of a long driveway was the name CARMICHAEL. And the name CARMICHAEL, in black letters shiny as tar, seemed to me astonishing. So suddenly, so openly—CARMICHAEL. It had seemed to me a very special name. In secret I'd written it out, how many times. And sometimes with only my finger, tracing the letters on a smooth desktop. On the Old Mill Road where Mr. Carmichael lived with his family—for it was known, Mr. Carmichael had a wife and young children—I dared to bicycle past the end of his driveway, and once dared to turn in to the driveway, hurriedly turning back when it seemed to me that someone had appeared at the house.

In math class when Mr. Carmichael handed back our test papers marked in red ink, though Mr. Carmichael spoke my name in a friendly way and may even have smiled at me I did not smile in return, I kept my eyes lowered out of superstition and dread for the red number at the top of the paper was my fate for that day: my grade. You would not have guessed, surely Mr. Carmichael would not have guessed, which of the seventh-grade girls was most desperately in love with him.

So long ago! You have to smile, to think that people like us took ourselves, and one another, so seriously.

And so on Old Mill Road beyond the Sparta city limits it wasn't surprising to me when Mr. Carmichael turned the station wagon onto the bumpy cinder drive leading back to his house. I knew this was where we were headed. And there was the mailbox with CARMICHAEL in black letters on the sides, stuffed with newspapers—this wasn't surprising to me. (So Mr. Carmichael hadn't been bringing in his mail, reading the local paper. Which was why he hadn't seen the front-page news of Harvey Fleet's "savage" beating.) "Won't stay long, Maddie," Mr. Carmichael was saying, "—unless we change our minds, and we do." The sweet warm sensation of the whiskey in my throat had radiated downward like sunshine into my belly, into my bowels, and below between my legs and my response to this was breathy laughter. Out of excitement—or anxiety—I was asking Mr. Carmichael silly questions, for instance, did he own horses?—(no, he did not own horses)—did he know a Herkimer County judge who was a friend of my father's, who lived on Old Mill Road?—(yes, Mr. Carmichael knew the man, but not well). Surprising to see how much shabbier—sadder—Mr. Carmichael's house looked now than it had two years before, when I'd dared to bicycle partway up the driveway. The large front lawn had become a field of tall grasses and wildflowers and the cinder driveway was badly rutted. The house that looked ugly but dignified from the road looked, up close, only just ugly; a squat two-story block-shaped cobblestone with a steep-slanted slate roof, the kind of house (I bit my lower lip to stop from bursting into a fit of giggling at the thought) in which, in a fairy tale, a troll would live. "Glad to see you're laughing, Maddie," Mr. Carmichael said. "Damn lot better than crying."

Mr. Carmichael parked the Dodge station wagon close beside the house. In the backyard was a children's swing set among tall grasses. Cicadas were shrieking out of the trees. Close up, the cobblestones were misshapen rocks that looked as if they'd been dredged up out of the earth with dirt still clinging to them. The back screen door was ajar as if someone in the house had rushed out without taking time to close it. One of the first-floor windows had been shoved open to the very top and a yellow-print muslin curtain had been sucked out by the wind, wanly fluttering now. The thought came to me *He is living alone here. There is no wife now.* With the cruelty of a

44

fourteen-year-old female I felt a stab of satisfaction as if I'd known my math teacher's wife, a youngish blonde woman glimpsed by me only at a distance, years ago; a figure of idly jealous speculation on the part of certain of Mr. Carmichael's girl students, in fact a total stranger to us. That Mr. Carmichael had young children was of absolutely no interest to us. "Won't stay long," Mr. Carmichael repeated, nudging me between the shoulder blades, urging me into the house, "but damn we are thirsty."

It was true. I'd been drinking from the quart bottle out of the glove compartment and I was very thirsty now, my throat on fire.

All going to die. Why's it matter exactly when.

This raw and unimpeachable logic emerges like granite outcroppings in a grassy field, at such moments. You will remember all your life.

"Welcome! 'Ecce homo.'" Inside it looked as if a whirlwind had rushed through the downstairs rooms of Mr. Carmichael's house. In the kitchen the linoleum stuck to my feet like flypaper. In grayish water in the sink stacks of dirty dishes were soaking. Every square inch of countertop was in use, even the top of the stove with filth-encrusted burners; in the hot stale air was a strong odor of something rancid. Flies buzzed and swooped. Mr. Carmichael seemed scarcely to notice, exuberantly opening the refrigerator door: "Voilà! Cold beer! Not a moment to spare." He grabbed a dark brown bottle, opened it, and drank thirstily and offered it to me but I could not force myself to take more than a cautious little sip. I hated the taste of beer, and the smell. I asked Mr. Carmichael if there was a Coke in the refrigerator and he said no, sorry, there was not: "Only just beer. Made from malted barley, hops—nutrients. Not chemical crap to corrode your pretty teen teeth." I saw Mr. Carmichael's eyes on me, his smile that looked just slightly asymmetrical as if one side of his mouth was higher than the other. Impossible to gauge if this smile was on your side or not on your side, I remembered from seventh grade: yet how badly you yearned for that smile. "C'mere. Something to show you"—lightly Mr. Carmichael slipped his arm around my shoulders and led me into a dining room with a high ceiling of elaborate moldings and a crystal chandelier of surprising delicacy and beauty, covered in cobwebs. This was the room with the opened window through which the yellow-print curtain had been sucked and here too flies buzzed and swooped. Around a large mahogany dining table were numerous chairs pulled up close as if no one sat there any longer, except at one end; the table was covered with books, magazines, old newspapers, stacks of what appeared to be financial records, bills, and receipts. On sheets of paper were geometrical figures, some of them conjoined with humanoid figures (both female and male, with peanut heads and exaggerated genitals), which I pretended not to see. Idly I opened a massive book—*Asimov's Chronology of the World*. It came to me then: a memory of how Mr. Carmichael had puzzled our class one day "demonstrating infinity" on the blackboard. With surprising precision he'd drawn a circle, and halved it; this half circle, he'd halved; this quarter circle, he'd halved; this eighth of a circle, he'd halved; as he struck the blackboard with his stick of chalk, addressing us in a jocular voice, as if, though this was mathematics of a kind, it was also very funny, by quick degrees the figure on the blackboard became too small to be seen even by those of us seated in the first row of desks; yet Mr. Carmichael continued, in a flurry of staccato chalk strikes, until the chalk shattered in his fingers and fell to the floor where in a playful gesture he kicked it. No one laughed.

" 'Infinity.' *Ex nihilo nihil fit.*"

It wasn't clear what Mr. Carmichael wanted to show me. He'd wandered into the living room, sprawled heavily on a badly worn corduroy sofa, tapping at the cushion beside him in a gesture you might make to encourage a child to join you, or a dog. Tentatively I sat on the sofa, but not quite where Mr. Carmichael wanted me to sit.

This room was not nearly so cluttered as the other rooms. You could see that Mr. Carmichael often sprawled here at his end of the sofa, which had settled beneath his weight. Close by was a small TV with rabbit ears on a portable stand and beside it a hi-fi record player, with long-playing records in a horizontal file, Beethoven's Symphony No. 7, a piano quintet by Mozart, a piano sonata by Schubert. . . . These were only names to me, we never heard classical music in our household; eagerly I asked Mr. Carmichael if he would play one of his records?—but Mr. Carmichael, said, "Fuck 'Mr. Carmichael.' You'd like to, eh?" Seeing the shock and hurt in my face quickly Mr. Carmichael laughed, and in a tender voice said: "Anyway, call me 'Luther.' No 'Mr. Carmichael' here."

Mr. Carmichael passed the icy-cold beer bottle to me, and I managed to swallow a mouthful without choking. Hesitantly I tried the name: " 'Luther.' " Biting my lower lip to keep from laughing, for wasn't "Luther" a comic-strip name?—then I did begin to cough, and a trickle of beer ran down inside my left nostril that I wiped away on my hand, hoping Mr. Carmichael wouldn't notice.

Another time I wanted to ask Mr. Carmichael who he'd been visiting at the hospital, and where his family was, but didn't dare. Against a wall was an upright piano with stacks of books and sheet music on its top. I could imagine a girl of my age sitting there, dutifully playing her scales. The living room looked out upon the vast front yard now overgrown with tall grasses and yellow and white wildflowers. The walls were covered in faded once-elegant wallpaper and in this room too was sculpted molding in the ceiling. On the coffee table near the sofa were ashtrays heaped with butts and ashes. I resolved, if Mr. Carmichael lit another cigarette, I would ask if I could have a "drag" from it as girls were always doing with older boys they hoped to impress. Mr. Carmichael took back the beer bottle from me and drank again thirstily and asked me which year of high school I would be in, in the fall, and I told him that I was just starting high school: I would be in tenth grade. "That sounds young," Mr. Carmichael said, frowning. "I thought you were older."

To this I had no ready reply. I wondered if I should apologize.

"You were my student years ago, not recently. How's it happen you're just going into tenth grade?"

Our math teacher's displeasure showed itself in a quick furrow of Mr. Carmichael's forehead and a crinkling of his nose as if he were smelling something bad—and who was to blame? He asked if I had a boyfriend and when I said no, the bad-smell look deepened. Stammering, I said, "People say—I have an 'old' soul. Like maybe—I've lived many times before."

This desperate nonsense came to me out of nowhere: it was something my grandmother had told me when I'd been a little girl, to make me feel important, I suppose, or to make herself feel important.

Still frowning, Mr. Carmichael said suddenly, "The Stoics had the right goddamn idea. If I was born a long time ago, that's what I was— 'Stoic.' Y'know who the Stoics were? No? Philosophers who lived a long time ago. Marcus Aurelius—name ring a bell? 'In all that you say or do recall that the power of exiting this life is yours at any time.'"

"You mean—kill yourself?" I laughed uncertainly. This didn't sound so good.

Mr. Carmichael was in a brooding mood so I asked him if he thought there might be memory pools that collected in certain places like the hospital, the way puddles collect after rain; in places where people have had to wait, and have been worried, and frightened; if there were places where you left your trace, without knowing it. Mr.

47

Carmichael seemed to consider this. At least, he did not snort in derision. He said, " 'Memory pools.' Why not. Like ghosts. Everywhere, the air is charged with ghosts. Hospitals have got to be the worst, teeming with ghosts like germs. Can't hardly draw a deep breath, you suck in a ghost." Mr. Carmichael made a sneezing-comical noise that set us both laughing. "Could be, I am a ghost. You're a sweet trusting girl, coming out here with a ghost. Or maybe you're a ghost yourself—joke's on me. Some future time like the next century there'll be explorers looking back to now, to 1959—what's called 'lookback time'—y'know what 'lookback time' is? No?" Mr. Carmichael's teacherly manner emerged, though as he spoke he tapped my wrist with his forefinger. " 'Lookback time' is what you'd call an astronomical figure of speech. It means, if you gaze up into the night sky—and you have the look of a girl eager to learn the constellations—what you see isn't what is there. What you see is only just light—'starlight.' The actual star has moved on, or is extinct. What you are looking into is 'lookback time'—the distant past. It's only an ignorant—innocent—eye that thinks it is looking at an actual star. If our sun exploded, and disappeared, here on earth we wouldn't know the grim news for eight minutes." Now Mr. Carmichael was circling my wrist with his thumb and forefinger, gently tugging at me to come closer to him on the sofa. "Eight minutes is a hell of a long time, to not know that you are dead."

I shuddered. Then I laughed, this was meant to be funny.

Somehow, we began arm wrestling. Before I knew it, with a gleeful chortle, Mr. Carmichael had kicked off his moccasins, worn without socks, slouched down on the sofa, and lifted me above him, to straddle his stomach. "Giddyup, li'l horsie! Giddyup." My khaki shorts rode up my thighs, Mr. Carmichael's belt buckle chafed my skin. Beneath the Rangers T-shirt he ran his hard quick hands where my skin was clammy-damp; he took hold of my small, bare breasts, squeezing and kneading, running his thumbs across the nipples, and I slapped at him, shrieking in protest. Suddenly then Mr. Carmichael rolled me over onto the sofa, pinned me with his forearms, and gripped my thighs, between my legs he brought his hot, rock-hard face, his sucking mouth, against the damp crotch of my shorts and my panties inside my shorts, an act so astonishing to me, I could not believe that it was happening. Like a big dog Mr. Carmichael was growling, sucking, and nipping at me. "Lie still. Be still. You'll like this. L'il bitch god*damn.*" Wildly I'd begun to laugh, I kicked frantically at him, scrambled out of his grasp on my hands and knees—on the floor now, on a carpet littered with pizza crusts, dumped ashtrays, and empty beer bottles. Cursing me now, Mr. Carmichael grabbed hold of my ankle and pinned me again, mashing his mouth against mine, his mouth and angry teeth tearing at my lips as if to pry them open. By this time I'd become panicked, terrified. No boy or man had ever kissed me like this, or touched me like this, so roughly—"Why'd you come here with me? What did you think this was—seventh grade? You're a hell of a lot older than you let on. Hot li'l bitch." With each syllable of *hot li'l bitch* Mr. Carmichael struck the back of my head against the carpet, his fingers closed around my throat. Fumbling, he tried to insert his knee between my thighs, he pressed the palm of his hand hard against my mouth to quiet me, I struggled, desperate to free myself like a fish impaled on a hook desperate to free itself at any cost, I would have torn open my flesh to be free of Mr. Carmichael's weight on me. Now he lurched above me, grunted and fumbled, unzipped his trousers, I had a glimpse of his thick engorged penis being rammed against my thighs, another time Mr. Carmichael grunted, and shuddered, and fell heavily on me; for a long stunned moment we lay unmoving; then he allowed me to extricate myself from him, to crawl away whimpering.

Somehow next I was in a bathroom, and I was vomiting into a sink. Must've been, Mr. Carmichael had led me here. In this sweltering-hot little room, which was very dirty—shower stall, toilet, linoleum floor—I ran water from both faucets to wash away my vomit, desperate to wash all evidence away. I could not bring myself to look into the mirror above the sink, I knew my mouth was swollen, my face burned and throbbed. On the front of my T-shirt were coin-sized splotches of blood. (Was my nose bleeding? Always in school I'd been in terror of my nose suddenly beginning to bleed, and the stares of my classmates.) With shaking hands I washed away the sticky semen on my thighs, which was colorless and odorless. Outside the bathroom Mr. Carmichael was saying, in an encouraging voice: "You'll be fine, Maddie. We'll take you back. We should leave soon." Yet the thought came to me *He could kill me now. He is thinking this. When I come out of here. No one will know.* But when I opened the bathroom door Mr. Carmichael was nowhere in sight. I heard him in the kitchen, he was speaking on the phone, pleading, and then silence, the harsh laughter, and the slamming down of a telephone receiver. A man's raw aggrieved voice—"Fuck it. What's the difference. . . ."

When Mr. Carmichael came for me, his mood had shifted yet

again. In the kitchen he too had been washing up: his flushed face was made to appear affable, his disheveled hair had been dampened. His badly soiled sport shirt was tucked into his trousers, and his trousers were zipped up. The moccasins were back on his feet. It was with a genial-teacher smile that Mr. Carmichael greeted me: "Madelyn! Time to head back, I said we wouldn't stay long."

In the Dodge station wagon, in late-afternoon traffic on Route 31 East, Mr. Carmichael lapsed into silence. He'd forgotten about driving me home, there was no question but that we were returning to Sparta Memorial Hospital. From time to time Mr. Carmichael glanced anxiously at me as I huddled far from him in the passenger's seat, trying to stop my nose from bleeding by pinching the nostrils and tilting my head back. So distracted and disoriented was Mr. Carmichael, as we passed beneath the railroad trestle bridge, he nearly sideswiped a pickup truck in the left-hand lane of the highway; behind the wheel of the pickup was a contractor friend of my father's. He saw me, and he saw Mr. Carmichael at the wheel beside me, not knowing who Mr. Carmichael was but knowing that it was very wrong for a fourteen-year-old girl to be with him, this flush-faced adult man in his mid- or late thirties. I thought, *He sees us, he knows.* With the inexorable logic of a dream it would happen then: my father's friend would telephone my mother that evening, that very night Luther Carmichael would be arrested in the cobblestone house on Old Mill Road. Mr. Carmichael would be dismissed from his teaching position because of me, of what he'd done to me; because of this—having been seen with me, in the Dodge station wagon this afternoon. And now, telling this story, I remember: Mr. Carmichael hadn't yet been dismissed from his teaching job, as I'd said. All that lay ahead of him. The remainder of his foreshortened life lay ahead of him. He would be arrested, he would be charged with sexual assault of a minor, providing alcohol to a minor; he would be charged with the forcible abduction of a minor, and with kidnapping. He would be charged with keeping me in his house against my will. Some of these charges would be dropped but still Luther Carmichael would kill himself in the ugly cobblestone house on Old Mill Road, hanging from a makeshift noose slung over a rafter in the smelly earthen-floored cellar.

All this had not happened yet. There was no way to accurately foretell it. All I knew was, I had to return to my father's bedside.

I was desperate to return to my father's bedside. Before Mr. Carmichael brought the station wagon to a full stop in the parking lot, I had jumped out, I was making my way into the chill of the hospital that never changes, taking the stairs two at a time to the intensive care unit on the fourth floor, avoiding the elevator out of a morbid fear that, at this crucial time, the elevator might stall between floors, now breathless from the stairs and my heart pounding in my chest as if it might burst—

Still alive! From the doorway of the intensive care unit I can see my father in his bed swaddled in white like a comatose infant, and he is still alive.

Why Does the World Out There Seem
Peter Cole

I.

Why does the natural feel unnatural?
Why does the world out there seem
so utterly foreign to these poems?
It isn't strange, and hardly hostile,
to the heart and eye behind their lines:
dirt exploding into spring,
leaves climbing the pipe to the screen,
the morning glory's funnel of blue,
the sap of it all coursing through
every fiber of all those veins.
Why does the natural feel so strained
when set beside the abstract figures
of speech's discourse linking us?
Poems, as Williams wrote, are machines.

II.

But maybe the natural's not what I mean,
so much as experience *of* the natural
merged with that which men have made.
No, not that. It's registration
of things one feels have already been
established as facts by eyes and mind.
Once is plenty. And that's the sacred.
Why the need to return to the scene
of each epiphany? Why the craving
for that halo? A kind of greed?
Natural lines on a piece of paper
are revelation enough for now,
as are speaking and listening to
you and what these words might say.

III.

Extending beyond information, but also
observation of that natural
world that observation reveals
as a miracle. Or not beyond—
beside. Maybe even beneath.
Or breached. That's the thread leading
back and possibly out or through:
to what or whom? Him? You?
I'm here, almost against my will,
having been led, as though by the nose,
by language. And in this abstract picture
I'm asking you to bear with me.
Reader. Readers. Reading. We
are in this instant's chain together.

IV.

A chain partaking of enchantment,
mystics have written, implying song,
and maybe the poem. Or just a spell.
Which might as easily be a hell-
ish hall of echoes or mirrored images
mixing in the hungry mind.
Or, diversion that doesn't feed
and draws one further from, not toward,
the pool of pleasure wisdom is.
Depending on the poem's design.
Strange how I've become a modern
poet of a medieval kind—
making poems for a different diversion,
as they point toward what's divine.

V.

Amusement derives from the animal's mouth
and snout, stuck there in the air,
as it stares, struck by words
it heard. In a manner of speaking
it muzzles as in what's not fair,

or wonder. And in the illogical moment
of what it means and how it works,
while the mouth is closed, nourishment—
if it's serious—enters through it.
And in a nutshell that's the sentence
and solace that sweet Chaucer meant.
The poem's gesture, changing, survives
in generations of aspiration,
leading us on . . . or into our lives.

Edge Boys
Charles McLeod

BOUGHT IN MOTEL ROOMS, in public park bathrooms, the edge boys
have highlighted their hair. The boxes of Clairol are plucked stolen
from shelves and tucked into boxer-brief waistbands. The store clerks
are busy asking for price checks. The edge boys have very white
teeth. They stride the linoleum, smiles shining out. The clerks think:
no one that pretty would take things. The doors whoosh to open;
here is the sun, here is the blacktop, shimmering. The edge boys
wear shorts that go past their knees. The edge boys wear oversized
T-shirts. They buy gum at gas stations and pace the grass strips
between pump bays and street intersections. When cars slow in passing, the edge boys blow bubbles. Tucked in their anklets are prepack-
aged condoms. They have earrings in both of their ears. Last week
was the last week of their high-school semesters. The edge boys are
ready to earn. In parentless houses, the kitchen tap running, they
work water down to their scalps. Blond with red streaks or brown
with blond streaks or black transformed to white blond. They wrap
the dyed locks in lengths of tinfoil and wait, watching game-show
reruns. Their yearbooks, in backpacks, sit signed and forgotten: *have
a great summer. i'll see you in autumn. thanks for being such a
good friend.* The edge boys are gay. The edge boys have girlfriends,
meek girls with glasses or cheeks stained with acne, who hide their
girth under loose batik skirts, girls who ask less per their subpar aesthetic and thus function as near-perfect foils, the edge boys needing
only to take them to movies, to malls, to infrequently dine them at
some neoned franchise and then later take their clothes off, this last
part disliked but understood as essential, as requisite for the upkeep
of hetero visage, mandatory for avoiding all manner of bullshit in
locker-walled, fluorescent-lit halls, so these girls' hands held in high-
ceilinged lunchrooms, these girls taken to prom, their taffeta dresses
like bright shiny sacks, their matching sling backs rubbing their fat
ankles raw, and the edge boys make clear on spring nights in late
April that it has been fun but just not enough, that it's in both parties' best interests to move on from each other, to let summer heal

wounds and meet up in fall, and by the week after finals the edge boys are working, are putting in hours, are taking their knocks, have had their foreheads put hard against corners of nightstands, have been bruised by closed fists, have been robbed, have been taken to dark lonely lots off the parkways, the mood changing, the date going wrong, and sometimes the edge boys flee into nighttime, hoping their sneakers don't scuff, as the body in youth will start itself over, can reset with nearly no flaws, but the shoes are expensive, were purchased, must last, possess sharp lines and clean looks, traits that the edge boys must also possess so the skin tanned in backyards on slow afternoons, the teeth brushed and whitened and flossed, the hair kept to flawless, shampooed and then sculpted, the back tightly tapered, sharp as the bristles on a brush—their image rechecked in the bathrooms of Chevrons as the day turns itself into dusk, and when the dye fades the edge boys repeat the process of dyeing, and when cars stop the edge boys lean through the frames of car windows, asking for rides to some other place, asking how much and for what.

And here the edge cities, the car-fervent boomburbs, Levittown's sprawling kempt spawn, more jobs than bedrooms, the streets dead by evening, the office parks sleeping it off; here the coiffed glow of postindustrial society, the middle class outsourced, the farmlands paved over, gone, practical know-how no longer important so goodbye to Pittsburgh's Steelworkers Union, goodbye to Baltimore's docks, the stevedores half starved from nothing exported, the labor halls places of rot, production supplanted by codified knowledge, the making of goods replaced by the selling thereof, the old urban centers unwanted, not needed, high crime and high rent, the drug-addled dozing at bus stops, so development set down in between freeways, acreage near airports bought cheap and built up, and from this Bethesda and Scottsdale and Reston; Irving, Texas, and White Plains, New York; here Costa Mesa in LA's choked basin; here Downers Grove and Ogden, Utah, here the midlevel skyscraper of mixed office/retail, the arterial road ten miles long, where sidewalks are largely parachronistic as sidewalks are *places of sloth*, made for the beggar and stroller, the uncertain, the person too full of free thought, for the edge cities are kingdoms of *the action efficient*, progress optimized, apologism constantly scoffed—realms of the stem cell, the spreadsheet, the lepton, where the hum of the lathe has never been heard, where absent is the din of the die caster's punch, these sounds replaced by the light constant clacking of flesh on computer keyboards, the new assembly lines well-lit partitioned desk cubicles one floor up from the whir of juice bars, and rolled out from these factories datum not item, patent not part, as the things we make now are not things at all, are service or research, advice or idea, theory mapped out or thought up—here Science unbridled, here plugs cords and wires, here bits bytes and pixels replacing the orchards, all produce imported by plane and then truck, here nanotech labs with federal contracts, here the cybernetics startup, *here green even sod between rows of parked cars outside of the Mall of America;* here wetlands demolished, here cell towers erected, here all the bees dying off, here bigger and faster and smaller and brighter, here the twenty-screen Cineplex showing ten action titles, teens texting on handhelds through all the slow parts, here drive-thru windows on pharmacy walls, here Zoloft and Lustral passed out like fast food, here tax breaks enormous for new corporate tenants, here regional outlets inside megacenters, here firms expert in hedge-fund investment and intellectual property law; here unclassified research in the hills east of Berkeley, Houston's Sugarland, Denver's Aurora, here Cool Springs between Memphis and Nashville, here Clearwater due west of Tampa, each place a nexus of postwar success, these cities we fought for, these cities we won.

The edge boys do oral. The edge boys do anal. The edge boys will do half and half. On laptops, in bedrooms, listings are posted, published to Web sites with classified sections accepting of this sort of fare. The edge boys were born 1990 or after. The edge boys can type very fast. Cross-legged on throw rugs, on low thread-count bed sheets, the edge boys' shoulders hunch over flat screens, searching for what to say next. When their eyes blink, the edge boys don't know that they're blinking. On walls are taped posters of rock bands or rap stars or harmonizing Caucasian quintets. Square fans fill windows, their blades quickly turning. The rooms of the edge boys are never a mess. The rooms of the edge boys are kept swept and dusted, clothes hampered, corners absent of lint—quick work that functions as high-gloss veneer should parents, at some point, peek in. The edge boys do poorly on standardized testing; for them it will be junior college at best. There is flash on the brainpan and their bodies hunch tighter and their fingers, crookedly, tap: *versatile bottom seeks high-class encounter. tan toned and ready right now. if you have the quarters come see my arcade. i have the best games in town.* The edge boys review; the edge boys make edits. The edge boys are junk food, sweet cheap and addictive, so the edge boys call themselves twinks. With driveways vacated, with the highways now humming, with the sun burning dew from the grass, the edge boys are mid-morning entrepreneurs, undertaking new enterprise, assuming all risk. The edge boys are merchant fleet, caravan, troupe. The edge boys are both song and dance. The edge boys offer companionship, not fucking: *any money exchanged is a gift for time spent.* Pictures are uploaded alongside the squibs, photographic self-portraits in which the edge boys are shirtless, their faces made blurry or blacked out, as the edge boys must show what they have to offer without revealing too much of themselves. A lawnmower whirs; a car honks a street over. Hummingbirds hover inches from blossoms; the edge boys can see them through cracks in the blinds. Light falls in threads onto desktops and dressers. The rooms of the edge boys are often so still that the edge boys sometimes believe themselves dead. From hallways chime wall clocks; it's seconds past ten. Windows are closed out and e-mail then opened and soon after the ads of the edge boys go live. The edge boys stand up and step out of lounge pants. The edge boys own phony IDs—crude fakes they self-publish on laser-jet printers while their parents, exhausted, succumb to canned laughter on prime-time TV—as the edge boys must be young look-ing but legal, twenty-one, twenty, nineteen, some age that confirms them as virile and nubile but rules out anything *statutory,* and with music put on and their wardrobe selected, the edge boys walk briskly to white-tiled bathrooms where towels hang folded in halves, the shower knob pulled out or turned right or left, the steam rising over the basin's glass door, the wall mirror growing fogged in.

And here the respondees, the white-collar lustful, alumni of Schools of Letters & Science, men in their twenties, their thirties, their fifties, men of all races and sizes, men who were born on Amer-ican soil and men who at one point were naturalized, men who have been with the company for decades and men only recently hired, men who lean left and men who lean right and swing-voting men who will cross party lines should they really believe in the candi-date, men with no voting record, men who watch sports ten hours each weekend and men who do not own a television, men who ride Harleys and men who drive hybrids; dumb men, who will not last through the next round of layoffs, and men who are workers up-standing, men who wear suits with ties Windsor knotted, men who wear lab coats and bow ties, men who are lead-end application de-signers and men who once worked on Wall Street, men with full knowledge of the Doha Round's implications and men unsure of where Doha is located, men with low tolerance for processing lactose, men allergic to peanuts, to buckwheat; bearded men, bland men, men with thin fingers, men who are wearers of rings, men with tan lines where these rings once were but most aptly *men of duplicity*, men of the mask worn under the skin, men of coarse acts and good hygiene, men at once members of neighborhood watch groups and blackguards for their local sex industry, and these men of the condo, the townhouse, the Tudor, these men of argyle and khaki, who stay late or rise early and work hard or don't, all of these men double-dealing—men of two forms, two positions in space, makers of both song and painting, men who are crooners of stanzas threnodic, peddlers of anapest, of trochee, men who know which sounds to stress and not stress to sell fables in a manner convincing: men of the midday trip to the dentist, men of cars whose oil needs changing, men who are fathers of very sick children, small boys or girls who abruptly fall ill at desks inside school buildings, and these children needing *care*, needing parent and transport, needing warm soup and cold remedies, so grave faces worn while approaching coworkers, or bosses in the middle of e-mailing: *I just got a call from, You won't believe this, He said* and *She said* and *Well they just told me—* lines near canonical for each of these men, these scholars entrenched in the oral tradition of lying, as the edge boys are canvas that can't be left blank, are these men's passion, their calling, what they would choose if there was nothing else, no yard work, no anniversaries, no pushing of paper or processing words to sustain and increase yearly salary, so all manner of untruth composed and conscripted, the devotion to craft close to boundless, and here is the cell phone purchased in secret, and here the bank account no one else knows of, and here the PO box for these bills and statements, rented the next city over, as the lunch breaks of these men do not involve food but do very much include *hunger*, so daily or weekly, in the stalls of work bathrooms, or in cars parked in the dark of garages, the ads of the edge boys perused via BlackBerry, flipped through using touch screens on iPhones, and when the right hue is found, the precise chiaroscuro, these men then envision their paintings: art made amongst cheaply starched sheets of queen beds in rooms advertised as having free cable, or the bought trysts transpiring well into evening, subject and object in states of undress at rest stops on the city's periphery, and sometimes the process goes very smoothly and on occasion the practice is rougher, but more important than outcome *sustained feasibility*, that these actions are able to be tried and retried, to be done again over and over.

Charles McLeod

The edge boys want their donation up front. The edge boys take cash and cash only. The edge boys will wear any items you like, providing they then get to keep them. The edge boys can tell you which parts of lots can't be seen from the street, from the freeway. The edge boys don't ever kiss on the mouth though the men that they meet *will lean in,* will keep trying, and by now, my midforties, still married, still scared, still fake small meek and unsure, a member of gyms, a father of daughters, as someone who dishonored oath long ago but has largely upheld every contract, as owner of a house now fully paid off, as possessor of matching brass shoehorns, as someone who never stood up for himself and finds richness in acts done in shadow, in darkness, the edge boys, for me, serve as *opera omnia,* comprise a life's work collected, and here *early works:* my third year at Lehigh, a major in civil engineering, freshly admitted to Tau Beta Pi and possessed by the deeds of Telford, of Jessop, both preeminent builders of canals, of artificial channels of water, this '83, Rock Hudson infected, the disease often still called gay cancer, AIDS known to Reagan, who was two years away from using the term while in public, and *winter in Bethlehem,* bright but cold days, the steel plant still up and running, the historic downtown lined with bare elms, the clothiers and bookshops brick walled and stately, and for ten months by this time letters to parents, verse that spoke often of Daphne: Daphne of Cleveland, Daphne a senior, Daphne who too soon was graduating, and included therein our fake union's minutiae, trips to Ohio or north to the Catskills or hikes to the top of South Mountain, the posts detailed but also disjointed, meant to seem rushed, to seem done in one breath, to convey I was in constant hurry, whereas in truth there was only course work and near-daily walks, done close to sunset, down to the bank of the river, brisk peregrinations from my Fountain Hill in-law past one side of St. Luke's Memorial, where often a nurse, in pink scrubs and peacoat, stood smoking by a low bank of generators, and with eye contact made and a quick nod hello his shoe tramps on the dirt path behind me, and these men my seniors by a decade or more—there were eight in two years, in total—and while I remember their faces and where they said they grew up and the deep grove of white pines we went to, I cannot recall a single one of their names or if they once ever told their names to me, but nonetheless *closeness,* something near respite, relief from a bleak way of seeing, as while I adored all the things human beings had made I mainly despised human beings: saw their design as shortsighted, their construction haphazard, their maintenance needing too much maintaining, but hidden by trees, dusk sinking to night, *the singing of near-perfect industry*, here pressure and density, here equations of state, here balance, breath measured, entropic, and when we were finished, had switched ourselves off and parted from each other's company, within me was calm, flat neutral and static, the job done, the stars still indifferent, and so over time, and through acts of this manner, I came to see love as *duty to work*, a viewpoint not that uncommon, as I held great affection for accomplishing task, for procedure done forthwith and fitly, and by May of my last year in North Appalachia, that region of limestone and sinkholes, I knew I would always live two lives at once, a life seen and a life more invisible, and knew also that these lives would transpire in parallel, would move forward in space at a similar rate while remaining at all points equidistant, but ignored in this thinking *Euclidean principle*, as according to Euclid *on a spherical plane all straight lines are turned into circles*, bend warp and wrap, are bound by their globe, and thereby become geodesic, and with earth a sphere this meant points intersecting, meant contact made between two different things that I'd thought I could always keep separate.

And here *midcareer*, the Near North Side loft, my wife holding a torn condom wrapper, the two of us poised on opposite sides of our kitchen's marble-topped island, light pouring in through the balcony's sliding-glass doors, reflecting from off Lake Michigan, this '97, the boom in full swing, the country choking on money, and with one arm akimbo the person I married releasing the ripped piece of plastic, the object suspended and then falling slowly to the smooth beige Biancone counter, and on this woman's wrist a chain of white gold, and on her finger a ring of white diamonds, and the condom itself, once contained in the wrapper, in a trash can at Anna Page Park west of Rockford, used in conjunction with a junior in high school, a boy named Brandon O'Cleary, taller than average and lithe and light haired and dressed in grunge-era trappings: ripped jeans and cloth high-tops and plaid flannel shirts, worn despite the damp heat of deep summer, button-down items undone by myself on at least ten separate occasions, the two of us coming to know one another per work for the firm that employed me, endeavors involving repeated site visits to dozens of area cities, as these places were ready to take on more people, were building hundreds and hundreds of houses, and along with these houses new schools and boutiques and plazas and fire departments, structures intended to be *flanked by*

small ponds, by fountains and banks of bright flowers, and lawns
would be needed and toilets and bathtubs and all this depended on
water, as without water no dwellers could dwell, and no shoppers
could do all their shopping, and no roads would be tarred and no
sprinklers would hiss and the juice bars would have no crushed ice
for their smoothies, so watershed checked for all types of pollutants,
farmland surveyed for new aquifers, and *here's where to pipe in to
existing storm drains* and *here's how to maintain water tables*—
all of this data determined and gauged, collected for further analysis,
and at night in hotel rooms in Schaumburg or Elgin calls home to the
woman I married: *I'm just checking in* and *yes things are fine* and
I can't wait to get home and see you, sayings that in some ways
were not utter lies as I loved my wife then and I still do, but with the
receiver set down on its cream-colored base a walk to my car to start
trolling, cruising each village—the malls and gas stations—for boys
who were in need of money, who were willing to part with one type
of resource in order to then gain another, as I wanted something soul-
lessly epicurean and the edge boys had this to offer, could promise
me dividend with low overhead if I was willing to become a partner,
and at tables in food courts not far from arcades or in restrooms out
west toward the toll roads, the edge boys and I would come to terms
quickly, as we were living within a bull market, and yes there were
blips—a kidney infection, a stop at a DUI checkpoint—but the tech
bubble was big and said bubble was growing and past the continued
growth rate of this bubble few other events seemed to matter, so
repeated foray while my wife sat at home with first one and then
both of our children, and the paychecks were big and I had money in
hedge funds and things just kept growing and growing, and the first
of our daughters grew out of her onesies and went to her first day of
preschool, and the suburbs expanded, spawned acres of homes, re-
plete with skylights and bird feeders, where young men and women,
the moon overhead, supplemented their own genealogy, while beneath them new pipes pushed out all their sewage, carried their
waste to *wherever,* but what I mean to say is there was no need to
think, only an urge to keep doing, so when the condom's torn wrapper touched down on the counter I looked at my wife very calmly,
crossed my arms on my chest, and leveled my eyes and explained
that conference in Denver, where by true chance I ran into someone
that I knew from my days back at Lehigh, and her name was Daphne
and she was from Cleveland and one drink had led to three others—
and the story was seamless (there were parts told while weeping),

and I beseeched my wife not to leave me, to accept my mistake and think of our daughters and think of the concept of family, something that I, for one night of my life, had so foolishly placed by the wayside, and while this tale was spun into something metallic, into something expensive and shiny, my thoughts went again, as they still sometimes do, to the image of Brandon O'Cleary, his long body leaning on a tall granite wall littered with weaving graffiti, his hair to midear, deep blond and unwashed and parted straight down the middle, the locks grimy enough to keep a clean angle, to roof his face in an A-frame, and Brandon liked music and Brandon liked pot and Brandon liked shooting home movies, and set up his parents' bulky camcorder on a tripod each Sunday evening, where before dusk and until shortly after he filmed from his small bedroom's window, the lens looking down the length of his street, looking, he told me, *at nothing*, at cars leaving driveways and children on bikes, at snowfall and rainfall and hail, and stacked in his closet were columns of tapes, some years old and some very recent, these acts of surveying disclosed to me while I set up my firm's *total station*, a device that like Brandon's sat too on a tripod, and was also used in surveying, and when Brandon approached and said *what the hell is that* I told him of angles and distance, of sight via prisms and data recording and how to look under and over and straight through the earth, how to see measure test and tell everything.

But now it is summer and I've rushed through my life, only to find other summers, more seasons of heat, doubleheaders and picnics, more evenings of lush thrumming stillness, more weeks of monotonous unchallenging work, more checks written for property taxes, more vacations taken to mundane locales: lighthouses or churches or statues or bridges, trips now made most often without me, my wife and two daughters wanting time to themselves, a concept I don't find surprising, as while I've been a good father in a number of ways I am also quite guilty of *distance,* of supporting my offspring with money, not love, of remaining *emotionally absent,* a shortcoming my spouse has said she equates to our children being not male but female, that I have had a hard time accepting my role in our family and that from this our family suffers, but when they pack up the Jeep for points west or east there is, within me, real sadness, deep melancholy that I've failed at my task, that I couldn't perform any better, that on car rides to St. Louis to lay eyes on the Arch or to Utah to hike in the Tetons, I am spoken of poorly—not called spiteful names in tones bright with rage but wondered at, frowned upon, questioned, the way the favored team's fans, having watched their club lose, leave the stadium bewildered and empty: *they should have done better* and *what were they thinking* and *man, I just can't believe that,* and to provide counterbalance to these feelings of shame I walk to my den and computer, boot up the hard drive, and sit down at my chair and see who is working this evening, who will meet me at street corners close to the mall, where the big summer sale is happening, where nightly the blacktops, like still inland seas, wait for the next day's sojourners, temporary residents of these declining Edens, as America is reaching its summer, that point where all bloom has happened, where what has sprung from the earth shows off what it's got and waits patiently for *decomposition:* the peaking of oil, the drying of rivers, the crops lying wrecked in their rows in the heartland or some other crippling paucity, and for this reason the edge boys are genuine artifact, Americana that's highly collectible, each one like the last one but also unique, made individual via small details: a birthmark or scar or small discoloration, a type of deodorant whose scent is brand-new to me, a way of dyeing their hair that I'd never thought of or a piercing in some place that I had not seen, and on these evening drives to the malls or motels, I allow myself time to wander my city, take in each billboard and juice bar and gas pump, every neon, glowing marquee, and here is the semi just in from the freeway, its trailer filled with plasma TVs, and here the grease franchise, burgers and shakes, cars ringing three sides of the building, the doors locked but the drive-thru window still open, its panes retracting hydraulically, and out farther from town landfill and power plants and all manner of *infrastructure unsightly*—squat concrete structures where sewage is treated, as the clean must be kept from the dirty.

And Brandon, my favorite, do they know what their acts bring, these people of cities on the edges of cities? Do they know that all this is ending? That how things are now is not how they will be? That this grand experiment's over? That the Feds have cut rates per blowback from subprime and still these places are failing? That homes being built now will never be lived in? That at the auto plazas, units aren't moving? That people work longer than ever before and earn less than they did at midcentury? That the petals have dried out and the stalks are all rotting? Because, Brandon, I know it, and this is why last night I put in my two weeks after being telephoned by a headhunter, an anonymous man two time zones away representing a firm working in *catastrophe modeling,* in the scientific prediction of disaster, in detailing what type of wrath to expect when the next Level Five descends on the Gulf Coast, or the big one arrives to shake down San Francisco, or the Southwest has its next batch of fires, or the Singapore Causeway succumbs to tsunami or a flood eats some county in Kansas, for these events, now, are just short of certain, and insurers want to cover their asses— need to know what kind of odds are in play, if gross loss will be millions or billions, and for this *computer-assisted scenarios,* software eschatological in nature, programs designed to map out the End Times second by second by second, and here's what to expect when the Bay Bridge collapses, and here's what this zip code will look like as rubble, and here's what turns to ash if winds blow from the west as opposed to blowing northwesterly and Brandon, the money's terrific, the sum offered much more than I would have expected for my input on our slow apocalypse, and for this reason I will again move my daughters and wife, and will sell my house and then buy a new house, and find yet another tree-lined tranquil street in a newly made master community, where each house looks just like the last one, some split-level in which I may hide a bit longer and wait while things turn truly sour, for coastlines to shrink and shelves to go bare and gas to hit twenty a gallon, and perhaps I won't ever see it, will expire before we fully lose balance, and fall from our perch on the roof of the world, spiraling downward and downward, and it was to be different, *there were to be bluebirds,* there were to be grills near the shore of a lake, a postwar aria of infinite refrain; we were to applaud, and be applauded. There was the promise of promise. We had solved something. The dead were brought back from French beaches and honored. The dollar held. Wheat grew. We made things of substance. But it all went perverted, we purchased each other, and we left you, Brandon, with *nothing,* with hair dye and game shows and modified food, with the ghost of Social Security, with lead in the paint on the walls of your schools, with electromagnetic pollution, with esplanades of red brick where the hollow walk shopping, the headsets of their cell phones like blinders, with some small bit of wealth that can never make up for the damage inflicted upon you and Brandon, I'm sorry, I should have known better, I should have made more prudent choices, but what I loathe most about the person I am is also the thing that completes me so Brandon, please, one kiss, I'm done asking, we have financialized your humanity, we have taken and taken, and there's no stopping this and there's no cure for this and so coated in fear lust and haste are our happenings that we forget wholly *implication,* that these cities, like rash on the skin of the land, are emblematic *of more dire virus,* and once in a host will not go away but replicate over and over, and, Brandon, my pet, we're low on vaccine, and the antibiotics are useless, and small bits of plastic float in our seas, debris no bigger than plankton, sharp brittle shards that won't biodegrade, not now and not ever—proof we were here, in our miserable way, have washed up on every island, and wrecked every acre and nautical mile, and spun the hand on our moral compass, and without any pride or belief in ourselves exist without any power, and supplanting this *war,* and replacing this *purchase,* and we give ourselves over to skirmish and item, and our guilt gels around us, forms into things that we can't escape so more things are built to contain them, and if we don't like how they look they can always be brightened so Brandon, keep bleaching, burn through every root, because if you're not pretty then you'll get no money, and if you don't feed us, we promise, we'll eat you.

Two Poems
Cole Swensen

AND AND

After Laurent Pariente's White Walls,
Musée Bourdelle, Paris, 2006

doorway without door after door
after moving through a small room

and through the doorway he saw

and the wall opened for him

through a white afternoon

and in one small room you'll find
a man bending down to pick up something small,
a piece of paper, folding over, a white after white we have tried to repeat
but a lengthened difference
                              was my home shadow
I lived in a series of interlocking rooms that can carry

and the shadow carried him home.

When a doorway outnumbers its door, and here we have an uncountable
opening in the shape of the empty, and in glancing to the left, in a series of
flight, the angled guest.

Thus a doorway is always a distance, and if there's a face in it, our corridors
have corridors within them
and he traveled seven days without ever leaving the house.

Laurent Pariente's walls are broken and something white follows you from
ocean to ocean.

Cole Swensen

Laurent Pariente enters the house alone; the body becomes its own room, and so he must walk on, which is an accumulative art, an intersection of time and space that is the body slightly lost, which is the future until he had no house.

If once a white shadow, over, wing, over

       want under

       want either

     and washed it asunder

     these were the corridors we wandered to pieces

gone acre, now naked, what army of silent

To walk into the deaf house, the chalk house, the flayed house that Pariente has built a house in which there are no rooms; there are only corridors leading to walk into the thought house, the sparrow home, the mathematical hand. We are constrained to live in houses, where starts anemia, thus amnesia, and are dreaming: the houses of the mind fall for miles. And it's relaxing, a matter of slowly giving, and often the fall is lateral, and you walk on without thinking.

Laurent Pariente has set out to use silence as a building material, and from there devolve houses composed entirely of angles. If sighted down to the vanishing point, if the earth goes ajar. Any doorway is a frame, which makes the face inside come alive. And she leaned on the door frame as if she had ages. Which makes the days harder.

Which is to say, geometry and light constitute a forest, which is in turn defined by its aleatory, its arbitrary, its errance is the geometry of a threshold seen across a salt plain delivered at regular intervals he placed a statue that became a monument because an echo becomes visible the more the forest grows larger from your listening, from your leaning in as though you were listening even harder.

are the days.

Space happens in pieces.

Pariente sculpts only what cannot be touched.

Interviewer: What do you think touch is?

Pariente: White.

Interviewer: What do you think white is?

Pariente: The face once all its impediments have been cleared away.

68

Interviewer: What do you think a wall is?
Pariente: Something, anything, that opens itself because it hears a slight sound
and so turns around a little too quickly and cracks open at the spine, simply
flays its own vertebral column, atmosphere layered, which is to say air—there
it turned; a wall is a spiral stair in a slower mirror, which is a wall ironed out
by fire
and I'm caught on the top step.

Wandering such hallways in the light
disturbs the careful balance of inside and out.

Interviewer: What do you think inside is?
Pariente: I thought of adding a small red square.

TO BE HAUNTED

To be haunted is to be lined with a separate time   one just slightly off-set
one   spotted mirror ajar   to feel above all   sometimes inside the arms
but more interior still   a man silhouetted in a window   naked, but lit
and where does the light   why does light fit   a window, an unshorn sail
a tradition of sightings   that credits the sighted   with unlikely
but what does it prove?   That a solid object fears the uncanny, that an archer
is more the thing empty   than an archer   stood at a crossroads, counting.

Haunting is an incommensurability between what we see and what we know.
The electric wires outside   set up a hum.   What occupies a fire within
could burn the building down.   And down and down.   A town
is a serial occupation in the same way that serial paintings take the same
place with the slightest   and inch it into difference   there's an animal
you can't quite name who stands between.   Incommensurably
who could not speak.   Gray that would not end   in endless gray
increments   the infra thin   dimensionless
denies the infinite   and so sadness   becomes dangerous.
There's an animal between us   and we can't find him.   In the margins
of fifteenth-century miniatures   creatures thrive beyond description.
It was from a love of animals   that humanity was made from humans.

69

Cole Swensen

Ghost: **from gast,** as in soul-sprite breath-life, sliced wreath   of a waning
neck   it comes from all over   has been called the back-comer
the night-child   guest of lack-print and glass-phoid   of shatter-this
and all the way back unto 1385   when the word was first connected
to the thing that wandered off from the body, a slight scarring on the surface
most words for ghost are pieces   of mica that carefully layered
will make a window out of fire. It's cold   and the faces at the window do
what faces usually do, they open   onto a genetic history   turns and
it's the eyes, everyone says   you can't say that's not alive.

Who was an ordinary man   who turned to light a stove   who shadow-
flew-on-wall   will nothing there awake   like anybody else   who,
picking up the mail   and so the shattered half   I watched a man
walking down a hill   who then came to him   watched I a man
and there within   who slices bread   who cut   and did not bleed
and straightened up   with the shears in one hand and the
zinnias in the other   the corner   of the eye is an enormous room.

He emerged from a doorway, she came out of the mirror, he simply appeared,
I turned around and there she was on the hearth, the carpet, the stairs. Ghosts
always look like they're alone, which is to say, are seen one by one and so the
field extends right there in the room or a vast plateau among wind. Holding
out her hand, she came in from the garden and held out her hand as if to say
take it, pointing to the small object therein, which turned out to be a tooth.

The ghost is in itself a boundary, is that   that distinguishes between the
past and the after   which is endless   and that a ghost itself   cannot be
older   than the way a dead child is instantly   than any of us will ever be
more widely, a tendency   toward repetition   which is itself a clock
that stopped   that endless   circling which traces a circle in the dust
on the floor the sunlight sketches an hourglass   was on again   the
revenant   but no, time only seems circular to those on a spherical earth,
something about gravity that   while a long line stretches out, the
errant of the heart   you know they cannot swerve or perhaps the notion of
cyclical time comes only from the sun   if you lived   anywhere else
you'd find you never see them again.

Natural Daughter
Sandra Cisneros

"BEFORE YOU AND YOUR brothers were born," my mother said to me, "before your father met me, he already had a kid in Mexico City. Illegitimately. With one of *las muchachas* who worked for your grandmother. A daughter."

It was 1995, Presbyterian St. Luke's in Chicago, the hospital where I was born and where my father was under the knife having heart surgery. While we waited in the hospital lounge, my mother bared her own heart to me, her only daughter.

"Sometimes when we were in Mexico visiting, this woman and her daughter helped out with our laundry. You used to play with the girl. But you were little, you don't remember."

I didn't tell my mother then, but I *did* remember. The face of this girl, my natural sister, traveled back to me like a *paloma blanca* fluttering across the expanse of forty years.

And though my father survived the heart surgery and accompanied us in the world of the living for two more winters, he never mentioned his other daughter to me. I never mentioned her to him.

There are some questions a daughter can't ask a father.

I thought about this sister a lot as I wrote *Caramelo*. After my father died, I wrestled with whether to exploit this family secret as raw material for my story. I had to promise my father's spirit that in the end it would all turn out *bonito*. But the novel was finished years ago. She haunts me still.

I thought my novel would force my family to sit down and talk, finally, like a real family, with one person speaking and the others listening. I imagined my six brothers and I having a moment like in

71

the *telenovelas* where the music rises and tears fall, but in the end we would all embrace.

But we never talk about things that matter. We talk about breaded pork chops, the Chicago White Sox, the dog's skin rash.

And because I don't talk about her, even thinking about this woman makes me feel like crying. So who could I seek out who could tell me about her?

As Divine Providence would have it, when I next telephone my mother in Chicago, guess who's visiting from Mexico. Señor Coochie is sitting at my mother's kitchen table as if willed into being. Señor Coochie is a character in real life and in my novel. He's also my father's *compadre* from way back, from the Mexico City of their youth, after Father came back from serving in the U.S. Army in World War II.

The first thing Señor Coochie tells me about my half sister is: "I think you're mistaken."

"I remember your father had a '41 Buick, a big yellow convertible. And good suits Señor Curiel the tailor made for him, and those expensive shoes. Italian leather. They cost a lot. He liked to dress good. Beautiful suits. Beautiful shoes. 1948, '49. I knew your Uncle Little first, that's how I came to meet your father. Through Little. Little and I were still riding bicycles, and we would see your father come and go in that big '41 Buick of his. What a car! He liked those big-shouldered suits. What I remember was the '41 Buick. But a daughter? No, I think you're mistaken.

"A '41 Buick. Beautiful, but it gave him a lot of car problems."

Señor Coochie is a master storyteller. He takes his time when he should take his time. He slows the story almost to a halt when he has your interest, and then speeds the story along like a dancer pattering toward the footlights, pausing right before a furious final pirouette.

"This was around the time when this girl Silvia was my girlfriend when we were just *chamacos*, just kids. She was maybe fourteen, so let's see, maybe I was sixteen or so. These days Silvia takes care of my house in Juchitán when I'm in Mexico City. I let her stay there rent free, because she's old now and I feel sorry for her, but, oh, my wife is jealous! She thinks this woman and I have got something going on. Look, she was just my girlfriend a long time ago. When we were just *chamacos. Cha-ma-cos.* But I broke it off, because she was fooling around on me. I said, 'Silvia, I think it's to your benefit if you and I go our separate ways. . . .' "

"But what does this have to do with my father?" I ask.

"Oh, well, that. No. I think you're mistaken."

*

After I interview her about the secret sister, my mother says, "So what else is new?"

It's been a decade since that first conversation we had in the hospital. I'm ashamed to say I was afraid of my mother's bad temper. She was angry with her mother-in-law for bringing the washerwoman around when she was there as the official wife. But this time, after she told me all she knew, which was about as much as I knew, she said, "That was the past. It doesn't have anything to do with me. So what else is new?" She sounds as blasé as if talking about the weather.

My mother doesn't like silences. She fills them up with "So what else is new?" Or with a detailed report of what she had for dinner. Or what she bought at the grocery store. Silences are to be filled in the way one stuffs a mouse hole with steel wool. That's what my mother's lists of food and talk that is just talk are all about. Syllables to fill the void, so the real stories that slink about in the dark won't come out and spook us.

I wonder about my mother. And I wonder about myself and my own curiosity, my nagging need to poke under the bed with a broom.

*

Señor Coochie calls me back a few days later: "I spoke with your mother about the girl. She said she didn't think it was true."

I'm surprised at my mother lying to him so coolly and ask—"Did she get upset?"

"No. But she did say this: 'If he has a daughter, she's probably in Korea, because that's where he was stationed between the wars.'"

Then he tosses this Molotov: "And I managed to get ahold of your uncle Old. Old said he doesn't know anything about your father and any illegitimate daughter. But . . ."

And here he pauses for effect.

"He did confess to having an illegitimate daughter himself! A girl he sees on Mexican television because she's a newscaster."

Before hanging up, he gives me this advice: "Look, the person you should really ask is your aunty Baby-Doll. She and your father were always close."

But when I do summon the courage to call Father's favorite sister, they tell me she's in Mexico. How is it when she lived in Mexico she was always visiting the US, and now that she lives in Chicago, you can never find her, because she's in Mexico City!

Maybe the antidote to my fever is to *not* think about her, like Mother: "That was before he met me. It doesn't have anything to do with me."

*

I telephone my oldest brother late at night when I know I'm sure to find him. He's a doctor and rarely home. He tells me a story, but not the one I'm looking for.

"You know the story of our tía Esmeralda in Mexico, don't you? How she was pretty, the prettiest of all her pretty sisters, right? She's a black widow."

"What do you mean?"

"She killed all her husbands."

"But *how*?"

"Well, *I* don't know," he says. "Poison maybe."

But what about the family secret about our half sister?

"Oh that," he says flatly, "I already knew. Papa told me in the car. He was already sick."

"And what did *you* say?"

"What *could* I say? I was in shock!"

"The girl used to play with us," I say. "Remember?"

"No, I don't."

"But *you* were the one who made up the game to see if she wore underwear."

"How do you remember those things?" he says.

"How do you forget?"

*

I think if I think the thought, my lost sister will materialize and tell me the story of her life. The one without our father. If she stayed behind in Mexico, it's probable she never learned to read and write. It's possible she made her living as a laundress like her mother. If she had children, maybe they made their way north to the border and crossed over. And maybe that crossing was safe and uneventful, or maybe it was dangerous and fatal, or worse. It's always worse for women, isn't it?

And if her children made it over to this side, I *know* how difficult their lives are here. Especially now after 9/11 when politicians want to build a wall around the country.

And I think about the recent immigrant rights marches and the sign one man carried: IF YOU DEPORT ME, WHO WILL BUILD THE WALL?

*

Brother Number Two and I exchange emails under the subject "The Missing Sister," like a mystery story from Sherlock Holmes.

Brother writes: *She might be related to us, but she's a stranger to me. Anyway, the way I see it, I have a lot of relatives I already know that I barely have time for as it is. What do you expect to get from all this?*

I don't know, I write back immediately, *I'm a writer. It's my job to think about things. I live my life facing backwards.* I don't tell him all of this bothers me because I was Father's favorite. His *reina.* How come Father lavished all this love on me and none on her?

My brother writes: *Why don't you ask Aunty Baby-Doll? She loves to talk about the past.*

If I could find her, I write back, *but she's an unreliable witness. You know how she always covered up for Father.*

My brother suggests I ask our father's friends. But most of them are gone already, crossed over the final border to the other side, where, as Chicano poet Levi Romero puts it, "*quizás están muy contentos allá en la gloria/porque no llaman ni escriben.*" They must be very happy over there in heaven, because they don't call or write.

My father's *compadres.* Even the ones who might be alive, how to find them? Drifters who worked both sides of the border, a little upholstery, a little buying here and selling there. Who knows what they did over there. They were never home, their wives and kids stashed conveniently on the other side. Sure, they sent money home. Some of them went to church every Sunday.

Just a bunch of ne'er-do-wells, big talkers, nothing-but-story. Bull-shitters. The kind of guys like Fellini's *I Vitelloni.* Just a bunch of big mama's boys. Babies with suits.

*

Everyone warns me not to revisit the story about the laundress's daughter, because it's not fiction anymore.

Now it's dirty laundry.

*

"You just want the dirt on Papa."

Brother Number Three is home when I call. He and our two youngest brothers, the twins, manage the upholstery shop my father left behind. It's Saturday. Brother is minding the kids while his wife is out.

"You just want the dirt," he insists.

"No, I just want to know what you think."

"I think everybody has secrets."

"Not me," I say. "My life is an open book." But as soon as I say this, I wonder if it's true.

Brother admits he knew. Cuco, one of Father's upholstery buddies, told him.

"Remember Cuco?" he asks. "He's the only upholsterer I knew who wore a suit to work, like a businessman." A fat man with slick hair hammering chairs in his white shirt and tie. "After Papa got sick, I used to hang around with Cuco and listen to his stories, stories about the war, stories about the relatives. He's the one that told me Aunty Oralia had a fling with Uncle Paco before she married his brother."

"You're lying!"

"That's what he said. He was a good guy for stories, I tell you that."

My brother adds: "Mama didn't like him, though, said he was a bad influence. Mama always suspected Papa was having an affair with

77

one of his seamstresses. Well, the seamstress was nothing to look at, but I don't know. I think, well, I went through things in my own life. But I'm good with my wife and my kids, you know. It's different once you become a father."

"That's the point," I say. "You have a daughter you're crazy about. Think about *her*."

"Wait, I'm not so sure Cuco is dead. I'll ask this guy who sells Poly-Foam. He would know. And you should try getting ahold of Aunty Baby-Doll."

He promises to call me back. But then he doesn't.

*

Brother says Father was always running away from his problems. I think about this for a while and consider its truth. When the washerwoman was pregnant, Father ran to Korea. And when Mother was pregnant with her firstborn in Chicago, Father ran back home to Mexico City. But he was scolded by his own father, who reminded him: "We are not dogs." And Father returned with his tail between his legs to Mother in Chicago, and he married her.

*

I think a lot about the reasons for my obsession while I'm driving the car, while I'm waiting at a red light. Maybe it's about abandonment. It's because I was abandoned by lovers when I was writing the book, not once but twice. It's because I know the worst thing in the world isn't having someone leave you by death. That, after all, is not their fault. But to have someone leave of their own volition, to have someone you love alive, existing on the planet, but choosing not to share any part of that living with you.

The weakness isn't having the child. It's abandoning it.

To me abandonment is worse than death.

*

Why do you suppose the grandfather didn't insist Father fulfill his obligation to the washerwoman? Was it because she was Indian? Mexico glorifies its Indian past, but the contemporary situation is another story. Indians are the ones who work the worst jobs, who are at the bottom of the social ladder. You only have to watch Mexican television to see all the stars are as white as Hollywood. It's the mixed bloods, the mestizos, who play the part of Indians even in the *telenovelas*. I don't know of any Indians who play Indians. And when there is a role for an Indian, it's a bit part as a servant, or in a Stepin Fetchit role that ridicules Indians. In Mexico the worst kind of insult is to call someone *un indio*.

*

The washerwoman's daughter. My father's natural daughter. What kind of father was he to her? It's like a *telenovela*. Did the mother fall in love with my father in his good suits and yellow convertible? Or did my father simply help himself to what was close at hand? He wouldn't have had a hard time. My father was always a charmer.

I wonder what she felt, this washerwoman, watching my mother and her kids, watching us, watching me play, while her own daughter with the same face as my father, the darker daughter, had to work.

We were always *amolados*, always traveling from Chicago to Mexico City and back on a shoestring. No seat belts. No credit cards. No stopping. Baloney sandwiches for dinner. Sometimes my father was so sleepy he'd swerve across the line. A truck would honk. That's when my mother would jerk awake and scream, "Alfredo! You could've killed us!" And then we'd pull over to the side of the road and let Father join us for a snooze.

He couldn't resist a baby. He borrowed them from their mothers at the supermarket just so he could get a chance to hold them. He honked and waved at kids when his car paused at stop signs. "Watch out!" we'd warn him. "Somebody's going to think you're a pervert." He didn't care. He was a lover of children even as a young soldier. Photos of him in Korea holding crying toddlers, hugging street kids, three or four in each arm. My father was always a man who loved kids. He raised seven of them.

79

Above all else. Above anyone, everyone. Including his wife. My father adored kids. How could the man I knew be the same one to walk away from a daughter?

*

I should've asked my father when he was alive. After lying on the operating table having a quadruple bypass, he had almost two more years of life.

My family suffers stories no one dares to mention.

The grandmother who had a child from another liaison before she married my grandfather. The uncle who ran off with the army payroll. The cousin in Philadelphia who shot his wife in a fit of jealousy and had the rest of his life in prison to regret his bad temper. The maternal great-grandmother who, despite being ugly, married five times and thus is suspected by this descendant of being good in bed.

We don't talk about these things. Father would get angry if I even mentioned them.

So how was I to ask?

I should've asked him.

*

Brother Number Four says he knew because of my novel. He's a geologist. His wife was born in Mexico, so they go back and forth a lot. It's because they've witnessed what it is to be poor over there. Every time they go, they visit an orphanage and bring gifts, donate a little money. This brother is the only one who says he wouldn't mind trying to find our sister.

"But how do we find her?" he asks. "Hire a detective?"

"I don't know," I say, "I don't know."

*

Sister, maybe your mother saw an opportunity.

I don't blame her.

Maybe she fell in love with his words, his big-shouldered suits, the fine car, the good shoes. Maybe he was the only gentleman who ever looked at her.

Or maybe he just used her. A player like the ones I fell in love with and imagined myself in love with for years.

I'd fall for a suit and a tie every time. A nice car. A good profession. An apartment in a neighborhood that was glamorous. Not like my neighborhood that looked like a mouth with open sores.

Maybe she thought he'd come to rescue her, like the stories on the *telenovelas*. Deliver her from the rooftop room and install her in a home of her own.

*

I want to see you, and I do see you, everywhere, in all the women I meet when I travel to Mexico or Bosnia or Italy. I see you in all the women, the poorest of the poor. That spring day in Sarajevo, an unforgettable picture of misery: a Gypsy with terror on her face, standing on the curbside, ignored, offering for sale half-dead lilacs wilting in the miserable heat. The *indígena* in the Tepoztlán market begging me to please buy another bag of *chocolate* even though I'd already bought one: "*Por favorcito*, it's not going well for me today. *Por favorcito.*" In Rome the Polish refugee knitting hats on the curb of Piazza Mazzini, her wares spread on a little card table; the Peruvian nannies afraid to talk to me, homesick but afraid to complain, sunning their little charges in the pebbled park of the Gianicolo; the Asian women at Piazza Navona, silk scarves draped from their arms as if they are the goddess Kwan Yin, each desperately shouting lower and lower prices just to make a sale. At Union Square, San Francisco, the homeless woman who says, "Thank you. You're the first person all day who looked me in the eye and treated me like a human being."

Everywhere, no matter where I go, I see you.

Sandra Cisneros

*

My phone machine. Brother Number Five: "Got your message. Call me back."

*

The most recent US census form arrives by mail, and I find myself confused by the most basic question.

"What are we?" I call out to Ray, my friend and life partner who is working in his study. "What shall I put down for what we are?"

We don't agree with being classified as "Hispanics," that slave name I connect with presidents who never even bothered to ask us what we call ourselves. What's in a name? Everything. If it doesn't really matter, why won't "wetback" do?

"Sweets, what shall I put down for what we are?"

Ray and I decide after some conversation to check off "other."

But then the census insists on details and offers ethnic categories.

We claim "indigenous" because we don't know how to explain it in one word.

But after I check off "indigenous," the next question baffles us even more: *What tribe?*

"Ray, what tribe are we?" I say, shouting to my partner at work in the next room.

"What?"

"They want to know what tribe we are. What shall I say?"

After some discussion we agree to write in "mestizo."

*

Brother Number Six says, "I don't know anything."

Then a knocking on the phone cuts us off, as if our father doesn't like us discussing his sins.

*

My youngest brother and his wife and kid come to visit me in San Antonio, Texas. Because they're tourists, we consider the horse and carriages parked next to the Alamo. We're eating ice cream sundaes and we hesitate. But the driver says, "Sure you can bring your ice cream on board." So we climb up.

I'm enjoying my caramel sundae and the ride when the driver, a big country woman from outside Dallas, starts talking about genealogies. How she's one-sixteenth Cherokee and one-fourth I-don't-know-what, and on and on. She is the color of boiled milk.

Somehow it pisses me off for her to claim to be Indian. So many Americans claim to be Indian, but I don't see them volunteering to assist their natural brothers on the reservation.

It might be the canvas sack collecting horse *caquita* under the horse's tail, or it might be the story she's telling, but my caramel sundae starts tasting like horse manure.

After I've had enough, I finally speak up and say, "Well, we're Indian too!"

She twists around from her seat in front of the carriage and says, "Oh yeah?" in a smart-alecky tone, and then, just like the US census, she asks, "What tribe?"

"What tribe? Well, I don't know," I say. "Our families fled Mexico during the Mexican revolution. But all you have to do is look at our faces."

My sister-in-law is the color of coffee with not enough milk, my brother and I the color of *café con leche*, the child the color of a cappuccino. My brother, his wife, child, and me, we look like Mexicans, Arabs, Jews, Moors, Sicilians, American Indians, East Indians, Turks, Greeks, Palestinians, Gypsies, Egyptians, Pakistanis, Iraquis, Iranians, Afghanis. We look like what we are.

And who the hell knows what that is.

*

Aunty shrieks like a parrot when I tell her why I'm calling. She calls the woman and the daughter both—*esa chamaca*—"that youngster." All the characters in her story are pronouns—*esa chamaca, ese fulano, este ratero, esa sinvergüenza.* That youngster, that so-and-so, this thief, that shameless one. I'm not certain if she's talking about the mother, the daughter, an older daughter, the man the mother took up with, or the man my natural sister ran off with.

"Now wait a second, Aunty. *Who* stole *what* money?"

"She robbed me," Aunty goes on without answering. "I'm certain *por Dios Santo* she was not your father's daughter. How could he be the father if he was in Korea when she was pregnant?"

Then she goes on: "*La chamaca* Luz . . ."

Luz! My memory was right about the mother's name.

"She was a clubfooted servant . . ."

Funny I hadn't remembered her clubfoot, but, yes, I do remember now the little polka of her gait, the way she labored under the tin bowls of wet laundry.

". . . a good washerwoman, excellent, but she did not wash her own body. How could a man as delicate as your father take up with a woman who was dirty and smelly?"

My aunt calls the washerwoman *mugrosa*, dirty, and *apestosa*, smelly, but I saw her as dusty and worn out from labor. I suppose if you had to hobble about washing clothes and pulling loads through a wringer washer on the rooftop in the summer heat, you'd be smelly too. "She had two girls, an older one, Teresa, from another man, of

84

course. And a younger girl whose name I can't remember. Because they were the kind of women who would get involved with anyone.

"Yes, she had a fellow who lived up there on the roof with her. But after the younger one was born, the *sinvergüenza* left them, and your grandmother would find her work. Your grandmother was just trying to be kind. Do you think she would've had her around had she known the gossip?"

"But I remember the girl, and she looked just like my father, only darker."

"What are you saying! She didn't look like your father! She went with us to Acapulco. You have photos of her."

I'm astounded. I thought I made up this part of the story. I thought I made up several parts of my novel, but later someone tells me it really happened. The things I think I imagined are true, and the things I remember as truly happening . . . ? But maybe it's the elder who was my father's daughter. After all, my father came home periodically on leave.

Aunty goes on with her story, still talking about the younger girl. "Somebody put the idea in her head about your father. That girl tried to get money from us after you'd all gone back to Chicago, and when she couldn't, she robbed us. I didn't call the police because of her mother. But let me look for the photos of Acapulco. And the letters from your father in Korea. I'll look and we'll set this all straight."

Is it only a good story, not a true one? And if it is true, is it too ugly for fiction, made dirty with theft and accusations, blackmail and bigotry, the same prejudices one class, one race, has about another?

Then Aunty proceeds to unravel another family secret, one she thinks I don't know. I do, but I want to hear how she will tell it. It's about when the grandfather was a colonel in the Mexican army, stationed on the coast at Tampico. He had a mistress there who was *el amor de su vida.* . . . But this is *my* version of the story, not Aunty's.

"Mamá moved us there for two years to keep an eye on him. One

85

day Little and I discovered that so-and-so talking to Father at the barracks. We chased her with sticks all the way back to her door, so she would leave him alone. Father was so mad he sent us back to Mexico City after that."

Aunty chuckles with pride over her victory over *la fulana* even though it happened more than a half century ago.

I want to ask her about her father. Didn't she think she should've beaten him up too? But I don't bring up this detail since she seems so pleased with herself.

Poking under the bed, all I've found is other people's dirt. Everyone has told me something I didn't know, or that they didn't know I knew.

And I wonder, are all stories like this, the natural events much more complicated than the artificial story each of us weaves with ourself as the hero, in the center of the universe.

Aunty tells me, "I went to visit your father at the hospital at the end and told him, 'Look, you're not the father of that girl. When Luz was pregnant, you were in Korea. The dates don't coincide. So there!'"

And then, as if she knows how I feel, Aunty adds to me: "You have nothing to feel guilty about."

"And then?"

"What do you mean?"

"What did Father *say* when you told him?"

"Nothing. That's the end of the story. What else could he say?"

Then it's my turn to say nothing.

Modulation
Richard Powers

DO

FROM EVERYTHING THAT Toshi Yukawa could later determine, the original file was uploaded to one of those illegal Brigadoon sites that appeared, drew several thousand ecstatic hits from six continents, then disappeared traceless, twelve hours later, compressing the whole arc of human history into a single day: rough birth, fledgling colonies, prospering community, land grabs and hoarding, shooting wars, imperial decay, and finally, much gnashing of teeth after the inevitable collapse, which seemed to happen faster each time through the cycle. The kind of site that spelled *music* t-u-n-z.

Yukawa—or the artist formerly known as free4yu—was paid to spend his days trawling such sites. When he was twenty-six, the Recording Industry Association of America surrounded his apartment, coming after him to the tune of $50,000 and four years in prison. He was now twenty-eight, out on parole, and working for his old enemies. His job was to study the latest escalations in the arms race that kept a motley army of hackers, crackers, and slackers running roughshod over a multibillion-dollar industry, and then to develop the next counteroffensive to try to reclaim file-sharing no-man's-land.

By Yukawa's count, the average illegal file server could satisfy half a million happy customers across the planet before being shut down. Most looters rushed to grab this week's tops of the pops. But even files with no identifying description could rack up hundreds of downloads before the well went dry. Much later, Yukawa guessed that the infected track might have installed itself onto as few as fifty initial machines. But as his friends in digital epidemiology were quick to point out, all it took to start a full-fledged epidemic was a single Typhoid Mary surprise package slipping through quarantine.

Richard Powers

DI

A week before the music changed, Brazilian journalist Marta Mota was grilling a strike brigade attached to the Second Infantry Division near Baqubah in the explosive Iraqi province of Diyala. She was looking for a story for the *Folha de S. Paulo*, some new angle in the endless war that hadn't already been done to death. The stress the combatants had lived with for years had broken her in three days. All she wanted was to get back to her apartment in Tatuapé and write some harmless feature about local rampant corruption.

On the day before she left Baqubah, she interviewed a young American specialist who called himself Jukebox. He described, in more detail than anyone needed, how part of his informal job description involved rigging up one of the M1127 Stryker Reconnaissance vehicles with powerful mounted speakers, in order to pound out morale-boosting music for the unit during operations. "What does this music do?" Marta asked the soldier, in her lightly accented English. The question bewildered him, so she asked again. Jukebox cut her off, somewhere between impatience and amusement. "What does it *do?* That depends on who's listening." When she pressed for details, Jukebox just said, "You *know* what the hell it does."

At his words, Marta Mota snapped back in time to Panama, listening as American Marines tried to flush Manuel Noriega out of his bunker with massive waves of surround-sound Van Halen. That was two decades ago, when she was still a fledgling journalist in her twenties, absolutely convinced that the right story could change the conscience of the species. Since then, in combat zones on three continents, she had written up far more soul-crushing sounds.

She asked what music the Stryker vehicle pumped out, and Jukebox gave a rapid-fire list: the soundtrack of the globe's inescapable future. She asked for a listen. He pulled out something that looked like those slender, luxury matchboxes set out on the tables in her favorite Vila Madalena jazz club. She inserted the ear buds and he fired up the player. She yanked the buds out of her ear, howling in pain. Jukebox just laughed and adjusted her volume. Even at almost mute, the music was ear-stabbing, brain-bleeding, spine-crushing stuff.

"Can you copy some of these tracks onto my player?" she asked, and fished her device out of her bag. She would write up the musical recon operations later, in Frankfurt, while on her way back home.

The sight of her three-year-old player reduced Jukebox to tears of

88

mirth. He pretended to be unable to lift it. "What does this beast weigh, like half a *pound?*"

RE

On the campus of a midwestern college dead center in one of the I-states, in the middle of a cornfield that stretched three hundred miles in every direction, a recently retired professor of ethnomusicology walks through a dusting of snow across the quad to his office in the music building to begin his permanent evacuation. Jan Steiner was supposed to have vacated back in August, to surrender his coveted space to a newly hired junior faculty member; it's now mid-December, the semester over, and he's still not started culling.

Born in the late twenties to a German-speaking family in Prague, Steiner came to the States just before half his extended family was rounded up and sent east. He moved from a Czech enclave in Queens to Berkeley and Princeton, and from there, he went on to change the way that academics thought about concert music. He has taught at his privileged college for as long as anyone alive, and he has occupied his office one semester longer than the college allows.

He follows the stone path through a break in a hedge and comes alongside the Doric temple to Harmony. For the first time in years, he notices the names chiseled into the building's limestone frieze: Palestrina, Bach, Mozart, Beethoven, Schumann, Brahms, and—after decades, he still can't help smiling—Carl Maria von Weber. It could've been worse; there's a University of California music building that celebrates the immortality of Rameau and Dittersdorf. His parents revered these names above any humanitarian's; beyond these names, they said, the rest was noise. Steiner's father went to his grave holding his son partly responsible for the twilight of these gods.

Once, at the peak of the iconoclastic sixties, Jan Steiner suggested that all these names be unceremoniously chiseled out of their limestone and replaced by thousands of names from all places and times, names so numerous and small they would be legible only to those willing to come up close and look. Like all his writing from those heady days, his jest had been deadly serious. The whole sleepy campus was outraged; he'd almost been driven to finding work elsewhere. Now, a third of a century on, when the college would probably leap at such a venture, Jan Steiner no longer has the heart to propose it again.

Before Steiner and his like-minded colleagues set to work, scholars wrote about music mostly as an aesthetic experience, masterpieces to be celebrated in religious terms. After his generation's flood of publications, music took its place among all other ambiguous cultural work—a matter of power relations, nationalism, market forces, class contestation, and identity politics.

Jan Steiner gazes up at the Doric temple's entablature, circa 1912, and squints in pain. Could he still tell Palestrina from Allegri, in an aural police lineup? When did he last listen to anything for pleasure? If this building were to collapse tomorrow, what would he advocate, for the replacement frieze? Just spelling out the solfège syllables of the chromatic scale smacked of Eurocentrism.

He lets himself into the building's side door and makes his way up to the second story. Even on a snowy December Sunday, the practice rooms are going full tilt. He walks past the eight cubicles of baby grands—Pianosaurus Rex in full, eighty-eight-key sprint. The repertoire has certainly expanded in his half a century on campus. The only fragment of sound in the whole polychordal gauntlet he can name is the John Cage emanating from the empty cubicle on the end.

Other voices, other rooms: he's given his life to promote that, and the battle is all but won. Scholarship has discovered the ninety-eight percent of world music it hitherto suppressed. Elitism is dead; all ears are forever opened wide. So why this pall he's been unable to shake for these last several months? Perhaps it's the oppressiveness that Paul Hindemith once attributed to Bach in his last years in Leipzig: the melancholy of accomplishment.

He unlocks his oaken office door and flicks on the light. The tomb is overflowing. Every flat surface including the dark linoleum floor is piled with precarious paper towers. Monographs bulge off the shelves. Folders and collection boxes stack almost to the fluorescent lights. But he can still put his finger on any desired item, in no more than a few minutes. The problem is desire.

Now he must judge every scrap. There's too much to save, but it would stop his valve-repaired heart to throw any of it out. Five decades of iconoclasm. The college library might sift through it and keep anything of value. But who in the last five years has set foot in the college library?

He drops into his desk chair and stares again at the awful severance gift from his retirement party. The department presented the mobile device to him in a teary ceremony: a clock, calendar, appointment book, phone, Web browser, and matter transporter, but mostly a bribe to get him to quit quietly. The thing also, incidentally, plays music. Even the name sounds like *Invasion of the Body Snatchers.* He should have known, half a century ago, that music, like the most robust of weeds, would eventually come in *pods.*

And this one came preloaded with every piece of music he has ever written about, recorded, or championed. Turkish hymns and Chinese work-camp songs, gamelan orchestras and Albanian wedding choirs, political prisoners' anthems and 1930s radio jingles: his entire life's work arranged for an instrument that everyone could learn to play without any effort. What were his colleagues thinking, giving him his own back? What he needs is music he hasn't yet discovered, any sound at all that hasn't disappeared into the oversold, derivative, or market branded. He grabs the device, flips it on, and blunders through the menu screens, looking for a song he might somehow, by accident, have blessedly forgotten.

RI

On the night before the exploit launched, Mitchell Payne was on his way from Los Angeles to the Sydney 8-Bit Chiptune Blowout. The first humans to grow up from infancy on video games had stumbled inadvertently into young adulthood, a condition that left them stricken with nostalgia for the blips and bleeps of their Atari childhood. And where there was nostalgia, there were always live concerts. The Sydney event was Mitchell's third such extravaganza. The chiptune phenomenon had hit North America ten months ago, which meant it would soon erupt into mass consciousness and be dead by this time next year. But until such demise, Mitchell Payne, leading Futurepop composer and perhaps the greatest real-time Roland MC-909 Groovebox performer of his generation, had found another way to help pay off his Sarah Lawrence student loans.

The one-hundred-and-fifty-grand debt didn't worry him so much. What bothered him, as he hunkered down over Palmyra Atoll for the next hour's installment of in-flight entertainment from the Homeland Security Channel, was the growing conviction that at twenty-three, he no longer had his finger on the pulse. He had lost his lifelong ability to keep one measure ahead of the next modulation. He'd recently scored only seventy-two percent on an online musical genre test, making stupid mistakes such as confusing acid groove, acid croft, acid techno, and acid lounge. He blamed how busy he had been, trying to master the classic eight-bit repertoire. He told himself that he had just overthought the test questions, but in reality, there was no excuse. Truth was, he was slipping. Things were happening, whole new genres crossbreeding, and he was going to be one of those people who didn't even hear it until the next big thing was already in its grave and all over the cover of *Rolling Stone.*

But he had more pressing worries. In Sydney, he'd be up against some classic composers, the true giants of the international chiptune movement. Without some serious art on his part, they'd laugh him off the stage. Fortunately, his material was beyond awesome. He pulled his laptop out of his carry-on and fired up the emulator. He flipped through his sequences again, checking tempi, fiddling with the voicing of chords. Then he peeked again at the climax of his set, an inspiration he still couldn't quite believe he'd pulled off. He'd managed to contrapuntally combine the theme from Nintendo's *Donkey Kong* with Commodore 64's *Skate or Die,* in retrograde inversion. The sheer ecumenical beauty of the gesture once more brought tears to his eyes.

When he looked up again, the in-flight entertainment had graduated to that new reality show, *Go for the Green,* where ten illegal alien families compete against each other to keep from getting deported. He watched for a few minutes, then returned to his hard drive's 160 GB of tracks. But before he could determine where he'd gone wrong in discriminating between epic house, progressive house, filtered house, and French house, the stewardess was on the sound system asking everyone to turn off and stow all portable devices in preparation for landing in Sydney.

MI

Toshi Yukawa took too long to realize the danger of the virus. He'd seen the chatter on the pirate music discussion boards, the reports of files that downloaded just fine then disappeared from the receiving directory. Some guy named Jarod would complain that his file count was broken after syncing with his Nano. Some guy named Jason would report that the same thing was true on his Shuffle. Another guy named Justin would confirm for his Zen. Then another guy named Dustin would chime in, "Get a Touch, you freaking noobs, it's been out for weeks."

Any file that hid itself was trouble. He ran some tests on the twelve machines behind his router firewall: five subdirectories were compromised. He could discover nothing else until he synchronized these machines with portable devices. After syncing, three different handhelds—a music player, a pocket PC, and even a cell phone—showed flaky file counts. Yukawa realized that he was looking at something technologically impossible: the very first backdoor infection of multiple music players.

The ingenuity of the code humbled Yukawa. The main file seemed to figure out what kind of mobile device was attached to the host computer, then loaded in the appropriate code. But the ingenuity got better, and worse. On next check, Yukawa's five suspicious desktop directories had multiplied to twelve. The malicious payload was attaching itself to other files.

What kind of person would want to punish music traffickers? There were the geek hacker athletes, virtuosi like Toshi had been, simply giving their own kind of concert on their own astonishing instruments, regardless of the effect on the audience. There were always the terrorists, of course. Once you hated freedom, it was just a matter of time before you hated two-part harmony. But when he saw how this new virus could spread, Toshi Yukawa wondered if he wasn't being set up. Maybe some of his colleagues at the Recording Industry Association had developed the ultimate counterstrike for a world where two hundred million songs a day were sold, and even more were borrowed. And maybe his colleagues had simply neglected to tell him about the new weapon.

Some days he wasn't even sure why the RIAA had hired him. So much music could be had by so many for so little that Toshi should have long ago been driven into honest work, say eclectic format disc-jockeying for Starbucks. There was pay what you want and genetic taste matching and music by statistical referral. Customers who liked Radiohead also listened to Slipknot. If you like Slipknot, you may also like the Bulgarian Women's Chorus. The vendors had your demographic, and would feed it to you in unlimited ninety-nine-cent doses or even free squirts that vanished after three listens. He owed his job to saltwater syndrome. Drinking made you thirsty. Buffets bred hunger.

And some kind of strange musical hunger had bred this virus. Whoever had made the payload had made something beautiful. Yukawa had no other word for it, and the way the thing worked scared the hell out of him. Three days into his hunt, he discovered that four other computers behind his firewall were now infected.

These boxes had gone nowhere near an illegal download site. The virus had somehow uploaded itself back up to shared music service software, and was spreading itself through automatic synchronization onto innocent bystanders.

A sick and brilliant mind: that's what Toshi Yukawa was fighting. He felt a wave of disgust for anyone who couldn't put such gifts to better use. Then he remembered himself, just four years ago: a collector so obsessed with liberating music that he'd all but stopped listening to it.

FA

Marta Mota woke up in her economy hotel on the Schönstraße near the Frankfurt Hauptbahnhof with a tune in her head. Not a tune, exactly: more like a motif. She couldn't altogether sing it, but she couldn't shake it, either.

It lasted through her hot shower—a marvelous indulgence, after Iraq. It persisted through the heavy black breads and sausages of German breakfast. It was still there as she handled her e-mail and filed another story with *Folha* on the Diyala campaign. She had contracted what the Germans called an *Uhrwurm*, what Brazilian Portuguese called *chiclete de ouvido:* a gum tune stuck in her relentlessly chewing brain.

As earworms went, this one wasn't bad. She'd spent an hour yesterday listening to the testosterone storms that the American soldier had copied for her. She'd needed two hours of Django Reinhardt and Eliane Elias to drive that throbbing from her mind. What she hummed now, she felt sure, was nothing she'd heard in the last five days.

She Skyped her mate Andre at the appointed hour. He was consulting, in Bahrain. The world was insane, and far too mobile for its own well-being. She only thanked God for dispensing Voice Over Internet just in time.

Andre asked about Iraq. There was nothing to say. Everyone knew already, and no one could help. She told him about the earworm. Andre laughed. "Oh yes. I had that for three months once. Kylie Minogue. I thought I was going to have to check into a hospital. You see? The Americans will get us all, one way or the other."

She told him she thought Kylie Minogue was Australian.

"Alabama, Arizona, Australia: it's all a World Bank thing, right?"

He asked how the tune went. She tried to describe it. Words were as effective at holding music as smoke was at holding water.

"Sing it," he commanded.

She swore colorfully. "Sing it! Here? In public?"

The man seemed to do nothing but laugh. Wasn't there grimness enough, out in Bahrain?

"The Internet is not public," he told her. "Don't you know that? Everything you do on the Internet instantly disappears."

She tried to sing a few notes, but it was hopeless. The earworm wasn't even a motif. It was more a harmony, a sequence of magical chords that receded when she focused on them.

"Where do you think you heard it?"

She had no clue.

"I read an article about why this happens, but I can't remember it. Would you like the garbled version?"

She said yes. That was the beauty of free communication. They could be as silly as if they were lying next to each other in bed. Andre recounted his jumbled article, something about a cognitive itch, some combination of simplicity and surprise, the auditory cortex singing to itself. He thought he remembered something about the most common stuck tunes coming from the first fifteen years of a person's life.

"You need an eraser tune," he told her. "A good eraser tune is as sticky as the original, and they cancel each other out. Here's the one that worked for me." And into his tinny laptop computer microphone in Bahrain, in a frail but pretty baritone she hadn't heard for way too long, he sang a few notes that rematerialized in her Frankfurt hotel as the theme song from *Mission Impossible.*

It didn't help, and she went to bed that night with the phantom chords taunting her, just out of reach.

FI

Jan Steiner sits in his windowless office, listening to his life's work. It isn't bad, as life's work goes. But all these sounds have become so achingly predictable. He can't listen to anything for more than thirty seconds without hearing political agendas. Somebody preserving their social privileges. Somebody else subverting them. Groups of people bonding together with branded tunes that assert their superiority over everyone with different melodies.

He has recorded hundreds of hours of what people now call "world music," and written about thousands more. He always paid the performers out of his modest grant money and gave them any rare recording profits. But he has never taken out a single copyright. Music belonged to everyone alive, or to no one. Every year, in his Introduction to Music lecture, he told his freshmen the story about how the Vatican tried to keep Allegri's *Miserere* a trade secret, refusing even to show the score, but insisting that, for the full mystic aura of the piece, one had to come to Rome and pay top dollar. And the protectionism worked until the fourteen-year-old Mozart, in Rome for a concert, transcribed it perfectly from memory, freeing it for performance everywhere. And every year, Jan Steiner got his freshmen cheering the original bootlegger.

The idea was simple: put your song out in the world, free of all motives, and see what other people do with it. When his scandalized colleagues asked how musicians were supposed to make a living, he pointed out that musicians in hundreds of countries had eked out a living for millennia without benefit of copyright. He said that most music should be amateur, or served up like weekly cantatas knocked out for the Glory of God alone.

He sits on his green padded office chair, tipped back on the cracked linoleum, under the humming fluorescent lights, listening. He listens to a traditional Azerbaijani mourning song, as personal a lament as has ever been put into tones. He found it gut-wrenching when he first recorded it, two decades back. Now all he can hear is the globally released feature film from a year ago that used the song as its novel theme music. The movie seemed to be mostly about potential residuals and the volatile off-screen escapades of its two stars. The soundtrack made more money in six months than any Azerbaijani musician had made in a lifetime, and the performers on his track—the one that had brought the haunted melody to North America—had seen not a penny.

Just to further torture himself, he switches to his other great recent hit: an ecstatic Ghanaian instrumental performed entirely on hubcaps and taxi horns that only six months before had been turned into an exultant commercial for global financial services. This one also made a mint as a cell phone ring tone.

He has no one to blame for these abuses but himself. All music was theft, he has maintained over a lifetime of scholarly writing, since long before sampling even had a name. Europe used to call it cantus firmus. Renaissance magpies used to dress up millennium-old Gregorian Psalmodic chants in bright polyphony. Whole musical systems—Persian dastgāhs and Indian ragas—knew nothing about ownership and consisted entirely of brilliant improvisations on pre-existing themes. The best songs, the ones that God wanted, were the ones that someone else transposed and sang back to you, from another country, in a distant key. But God hadn't anticipated global financial services jingles.

Back in the 1970s Steiner had predicted that the rise of computing would save music from death by commodity. Armed with amazing new ways to write, arrange, record, and perform, everyone alive would become a composer and add to the world's ongoing song. Well, his prediction had come true. More music of more variety was being produced by more people than any ethnomusicologist would ever be able to name again. His own illiterate grandson was a professional digital musician, and Jan Steiner finds the boy's every measure unbearably predictable.

He works his way through the towering stacks of offprints, pitching mercilessly. While he works, he leaves the player on shuffle, letting it select his life's tracks at random. By the time he leaves, hours later, he has thrown out two large garbage bins, and it's made no visible dent on the office. He stashes the player in his coat pocket as he leaves the building and heads back toward the snowy quad. Outside, it's night, and silent, the only track he can bear.

But as he rounds the corner of the Georgian psychology building, a tune comes back to him. *Comes back* isn't quite right, since this one is nothing he's listened to this evening. He can't quite say whether he's ever heard it before, or even what scale or mode or key it wants to be in. As far as he can tell, this track—if it is a *track*—has gotten away safely, innocent, never repackaged, let alone heard by anyone.

SOL

In Sydney, Mitchell Payne felt a song coming on. It had banged around his head since deplaning. This was dangerous: when melodies came to him out of the blue, it usually meant he was ripping someone off. He wasn't alone. There were only so many notes—twelve, to be precise—and they could be combined in only so many sensible ways. Someday soon, a garage band out in Cos Cob was going to string together the last viable melody, and music would be pure plagiarism and mash-ups, from then on.

The industry was already pretty much there anyway. Covers and remakes, quotations and allusions, homage, sampling, and down and dirty five-fingered discounts. A Korean kid covering a Taiwanese kid whose arrangement imitated the video game *Pump It Up* whose soundtrack mimicked an old Brian Eno performance uploads an electrifying guitar video of Pachelbel's Canon in D, already the most hacked-at piece of the last three hundred years, and immediately, people from Panama to Turkmenistan post hundreds of shot-perfect recreations, faithful down to every detail of tempo and ornament. . . .

The melody nibbling at Mitchell's brain as he set up his loopers, shifters, sequencers, and MPCs on the stage of the small Haymarket theater might have come from anywhere. It was at once oddly familiar and deeply strange. He cursed the snippet, even as it haunted him. He couldn't afford Stuck Tune Syndrome just before performing. He had to settle into the chiptune groove, that quantized trance that the children of Mario demanded.

But by the time he finished testing the gear, Mitchell was flipping. He stood inside the circle of banked electronics, his Mission Control of waveform generators, wanting to pull the plug on everything and crawl off to a Buddhist monastery until the monster tune scratching at his brain either came forward and said what it wanted from him or left him for dead.

While the house filled, Mitchell sat backstage in the green room answering questions from an editor of New South Wales's most prestigious online chiptune zine. What was the most influential mix he'd ever listened to? What would be the most important developments in the eight-bit scene over the next few weeks? If he could put only one video game soundtrack into an interplanetary spacecraft, which would it be? He could barely hear the questions over the stunning harmonic tension in his head. The stage manager had to call him twice before he heard.

Nerves almost doubled him over as he jogged out of the wings in front of a restive crowd already clapping in frenzied, synchronized downbeats. He had that sick flash of doubt: *Why do I put myself through this? I could retire to something safe, write a music blog or something.* But as soon as he got the backing tracks looping, the MSX emulator bumping, and his Amiga kicking out the MIDI jambs to the principal theme from the old blockbuster game *Alternate Reality*, he remembered just what Face-to-Face was all about, and why nothing would ever replace live performance.

SI

By the time Toshi Yukawa realized he needed help from coders be-yond himself, it was too late. He'd taken too long to isolate the virus and even longer to break-point and trace the logic, trying to determine exactly what the multiple payloads meant to do to the hundreds of thousands, perhaps even millions of music players already infected. The code was so idiosyncratic and original that Toshi couldn't under-stand it, even as it stared him in the face. The weapon was cryptic, evanescent, awful, awesome, protean, full of fearsome intelligence and unfathomable routines: a true work of art. He isolated a sub-routine devoted to hijacking the player and beaming out music in subaudible frequencies. Yukawa didn't get it: why spend such incred-ible intellectual effort to take over millions of devices, just to play a tune no one could hear? That had to be just a private amusement, a warm-up act for the headline show. Yukawa dug deeper, bracing for the real mayhem. A person who could write such code could sow destruction on an operatic scale.

Then Toshi stumbled onto a portion of the initializer that made his blood run cold. It checked the host's time zone and adjusted an-other routine that made continuous calls to the music player's clock. A timed detonator: the code was going to launch a synchronized event to go off at a single moment across all the world's time zones. But what event? The code was inscrutable assembly language. Delet-ing songs at random? Scrambling the firmware or flash memory?

Yukawa logged in to the best professional discussion board for tracking the thousands of viruses, worms, Trojans, and assorted malicious code in the wild. There it was: growing chatter about something already code-named *counterpoint*. Yukawa posted his discoveries, and four hours later, one of the big boys at Norton found the trigger date for Yukawa's detonator routine. A day obvious after the fact: *counterpoint* was set to premiere on December 21, the winter solstice. The day after tomorrow.

Time had run out. In two days, many, many people were going to be walking around earbudless, their billions of dollars' worth of portable media centers bricked. Personalized music would never be safe again. People would be thrown back on singing to each other.

A South American journalist reporting on the eternal hackers' arms race had once asked Yukawa what would happen if the white hats lost. He'd laughed her off, but here it was. Toshi sat back in his Aeron chair, gazed out his window down the glens that hid the unsuspecting venture capitalists along Sand Hill Road, and gave up. Then he did what any artist would, faced with imminent destruction: he turned back to study the beauties of the inscrutable score. He worked on without point, and all the while, unconsciously, under his breath, in the key of hopeless and exhilarating work, he hummed.

LA

São Paulo did not help Marta Mota. In fact, the relative safety of home only worsened her earworm. It got so bad she had to take a few days' leave from *Folha*. Andre actually suggested she get help. Only the fact that several friends were also suffering from a barely audible *chiclete de ouvido* running through their minds kept her from losing hers.

More confirmation awaited her online. She turned up hundreds of posts, each one plagued by unsingable music. A reporter to the end, she traced the blind leads. She found herself in ancient backwaters, Krishna's healing flute, Ling Lun's discovery of the foundation tone, Orpheus raising the dead and animating stones, the Pythagoreans with their vibrations the length of a planetary orbit, the secret music that powered the building of the Pyramids, the horns that felled Jericho, the drumming dance of Ame no Uzume, the rain goddess, luring the sun goddess, Amaterasu Omikami, from out of hiding in the rock cave of heaven. She read about African maloya, outlawed because of its power to stir revolution. She found a fantastic article by an old Czech-American musicologist tracing the myth of sublime sound, from Ulysses, tied to the mast to hear the Sirens, through Sufi mystics, Cædmon's angel-dictated hymn, and on into songs on all continents that yearned for the lost chord. God's own court composer seemed to be baiting her for a libretto.

On the solstice, Andre was consulting in Kamchatka. Marta worked late, too wired to sleep. She drew a hot bath, trying to calm down. Her player was docked in the living room, whispering soft, late Vinicius de Moraes, one of the few human-made things capable of temporarily curing her of the human-made world. Right at a key change, the music stopped, plunging her into the night's silence. Then another tune began, one that, in four measures, lifted her bodily out of the water. She sprang from the tub and dashed into the living room, nude and dripping. By the time she reached the player, the harmonies were done.

She fiddled with the interface in a naked daze, but the tune had erased its tracks. Whatever had visited was gone faster than it came. She shut her eyes and tried to take down that sublime dictation before it faded, but could make out only vague hope, vaguer reassurance. What was left of the tune said, *Keep deep down; you'll hear me again someday.* She stood on the soaking carpet, midway between bitter and elated. The song had ended. But the melody lingered on.

LI

Mitchell Payne was deep into a smoking rendition of *The Last Ninja* that was burning down the house when the music died. The backing track piped out by his 160 GB classic simply quit. The iPod brought down the master sequencer, which in turn crashed the Roland, a chain reaction that pretty much left Mitchell noodling away clueless on a couple of MIDI controllers in the empty air. The silence lasted no longer than it takes to change a track, an onstage eternity.

His first thought was that his old partner in crime, free4yu, had come back to wreak electronic revenge on Mitchell for walking away scot-free when their trading concession got rounded up by the federales. But before Mitchell had the presence of mind to power anything down, the iPod started up again.

The thumping audience fell silent and listened. The harmonies passed through a series of changes, each a strangely familiar surprise. Afterward, no two people described the sequence the same way. It was the weaving antiphony of a dream, the tune your immigrant nanny made you laugh with, the unsuspecting needle dropping onto a virgin *Sgt. Pepper,* a call to desert prayer, an archaic fauxbourdon, that tape you tried to make with your high school garage band, the last four measures of something amazing on the radio that you could never subsequently identify, highland temple bells, an evening singalong, the keys you pressed chasing after your grandmother's player piano, a garbled shortwave "Happy Birthday" from the other side of the planet, a first slow dance, a hymn from back when you were just setting out on the game of consciousness, all resonance, sphinxlike, aching with possibility, a little incandescent phrase transporting all listeners back into timeless time.

That's how the world described it the next day, those who were lucky enough not to rip their buds out of their ears or fiddle with their rebellious players. The nations' blogs resounded with endless variations on one simple theme: *OMG—did you hear that?*

The world on that day had half a billion music-capable mobile devices. If a tenth of those were infected and turned on when the tune got loose, then more people heard the ghost tune at the same time than were alive when music was first recorded into the Samaveda. And here it was again, after an eternity away: a tune that sold nothing, that had no agenda, that required no identity or allegiance, that was not disposable background product, that came and went for no reason, brief as thunder on a summer night.

For his part, Mitchell heard the song he'd been hallucinating for the last two days. And in that instant before the crowd broke out into stunned applause, Mitchell Payne thought, *This is it—a totally new genre.* The first person to transcribe the thing was going to make a fortune. *Bow, you sucker, bow!*

TI

The quad is dark and empty, the snow gathering. Flakes pour out of the woolen air. The sky above him is a lambent orange, scattering the lights of the town. Jan Steiner takes the long diagonal path toward the neoclassical English building. The phantom tune still nags at him. The harmonies take an amazing turn, he calls out in surprise, his foot slips on the icy walk, and he slams to the pavement. Hot current shoots through his brain. Pain such as he has never felt tears up the fuse of his spine and he blacks out.

When he comes to, he feels nothing. Some part of him understands: shock. He tries to stand but can't. His right thigh comes through his hip in a way that it shouldn't. The front part of his pelvis is as powdered as the snow.

He lies on his back, paralyzed, looking up into the rust of night. He calls out, but his voice doesn't carry much beyond the globe of his body's warmth. He always was a feeble little tenor, even in the prime of life. Those who can't sing, teach.

He rolls his head to the left, the empty Colonial anthropology building. He rolls to the right, the abandoned Brutalist auditorium. He can't see past his body to the music building, with the seven names on its confident pediment. Winter's first night. The college is closed, evacuated for the holidays. He'll lie here until morning, undiscovered. The temperature is falling and the pain starts a vast, slow crescendo. He can't imagine how the piece will end.

He's amazed that this fate has been lying in wait his entire life. He looks up into snowy emptiness, recalling the words of the stunned Mozart, when the natives in provincial Leipzig forced him to listen to their old Capellmeister's archaic motet they'd kept alive like some forgotten relic: *What is this? Here at last is something one can learn from.*

Then he remembers: invasion of the pod phone players. By a mighty effort of will, he manages to crane his shattered right hand around into his coat pocket. He shovels the device out onto the pavement in little Lego pieces. No saving call. Not even a diverting tune while waiting to go numb.

He inserts the buds anyway, to keep the warmth from leaking out his ears. World's smallest earmuffs. Snow is falling on the wool of his coat and his cotton cap. Snow falling on concrete, on frozen earth, freezing skin, snow on snow. In the hush, his ears sharpen. Through the dead buds, he hears the crushed device whisper a vast and silent fantasia: the wired world recovering a theme it long ago misplaced.

He lies still in the ravishing dark, listening to a need as big as lust or hunger, an urge with no reason on earth ever to have evolved. The only fundamental human pleasure with no survival value whatsoever: Music. . . .

Ah, music for a while,
will all your cares beguile.

A few measures more, and the cold returns him to Do.

King Cow
Shelley Jackson

—For Sean

KING COW IS THE FATHER of the tiny country we call The Foreground. Everything is concrete there. Everything has been concrete for forty years. King Cow himself is concrete, almost as concrete as his statue, which is made of concrete, with steel reinforcing and peridot eyes. No ghosts cross the bridges that connect our homeland to the mountainous mainland. Even echoes die out over the water, and weather finds somewhere else to go. Traffickers in dreams and omens have failed to establish trade routes to our cities, and obituary columns must outsource, since we have no dead, or if we do, we don't remember them, since memory too is a sort of ghost.

"The dead are among the world's most fearsome and disciplined guerrilla organizations. To safeguard our nation and our people, I am classifying all foreign bodies as haunted," said King Cow, in his Immensely Popular mask. "I am further classifying the entire mainland as nowhere, and naming it Nowhere." Cheering crowds tossing clover, greasing the statue of King Cow with fat. King Cow agleam! His eyes the day!

The king replaced his Immensely Popular mask with his Fund-Raising mask. Rain of amethyst, citrine, peridot. "Political hay is a cash crop," said King Cow jubilantly. "If I get any richer, I'll buy me some money!"

King Cow's names:
King Queen, The Chief Porker, Mr. Concrete Head, The Lord of Beef Cattle, The President of Procurement, The Ombudsman of Talks, Death Head of State, General Electric Pork, The Editor, The Department of Immensely Popular, .The Twenty-five-member Advisory Body, Mr. Similar, The Impenetrable Man Cow, The First Armored Oinker, The Rarefied Infrastructure, The Arm of Queen Elizabeth, The My My Fellow, The Sole Author, The Mother's Conjecture.

104

King Cow is the father of our country, but he has a mother's ways: he shares. Citizens clinging to his advisory body are rewarded with that perfect food we call M.I.L.K., or More Is Less. . . . (We don't remember what the K is for. Memory is a sort of ghost, and there are no ghosts here.) Last year, King Cow produced almost four thousand gallons.

King Cow's udders:
  Number of nipples?
  Seventeen.
  Jutting?
  Perkily.
  In hue, Pepto-Bismol or Mr. Bubble?
  The latter.
  Describe them.
  Leathery but moist, a bead of white forming at the tip. Slightly puckered around the holes.
  Why?
  Decades of giving suck.
  Describe the udder.
  The udder proper is swollen. Swollen and pendulous. In hypothetical state of repletion containing a net fluid volume of sixty-eight kiloliters, figure obtained by multiplying number of subjects by average suckle strength by time suckling by M, the milk constant.
  Is there anything more pleasant than sucking on the teat of our king?
  No.
  Complete sentence please.
  There is nothing more pleasant than sucking on the teat of our big, motherly king.

King Cow holds a gala. He performs a daring baton trick and gives a talk critical of King Kong. "He's a porker, but I am scientifically the biggest. My very body is feature length. My eyes are the day!" He puts on his Reputation mask.
  Spectators: "Woohoo!"
  "Take this clover away! Bring me flowers! Poppies, I think . . . ," he adds.
  Now trucks and Jeeps and motorbikes are crossing the bridges,

laden with seed. The entire country is under cultivation. Fields replace our tiny desert, our small jungle, our clover meadows. We are all farmers now and we are plowing and we dream of harvest and we wait for rain. That's how it is in the land of King Cow: his need is our need.

Recurring dreams of the populace in this period:
poppies
poppies
poppies
poppies
poppies
donkey eating poppies
poppies

One day a man with a telescope came to King Cow and reported sighting a fat female beluga whale under the bridge to Nowhere. "Go to increased surveillance," said the king, replacing Friendly Leader with Law Enforcement.

The whale was next seen posing for photographs near Port Foreground. From his Bureau of Investigation King Cow acquired two pictures: one of her fine, bold, nationwide abdomen, one of her small, sharp eye.

Under the mask, his face grew speculative.

King Cow dictates a memorandum:
Some bridges to nowhere take the form of a circle.
Opium is the opiate of the masses.
The letter K: do we need it?
Something was eluding him. "More poppies!" demanded King Cow.

Thirteen tons of poppies were brought. A mountain of poppies was raised in the forecourt of the palace. Scores of people were injured in a poppy landslide. King Cow looked at the poppies. His eyes were the day: partly cloudy.

King Cow found himself looking forward to his weekly briefings, where the whale was reported playing the sitar, doing a crossword, listening to a cellist. Fascination of King Cow.

Dreams of King Cow:
  whale playing in poppies
  whale playing in a jeweled aquarium
  whale in a veil
  Queen Whale
  King Cow being offered a cigar

If he had not banished ghosts, he would have said that he was haunted.

"I wish to woo," said King Cow to his advisers.
"Woo who, your Majesty?"
King Cow mistook this for jubilation and did not answer.
After some consultation, the advisers said, "Woo whom?"

King Cow went down to the water, surrounded by his retinue. He put on his new Courting mask. "My new world, my global warming," he called, "I am yours!"
"It's not mutual, pig," she replied.
"I'd like to be a little oinker," said King Cow, "but I'm all beef. Some people say my eyes are the day," he added nonchalantly.
"What's that supposed to mean?"
"Oh, radiant, I suppose. You know how subjects are."
"No," she said.
"I know a trick," he said, signaling for his baton.
"So do I. Close your eyes," she said.
He did. When he opened them again, she was gone.

King Cow raised a billboard facing the water reading "Discover King Cow!" and "Beef and Beluga, an Idea for Today!" and "Try My M.I.L.K." and "Now With Extra Fat: King Cow!"
He reshaped 1.5 tons of pork fat into a sculpture of the whale.

He hired the cellist to play day and night on the beach.
He dropped fliers offering a twenty-four-hour test drive.
Finally, the whale lifted her head above water. "You're bothering me, pig," she said. "If you don't desist, I'm heading south."
"You don't understand," said King Cow. "I'm asking you to be my *queen!* It's a concrete and lucrative offer! How can you refuse?"
"Like this," said the whale, and flipped a fin as she dove.

Headlines of the local news organs:
"Spurned!" "Rejected!" "King Receives Marching Orders from Cold-Hearted Beauty!"

King depressed.

Dreams of King Cow:
  whale attending a cello concert with a leading Indian sitar player
  whale denouncing King Cow's human rights record
  whale in a television commercial for M.I.L.K. substitute
  whale starring in a Hollywood movie
  whale receiving an Eastern-style massage from King Kong

King Cow woke panting. "Poppies," he moaned.
"It's too soon to harvest again, your Majesty," said his advisers deferentially. "But in the meanwhile, here are seventeen adolescent girls who would like to suckle, sir!"
"Poppies!"
"But your Majesty!"
"Poppies!"
"What shall I tell the girls?"
"Poppies!"
Every last petal was harvested. The land was scraped bare, until from shore to shore The Foreground was nothing but soil and concrete. The last poppies—tiny, bruised—were heaped around the bed of the king.
He gave them a weary look. "More," he said, closing his eyes. But no more would grow, though the advisers had the soil lashed, beaten, threatened with handguns, and tortured with lit cigars.

The king lay in his own manure. He chewed cud. He refused to give suck. Gradually his M.I.L.K. dried up, and the land went into drought. Many people died. Among them: every last member of the elite cadre that guarded the bridge to Nowhere.

In subsequent weeks:

Everyone's memory improved.

A man claimed to possess a haunted telescope.

The attorney general's office was heard to be investigating allegations of weather.

Seventeen adolescent girls claimed to hear the music of a phantom sitar.

A farmer swore that his boots were haunted by the ghost of a Manhattan socialite, who peered at him through the eyelets.

An electrical contractor believed his abdomen to be haunted by the ghost of a mathematician, who incessantly proved theorems.

In the once lush palace gardens, a ghost poppy issued from the soil.

In an effort to please his majesty, a proposal to euthanize the letter K was carried out. "Ing Cow is better than Ing Ong," said King Cow, with the ghost of a smile. His eyes were the day: brooding, rain-soaked.

Ghosts surged across the bridges, defying the posted signs and the barricades. Ghosts toppled the statue of King Cow, which crushed the now rancid statue of the whale. The ghost of a donkey trudged in a circle around The Foreground. A child spoke in the voice of an eighteenth-century mullah; a spa worker claimed to be Queen Elizabeth. A nightmarish letter K began appearing in books, and the ghosts of poppies grew everywhere, but thickest around the palace.

King Cow began speaking in tongues. In omens, echoes, equivalents. Nothing was concrete, certainly not his greasy fallen statue. He saw cosmic theorems in crossword puzzles. With every breath, he inhaled the opium of a billion ghost poppies. "I'm a mad cow," he cried.

The seventeen girls thought of a way to bring back the king's desire to live and with it, his M.I.L. They went to a shipbuilder and said, "For the love of the Ing and all of us, build us a whale of a ship!" The shipbuilder complied. In less than a year, the whale ship set sail, crewed by seventeen girls and a sitar player.

When he heard the distant sound of music floating over the wavelets, King Cow lifted his head for the first time in months. A bead of milk formed at the end of one of his nipples. The courtiers raced to lip it up. King Cow threw them aside. He galloped to the harbor, hooves ringing through the streets. On the dock he stood listening, his nipples weeping. The people clasped hands and watched.

Then the king plunged into the water, his beard foaming on the tide like sea brack. He swam steadily out to sea, following the ship.

Some think the girls betrayed the king. Some think they saved him. But ever since, whenever the water is not clear but creamy, and foam streaks the billows with white, we say that King Cow is in love.

The clover has grown back, but among it, ghost poppies still bloom. Our children have never tasted M.I.L.K. and do not miss it.

Three Poems
Charles Bernstein

DEA%R FR~IEN%D,

I sa%w yo%r pixture on
wehb si;t; no.t su%re
whhc one & w~ant to
tal^k or mee.t ver~y so.on
I am old ma%n 57 year$
ba%d tooth & sme.ll
ma.ke vr,y hr.d t mee%t
people. I a,m wr$iter
wr$ite po%re%y an,d
email writ.in,g al>so
se{ll goo;d stocks v;;ry
che~p & prozac~ s%ince
I a$lso can^t slee.p. bihg
bizness opportunity to
tel^l on~ly my fre;ndhs
if yo;u hav. som,e m@oney
to hehlp me/i expec%
prostr%ate c%ncer an;y da;y
nee~d mon~ey al.so m.y
broth.er in tr^.rble
willl snd y$ou my pi%cture
n.eed check f~irst
a.m poet wh;o l.ikes
yo.u al%%read#y
emmail   m$e at swifftpllay
@ssorrow.tv
a.m nhow you.r freind
& soul mat.e—

Binggo

LONELINESS IN LINDEN
—After Wallace Stevens

The fear and the hum are one.
Monuments of show gumming the works
Until the weather grows tired of the people
And the people grow tired of the dance.
Jamais, jamais, jamais, again.

The measure of the town against a dampening sky
Cobbling together six million tunes
Into more than the tones tattoo
Or their scrambled mosaic forecloses.

And if the fume and the hope
Are one? My monkey, from '49
Steps as silent as those songs
Along the cratered dark
Where Jews do Jewish things
No one pretends to understand
Or are they pilgrims on this night
When the fear and the hum are one?

WON'T YOU GIVE UP THIS POEM
TO SOMEONE WHO NEEDS IT?

Remember what I told you about purgatory?
Limbo? How all that's happening now is just
this waiting around till the big cheese makes up
her mind about you? She makes you the way
you are and then decides if it panned out; for
every ten half-baked cookies there's a gem
&, you know, just maybe you're one of those.
Then there's those take her name in vain—
whaddya call them?, the religious moralists;
she don't much cotton to them, not when
they try to take away a woman's right to choose
or bad-mouth folks almost as queer as she is.

Well, everyone makes mistakes. That's what
purgatory's for. Sometimes it happens that
while you wait you see what's what—start
accepting you're in a long queue for God
only knows what. And neither of you has
any idea what the hell the matter is or what
to do about it.

Contact
Paul La Farge

J. ALWAYS KNEW THAT they were coming, had always known it, even
before the band days, only he had always thought they were coming
for *him*. When they came then, when they actually came, and it
turned out that they were here for more or less anyone but him, J.
took it hard. He stayed drunk a long time and when he was not
drunk anymore, he took the bus to Detroit, which was the last place
he could remember having seen anyone from the band. J. didn't
know just what he hoped to find; the trails that led away from that
last gig were fifteen years cold, but he didn't know what else to do or
where to begin doing it. And in fact, in a saloon on Upper Michigan
Avenue, not far from the place where they'd played that gig, which
was gone now, along with so many other things, he found, propped
against a sunny wall by the plate-glass window, a person who could
have been the drummer, M., fifteen years later. He couldn't be sure
it was him. M. had been small and lithe and clean-cut, had had a
thing, actually, about hair, and would, from time to time, if J. remembered right, actually tweeze out his own body hairs, or cover his
chest with masking tape and r-r-rip, that had happened once, J.
thought. This person was the right height but shaggy, unshaven,
mustached, bellied. It could have been him. J.'s memory was not all
that it had once been. There had been some difficult years. J. got a
beer from the barman and sat at a table by the window, facing the
stranger who might have been M. He lifted his glass. The stranger
lifted his glass.—Hell of a time, said J. The stranger grunted. He gave
J. a familiar look. His eyes were blue, unexpectedly. Not eyes that
went with the rest of him. Had M.'s eyes been blue? The thing was,
in those days, the band days, they all wore enormous glasses, and it
was hard to tell much about them. Especially as they did not take the
glasses off, not even, some of them, to sleep. Those had been enormous days.—Didn't think I'd live to see the goddamn aliens come, J.
said. The stranger nodded, or seemed to nod. He might be a junkie,
J. thought. M., the drummer, had definitely had that problem, among
others. J. looked at the stranger's arms. It wasn't possible to tell, at

114

this distance.—What's your name, friend? J. asked.—Michael, said the stranger. That was not M. the drummer's name, J. was pretty sure. Not the name he was born with. They had all changed names, sometimes they changed names around, so that J. became M., and M. became L., the bassist, and L. became . . . it made you dizzy even to think about. And it was amazing that they had managed to keep track of who was who, although mostly that kind of accounting wasn't necessary. They only had to know which instruments to play and sometimes not even that. They had gone on without instruments.— I'm Jay, J. said. Like jaywalking, or a jaybird. An introduction that he hoped did not sound too friendly, just in case the stranger was really just a stranger. God, it was hard to tell, with people, what you were doing. It had always been hard to tell. Even before band days, in the little bright past that J. kept somehow out of the general murk, it had been hard to tell; there were people like his stepmother who were good to you one day but the next were suggesting that you'd be better off in prison, or trying to keep you from taking any food. Don't touch that! she said. It's not for you! But later when J. went to the icebox and helped himself to it, and ate it in front of her, she didn't say anything. The stranger didn't say anything. He did look about the right age, though, and the sun got through the thin hair on top of his head, and lit up a golden arc of scalp.—Have we met before? J. asked. I'm thinking, I might know you already.—Live in Detroit? asked the stranger, Michael.—Not really, J. said. I just came here on the bus.— I been here fifteen years, Michael said. I guess I probably don't know you.—What do you do? J. asked.—Do? Michael said vaguely. You know, I get a check, every month. This was J.'s situation also. Actually two checks. One from the government, because he had taken the trouble to fill out some forms, to keep some appointments, to be certified, disabled, on account mostly of his back. The other from a record label he had never heard of. They had reissued one of the albums. Every time it sold J. got forty cents. Strange times. The music on compact disc, in stores J. didn't ever visit, because they pissed him off. Then the aliens coming. No connection, doubtless, probably.— That's a good life, J. said. Michael shrugged.—Were you ever in the music business? J. asked.—That's a strange question, Michael said. Not particularly. That's a strange answer, J. thought. What would it mean to be particularly in the music business? His glass was empty. Of course they hadn't thought of themselves as being *in the business*, or, really, as making music. They were making contact. Not with other worlds, at least, not at first. Just with people. J.

remembered a long conversation he had had with someone, possibly M. the drummer, about how this was supposed to work. Our sound is like a plant, growing out into the room, that's why it's slow, man, J. had said. This must have been with a reporter. It was the answer to the kind of question only a reporter would have asked.—Plants take time. Contact takes time. We're growing outward, toward you. He reached his hands out to this reporter, who shrank back, the twit. That was in the middle period, when they played music. Afterward they would give up the instruments. Then the last concert, in Detroit. Then: dissolution. Now, aliens. Finally. Aliens.—I played a show here once, J. said. Why did he sound so wrong when he spoke? Played a show. They had made an attempt here was what they did. They had taken on a responsibility. To call it anything else was to belittle it. Even if what they did was run around in those glasses and not much else, and try to speak in the language that had occurred to them, the language of contact.—Is that so? Michael asked. Would that have been recently?—About fifteen years ago, J. said, leaning forward to catch if there was a response.—Might have seen it then, said Michael. I used to go out for a lot of music.—Might have *seen* it, man, you might have been *in* it, J. said. There, now he'd know. But Michael just shrugged.—Might have, he said. I did a lot of crazy things. Got up on stage, sometimes, probably. Now it was J.'s turn to doubt. Had the show been in Detroit? Had it even been J. playing? Maybe he was one of the people who climbed upon the stage, just a person in the crowd. It had seemed real but his memory was fucked. And *real* in those days meant something different, more like, *real to you.* That was how it had all been possible. Because they got away from what was just real. So, J. thought, let's just *say* that this is M.— Can I get you a drink? he asked.—I guess so, said Michael.—You're not a faggot, are you?—Not particularly, J. said, turning back just long enough to say it as he walked to the bar. And he hoped it stung.

A Bit of Nocturnal History
Lyn Hejinian

A straight rain is rare and doors have suspicions
and I hold that names begin histories
and that the last century was a cruel one. I am pretending
to be a truck in Mexico. I am a woman with a long neck and a good burden
and I waddle efficiently. Activity never sleeps and no tale of crumbling cliffs
can be a short one. I have to shift weight favorably. Happiness
can't be settled. I brush my left knee twice, my right once,
my left twice again and in that way advance. The alphabet
and the cello can represent horses but I can only pretend
to be a dog slurping pudding. After the 55 minutes it takes to finish
my legs tremble. All is forgiven. Yesterday is going the way of tomorrow
indirectly and the heat of the sun is inadequate at this depth. I see
the moon. The verbs ought and can lack infinity and somewhere
between 1957 when the heat of the dry sun struck me
like an erotic secret and now when my secrets erupt in the ecstasy
of cold rains and night winds a lot has happened. Long phrases
are made up of short phrases that bear everything "in vain" "all in fun"
"for your sake" and "step by step" precisely, I can only spring slowly.

*

It is the 73rd night of 1873, the year in which cowboys all wear baby blue hats
and long baby blue coats to match. Some cowboys come galloping toward me
over the horizon like bits of leaping, dust-raising embodied sky. They are as
free of the sky as they are of the false idea of them we've received from old
black-and-white photos. Their freedom is greater than what occurs during free
association. Their freedom surpasses everything that occurs during a flirtation.
The cloud of baby blue riders sweeps past me and they "pay me no mind,"
their freedom is greater than my rosy longings and yearnings and ochre
desires, which are less great than my rising sense of failure, or remorse, of
spreading shame. The cowboys recede.

*

Lyn Hejinian

For the Timtarians oppressed by the Planch, the claims of the dissident Planch intellectuals are unconvincing. "Where was your magnanimity," asks a dark Timtarian named Gus, "when our poor marched into your cornfields?"

Dissidence, when it has entered historical memory, can only be represented by fragility and mournfulness.

The Planch plutocracy will in the end be brought down by fragility and mournfulness.

*

the sky gaily nods
     . . . eggs

    to yield!

naked
    overjoying indifference
      its honors hairs

anywhere

the assassin feathers
    eight minutes
  after an instant's hesitation

*

I insist that I didn't say "political club" but "political run." We wanted to address *all* of those little irritations that distract one just at the moment the sunset is the most beautiful.

I believe that there has never been a historical moment more in need of lawns and gardens for the little ones to run around in after fighting both ideologically and practically against CEOs than this. The lives of the little ones are in a state of *transition* but they shouldn't be thrown into a state of *upheaval.*

Transition is fun, after all, though little ones need reassurance during it.

And, of course, one can't accomplish it in a single burst—that would upset the little ones. And, by the way, it's not something that will make you rich.

Probably you yourself have experienced moments in which a disjuncture between your professional persona (dignified, knowledgeable, experienced) and your persona as a granny (crawling around on the floor honking, pretending to be either a goose or a truck) seems suddenly terrifying to the little ones.

Then one day you'll gallop off, crossing a border from which there is no return.

You'll lose your personality—you'll no longer be vain, demanding, deeply insecure, vividly charismatic, and wonderfully intelligent.

*

Along comes someone down the street ranting about some "world parrot" and raising her arms as if raising arms to aim and shoot so realistically that she is spun completely around by the imaginary rifle's imaginary recoil and she
staggers out of view
She hasn't reappeared except in my imagination and that can't be represented
visually to others so she can't be represented and we will never know
how she got to that street at that moment since she wasn't needed
even though her being useful was not impossible
And much the same can be said of the bulk of things to be found

*

synonymous

. . . of vegetable

thinginess everywhere—clutter!
with vegetables!

surroundings

in a vision

119

Lyn Hejinian

and that explains . . .

but what kind?

and would another mind have . . .

with fish fault thought the what be out mind
        free
spoon halt cups
        bang in space pink

                                        and hating pink
            lacking pink

                        *

Some people insist on exercising the sincerity of their intentions
No sunglasses
I cannot produce any more posterity than my grandparents could and they will
        not begin to understand
In the course of a beautiful allegory a coursing god kills a child
Children return but only if their deaths are individually acknowledged
Deaths occur in a milieu without laws or so we think, finding them scattered
        unequally throughout the world
We have never yet remained all the way through the sequence of vignettes
        that's said to be their original
One death alone is enough to turn one's brain—we twist our imagination to
        the maximum
We are forced to cry stop but the horse trots on

                        *

The spoons have clattered
Aren't children little pears and observant birds
I note that the green blanket is askew again briefly
I have flung my sweater over the banister again
The corn cockle is beautiful

For months I've owed someone I'll call Amy Rossini a letter and tomorrow I'll
     write it but I can't explain
There was of course the matter of the curious descent into a mine and the
     terrible ascent of children hauling ore out of context
Brevity is not child's play though child's play is brief but over a long period of
     time
Today a man in a green leather hat advised me to sink my shovel
If I were to write a letter to Knut Handekker now he wouldn't remember
     who I was which in any case is not who I continue to be
Tchaikovsky died when he was 53
We'll celebrate my birthday wearing hats in May at the beach
Taking the espresso I say gracias
The house in which I toss is known by its address but it might have been
     named Credulity and called a film
Believe me
Long ago I was once in Seville in a blue dress that could be washed and dried in
     less than an hour
I want to speak of revolutions in beauty but I hear hordes counting down to
     midnight
The tales I used to tell myself no longer do
None of this is true

*

My stomach is important.
     If I tell you that I am nagged by worry at night and suffer from stomach
pains as a result, it is something you should remember because later people
may ask you about me.
     Because I'm a boa constrictor.

*

Sun!
     look ups

*

The picture appears suddenly in its entirety
It begins nowhere, and I'm faced with it
I'm against the wall opposite it facing an audience and replying to the many
     objections that the audience is lodging against existentialism

121

The picture raises no such objections, being ridiculous in its own right
It is there by virtue of a mere fluke with silent placidity
The picture is of a cow then?

I have to turn away

A cow?
Then?
There's a cow on a board?
Board, certainly, but no cow, and we term that a picture?

That it's of a cow rather than a battle is not a disappointment.

I never see cows in order

I neglect to do battle willingly out of cowardice

I'm avaricious, I want the picture

I would settle for a picture of the picture

*

Song giving way again
Every little narrative henceforth is in particular scientific
True, today the traveler goes from place to place at very high speeds
In braids (nice touch)
Given the requisite two weeks' notice but fired all the same: like a servant!

Man in the Moon
Stephen O'Connor

YOU STAY AWAY FROM them, Mama said. They don't like you. You've got your big head friends at the school. That's enough. You just stay here.

Mama didn't know anything.

You got a big head, the girl said.

No I don't.

Yes you do. It's gigantic.

No it's not. It's exactly the right size.

Your head is so gigantic, if it wasn't attached to your body it would float away. You better be careful, or somebody's going to tie a string to your head and give it to a little kid to carry.

My head is exactly the right size to be my head.

The girl just squinched up her eye and looked at me. After a while she gave her head a shake like she was so, so sorry. Then she said, Don't you have any brains at all? You got all that head and no brains inside?

That's what they told us at the Big Head School: your head's exactly the right size to be your head. There's no such thing as a normal head, they said. Don't let anybody tell you different.

They were all big heads at the Big Head School. The only little head there was Alf. And his head was so little it was more like an elbow. Golf-ball little. They made him do all the stupid work. With the toilet brush and the litter stick.

You walked in the door and there was a gigantic sign: THINK BIG.

There were signs everywhere: BE BROAD-MINDED. BIG HEADS ARE MADE FOR BIG IDEAS. THE BIGGER THE HEAD THE BIGGER THE HEART.

That was the main way you could tell it was a big head school. Everything else was normal. The blackboards. The desks. The trash cans.

123

That and the doors. They were all coffin shaped.

Why'd they have to do that? You know? Why couldn't they have made the doors light bulb shaped? Or keyhole shaped? Coffins! You know what I mean? *Coffins!*

Get out! the man from another country shouted. You are scaring my customers!

All I want is a doughnut, I said.

Go away! Nobody wants you!

Please. Just a chocolate twizzler.

You are scaring the children!

The man from another country grabbed a hammer from the box under his counter and ran around the counter with the hammer in the air. Look what you did to that little boy! the man from another country said.

It is true that little boy started crying when I walked into the store. What would be the point of denying that? And now his face was blue-red and he was screaming into his mother's neck. And she had, in fact, clapped her hand over his eyes so he wouldn't have to see me. But, even so, the person *she* didn't want to see was the man from another country. She didn't want to see what he was going to do with his hammer.

One chocolate twizzler, I said. I'll go if you give me one chocolate twizzler.

I will give you my hammer on your head, said the man from another country. I will give you two seconds and then my hammer is coming down.

One, the man from another country said. Two. Go now, or I will make a hole in your head with my hammer.

Please, I said. Just one.

With a head like that you should never have been born. Why did your mother give you birth?

I put a simoleon on the counter.

The man from another country made a clicking noise to his wife. He pointed with his nose, and she threw a chocolate twizzler out onto the sidewalk.

Go! the man from another country said. Fetch!

Can I touch it? said the girl. Then she said, It's warm! It feels like there's a fire in there. She hit me two times with the point of her knuckle. Is it hollow? She pressed her ear against my temple and she hit me two times again. Huh, she said. I bet I can't even reach my arms around it. I bet it's too big.

She pressed her chest against my forehead and her arms went out on either side.

Wow! said the girl. It's ginormous! Not even halfway!

I didn't want her to move.

Mama called them the ant heads. The ant heads don't like you, she said. They want to put your head in a garbage compactor. If they saw a boulder bouncing down a mountain straight at your head, they wouldn't say, Watch out! They would cheer.

Mama is a little head.

Why did you marry my father? I said.

Because I thought he was the moon drifting through the trees. Because I thought, There really *is* a man in the moon! I thought, Now *that* is a man who is *going* places! If I am married to the man in the moon, I will see everything. My home will be in the sky. I will have stars for earrings, clouds for slippers, and the sun will be my crown!

It's called the hate of love, they told us at the Big Head School. Inside the hate is the love for big heads. Bigger is better, is it not? It is because in the days before before, the little heads used to worship the big heads. They used to drape the big heads in fur and jewelry. They used to spray perfume into the air when the big heads went out for a walk because they wanted the big heads to always think the world was beautiful. The reason they did this is they thought the big heads could see the future. They believed that the heads of the big heads were so big because they were stuffed with everything that hadn't happened yet. This was all nonsense, of course. It is true that thoughts travel faster in big heads, but they have farther to go. So it all evens out. Eventually the little heads discovered their mistake, and felt betrayed. No more gold and fur and perfume. The big heads felt betrayed too. What? they said. What! Why is this happening? The lesson is: never worship anything. The lesson is: the love in the hate and the hate in the love. The lesson is: it all evens out. If we are lucky. If we wait long enough.

They don't know anything at the Big Head School.

It was the day after the men with torches and picks came to the Big Head School. We all got sent home for a surprise vacation. Because of all the repairs. The new roof and such.

So, do you want to know what home is to me?

Television twenty-four/seven. The smell of those little see-through socks that look like stockings for fat dwarves. Parrot shit. Parrot squawks. Mac and cheese.

Trees and more trees and trees again. Our house was a hiding place in the trees. Nobody knew it was there.

Mac and cheese. Mac and cheese.

Mama would walk a mile to the shop of the man from another country, but she wouldn't go a step further. All he sold was dough-nuts and mac and cheese.

She hadn't been into town since I was born, even though the man she had disgraced herself for had long gone.

Couldn't hold on to him any more than I can hold on to the moon, was what she always said.

So that day she said, Why don't you just stay home? They hate you anyway. Why don't you see your friends from the Big Head School? What did I send you to the Big Head School for if you don't see your big head friends?

Mama didn't know anything.

I didn't have any friends at the Big Head School. The truth is that big heads are not very nice people. That's just a fact.

So that was the day I started wandering through the trees like my father. Up over the mountaintop, down the other side. Nothing but trees and more trees. And I'm not paying attention to where I'm going. Just all brain scattered and foot tumbling.

And that's when I saw the girl for the first time. I followed my feet to the edge of the bluff, and there she was, just below, lying on a rock, her head leaning out over a stream.

At first she didn't see me. Maybe it was because of the noise of the water. So I just watched her. She looked to me like she was just about ready to start being a woman, but not quite. So maybe twelve. I was eleven. She was playing with this piece of stick. She'd let it go with her left hand. It would drift downstream and she would catch it with her right hand. Let it go. Catch it. Let it go. Catch it. That's all she was doing.

Then one time she missed it.

I must have air-sucked, because her head jerked up and she was looking at me.

She was a fat face girl. You know? One of those girls who look like a professional boxer. Or her face got stung by a million bees. All swollen browed and mushroom nosed and slug lips. No eyes to speak of.

Who are you? she said.

And I guess I said what I said because I saw how the shadow of my head just perfectly covered her whole body, even though she was mostly lying down:

The moon.

No, you're not.

Yes, I am.

Then how come you're dark?

I'm always dark in the daytime. That's why you can't see me.

I can see you now.

You're not supposed to.

She squinched up her eye and I could see she was trying to figure out if she should believe me.

Gotta go, I said. Big night tonight. Need to get some sleep.

See ya later! she said.

So after that I came down to see the girl every day. And sometimes I would see her playing her floating stick game. Or making a dam. Or just taking a nap on that rock. But she would never see me. I stuck leaves all over my head and crouched in the bushes. And I was careful never to suck air or sneeze or fart. Sometimes I would wait and wait and she wouldn't come, so I would go down and play the floating stick game myself, my head reflected like a cloud of cotton candy on the swirly-dimply surface of the water. Once I watched her the whole time she was lying on the rock playing her floating stick game. And I went down to her rock as soon as she was gone, and I put my hand down flat where she had been lying. And I could feel it. The heat from her body coming back up to me from the rock.

So then the Big Head School got all fixed up again. And the teachers told us to put our heads in a ring and do a Chinese Whisper of Hope for the little heads. The big head boy on my left said, I hope the little heads go to hell. And I said to the big head boy on my right, I hope they go to the moon.

That year the Big Head School canceled summer vacation. Our surprise vacation was enough, they said. In the school lobby they put up a new giant sign: BIG HEADS GET AHEAD.

The girl didn't come out to the stream in the winter. So I didn't see her until more than a year had passed. This time it looked like, ready or not, she'd mostly started being a woman. And I was mostly thirteen.

She still liked to play her floating game and make dams. But she also liked to lie on her rock and make big sighs. Sometimes she would make quiet noises that I think were a song. Then it was back to sighing again.

I used to call that being moony. She's moony today, I said.

One day I lay down on the far bank of the stream with my head under a bush. I am one of those lucky big heads with a little head face right at the bottom of my big head where I am mostly neck. I figured I wouldn't be so scary if she only saw my little head face first.

Hello! I called out when I heard her sit down on her rock. Who's there?

Foot-splash. Foot-splash. Foot-splash.

Who are you? she said, looking down at me.

Remember me? I said. I'm the moon.

No you're not.

Yes I am.

Why are you lying there?

I'm resting. Big night ahead. But now it's time to rise.

I had planned to say that all along. I thought if she thought my head was the moon rising in the trees maybe she wouldn't be so afraid. Maybe she wouldn't run away.

You got a big head, she said.

No I don't, I said.

Yes you do. It's gigantic.

No it's not. It's exactly the right size.

The day she pressed her chest on my forehead and stretched out her arms came and went. Then there was another day when she said,

128

They say the bigger the head the bigger the you-know-what.

Heart?

No, she said. You know.

I didn't know, so she pointed with her nose.

Oh, I said.

So, is it?

I don't know.

Show me, she said. Then a little later she said, I'll show you mine if you show me yours.

I said I guessed that would be OK.

So that was what we did.

Then she said, I guess that's pretty big. What do you think?

I don't really know, I said.

Neither do I, she said.

So she let her dress fall back down and I pulled up my pants.

Then there was the day I said, Why aren't you afraid of me?

It's because you're the man in the moon.

No I'm not, I said. Why doesn't my big head make you cry?

It's because you have little hands.

I do?

You have little baby angel hands. Who could be afraid of those?

Look, she said. She took one of my hands and she touched it to her mushroom nose. See? she said. Your hand's as soft as an angel feather. Then she put my hand on the top of her head. It's like a fly footstep. On her cheek. A mouse whisper, she said. Then for a long time she just held my hand in the air like she didn't know what to do with it. This way and that. Up and down. Then finally she put my hand on her belly.

What is that? I said.

My belly.

No. What does it feel like?

Nothing, she said. That is the exact feeling of something that never happened. And never will. That is the softest feeling in the world.

She smiled.

Why should I be afraid of that? she said.

129

Then one day: up over the mountaintop and just foot-in-front-of-foot down into the valley, and there I was at exactly the right stream, under exactly the right bluff, at exactly the floating stick game place, but the rock the girl used to lie on was in three pieces, and all the pieces had been spray-painted. One said, BIG HEADS = BIG BUTTS. The other said: WHY DO BIG HEADS HAVE BIG HEADS? BECAUSE THEY DON'T HAVE ANY ASSHOLES AND THEIR SHIT HAS TO GO SOME-WHERE. And the last one said, WHY ARE YOU ALIVE?

So after that it was television and parrot stink and parrot conversation:

My mother saying, Who loves you, snooky-wooky?

And the parrot saying back, Who loves you, snooky-wooky?

And then the parrot saying to me, Who loves you, snooky-wooky?

So I would lie down in the yard and look up at the stars and wish I could put my head into a garbage compactor myself.

And my mother would say, Don't worry. This vacation can't last forever. Soon you'll be back with your big head friends.

But the welcome-back-to-school letter kept not coming. And just when I was sure it was going to come, it wouldn't come again. Every time.

Then one day: bang, bang, bang.

I opened the door and it was the president of the Big Head School.

I regret to inform you, he said, that the Big Head School has burned down again and we are too tired to keep on rebuilding it.

Oh, I said.

The good news, he said, is that from this moment on, you are on permanent vacation. Congratulations!

Mac and cheese. Parrot shit. Mac and cheese. Parrot shit. Mac and cheese. Parrot shit.

Then Mama turned blue and fell to the floor in front of the television and there was a sound in her throat like the last little bit of water going down the drain.

Get Dr. Hand, she said. Quick.

She was giving me a beached whale look.

Quick, she said.

So it was up over the mountaintop and then what? I had never gone into town by myself before. I had only gone in the Big Head

130

School school bus. I knew that the girl came from the town, so that meant the town was on the other side of the stream.

Maybe.

Anybody have any better ideas?

The theme music to *Million Simoleon Lunch with Patti Kake* had just come on when my mother fell down on the floor, blue.

When I finally walked into town, the light was going powder orange all over the tops of the stores.

You could still hear the crackling of the cinders. Everywhere in the rectangle of black that used to be the Big Head School twists of smoke rose up into the sky like the ropes in swami rope-climbing tricks, only without the swamis. Someone had stuck a sign into the singed lawn that said, GOOD RIDDANCE Somebody else had dragged out the giant sign and changed it: BIG HEADS GET DEAD.

Children were screaming and hiding their faces in their mothers' skirts.

No! said the woman at the Visitors' Information Booth when I asked her, Do you know where I can find Dr. Hand?

Then she slammed down her metal window blind and I could hear her punching telephone buttons.

Sic'im! said the man walking the big tooth dog when I asked the same question, and slobber from the big tooth dog's mouth splattered all over my leg.

Sic'im! said the man. Sic'im!

But the big tooth dog just bent itself into a pretzel going all snarly and snapping-tooth ballistic after its own rat-skinny tail.

The man was a pin eye man, but even he wasn't fooled by the leaves I had stuck everywhere but my little head face.

And then I was lying on the ground.

And the man who had just hit me with his big stone hand was holding his hand in the air like he was going to hit me again. And his friend the big foot man had put his big foot on my chest.

Please! I said. Dr. Hand!

The man with the big stone hand and his big foot friend just laughed.

Please! I said. My mother! Mrs. Moon! She's blue! She might be dying!

131

It was hard to talk with the big foot man's big foot on my chest.
The two men only laughed louder.

Why are you laughing? I said.

Dr. Hand! said the big stone hand man, wiping tears from his eyes
with his little skin hand. Then he laughed so hard he had to cover
his mouth with his big stone hand.

What? I said.

Hand! said the big foot man. Hand! That's his name!

Are you Dr. Hand? I said.

The man with the big stone hand couldn't stop laughing.

Are you Dr. Hand? I said.

Now I knew why the girl was a fat face girl. She was the big stone
hand man's daughter, and both of her eyes were black, and her nose
was squashed flat and her lips were fatter than ever.

Is this the one who did it to you? said the man with the big stone
hand.

Anyone who cared to look could tell the girl had a baby coming
and that the baby's head would be a big head.

Her voice was so soft the man with the big stone hand made her
say it twice. Yes, Daddy, she said. And then again, Yes, Daddy.

Now get out of here before I throw you into the garbage compactor
instead of him.

Yes, Daddy.

I knew we'd catch you, the man with the big stone hand said when
his daughter had gone. It was just simple mathematics, he said. I
knew that if we just kept at it long enough, one of you would turn
out to be the one who did it.

Did what? I said.

The man with the big stone hand laughed. Then he said, You just
wait right here. When I come back I'll teach you more than you ever
learned in that big head school.

Later that night I heard a noise outside the bars of my window. I
couldn't move but I could talk. Is that you? I said.

Yes, said the girl.

Are you going to help me escape?

You can't escape, said the girl.

Why are you here then?

I'm praying.
What are you praying for?
For all the people who should never have been born.

The night I married your father, my mother said, all of the tree leaves turned silver as we drifted over, and all of the rivers and lakes showed us their silver faces. Chimney pots too glinted in our light, and the shingled roofs were triangles and squares of night-white gray. We drifted over mountains, seas, islands. And in almost every field we could spot the moon-glow bodies of at least one pair of lovers. Sometimes they would leave off what they were doing to lie on their backs and watch us cross the sky, and sometimes they were too distracted by one another to pay us any mind.

We drifted and we drifted.

The wind filled my veil and the skirt of my dress, and I discovered that no mattress on earth was as comfortable and soft to lie on as the sky. Stars were floating all around like unblinking fireflies. Your father gave me one for an earring. All the rest were sparkling in my eyes.

Why is everything so beautiful? I asked your father, my mother said.

Because this is the world that you were made for, your father said, and the world that you will live in from now until forever.

And I believed him, she said.

The Raven
Julia Elliott

WE WERE AT KRYSTAL, eating what my mother called a skin graft on a bun. I'd put on my raven mask to give our order, and my best friend Bonny, aka the Poet, stood behind me in her black beret and fake mustache, croaking, *Quoth the raven* after everything I said: *Six hamburgers (quoth the raven), three large curly fries (quoth the raven), three medium Cokes (quoth the raven).* I aimed my glistening black beak at the cashier and said, *By that heaven that bends above us, by that God we both adore, please give us some extra ketchup.* Bonny cracked up. But Brunell Hair just stood there looking pickled, her face scrunched up, dirty toe of her ballet shoe digging into the floor. She hated our guts but followed us around. She was Echo, scrawny as a wormy mutt, flouncing in a bruise-colored dress. Miss Joetta Shick, proprietress of Joetta's School of Dance, said the dress was chiffon, the color of dusk, of shadows, of gossamer insect wings and midnight passion flowers. And the feathers on my bird costume had gleaming rainbows down in their fibers.

"Thing of evil," said Bonny. "Do you have any cigarettes?"

"Nevermore," said I, and Brunell rolled her eyes.

"I'm having a slumber party," she said, "for my birthday. Right after the recital."

"Quoth the raven: Nevermore."

"Y'all're immature," said Brunell. Brunell came from a tribe of pinched-up possum-eating Pentecostals and she couldn't relax. Daddy said her people looked like they were being eviscerated, which means having your guts scooped out. Back in kindergarten, Brunell would follow you around babbling baby talk about hell. If you snatched a Lego from her, she'd say, "You'll burn." If you cut her in the lunch line she'd say, "You'll fall into the bottomless pit." If you pulled her pigtail she'd hiss, "No water will quench the eternal fires of hell." When she was little, she'd had the exact same creepy croak as that kid in *The Shining*, and we were always begging her to chant *Redrum, redrum, redrum.* Sometimes she would, sometimes she wouldn't—depending on where she was on the mood spectrum:

despairing, desolate, ghastly, bleak, melancholy, somber, or just plain dreary. Her smile was a twitch, uncomfortable and over in a flash. Her eyes were silvery and tormented and slightly froggish. She looked like an inbred angel from one of those old Flemish paintings my daddy liked—gray freckles, cornsilk hair, eyes goggling up at heaven—or maybe like a skinny vampire child who would float up to your window in a clammy cloak of fog, tap on the glass, and just stare at you until you went insane.

Despite Brunell's church bullshit, she was the one who'd somberly explained the mechanics of sexual intercourse to us in first grade, familiarized us with the meaning and usage of the word *fuck* (second grade), and haunted our tender minds forever with the story of a girl raped and mutilated, her body scattered through a forest where a satanic cult held their drunken *orgies* (third grade). Tapping into a dark underground stream we couldn't see, Brunell delivered disturbing information that turned our heads inside out. You never knew when she'd come at you with a big dirty monkey wrench and pound it into the mushy machinery of your brain. She'd be talking in that hillbilly drone of hers—about the pink pom-poms on her roller skates or her stuffed Garfield doll—when there it was, real and nasty, a slab of rancid meat on a lace tablecloth: a transvestite prostitute dying of pneumonia at Kuntry Kabins motel; a baby born without kidneys; an old woman left dead in her house for a month and eaten by her starving kitties.

That Tuesday night before dress rehearsal Brunell was going on and on about the electric curlers she was getting for her birthday, taking weird little rodent bites off her hamburger, when all of a sudden she bursts out with: *Joetta Shick wants your daddy.* She pointed a burnt french fry at me, ate it, then told us that Tonya Hutto, our cashier, had had three abortions.

"What do you mean *Joetta Shick wants my daddy?*" I asked.

"She wants to jump his bones," said Brunell.

"How do you know this?" I demanded, but Brunell Hair pressed her lips into a line and refused to speak another word on the subject.

Joetta Shick looked like a hyperthyroid mannequin—that's what my mother said—the kind of mannequin that would come alive in a horror movie and chase you down with a knife. My father didn't exactly agree with her, and this pissed my mother off. Yes, Miss Joetta's eyes bugged out like a Pekingese dog's, but she painted them

Egyptian style, and her mascara-thickened lashes were an inch long. She had cheekbones out to here. Raven black curls swished around her skinny butt. She painted lines around her skeleton lips to make them look luscious, and she kept her freckled chest powdered pale. Nobody knew her age, her past, or her true hair color. Everybody knew she had over a hundred antique clocks in her brick ranch house, that her Chinese hairless dogs had to wear sunblock when they went outside, that she did the flowers for St. John's Episcopal every first Sunday of the month—lush dark roses from her own garden.

Long and lank in a sheer-skirted leotard the color of a scab, Joetta Shick was fluttering back and forth across the Andrew Jackson Elementary stage, instructing a crew of fathers in her rich whine. As I sat in the wings watching Wanda Blitch's daddy struggle with the Fall-of-the-House-of-Usher inflatable castle (a Day-Glo orange toy spray-painted gray), I remembered something that made me wonder. Last year when we were trying to come up with a theme for our October recital, I'd told Miss Joetta my father'd written a book on Poe. I even recited a passage from "The Raven," and Miss Joetta'd paced around with a fevered look on her face. She got so wound up about the prospect of a dance recital based on what she called Poe's oeuvre that I didn't mention that Daddy, an English professor up at the community college, called Poe *the greatest comic genius in the history of American letters.*

"What if your parents got divorced and your dad married Miss Joetta?" said Bonny. She'd picked up my raven mask and was trying to put it on. I snatched it out of her hands, tearing a few feathers off.

"Shut up," I said. "Brunell Hair's full of shit."

But my telltale heart beat fat and obscene in my chest as I imagined my father kissing Miss Joetta. They were about the same height, whereas my mother was a little woman who kept her hair cut short so she didn't have to mess with it. She designed her own furniture and sold it to rich people in Charleston and Atlanta. She'd made almost every stick of furniture in our house, including my princess canopy bed with the built-in drawers, and of course she'd created my raven costume, researching bird anatomy for a month before carving the beak out of teak and rubbing it with ebony lacquer until it got just the right dark shine. She'd also designed the coffin for "The Premature Burial," the pendulum for "The Pit and the Pendulum," assorted gothic furnishings, and several grotesque papier-mâché masks for "The Masque of the Red Death" that she was supposed to

136

be bringing over from her workshop tonight.

"Your mama's here," rasped Brunell Hair.

Brunell was floating in a dark spot right behind us. I didn't know how long she'd been there, humming with weird thoughts.

"Hey baby," yelled Mama. She waved at me then walked to the other end of the stage where Miss Joetta was telling Pinkie Sprott what to do with his stack of Styrofoam tombstones. As my mother stood there balancing a liquor box full of masks on her hip, it seemed like Miss Joetta was making a show of ignoring her. When she finally gave my mother the look-over—bug eyes skipping over her pixie cut, her stretched-out T-shirt, her faded cutoffs, and chunky leather sandals—I felt little stabs of pity, then shame, then guilt for feeling pity and shame. But I felt sorry for Miss Joetta when I saw Mama smirking with superiority at her pancake makeup, the beads of sweat that seeped from above her upper lip, the tacky rings she wore on every single finger except her thumbs—Gypsy rings with fat, dark stones that I secretly coveted. I imagined my dance teacher pacing her rose garden at night, restless in some kind of billowy antique gown. I saw my father step from the bushes into a puddle of moonlight and this gave me an evil thrill.

I held my breath as Mama pulled her masks from the box. My mother was not a normal woman. She thought too much about everything she did. She couldn't just throw together some carnival masks with glitter and a glue gun like an ordinary mother. She had to make papier-mâché caricatures of certain people in our town, people she called money people: a real estate agent with a hairdo like a nuclear mushroom cloud, a Baptist preacher with a bulldog face who drove a Cadillac with silver doves stenciled onto its doors, and a baloney-colored politician who wanted to develop a whole swamp into a golf course with little Tudor mansions on its fake ponds. The night before when I went to bed, Mama was still holding her palette up to a piece of baloney, trying to get what she called Bobby Skink's hypertensive complexion just right.

"Those look awful heavy," said Miss Joetta.

"Oh, they're not," said Mama. "Just paper and latex paint. Kate gave them a test run this morning." Mama pointed at me and grinned her sarcastic grin. Miss Joetta picked up the amazing pig-nosed likeness of Tooty Tewksbury, which had a full head of ruby red crepe hair, and marveled at its lightness. "They'll work," she said. "Thank you, Edna." Then she dropped the mask back into its box and turned her attention to the gaggle of chubby third-graders dressed up as tap-dancing demons—they were figments of Poe's deranged mind. Every time something ominous was about to happen, they'd swarm the stage and start tapping like mad, plastic bat wings flopping on their backs.

I was out piddling in the night, crickets going full blast like a thousand teeny machines, the moon on the run. It was still warm outside, wet grass under my bare feet. I wore a long paisley skirt with my bathing-suit top. Twenty Gypsy necklaces tinkled on my flat chest. I snuck up to the square of light that was the dining-room window and peeked in. Daddy was hunched over a whiskey, the crisp wing of his hairsprayed bangs ripped to hell, making him look exactly like Jack Nicholson. My brother and I loved for him to yell, "Here's Johnny," roll his eyes like a homicidal maniac, and chase us around the house, which he would do, but he refused to wave an ax in the air. Mama was pacing around Daddy, taking quick drags off her smoke. Daddy said she had the constitution of a hummingbird—never gaining weight and always moving, talking, thinking, going, buzzing. He looked like he was having trouble keeping her fast little body in focus.

I watched Daddy pull Mama onto his lap and kiss her neck. She didn't close her eyes the way women on TV do, and I thought she'd look a whole lot better if she grew her hair long and wore some makeup. Plus, I was sick of her trying to teach me lessons with everything she did. For example, she'd turned Brunell's birthday party into one of those you-should-realize-how-fortunate-you-are Sunday-school scams, and she said I should probably go. I already knew how fortunate I was. I was glad I wasn't Brunell Hair. But that didn't stop me from wanting things. I wanted a home perm. I wanted boobs. I wanted some purple Candies with cork wedge heels and a pink Corvette with a sunroof. I wanted a disco ball in my room and lavender wall-to-wall and a pair of gold roller skates. I wanted a light-up mirror and a makeup kit with a hundred shades of eye shadow. I wanted a white Persian kitten and a raven black horse and a penthouse apartment that rotated at the top of a high-rise. I wanted a swimming pool shaped like a Hawaiian island with a video arcade and fluffy cockatoos squawking in gilded cages.

I wanted to jump out of my freckled skin into a long brown body with Coppertone legs that dwindled down to a pair of hot pink three-inch heels. I wanted to strut across a lit-up dance floor in a leopard-skin cocktail dress, luscious boobs filling my décolleté top like a double scoop of butter pecan, my hair an explosion of black curls, my laser-shooting cat eyes burning holes into anybody I looked at, except the tall dark pirate who would storm up on his motorcycle and kidnap me. We'd thunder up an Evel Knievel–style ramp and fly into the air, arcing right into the open door of a luxury spaceship that would shoot out past the moon, past Mercury, Venus, Earth, Mars, Jupiter, Saturn, Uranus, Neptune, and Pluto, past the Milky Way Galaxy, way out into the black purple light of deep space where he would kiss me on my glossed lips.

On nights like these, with the crickets all wistful and a restless moon, the things I wanted formed an ache in my gut. I turned away from the window and gazed out into the street. Sometimes, when I felt like this, I'd lie down on the asphalt and listen for the vibration of approaching cars. My heart would pound as the sound got thicker, then I'd hop up just before the car appeared. I was about to recline on the road, when what did I see but the silhouette of a woman, somebody tall, holding two skinny dogs on a leash, standing across the street next to our neighbor's vine-choked mailbox, one of her canines doing its business in the ditch. Now the only person in town with dogs that scrawny was Joetta Shick. The only person in town who wore exotic garments that billowed in the wind just so was Joetta Shick. But now she was hightailing it, striding toward the wood patch where the Bickle triplets had built their underground fort, dark fabric fluttering behind her like a comet tail.

Mama was spazzing out over the dining-room table she was making for this woman she called the Muzak heiress. My mother hated rich people, but only rich people bought her stuff, and therein festered her misery. The Muzak heiress wanted a birch dining table with fur-lined legs, and all morning Mama'd been stomping around the house with scraps of white polar-bear fur, shrieking, "I'm not a fucking upholsterer," so Daddy took me out to lunch to escape her hissy fit. I was finishing up my french fries at Frances Ann's Front Porch, a strip-mall joint posing as an antebellum house, when guess who walks up with her bald dogs: Miss Joetta Shick, wearing this silky black number with a big veiled hat, the noose end of a rhinestone leash chafing each of her bony wrists, her hellhounds looking antsy in the sunlight.

"Hello, Kate," she said. Then she moaned, "James," looked at the ground, squatted to mess with one of her dog's paws. "Good to see you again."

Where, I wanted to know, had she seen him? And since when did she call him James?

The dogs, pale and greasy, smelled like Panama Jack sunscreen. With the exception of the rock-star tufts of hair cascading over their gargoyle faces, they were completely bald, scrawny as hell, veins webbing their bellies, scabs and bruises and odd spots speckling them from head to toe.

"How do you pet them?" I asked, wanting to but not wanting to.

"Try petting their mantels." My dance teacher lit a Virginia Slim.

"Their hair?"

"That's right."

"Did their fur fall out or were they born like this?" I asked, and Daddy kicked me under the table. It seemed like he was trying to protect her feelings.

"These dogs were bred, Kate," he said. "Do you show them?" he asked Miss Joetta.

"Oh no. They're my *companions.*"

I squatted down by the dogs and got a whiff of their roadkill breath. Patting the frizz on the little one's head, I remembered all the mean things Daddy said about so-called purebred canines whenever a dog show came on TV, wondering why he chose not to express those opinions now. The dog whined and sniffed my hand, glanced toward the road, and whined again.

"What're their names?" Daddy asked.

"William and Wilson," said Miss Joetta.

Daddy laughed. Miss Joetta frowned. Daddy tried to look serious, but a constipated smile quivered his lips. A truck honked, and both dogs jumped like they were wired together.

"Doppelgängers," said Miss Joetta. She took the leashes in her left hand and swept an arc in the air with her right. "Are you interested in litra-toor, Mr. Cantey?"

"Literature is a nightmare I'm trying to wake up from," said Daddy. I gave him a look. His nose twitched like it did when he was about to say something smart-ass. I couldn't tell whether he was full of shit or not. When he launched into one of his lectures—this one about the farcical elements in the William Wilson tale, lighting a cigarette in the middle of the whole thing and getting totally full of himself—he looked so handsome it made my stomach hurt. Miss

Joetta leaned against a fake antebellum column entwined with plastic ivy and sighed.

"I *love* litra-toor," she said. "Poe, in particular. In fact, I don't know if Kate told you, but my autumn recital is based upon the oeuvre of the unfortunate poet, a mélange, if you will, of his most famous works."

"Oh," said Daddy, "that's what the bird head's for. 'The Raven.'"

"Duh," I said, but nobody paid me any mind.

"So my little daughter's playing the role of ghastly hopping hell hen," said Daddy. "How did this escape my attention?"

"Will you come see it?" asked Miss Joetta. She collapsed against the column, her black hat tilted back, two long curls jumping loose from her hairdo and bouncing around her face. She smiled what people call a radiant smile, flashing long teeth, her cheeks on fire, her shimmery pink lips disappearing. Her eyes throbbed at my father, and I wondered if it was true that toy dogs' eyes sometimes popped right out of their skulls when they freaked.

"I wouldn't miss Kate's performance," said Daddy, "for the world." He flashed his killer Jack Nicholson grin then turned to wave down our waitress. Miss Joetta went pale, said, *Good to see you,* and billowed off. After lunch Daddy was quiet for quite a while—he who loved the sound of his own voice.

The night was warm and drizzly, a bad night for hairdos: straight locks molded into crisp ringlets went limp and sticky; curly heads exploded into clouds of frizz. A box of Tampax poked from Miss Joetta's black vinyl tote. She kept fingering a cluster of pimples on her cheek. Her blusher wasn't well blended. She picked at her panty hose and screamed at Orvis Bickle when he dropped a plywood coffin, tumbling a plastic skeleton and scattering glow-in-the-dark bones. In less than forty minutes, *The Tell-Tale Heart of Edgar Allan Poe* was scheduled to begin and the backdrops for the opening piece were stuck—the giant heart diagram, the tormented mug of the poet. Elizabeth Ann Tewksbury—Miss Okra Blossom, head cheerleader, radiant performer of Lenore, Annabel Lee, and Madeline Usher—had yet to show, and sometimes it took an hour to make her tan skin look cadaverous. Plus two of the Dying Embers, three tap-dancing demons, and the double in "William Wilson" had come down with the chicken pox. Sandy Bumgarner'd puked on her orangutan costume. And the auditorium smelled like a clothes hamper.

141

Miss Joetta was all over the place: spraying the aisles with Lysol, scrubbing the vomit-crusted monkey suit, phoning the Tewksbury mansion for the fiftieth time. This didn't stop her from asking me, over and over, if *both of my parents* were coming.

"Yes," I said. "My mama *and my daddy.*"

"Elizabeth Ann's daddy goes both ways," said Brunell Hair in her blunt twang. She added that her mama'd let her open her electric rollers early so she could curl her hair for the recital. She said her birthday cake was the cutest thing on earth (Garfield lifted into the air by a cluster of purple balloons), that Tonya Hutto's mother wore fake breasts inside her bra on account of her double mastectomy, and that Mr. Dale Teeter's lungs frequently bled. Then she claimed that Elizabeth Ann Tewksbury, daughter of a real estate tycoon and a dentist, was coming to her slumber party. Bonny laughed so hard her fake mustache flew off. I shook my head and croaked, *Nevermore.* Brunell sucked her painted lips in and tried to shake her puffed-up hair, but it wouldn't move.

As if to expose Brunell's lie, Elizabeth Ann Tewksbury strutted backstage wearing one of those old-lady plastic scarves to protect her spill of golden curls. She removed her bonnet, said her daddy'd air-conditioned the Mercedes ahead of time and backed it right up to the front door so her perm wouldn't go kinky. Miss Joetta said, "Wonderful," and pounced on the girl with a jar of Merle Norman French Bisque. She dabbed her eyes with purple shadow, giving the beauty queen the dark circles of an incestuous photophobic sleepwalker. We had five minutes until curtain.

Light the color of congealed blood flooded the stage. From hidden speakers the thump-thump-thump of an enormous heart thundered, deafening but intimate, as though your own heart were about to burst out of your chest with a sputter of guilty blood. A big medical diagram of a ruby red heart dropped from the rafters and hung center stage. Miss Joetta Shick emerged, dressed up as a man (cap, fake mustache), and paced back and forth.

"The disease had sharpened my senses—not destroyed—not dulled them," she said, speaking deep from her diaphragm. "Above all was the sense of hearing acute. I heard all things in the heavens and in the earth. I heard many things in hell. How, then, am I mad? Harken! And observe how calmly I can tell you the whole story."

Although Joetta Shick didn't normally dance in our recitals, for

142

some reason she chose to begin and end *The Tell-Tale Heart of Edgar Allan Poe* with solo dances of her own that seemed designed to illustrate the suppleness of her body (I had my theories). With no music but the beating heart, she twitched and twirled, leapt and staggered, resembling a person trying to run through hurricane winds. After this prologue, first- and second-graders performed their "Tell-Tale Heart" routine, doing rudimentary ballet steps to horror music, dressed up as giant bloodshot eyes. The thunderous heartbeat popped back on in the middle of the song, and then tap-dancing demons swarmed the stage, sending the eyes running and screaming, only to be replaced by second- and third-graders dressed as black cats. The cats, wearing bow ties and sporting canes, shuffled through an impish jazz routine, at the end of which a coffin was wheeled onto the stage and Susie Horton, a bow-legged eighth-grader who practiced the art of mime, stood in a spotlight and pretended to be trapped in a confined space, growing more and more alarmed until the horror music went crazy and tap-dancing demons swarmed the stage. "William Wilson" was a blur because "The Raven" was up next and my heart was jumping in my throat.

I kept rubbing my feathers with damp hands and matting them. I fiddled with the elastic of my mask, paranoid that it would snap in the middle of the routine and send my beak flying into the audience. I was afraid I'd have a giggle fit, something I suffered from from time to time, and when I heard the earnest voice of Joetta Shick rolling into *Once upon a midnight dreary,* a laugh rumbled deep in my belly and snickered up through my throat. I bit my lip. I clenched my fists. I watched my best friend, Bonny, dance around with her buzzard quill, writing poems in the air to the mournful whine of violins, and I tried to empty my mind. I watched as each separate Dying Ember (Debbie Dyer, Kendra Jones, and Tina Skaggs) wrought its ghost upon the floor. I watched the rare and radiant maiden whom the angels named Lenore (Elizabeth Ann Tewksbury) leap around the edges of the stage as the agonized poet reached for her and Joetta Shick shrieked, *Lenore,* and Brunell Hair skipped behind Elizabeth Ann in her raggedy dress.

Miss Joetta was now whispering into her mike: *Lenore, Lenore, Lenore.* Bonny flung open the shutters that Mr. Brickle had rigged up, and onto the stage I hopped, *the ghastly grim and ancient raven wandering from the nightly shore.* I fluttered and preened my freestyle modern number as Miss Joetta croaked, *Nevermore,* with such passion that chills started flickering, not only up and down my spine, but, I felt sure, the collective spine of the audience, who could not fail to be blown away. I *was* the raven. My feathers, while blacker than the devil's goatee, gleamed with secret rainbows if you looked closely enough—hinting at possible delights on the distant shores of Death. Nevertheless, who didn't quake with fear at the sound of my portentous squawk? What mortal would not freak out over the sight of my lustrous black body perched on their window-sill? I felt the mournful darkness of the ominous bird, blooming in my heart like a beautiful night flower, and I leapt higher than I'd ever leapt before, so high that I could almost touch the fake full moon that dangled over my head.

That was when my father started laughing. Laughing fits, like alcoholism and big noses, ran in our family. And we never knew when laughter would fall upon my daddy like a nervous disease, wasting him to a wheezing spasmodic mess that my mother had to take charge of. That's why we'd quit the Presbyterian Church. That's why we always sat in the back at funerals and weddings. That's why my father could not be relied upon to chair a committee or speak before a large crowd, therefore impeding his advancement through what he called the bureaucratic cesspool of Bluebird Community College, "where dreams take flight." The longer my father restrained himself before a laughing fit, the harder it shook him.

My father's nervous laughter was an ancient song that spoke to my deepest blood, and I prayed for it to stop, knowing that it would not stop until my mother jabbed him with a sharp object from her purse, snarled at him, threatened him to his feet until he shuffled out into the hall.

Imagining this, I kept at the mechanics of my dance. But the fire that'd stoked every cell of every muscle in me was dead, and the look on Miss Joetta's gashed-open face—shame-laced horror—started my own fit. I sniggered. I snorted. Laughter slithered through my intes-tines like a tapeworm, queasy and pity-tainted. Every time I glanced at Miss Joetta's huge wet eyes or Brunell's smirk or Bonny's anger-wrenched face, the throbbing deepened, until a nasty donkey bray finally leapt from my mouth. I staggered to the edge of the stage where I fell to my knees to clutch my seething gut. There was noth-ing I could do. I let the contagion saw through me. I rolled and shook and howled.

Of course I was too distracted to notice Desmerelda Hair, Brunell's mama, standing up, righteousness shuddering through her scrunched little body and shooting from her pointing finger right at me, then at poor Joetta Shick. Miss Desmerelda was screaming. I sat up, straightened my beak, and scanned the audience. My mama was sitting by herself on the back row looking worn-out. Twenty-odd seats down, Desmerelda Hair stood trembling, her old-fashioned beehive gone crooked. She called Miss Joetta a spellatizing Jezebel witch. She claimed that my father and I were both possessed by her charms. She said the devil rocked through us, that demons flitted through our bloodstreams, that Beelzebub had taken command of our nervous systems. She shrieked that the whole show, with its black cats and ominous birds, its triumphant jigging demons and taunting skeletons, was the work of Satan, and that she should've known not to let her child take dancing. Her own mama had advised against it, knowing how well Satan could work his way into a body through rhythm.

"My mama can pick evil out of a person faster than a woodpecker pecks worms from dead wood," screamed Desmerelda Hair.

I looked for Brunell. She'd shuffled offstage to sulk in the shadows, her skinny shoulders heaving in her gossamer dress.

"Brunell," yelled her mama, "get your butt down here."

Brunell slunk away somewhere—I don't know where she went—and Miss Joetta came to her senses. She ordered us all backstage and read the prologue for "The Masque of the Red Death."

"Somebody oughta put a stop to this," yelled Desmerelda Hair, looking around at the audience, but everybody acted like she was the nastiest-smelling invisible lady who'd ever lived, and Brunell's mama stomped out of the auditorium just as the first masked dancers bounded onto the stage.

Joetta Shick stood in the wings with her battle face on—the face she wore at the end of class when we still hadn't learned a difficult step and she was hell-bent on making us. You could tell she was set on saving the show with nonstop perfection from there on out. I sat down by Bonny (who refused to speak to me) and watched Tammy Stucky bolt a pair of cardboard castle doors against a horde of writhing plague victims. Tammy was wearing the Tooty Tewksbury mask my mama'd made. As the rich maskers frolicked through their stately pavane, waving fake silver goblets and peacock feathers in their hands, the plague victims moaned and quivered. One by one, they dropped to the floor, twitched in lavish death throes, and lay still. When Judy Hicks, wearing a glow-in-the-dark plastic skull mask from Spencer's Gifts, knocked at the bolted palace doors, the real

Tooty Tewksbury appeared backstage, looking scary as hell, her mascara-crusted eyes rolling. Her husband dawdled behind her in his plaid golf getup.

Miss Tooty jumped right down Joetta Shick's throat, hissing and spitting: *How dare you make fun of me by putting that child in that mask?*

Miss Joetta: *What on earth are you talking about?*

Miss Tooty: *You know good and well you meant something ugly with that red-headed mask.*

Miss Joetta: *I assure you, no.*

Miss Tooty: *You made my nose look like a pig snout.*

Tooty pointed at Judy Hicks, who was twirling across the stage to invite the elegant skeleton into her palace. Joetta Shick looked at Mama's mask, then at Miss Tooty, then back at the mask again. Miss Joetta's eyes flickered and she started slapping her forehead. *Shit, shit, shit,* she said, *that goddamn little bitch Edna Cantey.*

Joetta Shick told Tooty that my mama was the one to blame. But Tooty Tewksbury wouldn't listen to reason. She snatched Elizabeth Ann by the hem of her decayed tutu (Miss Joetta'd buried it for three days to make it look rotten), and dragged her child down the steps that led out to the empty cafeteria. And that was that. Without the angel named Lenore, the rare and radiant Annabel Lee, the undead ingenue Madeline Usher (all variations on the middle-aged poet's diseased child bride, his cousin and his muse), *The Tell-Tale Heart of Edgar Allan Poe* was no more.

Miss Joetta sank to the floor with the drama that the situation required. She plunged her head into her hands and moaned. But there was a twitch of authenticity in her rich fit. Her hair had tumbled out of its chignon. And softened by the shadowy light, she looked beautiful. To us, at that moment, she looked exactly like a woman should look: harrowed and lovely with spilled hair. Little girls gathered around her with shy wet eyes enhanced by gothic makeup. We watched our glamorous teacher heave, sadness flickering between us, charging the humid air. Wendy Blitchington, a child who once wept when a boy in our class electrocuted a toad with a coffee can and a battery, patted Miss Joetta on her back. When our dance teacher squinted up at her, Wendy burst into tears and hid her face. A few others started crying. Miss Joetta blew her nose, patted Wendy's arm, wiped her huge leaking eyes, and stood up.

"You may change clothes and go home," she said. "The recital's over. I'm sorry. You have danced like goddesses. Most of you, that is."

146

Miss Joetta refused to look at me, but her eyes crinkled and I knew what she was getting at. I felt like a plague victim, so ashamed that my stomach disappeared, and I wanted to drop dead for real. I wondered if my mother had ruined the recital on purpose—maybe to teach me a lesson (deep down she scoffed at dance class, though not for the same reasons Brunell's mama did). I wondered if her disdain for dancing was tainted by something else.

I wondered and wondered. And Miss Joetta stood in the dark just at the spotlight's edge, watching as one wealthy masker after another caught the plague and died, playing their roles to perfection. Their performance was all the more harrowing because the recital was ruined, making me think of a beautiful opera singer squalling her guts out on a sinking cruise ship. Judy Hicks surveyed the piles of corpses and performed a jaunty jig. The crowd went wild when she took her bow.

After the dead rose and held hands and curtsied, Miss Joetta turned on her microphone, which squeaked with feedback.

"Due to unanticipated events," she said, "the rest of the recital will not proceed. I am very sorry. Thank you for coming." The crowd actually groaned. She put down her microphone and started gathering her things.

Fists clenched, I went to find my laughing fool of a bastard daddy. He was in the cafeteria, shuffling around moodily, strip-mined of humor and ashamed, tearing at his comb-over as his bloodshot eyes strayed over the crappy finger paintings of kindergartners. I was about to jump out from my hiding place behind the trophy case when Joetta Shick came bustling through the room, laden with tote bags and snarling. She stopped in her tracks as though Daddy were a wild boar. She was about to hightail it when he turned toward her.

"Joetta," he said, walking up to her. "Look, you don't understand."

"What is there to understand?" she said. "I feel so humiliated."

"I was not laughing at your amazing recital. I mean it, just one of the best interpretations of Poe I've ever seen. So elaborate, so ambitious, so many thoughtful details. And to organize all those horrible little children so brilliantly."

Joetta Shick just huffed. She refused to put down her bags.

"I have a nervous condition," Daddy said. "My father was a hysterical laugher, as was his mother. I think my daughter has the disease too. It's just, the whole thing was so complicated. You see, I was

147

also taking the audience into consideration. I kept watching Pinkie Sprott throughout the recital. He had his stupid church face on— didn't understand one iota of what was going on. Do you know what I mean?"

"James," said Joetta, putting down her bags. "This town is hell."

"I know it," said my father.

Joetta Shick put her hand on my father's arm.

"It's just that I'm a married man," said Daddy. "With two kids. And I love my wife, but I think you're a beautiful and intelligent woman. And maybe, in another world, in different circumstances. Well, you know."

Miss Joetta made a strange gurgling sound and removed her hand from my father's arm. "Goodbye, James," she said, then she picked up her totes once more, bags crammed with costumes and makeup kits, curling irons, rollers, brushes, combs, hair gel, hairspray, dozens of beauty products too fanciful or obscure to name, and walked out of the cafeteria.

A few months later she left town, the same week Brunell Hair tried to run away to Atlanta after her mama burned her Kiss records, making it all the way to Aiken on her bike before Desmerelda tracked her down. Rumors pulsed throughout school district three. Some people said Miss Joetta had relocated to Charleston to teach dance at a hoity-toity academy. Others said she'd moved to Florence to care for her sick mother. One group had it that she'd gone all the way to New Orleans to be a showgirl (never mind her age), and that she dabbled in voodoo. This is the story I settled on. And I took personal responsibility for helping Miss Joetta fulfill her enchanted destiny. Rather than getting bogged down teaching dance in this podunk town, mooning over men not sophisticated enough to appreciate her glamour, she'd gone on to bigger things.

I liked to picture Miss Joetta on one of those wrought-iron balconies in a Gypsy outfit, petting her bald dogs, watching masked revelers dance in the streets. These fantasies were lit up by a big silver moon, which made her dogs look like they were chiseled out of marble. And in the moonlight you couldn't see the lines around Miss Joetta's mouth.

Animal Communication

Mei-mei Berssenbrugge

I.

I underestimate the power of my connection with other people, with animals and events that are coincident.

Everyone's experienced talking with a friend, when conversation suddenly deepens.

Estimation supports the magic of deepening.

Days begin to skew slightly; we open to accident.

Though touching an animal differs from feeling vibrations of its spirit or thinking of it, not as moths, for example, meld light and thought.

They are a dimensional bridge to beauty, interacting between light and other worlds, i.e., intimacy can be the bridge.

II.

I begin by imagining I hear Jack's thought.

There's a sense of pervasiveness; particles go back and forth in me.

I write down today's encounters, including the mosquito, as a dream to interpret.

Certainly, one's tie to an insect is imaginative truth.

Not that my horse *represents* the union of intuition and imagining, she is that.

Turning her head to smell the wind, she shifts into its seamless dimension—mane, tail.

"Is that *like* saying the pond is my brain?" I ask, and frogs answer, "More like the shape of holding your thoughts!"

A horse doesn't change frequency to change form.

Form is part of my thinking this, like a willow seed's intent, intrinsic focus on willow trees.

III.

Jack tells me his dream of smelling violets.

I'm surprised at a cartoon of my dog in a lavender field.

He says the cartoon translates his dream into my imagining, "To you far away looks like space, light-years."

First, he says he's from another planet.

Then, he says it's a joke, if planets are wavelengths, like brain waves.

You could slow a pattern, and it coalesces into our planetary system; or a lavender cave solidifies with dream yoga.

There's transparency, lavender seen through a window, horse pausing, but the point of view is of glass, dream.

Karma is reformation, a distant remembering like feeling; something dim grows brighter.

Discontinuity becomes continuity, the memory sort of glittering as it flows, and sleep flows.

IV.

We had a life in town where beauty was discussed as a fountain and pool, flowing from within, reflecting inner and outer form

In other places it's incarnate, as here, a stream orchid under trees.

The effect is of deep, calming presence, of viewing a still pond beside your animal companion, of willingness to share the peace of home, stored in flesh.

Shade glows with no edge between space, grass.

As shade trees grow and the orchid grows, space around reflects inspirative beauty.

Like time passing of a fountain flowing, passage in space is our perspective opening to this beauty.

V.

Here, Jack's an ordinary terrier with hair over his eyes; "First, I lull you into complacent stillness.

I lie down beside you, you think I'm asleep.

Then, with my touch or glance, you can hear thought.

I evoke potential, the way honey evokes its energy grid in bees, a morphic field evolving with willows."

The rich dignity of honey expects magnetism.

Here's Buddy, a horse laughing, and owner Carol, Dawn and Barney, Inka and her llama, Tera.

Here's Raphaela Pope and her gray parrot, Dax, who told me Elmo from Sesame Street loves him.

Jack dreams he's a polar bear standing upright.

He shows me a chakra on the bottom of each foot, connecting to a grid in earth that maintains gravity, so we can be held here in our bodies.

"I anchor one grid line for Dax."

Three Poems
Reginald Shepherd

I'VE KNOWN THE GARDEN

The earth is an inventory of bones, the fossils sing,
thick with mud-headed myth, an unclassified
species of shadow: the crumbling architecture
of half-surveyed pasts beckons like a heat mirage

across the glacier-scarred desert, full of glare
and false outlines, canyon-blind, all
weatherless. Pieces of summer
come apart in my hands and I call it

prehistory, sea-shaped rocks
swim in my palm. I call it stratigraphy,
a place of blank road signs
pointing in all directions. I talked them out

of memory, let their stone flags sleep
amid the sediments. There's a muse for geography
and winter, a muse of fever
and distance, but there's no afterlife

for them. The carboniferous forests
left their coal behind, tree ferns
and lycophytes pressed fine-veined leaves
between black and combustible pages,

our open-pit understanding of the earth
almost legible in hindsight's seamed light.

E LUCEVAN LE STELLE

I.

Then nights poured out their gathered
darkness, having no there, assorted stars
spilled out in several colors
all resolved to white, resolved to be
more virtuous in the speckled,
spattered future rolling out, unfurling
like a midnight sea reflecting on the
little lights scattering sentimental rain
across its monotonously variable
surfaces, broken-off
pieces of weather
not well enough to be left alone,
adrift with others more thoroughly lost
and not to be navigated by.

II.

The stars shone as they had to, burning up
the visual spectrum, burning the invisible
too, taking lucidity to task, it being their task
to consume themselves seen and unseen, faltering
in the atmospheric interference, shifting
toward red or blue depending
on their direction, all stars
scattering from a core of light till they collapse
again, coalescing into a predicted darkness
from which emerges
again as if for the first time another
configuration, time being circular
like them, burning in the meanwhile, burning
both ends of it, sleepless as anyone.

III.

There was no light, but there were lights
dusting the dark drowned
in itself again, stealing the sky

from blue to black and white
pinpricks annealed into an adamant
-ly wavering being seen, blind animals with Latin names
making days of burning hydrogen all night
long, on some other side
of the world, an argument the sea has almost won,
its tidal ruins ticking off the hours
with the moments floating in them,
reflected faith shaken out across salt waves
stained by so many stars
more lost than left behind.

WHAT NATURE DOESN'T SHOW

It's always raining in my dreams,
I'm always lacking something
that I need, an umbrella, shoes, my peace
of mind, or just the right direction
home, another piece of my mind
I'll never find, far from what I'd want
to be. I carry these things
far into the night, or one just like
it, whitening into dawn
while rain wipes away the wax-paper
moon, the damp overgrown yard
moves into meadowhood, another
lush polluted pastoral. The wind
is simplified in such weather, wet windows
hold memory at a distance, drowning
liquid stars: a loss too far away
to reach the human world, barely touched
by the finger of fact. The body
is a body of water too, rain makes of me
a lake or pool or puddle, any fluid gathering
expanding and contracting
to the rhythm of imaginary tides'
forgotten or misplaced intentions.
I wonder, who invented water?

The Problem of Impairment
Rick Moody

THE MANIFEST LAYER OF this essay concerns the Pogues show I saw in March of 2007 at the Roseland Ballroom in New York City. Or, to be more precise, the manifest layer of this essay concerns the Pogues show I *intended* to see on March 15 of 2007. My cohorts in this *excursis*, doomed from the start, were my bandmates (in the Wingdale Community Singers) Hannah Marcus and Nina Katchadourian, as well as novelist Fiona Maazel. Hannah and I met in midtown west, excited at the prospect of the event, however doomed. We made our way toward the venue. Fiona and Nina were there already (having come from the southerly direction). Their telephone call from the vicinity of Roseland, however, contained the inevitable bad news. The Pogues show was rescheduled, owing to an injury suffered by lead singer Shane MacGowan. The gig was too good to be true, it seemed—the Pogues, St. Patrick's Day—and now things had unraveled, as things do. We arrived at Roseland, aggrieved, and there the reports became more complete. Shane MacGowan had slipped and sprained his ankle, it was said. Tickets would be honored the following night, it was said. And yet even the official security guys out front of Roseland were in on the ironies of the moment: "Shane MacGowan has injured himself! Read between the lines!"

Which is to say: Shane was too ill to perform. Shane was, most likely, too drunk, too incoherent, too semiconscious. He may well have injured himself (he had, in fact, as you shall see), but the injury probably had much to do with the advanced stage of alcoholism with which the singer was afflicted. We all scattered in the direction of home, wondering if there would be a show the next night or not.

Now to the backstory. The Pogues were the most important and most original band of the godforsaken 1980s, on either side of the Atlantic. However, I resisted them at first. At least, I resisted their first great album, *Rum Sodomy & the Lash*. I was drinking then myself, and I liked anything that had a self-destructive aspect (the Replacements, for example, or the New York Dolls). But I also believed I had an intellectual obligation to support music that was loud, dark,

Rick Moody

and challenging: Sonic Youth, Hüsker Dü, Pere Ubu, the Minute-men, Black Flag, and so forth. But upon my release from the psychi-atric hospital in July 1986, on the occasion of my first sober days, I had a sort of epiphany. It occurred to me that maybe it was OK to like whatever I liked, regardless of whether it cohered with the re-quirements of artistic credibility or doctrines of cool. It was about this time that a friend gave me a copy of *If I Should Fall from Grace with God*, the Pogues album that succeeded *Rum Sodomy & the Lash*.

What I had found folksy before, I found, nearly all at once, com-plex, mature, proud, sad, and very, very catchy. Indisputably, this album was one of the indelible masterpieces of postpunk rock and roll! There wasn't a bad song on it! Naturally, I soon saw the video for "Fairytale of New York," the album's best-known composition, and I marveled at the dark, forbidding dissipation of the lead singer. Even at this early stage, he didn't look terribly upstanding. The song was (manifestly) concerned with drunkenness, and so a simulation of intoxication was to be expected. But this was more than that. This was both the filmic simulation and the thing itself. Distracting from the darker themes, however, was the fact that the composition was masterful. The melody, the piano line, the dueling put-downs of MacGowan and guest chanteuse Kirsty MacColl, the sublime string arrangements, the Christmas imagery in the lyric, the drumming (you just can't talk about the originality of the Pogues without talk-ing about Andrew Ranken's drumming). I can think of only a few songs in my life, and I really mean this, that I have loved as passion-ately right from the first notes and from which I have never once turned away. I still can't hear "Fairytale of New York" without cry-ing. In fact, I watched the video today—in order to write these lines—and I cried again.

I could have been someone . . . Well, so could anyone . . .

And the rest of the album is just as extraordinary. It holds up today. Twenty years later. It triumphs. It sounds as wild, passionate, out of control, and heartbreaking as it did back then. Whereas so much other work from the period has dated—the Cocteau Twins, New Order, the Cure—the Pogues sound just as relevant. They're timeless and indomitable. From the first song on *If I Should Fall from Grace with God*, the Irish-music-at-punk-rock-tempos of the title track, to the last song, the genuinely stirring "Broad Majestic Shannon" (*Take my hand and dry your tears, babe, take my hand, forget your fears, babe*), the album veers from punky, drunken screeds like

156

"Bottle of Smoke" to world-inflected workouts like "Turkish Song of the Damned" and "Fiesta," where the folk instrumentation of the Pogues—acoustic guitar, tin whistle, banjo, accordion—suddenly enables them to sound like a klezmer band or a qwaali outfit or jazz combo. They're jaundiced and romantic, incisive and undependable, wise beyond their years, startlingly adolescent. They'd been a punk band with Irish music leanings before *If I Should Fall from Grace*, one that didn't have a reputation for instrumental prowess, but suddenly they could play *anything*, at any tempo, and make it energetic and moving without sounding shallow or sentimental—the way Madness always did, among their contemporaries.

Above the racket, Shane MacGowan bellowed, exhorted, ranted—who could tell if he was tenor or baritone—spitting out syllables that couldn't possibly be spit out that quickly, rushing the beat, his tuneless but expressive voice perfectly suited to the tempos and careening disorderliness of the compositions. The others in the band could sing, true, and did when Shane was forced out in the nineties, but MacGowan had some kind of fervent *vision*, some mad need to discourse, and so the Pogues just couldn't be the same, and weren't, without him. Even when his lyrics were tossed off, as they often seemed to be, scatological, irritable, provocative, there was something in them that was continuous with the heartache and sublimity of the Irish folk tradition. The Pogues made Irish music contemporary again, but without diluting its convoluted pathos, rescuing it from the banality of musical tourism, while striking a blow against what was, at the moment of their ascendancy, a virulent and popular strain of British anti-Irish racism.

I couldn't stop playing *If I Should Fall from Grace* for a long while. Long enough that I was just feeling I was thoroughly schooled in it when *Peace and Love* came out. The successor album. *Peace and Love* had, it seemed, many of the same concerns as *If I Should Fall from Grace*, and it was just as lovingly arranged and produced, just as worldly. But there was also something less focused about this album, as if the cracks in the edifice were beginning to show. Shane was still in charge, still writing about dog racing or Christy Brown (paralyzed Irish scribe), but the songs were slighter, as if they were being so carefully arranged to conceal a less generous supply of genius. The other Pogues were filling in between MacGowan compositions or cowriting more copiously with less felicitous results ("My Blue Heaven," e.g., a mere Brit pop song, and not a very good one). That said, *Peace and Love* remains a strong album, for "Misty

Rick Moody

Morning, Albert Bridge," "London You're a Lady," "Cotton Fields," and the tragicomic "Boat Train," the last of these recounting a ferry ride across the Irish Sea, an Irish protagonist bound for London, the cultural uncertainty thereof, and so forth. There was so much music coming out of the Pogues, even at three-quarters strength, that there was something arresting on any album they released.

An EP followed *Peace and Love,* and it prominently featured a pop song called "Yeah Yeah Yeah Yeah Yeah" (two more *yeahs* than the Beatles), and it was also great. It included one of the few good Stones covers ever: Spider Stacy, the tin whistle player, singing "Honky Tonk Women." This abbreviated release amounted to an unalloyed gem of instant pop, but it was followed in turn by the *last* Pogues album, *Hell's Ditch,* produced by the eminent Joe Strummer. Abruptly, to even the casual listener, it was clear what was happening. Shane's voice was beginning to fail, and the material had become fragmentary, dissolute, recorded in a way as if to try to make the record cohere even though it couldn't or wouldn't. *Hell's Ditch* was unable to conceal the fact that the singer had trouble enunciating, whether by reason of inebriation or missing teeth, and his intonation was little better. If they'd had an auto-tune plug-in back then they could have cleaned him up, but not in 1988. Shane remained Shane, unexpurgated, while the music around him filled in, with a general anxiety. The production feels forced, full of instrumental geegaws resembling the less effective and cannabis-enhanced portions of the Clash's *Sandinista!* album. Strummer must have tried to mobilize the troops, only to find that there was no general competent enough to halt this retreat.

Here the story ended for a long while. There are many versions of the did-he-quit-or-was-he-fired variety. You can imagine how hard it must have been. By all accounts the band toured relentlessly, and Shane MacGowan was probably trying to balance, on the road, the amount he needed to drink in order to avoid withdrawal with the amount that would render him unable to perform. This is how alcoholism goes. Other members of the band straightened up in the meantime, as if trying to shake off their legacy. Perhaps the most drunken rock-and-roll group in Europe was, it turned out, less chaotic than its reputation. The choice for the remaining members of the Pogues seemed to be: watch the singer kill himself, since he was unwilling to act on his own behalf, or break up a collaboration that had become phenomenally successful. They tried for a while to find a third way.

Rick Moody

Therefore, Shane (who claims to have been fired) went off and formed his band the Popes, a roadhouse outfit with Irish inflections that never amounted to anything much. The rest of the Pogues carried on for two albums, the second of which, *Pogue Mahone*, sounds like the Faces, in a good way, full of bluster and barrelhouse, but which, for all its competence, could never be the Pogues, not as we once knew them, a band with historical vision, imagination, cultural longing, and very human passions.

I lived on the Pogues for the first four or five years of my own sobriety, despite their besottedness, their dwindling into ignominy. There was no one else I liked as well, although I also investigated Van Morrison, and, to some degree, Warren Zevon and Tom Waits. I failed to accept that Shane wouldn't do what he needed to do to continue making the astringent and luminous music he'd made earlier in his life. Perhaps because I'd done what I imagined he needed to do—got sober—and it didn't seem so impossible or even disagreeable. True, I had a few ideas about alcoholism and recognized that the sufferer didn't always have a choice. Relapse, as has often been said, is the order of the day. But I'd managed to claw my way to sobriety, and I thought Shane ought to have been up to it, and I was disappointed when he wasn't.

Why wasn't he? It *is* important to remember that MacGowan, while born of Irish parents, was raised mainly in London, and his cherished construction of Irishness, the Irishness that's at the center of the Pogues' oeuvre, the identity politics of the Pogues (if you will), is the *diaspora* version of Irish culture. A number of Pogues have said as much publicly. The Pogues, in recreating Irish music in London, with Englishmen among them, were recreating a lost thing, a compendium of Irish music for expatriates and second-generation Celts. What's the relationship between this diaspora and alcoholism, you ask? Well, alcoholism, in my view, is an *illness,* or at the very least alcoholism behaves like one, and though there is a significant likelihood that it is either genetic or that some disposition to its rigors is genetic, there's also the melancholy of diaspora, the loss implicit in expatriation. There is the nearly sacramental notion about drinking that is so central to this recreated Irish identity. Diaspora doesn't cause Irish alcoholism, but it certainly doesn't help. Irish civil conflict and terrorism—the Troubles—don't cause alcoholism, but they don't help. Viewed through the prism of these difficulties, the alcohol problem in the Pogues is more poignant (in addition to being an *illness*), it's about losing a culture, wanting to preserve it against great

159

odds, and accepting self-destruction as a reasonable price to pay. This is the kind of Irishness that I sometimes feel in myself, the Irish-American melancholy of my mother's side, the Flynn side.

When I've been in Ireland over the years (and I guess I have been a half dozen times now), I've had the Pogues playing on my iPod like a soundtrack, as though they were the only way to articulate this sensation of returning to greensward and barren mountaintops, stone walls, sheep wandering everywhere. I always go scouring the local record stores looking for other Irish bands that offer this romantic essence of the Irish folk tradition that the Pogues convey, whether they want to or not. Back to the Clancy Brothers, or the Dubliners, or Christy Moore, or Ewan MacColl, or even the Horslips or the Boomtown Rats. None of these bands has ever, for me, been quite as moving and reckless and incendiary. As an Irish-American (one with a lot of British and Scottish DNA circulating in him too), I always feel like I can't put my finger on the soul of Eire, can't participate in it, can't be part of it. To my Irish acquaintances and friends, I'm just another American coming over for holiday and buying a tin whistle to take back to New York.

On one such trip to Ireland, I happened to watch a documentary about Shane MacGowan, *If I Should Fall from Grace.* It was available on the flight over. This is noteworthy. Because Shane Mac-Gowan, as depicted in the film, is a haunted, immobilized, all-but-incoherent husk of a man whose claim to fame seems tenuous, long past, and who, if the documentary is accurate, lives in a hovel with a long-suffering girlfriend and doesn't do that much besides, well, servicing his addiction. That Aer Lingus should consider this biography a legitimate promotional tool for Irish tourism is surprising, and yet in the end is this not what Irish culture is like, at least on occasion? Irish culture is full of paradoxes. For all its vestigial Catholic (or Protestant) conservatism, Ireland is ravaged by its unstoppable excesses. It's full of bitterness, mood disorders, self-slaughter. It tolerates more alcohol abuse than any place I have ever been on earth. And yet never does Ireland shrink from the acknowledgment of its shortcomings.

Shane, in *If I Should Fall from Grace,* the documentary, looks like he could weep bloody rivers at any moment, like he won't lift a nicotine-stained finger to prevent his next indignity, and just when you think you can't possibly feel any greater compassion for the man, he offers the kind of stinging vengefulness and offhanded arrogance that you would associate with an artist well aware of his gifts, or at least

the gifts he once had. Shane is hopeless, vindictive, but very percep-
tive. He drinks continuously. That he is still alive, on the basis of the
film, seems difficult to fathom. He's fifty-one, as I write these lines,
but he looks fifteen or twenty years older, and he totters around
stages like he could fall over at any moment. Which apparently he
does.

Knowing all of this, knowing what I knew about the Pogues, having heard recordings of him in the latter days, mediocre recordings,
in which he can barely get through the lyrics and is incomprehen-
sible during stage banter, I nonetheless greeted with enthusiasm
the news that the Pogues had begun playing reunion gigs. Why?
Because when you revere a band, when you have that fervent connection with a band, you always believe the romance can be renewed. As with absent lovers. There have been other rock-and-roll
bands for me, wherein the inevitable loss and heartbreak have long
been delayed. The Who, whom I saw play as recently as the last tour
before John Entwistle's death. R.E.M., whom I kept expecting to be
vivid and uncanny in the nineties and who just were not. Big Star,
whose recent reunion album is one of the great disappointments of
such efforts. With these experiences in mind, I had few illusions
about the Pogues. I thought Shane would probably be awful. But
the Pogues still seem to stand for something, not only for an idea
of music, but for a culture. As such, in an era of maₙₙₑᵣᵢₛₘs, they
are alien to what rock and roll is now, to a form airbrushed, stylized,
corporate.

So: on March 16, 2007, the four of us who had convened the night
before got back in the line at Roseland to try to see the Pogues play
again. Could the gig possibly come off as planned? We had our
doubts. Still, upon our arrival, fashionably late, the opening band was
to be heard in the distance, some indie rock aspirants, whom we immediately recognized, in fact, from our own shows the prior fall in the
Hague. These guys had played there too. Nina Katchadourian, in fact,
had been forced to sit in front of these whippersnappers on the plane
home, all of them unshaven, unwashed, none older than twenty-
eight or -nine. Really strange to see these youngsters up on the stage
before the Pogues, in a packed house, a house with the kind of great
anticipatory nervousness that I don't often find at shows anymore.

And then the lights went down. Out the Pogues came. It was the
whole band, understand, the band from its peak, all eight of them.
Spider Stacy was the first to seize the microphone and to venture an
overdue apology: "Sorry about last night. Shit happens." A mocking

simulacrum of the rock-and-roll entrance. Then the band launched into a couple of numbers to warm up the crowd, and the band was as tight as a band can be, full of cocksure vitality. Then, when the players were situated, exercised, and the crowd was ready, they *wheeled out* Shane. Yes, they wheeled him out in his *wheelchair.* There was a handler, a Shane handler, an old biker sort of a guy who seemed as though he wouldn't have been out of place at a Hawkwind reunion, and he was wheeling out the injured Shane MacGowan, as if Shane were some kind of gerontological specimen who could only be witnessed under controlled circumstances. *You see, ladies and gentlemen, there is no reason this fellow should be breathing.*

We'd managed to get close to the stage, stealthily, during the opening act. I'm not sure how we managed to accomplish this exactly, since the median age in our posse was probably forty-two, and there were many other eager Pogues fans, kids from Bay Ridge and Bensonhurst, who'd probably come to the Pogues via the Dropkick Murphys, and they were more eager. Still, somehow we managed to get near, and the only problem was that once near you could make out Shane's waxy, gray pallor, and his matted hair. Everybody else in the band looked pretty good. Older, to be sure, sporting a few extra pounds, but stylish and mean. Then there was Shane. When he tried to talk between songs, you couldn't understand one word of it. I don't know how the man chews. And there is a weird, ghostly cackle that issues forth from him when he's told some mandarin one-liner that he finds particularly compelling. Something between a snicker and a wheeze.

Very sad. Very hard to watch. Excruciating in some ways. But you know what? It was also an amazing show. Probably one of the best gigs I've seen in a few years. In fact, a number of nostalgic "reunion" gigs I've witnessed in the last three or four years were compelling: Rocket from the Tombs (featuring members of Pere Ubu, the Dead Boys, and Richard Lloyd from Television), Red Krayola (in which David Grubbs, another member of my band, occasionally serves), even Aerosmith at Madison Square Garden a few years back. Fleetwood Mac at a big stadium event in Washington, DC. But the Pogues were better than all of these.

They played every song you would want them to play. Without remorse. All of the best stuff from *Rum Sodomy* and *If I Should Fall from Grace.* They played at their usual breakneck tempos. And the members of the band were obviously having a great time, enjoying themselves, because they all got to take turns singing lead, in order to permit Shane his frequent breaks. The audience knew every word and sang along ceaselessly. And, best of all, there was a churning, writhing mosh pit in front of the stage throughout. I don't know if people *mosh* to the Pogues in England, Ireland, Scotland, and Wales, but they do in New York City. The strategic decision for the older members of the audience was: *do we participate?*

Though I sound like an obsolete appliance in saying so, I did like to get into it when I was younger. Once upon a time. Moshing, pogo-ing, generally causing trouble. But the last show at which I really tried to mosh was a Ramones gig in the early nineties. Dee Dee Ramone had already retired to shoot dope somewhere. The Ramones played by the numbers. I was wearing eyeglasses in those days, and I got worried about someone knocking my glasses off, and I moshed for a few songs, and then I decided that I was too old for moshing.

Despite the fact that I am in my later forties, I somehow felt, on this memorable occasion, that I wanted to dip my toe into the edge of the maelstrom, just as, independently, my friends were being borne away into that undulating mass of Irish-Americans. Even Hannah Marcus, who doesn't have a punk-rock past, and who is Eastern European by extraction (in fact, our group consisted of two Jews, an Armenian, and an Irish-American—a who's who of diaspora), drifted off into quarters where I couldn't see her any longer, except during the ballads.

I found, as I hadn't since my twenties, that the mosh pit is a caring and loving community. If someone falls, he is picked up. No pushing is more than affectionate, and when you are pushed you are invited, or even compelled, to push back. No one's ass gets grabbed nonconsensually, and when a song stops, so does the madness. From "A Pair of Brown Eyes" to "Thousands Are Sailing" to "Rainy Night in Soho," the Pogues played everything, and everyone got sweaty and covered in beer, even if they didn't drink, and they danced.

So why this horrible feeling the next day? What was this hangover feeling *after* the Pogues, when I hadn't drunk at all and had got to bed at a reasonable hour? Thus do we come to the subliminal layer of this essay, which is perhaps no longer terribly subliminal at all.

Remember the common witticism about Eric Clapton, that he *played better high?* People have been saying this for a long time, that Clapton *played better high*, that the best Clapton shows were the ones in Cream when he was probably smacked out and drifting in some psychedelic blues-rock ether. Later, when he got clean,

163

the theory goes, Clapton started recording the horrible pop songs like "Wonderful Tonight" or "Tears in Heaven." Personally, I don't much like Eric Clapton either way, no matter his blood alcohol level, but whatever your feeling about him the witticism is *inhumane.* Thoughtless. Rude. Unfeeling. Historically shortsighted. Dim-witted even. And it's not only Eric Clapton whose mythology is thus inscribed. How many great rock-and-roll personalities have been encouraged in their ability to self-immolate before the audience? Lots and lots. Certainly any number of punk rock icons—Sid Vicious, Iggy Pop, Stiv Bators, Johnny Thunders, Richard Hell, Kurt Cobain, Bob Stinson. Plenty of older, more established players—Jerry Garcia, Brian Jones, Keith Moon, Jim Morrison, Syd Barrett. Sandy Denny. I'm leaving out the cartoon players in their hair metal bands who all seemed to thrive only with needles in their arms. Nikki Sixx, e.g. Not to mention the jazz world: Miles Davis, John Coltrane, Billie Holiday. Did they all *play better high?* Did Miles Davis *play better high?* Is it possible to utter a sentence like that without being shamed by the perception?

The same conundrum presents itself in literature, where the examples are legion too. William Faulkner, F. Scott Fitzgerald, Ernest Hemingway, Dorothy Parker, John Berryman, John Cheever, Anne Sexton, Frederick Exley, Jack Kerouac, William S. Burroughs. Many, many others.

The problem with impairment, the problem it raises for the discerning enthusiast is: can you love the artist despite what he or she has become? Or must you love them in the process of unbecoming? Can you bear witness to impairment without participating in it? Is it possible to love the drunk and hate the drink? Recognizing the infirmity, can you love an artist nonetheless?

The problem gets more reflexive, and paradoxical, when you attempt to consider whether the work itself somehow *depends* on the intoxication. In the documentary *If I Should Fall from Grace with God*, Shane MacGowan's girlfriend, Victoria, says, "Maybe he was put here on earth to write about the experience of drinking." In just the way that Frederick Exley, in *A Fan's Notes,* has the one purpose only, the purpose of delineation and articulation of drink, and having discharged it magnificently he is all but blocked from that point on. If Shane MacGowan is drunken precisely so that he can give the best rock-and-roll account of blackouts and cirrhosis and dementia, then have we a right to complain about his investigations? To lament them? Imagination would suffice, you'd think. Shane might have written "Boat Train," e.g., or "The Sunny Side of the Street," in which he boasts that he will never reform ("I will not be reconstructed / Gonna stay right here on the sunny side of the street"), without having to destroy himself, his voice, his livelihood. But in this case, for reasons I cannot articulate, imagination did not, does not, will not suffice.

I remember meeting John Barlow once, lyricist for the Grateful Dead, at a party, and I remember asking him about the band, because the band was still trudging along at that point, and I remember a cloud passing over his face. Someone told me later that evening that "everyone was worried about Jerry." What to do about Jerry? Jerry Garcia stayed on the road until he died of it, just as John Entwistle, who went into cardiac arrest in Las Vegas, in the company of two hookers, died on the road, died from being an artist, died of the inability to do other than he had always done. The other members of the Grateful Dead couldn't do anything to stop Jerry, just as they hadn't been able to do anything to stop keyboardist and vocalist Pigpen, who predeceased him.

And if the extended Pogues family can do nothing about Shane, we can rest assured that the casual fan, or even the extremely partisan fan, can do nothing either. But it makes the experience of watching the Pogues perform a bittersweet thing. I, for one, don't think anyone ever, at any time, has made their best work high. I think people have made great work *despite* their shortcomings. I think most artists make their best work when they are sober, well rested, and able to take in the complications and crosscurrents of the world happening around them. And these artists will make more of the work we revere them for if they aren't poisoning themselves day after day.

Impairment, in the end, knows best the drama of itself. The truth about Shane MacGowan's lyrics is that by the end they stopped conveying the Irish heartbreak they had in the earlier records. They became mannered, silly, occasionally even embarrassing. As in all cases of impairment, what I hear after a point is the *illness* talking, and what the *illness* says is that it has seized control of the organism, and the organism henceforth will not have volition with respect to its wishes, its ambitions. And now when you hear the organism speak, not to mention when the organism makes its art, you will hear this other voice, and therefore the organism has these *two voices*, and the two voices are the voice of the organism and the voice of the *illness*, and the *illness* may be forced, where its needs are not being met, to cause the organism to *dissemble*, to act contrary to

165

itself, to berate loved ones, to neglect itself, to confuse things deliberately; the *illness* may even cause the organism to *fail*, generally speaking, because the *illness* requires that the organism first attend to the requirements of the *illness* and only when there is time left over (and there is less and less time left over), should the organism concern itself with the facts of its daily life. What is this thing that inhabits me but is not myself? Which is somehow inimical to myself? Let's not romanticize the travails of the organism, yes, but neither should we shrink from an honest appraisal of the organism's impaired state. It is not that we want to *watch*, nor that in watching we are complicit, but that sublimity is such a rare thing that we ought to honor it even when the artificer is unable to do so himself.

Beef
Edie Meidav

WE TAKE ADVANTAGE of that friendliness that Southerners are supposed to have, you know, the gentleman thing. What happens is I
come up close to the door, press my nose to the glass everyone has
out here, and one of these people comes to the door, could be an old
lady, could be a guy, it doesn't matter. I start talking real fast, sort of
snowing it over them, which is why the guys call me the Tongue, as
in, you want something, get the Tongue. Meat, beef, I've got a lot, I
say, I'll give it to you, I'll give it to you, cost me three hundred but
I'll give it to you for one hundred fifty, I'm almost shouting, *I'll give
it to you*—and behind me the other guys are holding these black
cardboard boxes we use, and our van is puffing steam, our van which
is also painted black, paint so thick we can't even use the rear lock
and have to open it from the inside.

And if the people who open the door raise their objections, like: I
don't have room in my freezer, I tell them, look, I've known freezers
in my time and people don't know how to use them, no need to get
namby-pamby on anyone, and I sort of shoulder it past them to the
kitchen and start arranging things better, because one thing people
don't know how to use is space and one American thing we know
for sure is space. I start shoving in the beef, packages of sirloin and
T-bone and all that, racks and hamburger patties, and I'm opening up
the box and hefting stuff in there, and if they say they don't want
to keep the box I tell them no worries, it's fine, I'll recycle, I've got
everything flat before they say lickety and before they say split they
find themselves whipping out a pen and writing out a checkarooni
for one hundred and fifty buckarupees, and if they don't, it's essen-
tially highway robbery, because now we've got all our beef in their
freezer, unpackaged, and possession is nine-tenths of the law, what
can they do and anyway we're gone before they think better.

And hey, it's not like we're taking anything from them, they get to
have beef for a month of Sundays, sauce it up any way they like it,
some people would die to eat beef, and OK it's not that prissy stuff,
none of that pure free-range cock-and-bull stuff, that grain-eating

mushmush, this is real cow slaughter. We're talking choose your cut and take it between your jaws, bloody or barbecued or what have you.

This is what the lone cattle farmer has to do in our time. I mean, I'm not that guy but I'm hired by a guy who works with a guy who works with that guy, one local guy who'd never let me use his name but I feel for him, I do, and anyway when I got out of the hoosegow after those domestic incidents what other jobs were open to me, I mean it wasn't like some national company was going to hire me to drive a brown truck delivering parcels or anyone would trust me decorating their cakes or whatever pissant job people find when they need to get by. If my mom weren't sick I wouldn't be doing this beef racket, because that's what it is, a racket, who are we fooling here, but money is money and truth is, it's sort of fun, the choice of a house, the way you zero in like a detective, circling. Trick is you got to look for markers that someone isn't really comfortable in his skin, like maybe you see someone with one of those cutesy mailboxes that show they're living out here because they think it's quaint, not someone throwing their trash out unbagged on their lawn but someone poking a rake at leaves as if yesterday someone introduced the whole idea of rakes to him. Or you see someone wearing his jeans a little too tight. Once you're done spotting, don't move in right away, you wait a while and come back in an hour, you have your guys with you, and the thing depends on speed, which means that after a good take, inside the truck, you are high as kites. This is pure adrenaline without guilt to tug it down, because after all didn't you just sell a decent product at decent markdown?

The only other job I've been able to get is working for the campaigns, I mean, at night, going around and removing signs the other guy has put up, people know me around here, in the electioneering scheme of things they don't call me Tongue, they call me Steam because I get away so fast, as in: you need a job done, you call Steam. Only it's these new people, the out-of-towners and northerners who drift south because their cities are turning into habitats for rats living on top of each other, prime targets for terrorist bombs, it's the escaping rats who don't understand the way we do things. Just for the record, the way you collect election signs is you stack them on a corner at night and then come back an hour later, no one really notices. All these endeavors depend on patience, you got to wait that hour before you scoop up the other guy's signs and then go drive to the river and throw them in the water so that even if they want to use them, the signs would look all bad and waterlogged and who's going to vote for someone with mildewed advertisements? A sign you should kick yourself out of the race, right? And the river's always better than going to the county dump, because anyone can dig up a sign from a dump.

When I was in Basra I was called Steam for a whole nother reason. I was in Basra, but back in Bentonville, where I lived for a little bit just out of high school, I had Cherilyn waiting for me. Cherilyn I'd met when she'd auditioned for the kind of bar where the bartenders dance and sing on top of the bar and she hadn't made it, they'd told her she was tops in the personality department but wouldn't be good for sales, she'd been sitting curbside outside the bar, crying just before happy hour on a Friday, a girl whose cheeks were so fresh you felt you'd get the first bite out of an apple, if you know what I mean. She felt I understood the troubles of her life and why getting this bar job meant so much. All the other guys in my unit were jealous about Cherilyn, whose ma had gotten her wallet photo retouched so that no matter how many times I took it out of my kit Cherilyn still looked like one hot apple.

The bad thing that happened two days before Christmas in Basra was basically I was eating turkey soup out of a can when we hear this explosion and everyone goes down, I mean everyone, and even my can gets knocked out of my hand, all I have left is the spoon in my hand and that's the dumb luck of a survivor. The only guys who didn't buy the farm that second were me and the corporal, who was about fifty yards away pulling down his pup. That one-night recon ended up, basically, a life sentence because in the bargain I lost everyone but the corporal, who hadn't been especially a friend of mine, though the moment did bond us, especially after we had to haul one of my buddies to the medevac that came too late because how can anyone get there in time to keep life flowing?

The soup incident is why I got a purple heart, even though it didn't take much bravery on my part, just the dumb luck I have, they gave me a heart to make up for all those other lost hearts, which is also why I got to see this head-shrink now because some wires got crossed, I mean who wouldn't need help. Like say you stared down the mouth of a nuclear reactor, wouldn't you think you were ready

169

for some help? Not everyone gets blown up and just has his stupid soup spoon left in his hands.

Which probably in a roundabout way explains how I got into the beef racket, the whole thing with my buddies and then Cherilyn walking out—we had a few domestic incidents, cops called, all that, but really she walked because I didn't hang on her every word and then she fell in love with some fellow boytoy prisoner friend of mine who only thought about lifting weights so he could update his photo on the prisoner Web site at the same time as he was legally changing his name to Dream Big—all that just did a number on me, and when I got out, Tony suggested I help him out in a new business venture with guaranteed profit each month, he kept saying, guaranteed, right when I was ripe for anything guaranteed, prayer wasn't doing the trick and also it had gotten too depressing staying at home with Ma all the time waiting for the veterans' check to thud in with all the other mail asking us to go out and buy things on the cheap. And I wasn't ready to start calling anyone Your Honor. You can see how it made sense.

So what happens is I've stocked the beef in someone's freezer and even got them to the point of sale, that's what it's all about, you get them to use their pen and sign the check and put it in your hand, and any objections they raise along the way you're like OK, I understand, your answers ready like little soldiers. And then we're out the door, vanished like the shine on some Christmas decorations the day after you've taken the tree down when it doesn't really matter anymore that you just had all this expectation hanging on getting something. This is not evil. If it were evil, I'd be a liar or someone would've stopped me already, because I'm not such a big guy, a fact that I got reminded of a thousand times a day in the hoosegow. It's just that my bald head makes me look taller or tougher, I can't stop shaving it since I got home from Iraq, so though Cherilyn used to say I had superkind eyes or at least did until the day she stopped saying it, it's probably my eyes draw them in while my shiny head is probably what keeps people from slamming and locking the door in my face. They're scared.

And you'd think that even after we leave they'd stop the check but they never do, probably stand a long while in the kitchen shaking their heads, trying to figure themselves out. Probably feel too foolish to want to explain it to Tanya at the bank, as in, Tanya, please stop my check because I just got taken in by the Beef Boys, which is the name we incorporated as, the name we ask them to use for the checks, and Tanya isn't about to help them out either, being that Tanya's a good local girl who understands that everyone out here does what he's got to do. Especially because out here we've got God country on our side, that's what we call it on days when you see dads standing around with their sons around the back of a flatbed, unloading a two-hundred-pound hulk of deer, everyone struck dumb by the fact that they're still living and that stupid animal just kicked it.

People ask OK did something happen in Iraq that made you go into this line of business and usually I don't talk about the soup-spoon moment, it's too much a tearjerker, so I can't think of anything except the one thing, which is that time we were crossing this little bay, which I won't name because it was supposed to be a no-fly zone, but our fuel supply was low and we see this little action hero sort of gasping somewhere out in the water, and I was not myself that day, I can't explain it, I asked Johnny, who'd been pressed into flight even though as corporal all he'd ever done was go to some military academy and get shipped out too young, barely knew how to man a copter, given that he was younger than I was, a fact I never let him forget, but on this day I was trying to eject something out of my throat, so I said let's go down, Johnny, I think that hero's one of our men, which I didn't really, but how can you explain days when you're not yourself? Everyone has them, I'm as good as the next guy. Still we get closer and I see the hero's not on our side, not at all, he has one of these superlong mullah beards, as we call them, not mullet as in long bad haircut from some 1970s band but mullah as in superevil trainer of young jihad minds trained to battle the USA.

Like the guy might be one of the priests those guys have out there. But something's hitting me, maybe because it's morning of Christmas Eve and we all should've been home two months ago or I don't know, I've gone a little soft on account of the soup-spoon incident, so I feel soft toward him, and this even after what I'd seen the day before. We scoop Mullet up in our copter, I say mullet because their hair is long in front not in back, and we're supposed to be heading to Basra to pick up some replenishment of our medical supplies, which have run low given our events, plus the fact that we've been bunkered in Bazookistan for two and a half months. And there Mullet is in the helicopter with us, spitting up water and smelling like something just dragged through major sewage, if you know what I mean, probably soiled himself. The problem is he doesn't speak much English and the Arabic rattling in my head is really not that useful, stuff like *koos emuk*, which means *your mother's private parts!* And other choice words that I won't share here. I don't know why, but certain things stick better than the *how are yous?* And *please turn around and raise your hands over your head* that we had drilled in us during pre-op. I can't help it, my head's not really sorted out for languages, but at least I remember one or two choice elements.

So here this guy is gasping and I hit on it, like something we could do for him, give him back some dignity, I go digging in my rucksack and pull it out, it's a little mushed, but it's still OK, this hoagie like we used to call it back in training camp near Philly, I pull it out and true the meat is mushed and true it's dripping but still it's prime USDA, sent in a Hugs from Home package filled with diaper wipes and graham cookies when what most guys really want is magazines and beef, even if ladies and beef both come freeze-dried.

And the guy at first looks happy when he sees the puffy part of the bread, he's skinny like a bird and hungrier, because even if someone has a different color skin and different way of thinking you can still figure out the basic human things, this is one thing I've learned, hunger anger love self-defense, but he's saying something we can't understand, muttering and spitting out a kind of question, so we're just smiling and saying *aiwa* and *la,* kind of at the same time, yes and no, which are words that even I can remember though neither of us really at that moment remembers how to say much else.

So what he does is take a bite and chews and it only takes him a half second before he spits it out and says something that I think might be the word for infidels but could just as easily be the word for disgusting, and that does it, I mean I've had it, what with the soup thing with my buddies only the day before and here I am sharing my last KP with him when we had a three-hour flight at least to get to Basra, me with my low blood sugar and him with the nerve to spit it out because it's not cut to his liking or whatever. It's cut wrong supposedly because the animal suffered and I'm like who doesn't suffer? Is suffering a reason to reject someone's courtesy? I say not.

So I say: let's drop him.

Just like that, let's drop him.

Plus the corporal doesn't even bat an eye, he says aye-aye, sir, kind of roasting my bones because I'm a private but I don't care, he's with me on the dropping-of-Mullet idea. So we're over some compound, I can't tell what it is, one of those secret government installations that are everywhere, they're on the maps like empty rectangles with squares jostling around inside, and we just do it, we force Mullet out, we drop him inside one of those cement blocks, maybe everyone has fled, maybe he gets locked inside, who knows. These guys can be supercrafty, have subterranean tunnels like moles. And Mullet can't believe we're doing it to him, I can still see his narrow longbeard face looking up right before we pull away, shielding his eyes from the wind of the copter blades but still shouting at us. OK, so even after I say that Mullet will figure out a way to escape because he has Allah on his side, the corporal seems too rattled to even crack a smile. When Mullet really deserved something, treating us with such inhospitality when there we were trying to rescue him, plus I shared my last sandwich with him, and the best thing he could think to do is call us infidels?

Which is all kind of a tangent but maybe it explains why I got so bothered last Saturday when we came to this prissy kind of door, the kind with painted birdboxes in front of it, as if our birds here don't have any place to go find shelter, and the guy who shows up at the door looks concerned, has one of those pasty northern cityfolk am-I-doing-it-right, I'm-still-a-foreigner-here sort of faces. He actually has paint stripes on his clothes, so I figure he must be one of those gentleman artsy painters because there is no way in freezing buck county that the guy is a house painter, I'd never let him touch one of my walls, inside or outside.

His wife has vanished like an aroma upstairs, I just saw her white ankles vanishing, and it is probably out of fear of the evangelicals who run rampant in these parts and who you got to be on guard against because they'll talk your ear off for a million months of Sundays and never let you get down to business, and they almost put us out of business because now some people don't even answer their doors.

But this is one pasty-looking mother staring at me, and he starts trying to out-egg me, you know, talking some breed of stuff about how he doesn't need beef, doesn't even eat it, being one more of these blue-veined vegetarians starting to infest our land, and I'm smiling at him like I can't believe this, like what kind of guy would you really be in bed, I mean I'm not exactly about to say anything, insults tend to put off sales, first thing you learn, because I'm not in the intimidation racket, just into the speech-and-speed thing. Then he starts asking all sorts of questions and it's not like I have any ready answers to his questions, and I'm starting to get a little pissy, because things

173

are not going according to plan, and it's when he says what are you fighting about? I try not to lose it and say I'm not fighting, that was before, and when he asks is the world black and white I say only if you say so and for whatever reason I'm thinking of our copter and I see this painter smiling in a way that makes him seem twice as crazy. He starts taking the beef, just ripping open the packages and throwing beef onto these massive iron skillets he has, I'm not kidding, frying up our goods in his kitchen, which is painted all these godforsaken colors, aqua or pumpkin or whatever they call those colors, cooking it up, and I would've left by now but I'm not kidding, the guy's wife is quicker than she looked, she came back smiling herself, smelling of vanilla perfume but basically using surprise tactics that made this one vet look bad, because she got me tied to their kitchen chair with two extension cords that for the life of me I can't undo. Must have had a brother in the Boy Scouts or what have you. At this point I'm bellowing like a ram in heat and stomping all what out but who's going to hear me out here? No one. And she keeps interrupting her husband whose eyes could be those of a serial murderer, I'm not kidding, keeps interrupting to say you want me to call 911?

You're not supposed to do this, I say, trying to calm everyone down including myself. How it's supposed to go is you're supposed to let me free now. Right here you should be signing the check and—

And he says we'll just keep him here. The thing they used on me was surprise, which I'm still feeling embarrassed about given how you'd think basic training plus my current line of work would have prepped me for better, but he's frying up the beef and I'm sitting there tied up and then he's serving it to me, not with sauce or anything, holding my nose to make me open my mouth and at first I'm just spitting it out onto my lap or the floor, wherever I can reach, and I'm thinking what kind of justice is this, me forced to eat my own beef, but the more I spit the more he shoves it in so I figure I better just start swallowing. If it's so good, he's saying, you think we're rubes or something? People you can just get something over on? And I keep eating, it's OK, not raw or anything, not like the desert lizard flesh I had to eat once, but it's also sort of disgusting, it's like I can see the meat there on his counter, the Freez-R-Pak starting to melt, losing its value, as Tony would say, and I can't tell which is killing me more—the fried meat or the sight of profit dwindling. And my voice is weaker than I mean it to be. I say, if you don't mind, would you please mind just putting those packages back in the freezer?

Because for everything that I sell for one hundred and fifty, I've had to shell out fifty, so it's like if everything goes bad, I mean I could sell it but I don't want to get anyone sick with E. coli, that's not my business, I never volunteered for the nerve-gas patrol if you know what I mean. I just don't want to lose money, you understand. I'm thinking of Ma at home waiting for me to bring her home a carton of cherry ice cream like I do whenever I make a decent sale, and I'm almost about to explain but the guy's talking too much, out-tonguing me basically. Meanwhile the guy's wife has disappeared again when I'd had the sense she was my only hope, something about her white ankles and vanilla scent and the way she knew to tie knots.

Not to go on too long but I'd say my guys apparently had vanished from outside, worse than steam, showing no loyalty, and I'm sitting there about three hours, telling by their folksy-cute kitchen clock that cuckoos in the voice of every different kind of bird. Three hours later and this crazy couple finally decides all right, it's enough, they're going to untie me. They've made me eat all the beef, the guy has even said back to me the thing I had said to him, which is that possession is nine-tenths of the law. Being tied up had gotten me confused and I'd started saying things out of sequence.

So that was yesterday. At least I got out with my pants on.

We have enough houses tucked away in the hills that I could be in business for a whole nother year before shifting to another line of work, and it would help out Ma with her payments for her lung cancer, that stupid doctor she goes to once a week who makes her breathe into a breathalyzer or whatever just to chart her lungs. None of it makes sense, and nothing lasts forever, I tell my ma whenever she complains but she sort of chucks me on the head and says Jimmy you used to be a decent kid, used to be able to figure numbers in your head so quick, and I let her treat me like I'm six because the old lady has gotten some marbles loose and there's no way I'm ever going to forget I'm all she has, this is why I'm so steady with the cherry ice cream except for yesterday. Not to mention that she has reminded me that I'm all she has practically every day since my dad was locked away and me only eight and allowed to see him once a month at visiting hours. Which is all a long way of saying I've changed my tactics, I'm a reformed man. Which also means I see the world in a new way and look, you gave me your time, it hurts me but I'm just about ready to give it to you.

Three Poems
Rae Armantrout

PROVENANCE

It's characteristic of X
to place his anxiety here

between "time"
and "alive."

What can you give me
for this glimpse
and its provenance?

I've got one just like it.

What interests me now
are spin-offs
of spin-offs.

The narrative
that rescues us
once more

in a less probable way.

By sailing
upside down at dusk
we've returned
from the land of the dead.

RESOUNDING

Are you still interested
in the image

of this island
as a brown shoulder

or breast

half hidden
by clouds?

Are you turned on
by chimeras?

The impossible woman,

part igneous,
part surge.

*

Go be
embedded,

beaded, pebbled.

The fickle luster.
That's right.

The fretwork
of disaster

Go on be
half

shrouded by

UNBIDDEN

The ghosts swarm.
They speak as one
person. Each
loves you. Each
has left something
undone.

*

Did the palo verde
blush yellow
all at once?

Today's edges
are so sharp

they might cut
anything that moved.

*

The way a lost
word

will come back
unbidden.

You're not interested
in it now,

only
in knowing
where it's been.

Gumbo Limbo
Brian Booker

THE VERY EXISTENCE of the town of Gumbo Limbo, based on a murky distinction between land and fog and the gray-green waves, had always seemed diaphanous at best, and in fact Gumbo Limbo may not be there anymore, and so far as I can see, it probably never was. But in the time I am thinking of—when a frail guest arrived on the shore, and lies spread like smut in a rotten hull, and rains of an impossible duration nearly smudged the village away—a boy did live in Gumbo Limbo. His name was Liam Murgen, born Van den Heuvel. He was the one who befriended the guest. Both of them have long since left. This was all quite a long time ago.

The boy lived there because when he was a very little boy his parents died in the scenic railway fire in Canada, so he was sent to live with an uncle far down south in Gumbo Limbo. It turned out the uncle was dead, but the boy was taken in by the local apothecary Murgen, who'd been a friend of this uncle. In those days the boy had little else than a box of clothing and toys mislabeled "Julius." He'd harbored a vague notion that his parents were resting in a fancy sanitarium in Massachusetts or Maine, and would return when the fire (which he imagined to be still raging in the remote north) was over. In his mind's eye he saw a mostly faceless man and woman reclined on a balcony under a canvas awning striped yellow and lime; a nurse or butler pressed cool pink cloths to their foreheads and served them chilled milk in crystal tumblers on a sapphire tray.

The boy no longer much imagined these scenes. He'd assumed his guardian's name, and was not unhappy residing with the elderly man in the apartment over Murgen's Apothek in Barnus Lane. He watched all the people of Gumbo Limbo in their gradual, inevitable parade through the pharmacy, suffering in greater or lesser degrees. He saw how while one customer burdened with the most flagrant of maladies might struggle in futility to conceal them, another, with no evident disease of any type, would flaunt his imagined ill with ostentatious mummery. He saw the discretion and care with which Murgen dispensed remedies for these afflictions, whether or not they

179

were visible to the eye, whether they abided in the mind or the flesh. So the customers came with crepitus and albugo, quinsy and railway spine, split nails and sclerotic teeth, light sleep and dyspepsia. They came with rodent ulcer, stammer, and lily rash, St. Clair's disease, limping, and glomus. Murgen pressed granules of medicine into hard little tablets, mixed acetous tonics and dissolving powders, compounded pots of waxy or oily unguents. He fermented widow's wood, crafted a debriding agent from the beards of blue mussels, and desiccated the milk from a rare deep-sea orchis. Sometimes these medicaments salved the maladies but most of the time they did not. Murgen gave free treatments to those who could not afford them, like Mr. Hannity from the swamp who came with an egg of a tumor on his face and went away weeping with gratitude and no hope, no hope. Murgen tried not to lie and to those supplicants who wanted to be deceived he mostly kept silent. He knew their secret deformities and the fear those deformities wrought in them. He knew why they employed him: to kill off the half-dreamt, half-real monstrous versions of themselves they so hated and cherished.

Murgen cherished Liam, and worried for him. He believed the boy was losing his eyes. A customer standing near the medicine counter might have seen, through the wooden grille separating the front store from the back office, how Murgen would sit the boy across from the eye chart, and, with practiced fingers trembling with palsy and personal concern, retrieve from the optical rack lens after thick glass lens, fitting them in the viewfinder and quizzing the child:

—Number one, or number two? Is this one a little clearer, a little sharper?

The boy didn't know; he couldn't tell. Then:

—There. Something.

Refracted convex in one of the big glass jars on the shelves—some of them dusty, their labels nearly illegible—Liam thought he'd discerned something clear and sharp.

—No. It was nothing. I'm sorry.

Murgen would sigh.

—That's OK.

But it wasn't OK. The eyes were sick. Murgen feared to try his tonics on the child because in truth he couldn't quite believe in them. Often now a morbid doubt crept in. He'd have gladly wrought an optical potion employing the blackest of diabolical arts if he thought its chemical burn might rend the veil on the boy's vision. But there wasn't any magic in Murgen's craft.

—Still, muttered Murgen. Sometimes I think that boy sees everything.

It was true Liam's dreams were still optically clear. And that was why, on the gray and mild winter morning when the boy discovered the strange visitor, he woke early and hurried down to the seashore with the peculiar sensation that he'd had the exact same dream as somebody else—he didn't know who—and furthermore (although, by the time he reached the dunes and broke into an urgent lollop, he'd forgotten what the dream was about) would see reproduced there in exact clarity the very thing he'd grasped in the dream, and then lost. But when he got there it was all gray on gray, beach and sky dissolving in a colorless mist: not the lapidary dreamscape, but the murky pannic haze of the boy's waking eye. And yet something out there held its form between the solute phases of saltswell and sandflat: a darkly saturate spot. A thing washed up. The boy came closer: it was a creature, that was true. But even up close it was hard to tell what the creature looked like. Was that a fin or lobe—some kind of sac? A slippery part, some scales—a portion of claw? Maybe the adumbration of a face. But it was tricky, similar to the way the mouth on a stingray's underside resembles a miniature little smiley face, but when you flip it over, it turns out the real face is on the other side: the eyes two wide-set dull expressionless beads. You'd rather have the more perfect little face on the underside. How much certainty ought one invest in a face, for fear it could be the false one? In the spirit of friendship, at least, one grants the benefit of the doubt to each and every possibility of a face.

—Hi, said the creature.

—Hi, said the boy. What are you doing here?

The boy bent his ear close, for the creature seemed to speak in the quiet susurrus of the listless surf itself.

—There is nowhere else, it said. No further to go. Isn't this the end of the sea? It keeps putting me up here, always at night. Always at night.

The creature sounded melancholy to Liam.

—Are you cold? the boy asked.

—I start to forget what it's like to be in the water, it said. I forget water. And the air is cold. But I also forget that it comes again, the tide, and takes me back in. Then I remember water, and I'm not cold. But the next night it sends me up again, to the edge, where I'm cold.

—What do you do when it rains? asked the boy, for even now a light prickling of rain had begun.

—When it rains on the sea? You can hear it, but can't feel it. It's just more water. Hardly that. More like the shadow of a cloud. But up here on the shore I can feel it.

—Do you like it?

—No, said the creature.

The boy nodded. Then he said goodbye and ran back home, because he knew Yak was approaching in his rolling chair, coming along the road behind the dunes, and Murgen had told Liam to steer clear of Yak, who was a crazy person, though wealthy, a shrimp speculator and owner of lime mines up-country.

That night Liam dreamt of a creature. He saw it lying on the sand in the dark. He woke early, and in the dawn light went back to the seashore, and again the visitor was there.

When Liam touched the creature it was cold; it quivered slightly and sighed. It was rough like a cat's tongue.

—Are you sick? the boy asked.

—It's different in the sea, replied the creature. Things have wisps and tatters, trail parts of themselves. Parts drift, tangle, and separate. It all ebbs and flows together, in and out of one thing and another. You're always inside everything, and everything is around you, and you move in it and it moves you around. But on the beach here it is different. On the beach, yes, here I might be sick.

—Are you sad?

The creature didn't know; it wasn't sure what sadness was.

—What do you feel like? asked the boy.

—Pick up that whelk shell, said the creature. Put it to your ear. Listen.

Liam did so.

—That's what I feel like, said the creature.

Boy and creature spoke a while and although the creature often gave ambiguous replies to the boy's queries he thanked him for his friendship, because in the course of their talks they'd become friends. At night the boy dreamed and when he woke he was sad at first, but then happy, because he remembered his friend was really there in the dawn on the shore, and it was.

But kneeling in the sand the boy found a loose scale, a translucent tooth, a husk of something that snapped like a seedpod. He rolled the fragile bits in his fingers; he feared they were part of the creature, who was coming undone from the strain of being washed up night after night. It needed to be in the water all the time and for some reason it couldn't be, the sea wouldn't let it, though of course the sea has no mind and therefore is not to blame.

The boy didn't want his friend to disintegrate. He decided, with some reluctance, to confide the matter to Murgen.

The next day he led the old man to the spot.

—There it is, said Liam.

Murgen craned his head—his hips were stiff—and peered toward where the boy pointed. Murgen seemed uncertain; there was a smell; he couldn't make much of what he saw there. He'd heard of the gourami, a fish capable of breathing the air. He'd heard of things caught in the nets by fishermen in Ireland or China.

—We should put it out of its misery, I think.

—No! cried the boy, crouching protectively over the creature. Wordlessly the boy queried his friend. The creature indicated the waves—and just then there washed up a tiny snailshell. Liam picked it up and saw how the inside glistened royal purple.

—Look, he said, showing Murgen. It's a gift. Like him. The sea keeps giving him back to us.

The elderly man fondled the rare shell and handed it back to the boy, who put it away in his pocket.

—I remember an old story, Murgen explained to the boy, about a siren who slipped through the dike in Holland. She came to live among the people. Nobody could make out her speech, but they taught her to weave. They said she worshipped the cross as if by instinct. It was argued that she was not a fish because she knew how to weave, but was not a woman because she was able to live in water.

Murgen's mind was drifting. The boy made no reply.

Murgen nodded. He agreed to the boy's wishes. The old man helped the boy put the creature in a big pickle jar of clean water. First they dropped a little cake of sodium in the water and Murgen stirred with a wooden stick until the cake had dissolved. They brought the jar to the back room of the apothek where it was safe. Liam asked the creature if it felt OK there and the creature said that it did, but could they put the jar up on the high shelf because it felt safer and more comfortable up there, and so they did.

Now in the mornings when the boy came downstairs he went to the back room of the shop and climbed up on the stepladder to see how his friend was doing.

And were it not for Murgen's shop assistant—a youth by the name of Tim Rutter—the trouble in Gumbo Limbo might never have gotten started, and they all might have continued on OK.

Rutter was a lanky, feral-eyed person with oily skin and a streak of cruelty that must have come from somewhere. He'd become attached to Murgen's shop some years back. He was not a good assistant, and customers patronized the apothek despite his presence. Rutter hosted a repertoire of malfeasance not so much methodical as it was impulsive, arbitrary, and weird. Not only did he overcharge the customers and keep the money, but he hocked phlegm in the philters and touched himself behind the counter when a pretty girl was in the shop, or sometimes a boy, or sometimes no one at all. He seemed too clever to be truly retarded, as the physiognomy of his head and face might have suggested, though some found the feral aspect perversely attractive or even irresistible. In fact he was an almost wholly unremarkable youth, except that he suffered from an irregular form of Saint Vitus' Dance, whereby not a fit but a sudden glazed expression stole over him, a mask that suggested to those looking at him an odd mixture of contentment and consternation that seemed not to belong to his person. The frequency of the spells varied, but they tended to last several minutes. Privately Rutter referred to his condition as "the morbus," because that is what his aunt, a Mrs. Torpin, told him it was called. This aunt characterized her nephew's rapt visage as peaceful, on account of Jesus was stroking his cheek in those times. She tried to take advantage of the spells to whisper in her paralyzed nephew's ear of the need of controlling his weakness.

Many people in Gumbo Limbo suspected that Tim Rutter had caused a dreamy, wild-haired girl named Oona LeMur to become pregnant after she welcomed his attentions, having evidently confused certain instances of the boy's hypnoid countenance with a complicated physical ardor. Oona lost her baby, though nobody knew for sure if the child had miscarried or if Rutter had employed some artifice he'd found in the pharmacy. Afterward Oona developed what they called the "woman's epilepsy"; she wandered the quayside at night pushing an empty stroller, and after a while they put her away in a home.

Then there was the matter of Liam. Tim Rutter had always despised the boy even more than he despised his employer, Mr. Murgen.

184

But after the business with Oona LeMur his malice intensified— despite (or even because of) the fact that the old man, who was absentminded and didn't care for gossip, knew nothing of his assistant's connection to the girl's aborted pregnancy. Not only that, but Rutter's hatred became even more maniacally focused on the person of the little boy. Perhaps Rutter had a notion that the boy had seen something, or knew something that most others did not.

—I dislike that crazy little blind boy, said Tim Rutter to Bobby LeMur, Oona's older brother, whom, oddly, Tim still counted among his reliable acquaintances.

—What's wrong with the boy? asked Bobby.

—He pees his trousers, said Rutter. He's ugly. I heard he has got water on the brain. Murgen is a fool for keeping him.

Rutter said that he couldn't even be sure Liam was a true boy and not a strange sexless large-headed imp of some kind. Rutter also knew about the special jar that was kept on a high shelf in the back of the shop. He knew of it and despised what was inside it.

—I can hear him creeping back up in there, said Rutter. Saying baby talk to it. He is a spoiled child. I don't think he is blind at all. I think he fakes it for attention.

Liam knew that Tim Rutter knew about the jar. The boy couldn't see the strange smile on Rutter's face as the older boy watched him through the wooden grille, but he sensed the expression plainly enough.

Liam asked Murgen if they could hide the jar someplace else.

—But why? laughed the old man. Who is going to mess with it?

The boy suggested, without naming him, that Murgen's assistant might mess with the jar.

Murgen laughed again.

—Timothy? What would he want with a thing like that?

But the boy wasn't convinced. He carefully removed the label from a bottle of quinine and reglued it on the creature's jar, hoping it might serve as a disguise. The boy asked the creature if it minded the label and the creature said it did not.

The very next morning, an unidentifiable boat was spotted in profile on the horizon. By noon an observer from shore would have noticed the boat had doubled in size and rotated slightly toward land. In the afternoon a fierce little squall passed over Gumbo Limbo, obscuring the boat from view. Purple clouds heaped up over the village, rain spat and lashed, wind drove sea nuts and the grit of oyster shell against the windowpanes. The listless surf beat itself into an angry froth and threw all manner of slimed and twisted wrack upon the sand.

When the squall had passed the strange boat was gone. But in Gumbo Limbo there was a weird hollow noise, a kind of dysphoric reverberation that seemed to come from everywhere at once and no place in particular. It made people feel like their heads had been filled with rubber. A man returning from the cinema house said he'd been issued a black ticket, and so had refused the admission. He said he had gone to the cinema every week for the past eleven years. He believed the perverse ticket meant that he'd been sold a viewing of a nightmare not his own. When released from his hand the ticket blew away down Mutus Street in a vortex of queerly charged wind.

The windless rains followed. It rained three days and didn't stop. Gumbo Limbo receded behind a curtain of rain. The line between sea and sky dissolved, the line between sky and land. Nothing was dry. The lanes were canals of mud. Brine shrimp proliferated in the puddles. Instances of the sea louse and sea weevil were noted. A week went by, ten days. The rain was quiet, vertical, whispering, incessant.

Mushrooms with unusual ocher labia sprouted in the cellars; rare black molds got a death grip in the walls. Mucus ran freely. Slimy heaps of refuse rotted in the breezeways. Some folks went a little deaf. The giant seedpods of some strange profligate plant crunched softly underfoot; the agglutinate seed husks clotted the mechanisms of local vehiculation. Two weeks into the slow deluge a kind of dentriform barnacle, lilac in color, had attached itself by way of a gummy tendon to every latch, newel, baluster, and gutter pipe; by the seventeenth day the peak of each chitinous bud had split and extruded a tiny fiddlehead nub that within hours had unfurled, with obscene grace, into a false wind foot or storm tentacle. Citizens who sought the apothek were obliged to ford a canal of mustard-colored slurry. They complained of head noise, skin blight, and geographical tongue, dysbasia, night terror, and partial paralysis of the eye. Murgen shook his head and prepared tonics and poultices. Three whole weeks. The rain went on. Instances of the marsh weevil were noted. In the unremitting gloom moods festered. Voices grew hoarse and decayed into angry whispers. Cases were mentioned of instantaneous death caused by lagoon-borne spores lodging in the lungs. It seemed that in some people the excess moisture had caused a

186

perilous loosening in the delicate structures of the mind. Citizens complained of cryptopodia, cephalopathy, late rickets, anoesia. Snails and slugs reared their soft blind antennae from bed knobs and cupboard handles. In the cupboards themselves the water beetle clicked through the long minutes of the night.

The rumors Tim Rutter had begun to sow germinated in the fertile rot of Gumbo Limbo. Slouched on the porch railing of Mrs. Torpin's home, he muttered to his companions—boys of brighter countenance than he—about a special jar on a high shelf in the back room of the apothek. A jar in which old Murgen kept a thing that, while in the technical sense unspeakable, it would not be past his powers of description to describe, should he decide to do so. As Tim Rutter spoke, hard little pockets of muscle stood forth on his jaw; the thin lips from which his news issued were crooked to the side, yet the listening boys felt that Tim's account, while definitely odd, conformed with what they felt they might already in some sense have known.

For indeed the attentive customer could have attained a partial glimpse, through the wooden grille, of a museum of the sort many apothecaries keep: specimens of local natural history as well as rare examples of corporeal perversion (e.g., omphalopagus, crinoia, cutaneum cornu), preserved in transparent mineral spirits for the edification of specialists. But to those laypeople inclined to be offended or appalled by jars of such prodigious content, their mode of display (obscured but not concealed by the wooden grille) might seem to reflect a subtle audacity on the part of the custodian—an implicit peepshow, an inadvertent medical pornography. The pickled specimens could, in this way, be viewed as artifacts of life partially developed and misformed, stuck in time, suspended in globes of fluid, marinating in their own juices, unable to properly decay, disappear, pass on to the next, the other world. Or else such examples of death enjarred might appear to conflict or, worse, conflate with the palliative, life-preserving purpose of the vessels of medicine alongside which they were shelved, making of the whole enterprise a relativistic and charlatanous fraud. The keeping of this sort of private museum might be one reason there has always been something suspicious about apothecaries, even kind and old ones like Murgen.

Whether or not the youths arrayed on the Torpin porch believed the insinuations of Rutter is neither here nor there. They listened and would later repeat what they had heard.

Tim Rutter spat over the railing; the ejected matter plopped like a

livid frog in a seething brownish pond. He asked:
    —What kind of abortions he got in those jars, anyway?
    The question scarified the fellows; and they went home pruriating a little.

Liam climbed the foot ladder, full of misgiving. He'd had a bad dream and no breakfast yet to dispel the gray net the dream had cast over his mind. He'd dreamt his friend the creature had rebuked him—had called him a name like "goony" or "fat ass," or leveled some cutting accusation, such as the boy had failed to protect or take proper care of it—then left the jar and gone back into the sea to become an argonaut, a night voyager that lives in a spiral shell, a narrow twisting house of diminishing chambers.
    In his dream Liam heard a muffled scream and ran down to the beach. He saw a gray-bearded old man hauling in his net—he dragged his catch through the surf and dumped it out on the sand. A little girl came running up to look at the fisherman's find. She jumped back and shrieked with terror or delight, while the old man, expressionless, worked at untangling his nets. . . .
    When he woke, the boy tried to feel better about knowing it was only a dream, but the hurt feeling lingered until, having mounted the foot ladder, he found his friend laughing quietly in the jar.
    —Do you want to know a funny song? it said.
    —Sure.
    —It's called "Turkey Foot," said the creature, who taught the boy the song. It was a very comical song and tears filled the boy's large eyes and rolled down his face because his friend's joke had caused him to laugh so hard.

Oona LeMur dreamt the moon released her baby back into the sea. Its sea mother called the child back to herself.
    A livid morello bobbed in the brine.
    It was going to be named "Nelly" or perhaps "Merceau."
    It had happened like this: the bone-globe moon tugged and tugged until the bulb broke; it slithered out, oyster and seed pearl, over the cup's lip, down the whelk's tube, the finite whorl, the spiral steps, nautilus the night voyager, hidden eye and sealed chamber, round and round to the vanishing point, till moonlight on cuttle-white bone lit tiny stapes, no more than a whisper, sea-polished glinting and gone.

—I named it Merceau, she said when she woke. It is out there in the wide world now. It has gone to an olden home.

—Old Murgen, he made a sin, said a man called Crippen who was known to be congenitally morose.

—A bad sin, he said. I believe it cannot be put right.

The talk that led the man to his conclusion had come from many quarters. But the first and most influential testimony had come from Mrs. Torpin herself. Torpin was a woman who even before the long rain had suffered greatly in her nerves, and whom Murgen had treated, at her own insistence, with salves of black mercurial lard, green belladonna, and even a pale silken hood thought to restore sense to the lunatic mind. Mrs. Torpin maintained that Murgen had captured a she-beast with no hind limbs and malformed breasts and hands that were flippers or flattened lobes.

—Like a mermaid, she said. Or some type of female siren.

The apothecary, she said, was keeping the mermaid hostage in a bottle. The rain would not stop on account of her fury. The unwholesome liquid had pickled and shrunk her. Yet even as she physically weakened (her skin or scales had yellowed and begun to slough off), her mental powers only intensified. Mute, she convulsed in her jar.

—Truly the rain will not stop, declared the elderly woman, until the mermaid is freed back into the sea where he got her.

It is always a difficult matter when someone else's nightmare gets caught in the tangled net of your dreams. A man named Onder said the creature had the head of a horse and the tail of a fish, but no one believed him. A man named Frye held that the creature was a tardigrade, otherwise known as the water bear, but no one believed him either. Nonetheless, everybody soon knew there was a mermaid ashore—or something close enough to a mermaid—and that Gumbo Limbo would drown like Atlantis, under an unbroken waste of waters a mile deep, unless the apothecary could be made to release her.

—If she is taken wrongfully from the sea, said Mrs. Torpin, truly the sea will come to her. Wherever she is taken, there too will the sea follow.

The man who said he'd been sold the black ticket began to advertise a ten-cent fee for people to come inside his home and view something he called a "sea movie," a hastily crafted zoetrope or flip book that might or might not have been purported to show a picture of the mermaid.

It is a difficult thing when not only two but many people feel they have shared the same dream. When they feel they're still in it together. When suddenly everybody is.

—Murgen made a sin, declared Crippen. A strange and awful sin.

Murgen himself, catching wind of the notion that a mermaid had been seen in the village, formed a hypothesis that a case of the sironomelia or "mermaid syndrome" had at last befallen some unfortunate family. He said to the boy Liam that never in his long experience had he seen such a case, though he'd read of it once in a medical book and the description of that particular birth deformity was so terrible it made him weep.

Mrs. Torpin's porch roof sagged under the weeks of water, seemed ready to break off like a slab of soft clay. Tim Rutter's urine arced in a long jet over the rotten railing into the soup of the submerged garden. He said:

—I saw Murgen's little retarded boy teasing the cripple fish-lady in that bottle.

Then he fell silent. Bobby LeMur watched Tim Rutter, who was dribbling pee onto his own foot. He stood there holding his cock and gazing into some unfathomable distance; the queer glazed contented expression had stolen over his face.

Bobby LeMur frowned. He had never cared much for this Rutter fellow.

Murgen didn't sleep, didn't dream; he lay on his cot and listened. A murmured demand rose in Gumbo Limbo. There was a freshly rotten stench, of something damp and spoiled, and many people gathered by the water. The sanitary wagon with its pale canvas hood drew up.

Mrs. Torpin, standing atop an upturned shrimp bucket, flapped her short, fat arms like a penguin and effected subtle evolutions of her theory.

—She is alive! cried the aunt, alluding to the mermaid. It's her baby—her baby has been abandoned in the sea. The mermaid must be freed unto the sea so she can nurse her child there.

Torpin painted for the crowd a picture of a baby floating in a cold limbo under the dark swells, a hungry baby crying out for its mama in the darkness far below the rain-pocked ceiling of the sea.

190

This news of a baby fanned the outrage of the pervasive stench: a chlorotic woman named Lucy Graves, who'd never been known for a morbid sensibility, suggested the mermaid's baby was dead. But such a thing was too awful to contemplate, for by that logic the rain might never stop, even should the furious and damaged mermaid be released.

From his window Murgen listened to the silence that followed the pronouncement of Lucy Graves; he listened while the wind drew vast curtains of rain across the dark plain of the sea and he listened while, on the forty-seventh day of rain in Gumbo Limbo, the citizens coagulated in groups that, by the time they'd begun to clog the narrow lane before the apothek, had formed into a veritable mob.

At the head of the mob were Tim Rutter and Bobby LeMur. The perversity of their alliance was not lost on LeMur, but at the moment he had no other idea of where to be or what to do.

Rutter's face was red and strained and his sweaty arms gestured wild and inarticulate. An exhilaration swept through him like he'd never known except when he was fornicating with Oona LeMur. He shouted at the crowd, rehearsing and reifying and embellishing the dicta of his aunt: that Murgen the apothecary had a mermaid or other variety of fabled she-beast held hostage in the shop; that the mermaid was shrunken and deformed in Murgen's bottle; that she raged impotently in a slightly viscous lime green solution; that, in addition, old Murgen had unnatural designs on the female creature; that for all anyone knew he may have already begun to pursue those designs; that the rain was a curse cast by the mermaid to punish Gumbo Limbo for the apothecary's secret crimes against her; that truly the rain would never end until somebody set her free.

As the words escaped his mouth Rutter felt that he believed them; as he convinced himself, so he hardened the resolve of the mob. They scooped up clots of mud and oyster shell and flung them at the shop. Two men climbed a drainpipe on the side of the building to try and get a look through the transoms at the famous hostage.

Murgen knew of the secret monstrosities wrought by nature in the bodies of God's creatures. And he knew it was their fear that made them truly monstrous. He suspected their rage had something to do with the boy's special jar but he wasn't sure what. He looked for Liam in his room above the shop but the boy was not there. A clamshell thick and heavy as a horseshoe hit the window and cracked it. Rain blew in. The old man went to the window; he held his hands before his face and wept and begged the people to stop. He raised his

191

voice to ask why they were angry with him, with the apothek, but the sound was swallowed in the din of the crowd. Blinking into the wind, he tried to survey the crush of faces in the lane. He saw his assistant was among them.

—Is that you, Timothy? called the old man, hoping for acknowledgment and help.

But the dead-eyed youth was buffeted and sustained in the surging press of people; his mouth hung open in a loose smile of childish incomprehension.

Again and again the mob surged against the apothek. They had nearly smashed out every last shard of the display windows and were beginning to climb inside when a man appeared in their midst, a medical physician named Grover Stiles. Stiles was a large man and he pushed to the front and told everybody there to shut up and listen. He said Gumbo Limbo was sick—sick with rain. He told the people they had water on the brain and implored them to be still and regain possession of their persons. He told them they saw mermaids everywhere they looked. He said that he was going to walk into the apothek and have a communication with the apothecary Mr. Murgen.

—I intend to enter that store, he said, through the doorway, not the window, and take an accounting of what all is in there and what is not.

So in the few moments of chastened bafflement the physician had purchased with his speech, he entered and went upstairs to where Murgen sat on the glass-strewn floor with his back to the open window, weeping.

—I gave Leroy a syrup, he muttered, a syrup for the cancer. But the cancer come back.

Stiles nodded. The apothecary's reason was impaired.

—It is not about a cancer or a syrup, he explained to the elderly man. It is about this rain. And something those people think you got hidden down there in a bottle.

—That is all made-up lies, said Murgen.

—It may be, said Grover Stiles.

Murgen agreed to let Stiles search his shop in hope that the mob might desist. The physician came downstairs and announced that a deal had been brokered: he, Dr. Stiles, would search the premises. If any mermaid was discovered she would be returned to the sea forthwith.

There rose a skeptical noise. The mob invested scarcely more trust in the doctor than in the apothecary, since in those days, as in ours, it was much the same business. A man named Horace Sympus stepped forward and demanded the liquid of the jar in question be tested for iodine to determine if the beast had lactated. Grover Stiles denied this request, but said he would permit Sympus to join him in searching the apothek. Sympus agreed on the condition that he could in turn appoint two additional searchers, forming a citizens' committee of three plus the doctor. Stiles agreed. Sympus looked around and couldn't see anybody he knew, so he indicated at random a small round-shouldered man and a stern sour-faced woman, whose names turned out to be Clive Dungeon and Chimpiffany St. Clair. The four then entered the shop through the doorway.

Murgen stood behind the counter, steadying himself. He tried to recall who these people were. He believed he'd treated the St. Clair woman for the limbic fever; to Sympus, who'd come confiding the shameful anomaly of his infant son Lyle, Murgen had been able to offer only condolence and discretion. Dungeon he'd neither seen before nor heard of. Murgen feared them: whereas before they'd come for help, they now came to ransack his shop because the wicked youth's mad aunt had told them lies about a decayed girl in a bucket.

They searched the apothek from top to bottom and front to back, and in the back room they found the wreckage of Murgen's stores. Somebody had smashed a cobblestone through the deadlight. Glass and spattered liquid lay everywhere; volatile powders clouded the air, and the room was filled with the bitter smell of potent chemicals.

There lay a piece of darkish matter on the floor that must have come from one of the busted bottles. Clive Dungeon prodded it with the toe of his boot, but Murgen stopped him:

—That's nothing to do with it. That is only my concern.

Then they saw the big-headed child huddled in the corner with his skinny arms hugging what looked like a two-gallon jar. The boy wept over the jar and his knees shook.

The doctor approached the child and asked him what he had there.

Liam, gazing up, could not make out the face that was speaking to him. He said it was a creature, a creature who had been ill and was his friend.

—I am going to need to take a peek at your friend there, said the doctor.

The boy shook his head. His eyes were rheumy and unfocused and he blubbered softly.

Murgen wanted to say something but the words caught up in his throat.

The three members of the citizens' committee closed in. The doctor knelt and gently moved the boy's arm off the jar. The boy cried out sharply. Then he began murmuring to the jar.

—Where are we going to go? Liam asked the creature.

His friend didn't know. It was comfortable in its liquid, unmoved by the great calamity.

—Do we have to let you go?

Liam could imagine what would happen: the old man would put a hand on his shoulder—*We got to let it go, son*—and together they would carry the jar down to the seashore. In his mind's eye the boy saw how the villagers followed at a cautious remove like a throng of sodden mourners. He saw how the long rain had smoothed the features from their faces. Then the boy and the old man knelt on the sand; the ground-glass stopper was pulled, an odor wafted up; the jar was tipped; with a gulp the thing slid forth, landing with a meaty splat on the sand where the foam purled over it; and tipped all the way over, the jar's dregs petered out, the piddling faint green afterbirth of this sad seashore expulsion. *I forget that it comes again, and takes me back in*, his friend had said. *Then I remember water.* The friend receded into the neutral gray distance where sea and sky dissolved and Liam saw the rotten ropes of the fisherman's net, hemp gnawed by sea lice, the scream of the little girl, the awful discovery. *There's nowhere else, no further to go. Isn't this the end of the sea?*

—I just need to be able to see what's in there, said the doctor.

Grover Stiles peered into the liquid and frowned. He retrieved his spectacles from his coat pocket and had another look.

Then he glanced up at Murgen. Sympus looked to Dungeon, and Dungeon to Chimpiffany St. Clair, across whose sour face a strange placidness had settled. St. Clair looked to Sympus and Sympus to Grover Stiles, who nodded and cracked his knuckles and stood and replaced the spectacles in his coat.

The crowd packed in the lane received the news with despair. The rain fell on their hats and shoulders; heads bent, they stood in puddles in blank amazement. They were bereft. Anyone who had harbored in his mind a special picture of the secret captive in the apothek felt robbed of the chance to see that picture brought out alive in a jar of fluid. None of it was real but the rain.

Gumbo Limbo woke to the same rain after a night of dreamless sleep. In the gray dawn light Tim Rutter stood in the empty, sludge-washed lane before Murgen's Apothek. He'd been up all night drinking a potent alcoholic clam broth. He was drunk and exhausted and vexed. He hollered in the lane and flung bits of refuse at the shop. A few people wakened by the noise, or who, like Murgen, had been unable to rest all the night, shuffled out to witness the commotion. Rutter cried forth deranged slanders against Murgen and the apothek and the boy. He said the boy wasn't a boy at all but a hermaphrodite with the God-granted bodily parts of both the male and female species. He said the old man and the child had deceived the search party and all of Gumbo Limbo, but he knew just where they had hidden the grisly specimen: he meant to smash out all the remaining windows and go in there himself, this very minute, and haul the thing out in the plain light of day.

The crazed youth was shouting such things when, as tended to happen, he was struck dumb. A paralytic innocence smoothed his contorted face. And all of a sudden that charmed countenance was transfigured by an unearthly light. The light seemed to emanate from everywhere and nowhere at once. The sun shone through: and it made Tim Rutter's face look a little green.

The clear weather didn't last for long. A mist rolled in, though a kind of dry mist, softening and soothing away the vision that had emblazoned itself in such hard and burnished outline in the mind of Gumbo Limbo—a desiccant mist that seemed to dry up all the rotting remainders of nightmare and panic, the wet stench of the terrible festering wrack—a mist that swept down the coastal plain from higher, drier ground, and a wind blowing dust through the village and out into the sea.

It has never been known for certain whether Murgen and the boy remained in their home for a few days, quietly sorting through the broken things, or whether in fact they left Gumbo Limbo in the rainy predawn hours of the night following the mob and the search. Or whether they almost didn't make it out of town, the causeway being flooded, the marsh waters lipping the highway's edge, so that it might have appeared to a distant observer that their odd vehicle was skimming the surface of a vast gray lagoon.

And the boy, going blind from a secret cause that was a mystery to the old man, said:

—What do you see out there?

—Nothing but water. Water and sky.

—All the same?

—All the same. Lovely. And it looks like the rain has stopped.

The big glass jar sloshed on the seat, wedged between the boy's thighs, his hands on the lid.

The old man said:

—Maybe we'll just let it go somewhere out there.

Like the rain ponds and storm pools that took some time to drain, the rumors lingered. There had been a mermaid, but she'd grown so shriveled that no one could recognize her as such; or she'd shrunk to a size where the water in the jar suited her, and she stopped raging, and so the rain stopped. Or Murgen's boy did have a secret jar, but with nothing in it except a dead seahorse or maybe a horseshoe crab, which through blindness or insanity appeared to the child as something more—and the old man, not wanting to hurt the boy's feelings, had kept silent so as to protect his belief for a little bit longer. Or else a truly unmentionable thing had been quickly disposed of, out the back door in the night.

Liam dreamt he'd woken up with a disease, a seasickness that was an emptiness inside him, or a failing heart, blood like seawater washing in and out of a grotto, a stony cave. He realized the creature was his heart and the creature was gone, back into the sea whence it came.

—What do you think it means? he asked.

—I don't know, said his friend.

Asking your own heart a question: how could it make a reply? It says only one thing ever, no matter the question you put to it. And even if you never ask one question your whole life, still it says that one thing, always and only that one thing:

—*I'm here. I'm going. I'm here. I'm going. I'm here.*

The boy cradled the jar with a sad feeling of happiness in his heart: the feeling you get when you wake up from a bad dream to find out it's not true, it's still OK, and will be so for a long while yet, as far as you can see.

Two Poems Inspired by
the Dreams of Emily Dickinson
Martine Bellen

WHEN ROBERT SCHUMANN MET
HANS CHRISTIAN ANDERSEN

She rubs a match against the wall.
    (running/falling)

    Mood: Green

It bursts into flame and where light sprays, the wall becomes transparent
And she sees the steam of roast goose stuffed with apples and plums—
A psychical consummation for the suppressed wish/desire.

    Mood: Forest fire

How fire burns
Her grandmother
And her cottage-cheese cottage of whooing owls
With dancing sirens massaging microzones of body.

Her three magic peas. She sleeps on peas, seven Ps on her forehead,
In sea green soup, pea fog on her mind, pea dreams, drowning in peas.
Echoic images shadow her through dark avenues—P Street—They wear
Peacoats and breathe down her neck
Their breaths shake her skeleton. Sigh!

(She might be left outside to fry
In a forest without letters for trees—a long, quiet, resting forest . . .)

"Peas, I AM a poor little girl with neked feet."
Elements need not have *x* in common to freeze.

It's all about shoes. Father was a cobbler.
Memory, like music, swirls around the cortex.

It's running tones
Toes and trees and stories // Sliced braising tongue

When the content oversteps the personal censor, she thinks, "I was only a
dream. I was only running for running's sake. It wasn't as though I wanted to
arrive, to win. I am only living because I am born."

How much has to do with scoring?

In logic, "mood" and "modality" convey possibility / impossibility, existence /
nonexistence, contingency / necessity. "Mood" in grammar, derived from
"mode" with its elongated vowel, is associated with states of mind (e.g., a
good/bad mood).

   Mood: Knifed

Red's the central character that might live inside her. No matter how beat up
      she gets
Her flesh is without wound. It's more comfortable
When the damage is seen.
Once the music stops
The words stop
Even though it was a gnarly, old-growth forest,
Unyielding, impenetrable, at least she was walking through a friend.
She could run through it as though it were a forest in a fairy tale,
Read through it, red through and through

One person, who is dependent upon another, will at some point in time make
a remark bound to be disagreeable to the second one, and because of it, a
simile is born.

It's as difficult to build a daughter as to build a Shinto temple.
It's especially difficult to build an ocean,
And even more difficult to build *on* an ocean.
The floor slopes forward, the sitting mind wanders,
Pillars and perspective lines tilt.

The one who crosses the ocean acts as a drum, throwing sound forward—none
Should be wasted. (Water beneath her for optimum resonance.)
She slips words down her teeny throat
Just in case a line is later needed.
Emily has never seen the ocean (nor the sea).

. . . open a closet and mourn the death of white dresses . . .
. . . close the mouth and prose . . .
Just in case some dreams are forgotten.
This bridge is not a symbol, but a way of finding
Herself, of running into the forest.
Her bird body has drifted away. A letter in the mail. Emily's e-.
How far across time can the voice reach?

The human form. Fox-form. Formlessness.
Tangled letters in scripted forests—underbrush and calligraphy. Spirited.
Suddenly all worldly attainments
Vanish. Her youthful flesh.
Calling out among the ivies, thieves, pines.
A loon song and the clicking of cicadas. Lone song. Plainsong.
We feel awkward at first light on the far side of the bridge,
Devoid of limb and limn, seeing and sound
Seafaring // the soundness of reason
Its soundlessness ghosting
A faded boy
I got so I could take his name
He put the Belt around my life
Mama never forgets her birds.

THE PHILOSOPHY OF HOUSE-KEEPING
"She died at play / Gambolled away / Her lease"

*Five Chinese brothers live with retarded cats, wander the edge of the
woods in wait. The five brothers with one name, one nature, with five
gills, five gifts, housed in one body with five doors. As Emily dreams, she
floats to the top floor, head in clouds, laughing helium. A cup of cinnamon
tea. She visits the five chiming brothers who save her from drowning,
burning, fading, shrinking—nightly she retreats into a spectral episode and
the brothers draw her near—sing to her / recite her favorite lies, bouquets

of jasmine and buttercup pregnant with songbird scent. A goldfinch Eucharist flutters against her teeth (ooh!), attempts to escape belief. In one dream she's a porn star—wraps her diminutive thighs around a pole, how she wraps her mind around death, poem after pole, after poem, and then she's Frankenstein's construction—a patchwork of putridity, baking loaves of gingerbread**, sifting sugar, licking tears from hummingbird eyes, always she's Emily recalling a world in a house, the objects in a kitchen—desire, hope, love—now*** rolling pins, an herbarium, the wire mousetrap. She embraces each noun that will vanish when she dies to the nothing it came from—the word—the way a cloud pie**** flies like a bee buzzing past the ear, flakes, and tenderly melts. Night blows out the single star for fear.***** Trombone air. Troubadour.

What kind of a world do we love in?

NOTES. *A poem without "I" wanders purgatory, swims through tormented seas of unsewn sheafs, travels farther into summer than birds.

**The lost chapter on bread baking.

***Language is a machine that brings abstractions into being, semiconductor that permits contact between light wave and light bulb; its antonym: death, which acts as a microtransformer of objects, reversing them into concepts. Without the authority of one fatal tongue, words fall into the vast vat of sound.

****Place ½ cup of cloud in glass bowl. Saturate with lemon water. A pinch of salt from teardrops. Introduce feathery chartreuse, magenta, cobalt, and cream—slowly stir in memories of pleasure until light and well blended.

*****Without a child she will always be a broken pine, burning the oven.

COMMENTARY. She who wrote: "To die—takes just a little while—/They say it doesn't
        hurt"
        —How willing to expire might she have been? As a specialist
        in dying and a meticulous record-keeper
        of the dead—their possessions, thoughts, senses—
        She inhabited a world that could be trusted
        To forget.

Self-Portrait with Sicily
Frederic Tuten

"HAVE YOU BEEN away a long time?" asked the short Sicilian, looking away from me.

"Is it my accent that makes you inquire? Do I sound foreign?" I
added, alarmed to think that I had changed so obviously over the
years. He did not answer but went on hungrily eating hunks of bread
he tore from a brown paper bag.

The train turned, mountains on one side, the cranky sea on the
other. Lemon and orange trees, fields of wild rosemary crowded the
sky and invaded my memories.

We were moving so slowly that I could see my grandmother
through our kitchen window as she was spooning snails into a boiling kettle. "Pull down the shade," I called out, wanting no one to
see that we ate snails, because when I was a boy no Americans
my age ate them—worms with oily shells. Nor did they eat the dandelion leaves my grandmother—a black silhouette—plucked from
the Bronx Park fields, just some few miles from the outskirts of
Palermo, where street lamps spread rectangle shrouds on the winter-
night streets.

"You people eat grass and worms," the kids cried out when they
wanted to start a rock fight with me. Small rocks, hard stones. I still
have a scar over my left eye, the one with which I can see the man
in the moon and his bucket smile.

She was making the evening meal, my grandmother, and soon we
would be at the table putting oil and salt on our bread. And soon
we would be eating snails drowned in olive oil and garlic. And then
a dandelion salad, bitter like the Bronx winters, the kitchen oven and
burners left on all night for the heat. Sometimes there was wine,
even for me at ten, from Segesta, where two thousand years ago the
Greeks planted temples and sacred groves in whose tranquil shade
they turned their minds to reasoning out the world. All that reason
wasted in the hills, where hot tempers rule.

"But now you've returned," the short Sicilian said. "Now you've
come back home."

There were not many automobiles below us in the Bronx streets when I was a boy. It was wartime and the gasoline was rationed. Few had cars, and those who did were careful about driving aimlessly here and there just for the carefree joy of taking a spin. In early winter mornings, when I was still half asleep, I could count the handful of autos on the road by the steel rattle of their tires chained against the ice. Everywhere was ice: ice coating the tree branches; ice sheeting the black mountains; ice chilling the little stone houses dotting the frozen hills; ice in my bed, piled up with coats for blankets. My grandmother left little chunks of stale bread soaked in muscatel on the windowsill to revive the sparrows freezing in the icy winter.

"Poor creatures," she said of them, as they shivered on the windowsill, their beaks blue from the cold.

"I have never left Sicily," I said to the short man, a bit sharply. "Why would you think that?"

Another Sicilian, in a hunter's cap, laughed, as if he had just woken up from a good dream, through whose mist he had found a cave of hidden gold coins as thick as chestnuts. Two gutted hares hung from the staff standing beside him. A double-barrel shotgun rested on his lap like a sleeping child. I liked his fat green cap and his green hunter's jacket, brushed to a sigh of its used-up life; I liked the way he tried to make himself seem prosperous, though his tired half boots had cords for shoelaces, and red patches spiced his dull corduroys.

"Do you have some matches?" he asked, half loading his pipe, his tobacco a peat of leaves and shredded debts.

"Would it not have been polite to ask us whether we minded your smoking in such confined quarters?"

I was gentle in my question, leaving him room to answer me with his dignity intact. You must always leave a man his dignity, unless you hate him. Unless you want to take the chance of his shooting you from behind an orphan tree on a lonely dirt path under a moon stained red by the dying sun and by all the disasters, great and small, that had befallen the day. Stained by the death of a strong goat, say, or of a fierce cat who has kept the rats from bothering the grain or by an insult that burns and burns in your heart or by the departure of a hungry son who had gone to work in the factories in the North and who one day would reject all memories of home and who would not even send a threepenny postcard back there.

"I wanted the matches for later," he said. "For when we arrive in Palermo."

"Palermo, is that where you're headed?" I asked the hunter.

"No, why would you think that?" he said, parroting me earlier, when I asked why he thought I had left Sicily. The other Sicilian laughed, and I did too, seeing how clever he was, the hunter, as all Sicilians are. Except me, my head filled with books in weary bindings, my head stuffed with dried memories in place of quick thoughts.

The short Sicilian stuffed more bread into his mouth, ballooning his checks into a wide pumpkin grin. I was happy for him.

"Are we Sicilians still as hungry as we were fifty years ago?" I asked the bread eater, asking all of Sicily, where, when I was a child, some had much and even more than much to eat and others sipped bowls of warmed water for their dinner.

"Because you are fed, do you think the world is fed?" he replied, licking the little shreds of bread stuck between his teeth.

"We Sicilians are always hungry," the hunter said. "It is in our nature to be hungry, food or no food."

"Is that why we eat sparrows?" I asked.

"To consume sparrows is in our nature," said the hunter.

"To eat baked sparrows is much in our nature," the short Sicilian said. "To eat even their crusty beaks."

"In my region, we do not eat sparrows," I said. "In my region we feed them."

"The region of plenty, I suppose," the bread eater whispered above the grinding of train wheels, whose heedless sparks set fire to towns and villages and wooden shacks along the way.

"The region of pity," I said, "is where we lived, the region of pity." That remark seemed to keep them pensive for a while, leaving one to gnaw on his bread and the other to feed on his hunter's dreams.

Now the train was gaining speed, traveling through flaming fields, hot fires the farmers had set to burn the dead stalks of corn, their ash to enrich the depleted soil and return its honor. The train slowed into the station, empty like an abandoned factory. Tucking the paper bag under his jacket to shelter it from the cascading rain, the short man rose and, with great courtesy, said, "I leave you and I salute you."

"I will miss you," I said. As I would, missing the sparrow from the windowsill, missing a cloud as it sailed away beyond my view, missing those who had left me even before they had died, missing my life as it sped faster and faster away from me.

Now we were again out of the station and into the countryside, where the sky was sending down a torrent, flooding everywhere lands high and low, engorging the newly planted corn and drowning everywhere the chickens in their coops and snails in their shells. In Sicily, the sun either burns the earth down to powder or the rain turns it into lakes where families of vipers enjoy their swim on Sundays, when Sicilians at mass pray for a fat roast chicken and potatoes for dinner.

No sooner had the short man left and the train made its way again than a young man with a mandolin under his arm entered and, sizing us up as men who did not have the coins to pay for a tune and a song, went into another compartment. Two plainclothes policemen in black silk suits came into our compartment as if they owned it; they looked about and one, with nails for eyes, gave us stern, schoolmasterish looks, as if we had been caught passing smutty notes to each other under our desks.

The hunter doffed his cap to them, to show them he knew his place. I wore no hat but made a little salute and a bow of the head, letting them know that I also knew mine.

"Have you seen here a man with a bag of bread?" the tall one, with grilled-mutton hands, asked.

The hunter and I looked at one another. He shrugged. I shrugged. Then I said in a respectful voice, "Not me, sir."

Then the other man, with nail eyes, said to the hunter, "I did not hear you speak."

"I saw no such man, Captain," the hunter said, doffing his cap again, deferentially.

Then mutton hands says, very softly, so as almost not to be heard, so as to make us strain to understand his words, "You're too slow to answer when addressed by significant people."

"It could be taken for an insult," nail eyes adds, with a smile to kill a subtle eel.

Then he goes, "What fine hares you have there. Very fat and filled with honey, very ripe for a stew."

"I'm sure," the hunter says, with measured dignity, "my wife would be as happy as I knowing that these hares will grace your table tonight."

The men did not smile.

"Your excellencies," he added, offering them his staff and hares.

The train slowed into the station. "Keep your dinner," nail eyes said, "with respects from us to your famous wife, if you find her still at home when you return."

They disembarked at the next station, scurrying down the platform, to apprehend one or another poor man who came into their
suspicious view.

"They always have an insult to humiliate you or to provoke you
into regrettable foolishness," the hunter said. "Why is it always like
that?" he asked the hares.

"Power," I said, as if that explained the world. Then I added without thinking, "Sicily."

"But we are in the Bronx," the hunter said.

"It's the same thing," I said.

He studied me for a moment, then asked, "Would you like them?"
indicating the hares.

For a moment, I thought of what a fine stew they would make,
cooked in red wine, with some carrots, for color. But I remembered
that I now had no place to cook them, no home and no stove. I
thanked him for his offer, saying that I had a long journey ahead and
thought it best to make it unencumbered. It was a reasonable excuse
and he accepted it with a dignified bow. It seemed that all the police
unpleasantness that had threatened to sour our way had been settled
and we were now ready to continue our journey along the neutral
grounds on which it had begun.

But when the train was some minutes from the station, he rose,
lowered the window, and, as we were climbing over the Bronx River,
he let fall the staff and dangling hares into the muddy water below.
He grinned at me, pleased with his costly triumph, and rubbed his
hands on his pants, as if to wipe away the grimy memory of the
policeman's insult.

"Well, that's finished," he said, with the finality of a newly dug
grave.

There will be other hares, I wanted to assure him, even bigger and
ones with more honey than those you have just shot. You are still a
young man after all, I wanted to say. But that was not true. He was
not young. But not old either, having the age of a man who has come
to know who he is without falsifications. He must have been fifty,
the age, I supposed, when a man has attained wisdom, which, I imagined, would one day also be mine, like a great inheritance, like a
vineyard on a hill taller than the rain and clouded from the scorch-
ing sun.

Finally, I understood who he was, the hunter, and I said, "Are you
not my uncle, Umberto? The one who owned seven mulberry trees
and left for America after the Great World War? Are you not the one

who gave me five dimes in secret after Sunday mass, a secret between us lest your son be jealous of your gift to me?"

As we Sicilians are jealous of gifts given to others and worried by the intent of presents given to us, as we Sicilians are worried by everything—a life of worries that not even death has the power to end. We worry in the grave and worry in the few cents' worth of our ashes. I wanted to say all this but thought it unnecessary for the occasion, thinking also that he had known all this, as he was clearly a wise man without falsifications.

"You are that uncle," I continued, "whose quince tree I climbed one day and shook the crows from their strong roost in the clouds."

"You were a good boy, you and that girl too," he said, at last, "saving my quinces from their beaks. Those crows," he said, as if he wished to break their wings and bake them in a pie.

"But they were hungry, those crows," I said, "like most of us in Sicily. Like all of the world who labor and from whose labor others summer in mansions by the sea." My voice trailed off, ashamed at the obviousness of my remarks.

"Your grandmother," he said, changing the subject and gracefully saving me from further embarrassment, "liked to drink a glass of muscatel with a raw egg when she was feeling sick. She was always sick," he said. "She drank the muscatel that I made myself, from my own grapes," he said proudly.

"She was infrequently sick," I said, not liking his speaking of my Nonna in that way, as if she had been an invalid. She was, of course, but who wants to review all that. I also did not like that he was so boastful of his insignificant vineyard, the size of a pale sneeze.

The train was coming to the station where my grandmother was to wait for me, and there she was, on the platform, standing exactly at the spot where my door opened. My uncle gave her a polite smile and she to him. I stepped onto the platform, turning to say goodbye respectfully, and he saluted me. Imagine that, I wanted to say to my grandmother, imagine that I would meet my uncle in a train after not seeing him all these hundreds of years, or so it seemed. "But nothing is unusual in Sicily," my grandmother said, reading my thoughts, as she always had, even from miles away.

She took my hand, as she always had when I was a boy, leading me through the marketplace, barrels and bushels and baskets of snails and olives and salted cod, dirty white like leftover snow, fronting the shops. To my surprise, because it was our usual marketing day, we stopped at none of the stalls but walked out of the district and followed a path through a wood, stands of cypresses flanking our way like blackened arches of a burnt-down church.

"Where are we going?" I asked.

"A surprise," she said.

I became worried that it might be like the surprise she had given me when I was a boy in short pants. One cloudless, burning summer day we took a similar path through similar woods to come upon a smallish Greek temple dedicated to the goddess of plenitude standing in the cypress groves on a cliff above the sea. My grandmother, mixing a bowl of honey and wine for the goddess, ordered me to pray.

Pray, she said, that we can pay the rent, pray that we can pay the electricity to light us through the coming winter. Her offering and our prayers were soon rewarded with a soaking rainstorm, the goddess imagining, perhaps, that we were farmers praying for water in a land of drought. My grandmother was never clear in her prayer, I suppose. Or perhaps over time, the goddess had become less Greek and more Sicilian, a trickster, granting favors but not the ones prayed for.

"I don't want a surprise, Nonna," I said. "I don't like it here anyway; this place is filled with memories of nothing alive."

I need not have worried because we soon left the temple and the cypress grove and walked into a field of frozen lava, pocked here and there with little caves leading down into the underworld of shades.

"There is someone here who has been in my dreams these last three nights, and who has been asking for you," my grandmother said. "It would be disrespectful not to make the visit."

She was right, of course. The dead—lest they sour in their loneliness—must always be visited when they inquire after you.

"Who was in your dreams?" I asked, hoping it was not my mother, whose grave I failed to visit on the last anniversary of her death. And a few before that as well, I remembered guiltily.

"No, not she, but another who still thinks of you."

"My wife?" I said, a bit annoyed.

"No, not she, though I'm sure she remembers you all the time, now that the ninny has time for reflection on her life."

My wife had once gone to America to visit her married sister in New York, and when she returned, after only four weeks, she refused to wash the dishes after dinner, saying that she and I should share the job, as the equals that we were. She came back with other such modern ideas, which my grandmother found unnatural to life and demeaning of me, the man of the house, who should never wash the dishes lest he become a woman. I never cared who washed the dishes or who swept the floor, having always done my share of both.

But my grandmother rarely spoke to my wife after she made her declaration of domestic liberation. Grandmothers are even less forgiving than mothers, who themselves also never forgive wrongs done to their sons, I reckoned. The truth is that I never loved my wife, dishes or no dishes. I never loved her in bed, where all life's opera starts and ends. Let's say that she and I were all recitatives and no duets, no grand soaring to the heavens, no ecstasy. Let's say that one does one's duty when called upon to save one's honor and the honor of the other. But duty does not ignite fires.

"Let it go, Nonna," I said. "All that is long ago and no one is pure."

That was true, of course, no one is pure, or half pure, but I wished it were not so, and that we could all live as we did when we were children. But then I recalled how children are mixtures of sweetness and guile, how children can be murderous and jealous, how children are midget versions of ourselves, the grownups, who betray with every breath the purity of each clean dawn.

"Yes," I added, "only the olive oil is pure in these days."

"*Figlio mio,*" she said. "Today the olive oil is often mixed, the good with the inferior."

"Even here in Sicily?" I said.

She tilted her head to give me her knowing look, the one she used to stare down the butcher when he tried to switch rabbit for veal, the look she used to show the world she knew what was what.

We soon came to a declivity, a pocket in the earth the size of a wheelbarrow, from which rose a cold mist that chilled me on the spot. A voice came through the mist or was centered in it, a voice drifting in and out like from an old-fashioned radio with weak reception. I knew that voice. Marie's voice.

How happy I was to hear her! Missing her as I had all these years. Missing her so that nothing else but she filled my bed at night, even when I was not alone in it.

We were in our teen years when we first made love. In the Bronx Botanical Gardens, that was, behind some thick bushes ripe with clover and on a bed of daisies and dandelions still moist with spring rain.

"Will you love me forever?" she asked, without flourish.

"Yes," I said. As I have, even after she married a schoolteacher who had gone to a university, and even after she died at nineteen in

208

childbirth. The child went with her. In Sicily, we die young. The measles, the smallpox, the heartbreak of unrequited love. She had married the wrong man, she confessed to me one day, a case of mistaken identity, she said, thinking he was me, just older and more settled in life with a classroom and a pension.

"Marie," I said, "how are you?" It was banal, that, a commonplace and hollow greeting of the living to the living, but I had meant it, wanting to know how she had fared all these years of being dead and what, so to speak, was her present state of mind.

"It's cold here," she said, as she used to say at the movie house when the air-conditioning had been turned up too high and the film started to lose significant interest because it was only the cold you were thinking about and not the lovers kissing on the screen.

"I wish I had a sweater to give you," I said, knowing it was a foolish idea even as I said it. But one never knows how it is with them or how to treat them, there in their caves of shadows or in the cold mist that embodies them when they come to visit us briefly on earth.

"Don't worry yourself," she said. "I just wanted to say hello, to remind you to cover your uncle's quince trees so that they will not die in the frost."

Sometimes I did forget. I had lost seven trees through my negligence one year, when fall had sprinted to a sudden, unannounced killing winter.

"That is thoughtful of you, Marie, to be thinking of me and my uncle's quince trees."

"We were friends, weren't we?" she said, her voice trailing off, returning to a faraway place in eternity.

"Friends," I said, rushing to embrace her vanishing mist before it was gone. But it was gone, and without a goodbye.

"Grandma, that was not a good visit," I said. "I'm now worse off than before I came."

She did not hear me, my grandmother, because she was no longer there and neither was I, who was now back on the train weaving its way through Sicily, stopping at every station grand and little at every village great and small. The hunter had returned to his seat and the bread eater to his. Each nodded to me, then went about his silent, brooding business. The bread eater looked hungrier than ever without his bread, the hunter forlorn without his hares.

"I should have reconciled with your grandmother long ago," my uncle said abruptly. "But then, you know how pride is—harder than granite. And then, when you are ready to make up, it is too late."

Before I could answer, the short Sicilian said, "I should never have stolen that bread. Just for hunger, just for hunger. Now I'm chased all over Sicily for a few crusts."

Before I could answer either of them, not knowing in fact what to answer them, the compartment door opened with a sly rush. I looked, thinking to see the two policemen reappear, but instead the young man with his mandolin entered, flashing us a jackal grin to show us he was friendly.

He began playing a Neapolitan love song much favored at weddings. A tearjerker it was, sung at the end of the evening, after dinner and dancing and when the wedding guests were in their sentimental cups.

"Across the sea of time, I think of you, across the sands of time I think of you, of you, of you, my love," he sang, as the train rattled about from town to town, making no stops.

The longer he sang, the more I began to remember him. Until I finally fixed him as the singer at my own wedding years and years ago. He had not grown older, which was the reason I had not immediately recognized him, because who does not get older with time, with the passing of thousands of weddings and countless other festivities?

If I were ever to get married again, I thought, I would never hire him to sing. Somehow, I blamed him for the souring of my marriage; he had put a bad spell on it from the start. I wondered how many other marriages he had jinxed with the sweetness of his song, with his singing of eternal love that only taunted the gods to do their mischief and shatter all conjugal dreams of joy and permanence.

These were my thoughts as we rode high above the Bronx River, the botanical gardens in view, burning in the summer heat. My traveling companions did not seem to notice the conflagration, so intent they seemed on their own thoughts and memories. The singer sang away, one song to another, indifferent to the fires below and to the heat in the compartment. He had many songs left in his bag, an eternity of them.

I could see now that all the trees were on fire and the river too, all the flowers in the botanical gardens and the roses turning into fists of flames, the earthworms and grubs and caterpillars, everything that lived in and above the soil was burning. My grandmother's black dress burst into flames as she was tearing the dandelions from their roots, and the children who were mocking her flared into packages of fire. The Greek temple where my grandmother and I had prayed crumbled under a cascade of smoke and dust, the goddess who had lived there taking flight in some passing clouds. Everything in the Sicily below us was on fire, everything in the Bronx was burning away to ashes, everything but me and its memory.

—*Homage to Elio Vittorini*

Moonlight Dance
Can Xue

—Translated from Chinese by Karen Gernant and Chen Zeping

I BELONG TO THE MOONLIGHT; the lion belongs to the darkness. The strange thing is that the lion is always walking back and forth, bathing in the moonlight in the wasteland, and I am generally tilling the humus soil with the earthworms. I only till, never harvest. Sometimes, I work my way out of the ground to stand beside the shrubs and wait. When a bat stops to rest, I jump onto her back. Then, carrying me, she flies to the ancient cave. I don't want to describe my experience in the dark cave: it's a place eerier than hell. Even in the daylight, every now and then the tragic cry of slaughter comes from the cave. I wait in the cave until nightfall, when my friend carries me on her back and flies toward the forest. When she stops on a pine tree, I leap to its highest branch. From there, I look out: the wasteland undulates in my field of vision, and the lion is anxiously looking for food. His objective is the zebra on the opposite shore of the stream; my objective is the lion. But why does he never attack? Does he like the high he gets from being dominant?

It's dark, and my friend has flown off. The branch is swaying in the wind, and I am holding onto the branch, clinging to it with my belly. I imagine myself canoeing in the ocean. The moon has risen, and I see the lion at rest. The zebra is also resting. Only a shallow stream separates them. How does the lion dispel his hunger pangs? This is his secret, and it is also my secret question. The moonlight dyes his long mane silver. His face is as ancient as the rock beside him. I'm enthralled by his face, but his face also troubles me day and night, because I can't find the solution.

The forest becomes noisy as usual: in the moonlight, these fellows won't be quiet. There are all kinds of sounds everywhere. Branches crack with a sound so vigorous that it's as if they want to turn the entire forest into ruins. Luckily, there are fireflies here—so many that they stream like waves of stars before my eyes. Some—the wingless ones—pause on the withered leaves on the ground and shine silently. Their light can reflect only a little spot under their feet.

These are blind insects. I once tried to lure these wingless fireflies to go with me into the earth. They ignored me; they're too proud. It can also be said that they are complacent and self-sufficient. Their idea is that they till their own bodies. The lion has turned around; his back is to me now: what a sorrowful view it is. Now even the zebras are in a stupor; trusting to luck, they've entered dreamland.

On vast Mother Earth, silhouettes of some other lions have emerged. They aren't real lions, but a trick of the moonlight. These illusions form a single line, extending to the horizon. Have you heard the lion weep? No, the lion's weeping can't be heard. My vision is blurred, and I'm weary from standing on a high place. I have to go down. Once I'm mixed in with those noisy fellows in the night, I relax, body and soul.

I know that my friend is working right now, so I'd better walk back. I walk a very long time before reaching the land I was tilling. In the moonlight, the large expanse of dark earth looks a little like a gloomy graveyard. Below the bosk is assembled a heap of wingless fireflies. What is this all about? Is it some kind of ceremony? The heap of tiny fires was gleaming, and gradually grew dark! Beside the land I was tilling, they burned up their inner fire. These tiny insects had limited choices. I smelled the charred flesh: the odor left me in a bad mood. From the cave, I burrowed underground. I slept as I tilled. Sometime in the middle of the night, I encountered the earthworms. There were two of them—one above me and one below me, and they kept advancing along with me. It was always like this. I couldn't see the earthworms, and yet they were always with me. As soon as they came toward me, I sensed them at once, for in the depth of the soil, the sensors were subtle. I could even sense their mood. The one above me was brimming with enthusiasm; the one below me was a little depressed. They were both time-tested believers. What did they believe in? They believed in everything, just like me. It was a faith born of the source. We were the moonlight school. The dark field was the place where we carried out our faith. I am going to fall into a dream: I knew I would dream of my grandfather. My grandfather was a creature between an animal and a plant, a little like the ocean's coral. But he was born in a place deep in the earth. In his lifetime, he couldn't move. He was always in the same place, thinking, thinking. After he died, it is said that his body fossilized in the place right under where I'm tilling—deep down, very, very deep. There will always be a day. . . .

213

I awakened. It was another day. Without emerging from the ground, I felt the heat from the sun's rays. I was anxious to know how the lion was doing. When I left him the day before, he was weeping. As soon as he wept, my brain went blank. He was so gloomy inside. Why did I care so much about him? Because he was king of the earth? Or was there another reason? Anyhow, my caring for him was connected with my faith: I hadn't chosen this; rather, I had been born with it. I couldn't go out yet, for my skin couldn't stand the sunlight. I had to get a lotus leaf from the pond beside the field and cover my head with it.

As I was swimming in the pond, I saw the corpses of lots of winged fireflies floating on the surface. Alas, those corpses of the moonlight nearly brought me to tears! I selected a lotus leaf, placed it on my head, and swam to shore. Something in the water pulled at my foot: it was an old fish who lived at the bottom of the pond. I was too weary to go to his home. The old fish was the most boring fellow in the world, and his home wasn't like a home, either: it was no more than a clump of waterweeds in the silt. Most of the day, he was in a daze as he squatted in the clump of waterweeds. He didn't think about anything; he was a fish devoid of any thought. He called me "the tiller"; I knew that was a slight. He also called my work "repairing the globe." "The world can't become square just because you're repairing it," he said. Of course, the old fish was experienced and astute, but his experience and astuteness for sure didn't come from his thought; it came from—how to say it? A certain instinct. He was one step ahead of anything that happened in this pond. For example, just now, when I was still in the field and he knew that I was about to arrive, he overcame his inertia and swam up, squatted in a cave beside the pond, and waited for me to pass by. I wouldn't go to his home; he knew this, but he was still unwilling to give up. Since quarreling with him the year of the hailstorm, I had vowed I would never step foot inside his house. That hailstorm was different from ordinary hailstorms: thickly dotted egg-sized hail fell for a day and a night, and a thick layer of it piled up in the pond. The old fish hid in an earthen cave next to the pond; the earth caved in and sealed the cave entrance. He slowly bored his way out; he struggled for two days before escaping. It was only because I felt uneasy that I went into the pond. That day, he and I resorted to staying in the stone cave. I was trembling from the cold; I was almost frozen stiff. In the beginning, we talked about this hailstorm, and then we began arguing, because I was well intentioned and advised him to move into the stone cave, but he not only wasn't grateful but cursed me for being a "coward." He said he couldn't imagine bamboozling himself. "Where is your home? Isn't it under the pile of hail? Why don't you go home? Why do you have to hide here?" I countered. At the time, he kept opening and closing his big mouth. He must have wanted to refute me, but since he couldn't think, he didn't know how to refute me. The old fish didn't say anything, but the expression in his eyes terrified me to the core. It was a steely, bewitching expression. I felt completely defeated by him. I can't say for sure how he had defeated me, but anyhow, I had suffered a deadly attack. I was in low spirits for several days. Luckily, I had my work: tilling was an omnipotent magic device. It could cure any injuries to the soul.

With the lotus leaf on my head, I streaked ahead. As I ran, I whooped impudently. If I didn't shout, my body would dissolve in the sunlight: I was convinced of this. Finally, I reached the old poplar tree, and concealed myself in the dense branches and leaves. This was much better for my skin. I climbed up to the highest branch. The zebra had already left. I heard that the zebras were just passing by; they were on their way to Africa. They belonged to the sun. Was it because of this that the lion was profoundly awed by their stripes? The lion was blocked by a large rock; I could see only the profile of his head. What was he thinking about? At night, did he launch an attack against the zebras? I really wanted to shout at him, but I knew that my voice couldn't carry that far. And besides, he wouldn't pay any attention to me. When I thought of the animals that he ate, I felt disgusted with him. I abhorred killing. I—and the earthworms too— ate only the earth, and even that, we didn't really eat. We merely let the earth travel through our bodies, that's all. We were benign animals. Underground, we dreamed of the moonlight and dreamed of our ancestors. Although he was disgusting, our esteem for him took the upper hand: after all, he was the king who dared to subdue Mother Earth. For example, right now: I was watching him with tears in my eyes. Did I fall in love with him? Nonsense—who could love a lion? He started moving. He was walking toward the riverside, and in the sunlight, his shadow was thick and black, as though another lion, a black one, were walking behind him. He was drinking water; he drank for a long time. How could he drink for so long? Was he extinguishing an inner fire? An oriole dropped to his head. The little fellow began singing at once; it was such a sweet, clear sound—so resounding! Even I could faintly hear it. The lion stopped drinking water; he was listening too. He didn't move lest he frighten the little bird. I noticed that while the bird was singing, the lion's shadow disappeared. When the bird stopped singing and flew away, the shadow returned. The lion squatted with his back to the sun, and the shadow circled around in front of him. His image gave me an impression of agony. I wanted to go back, for the moisture on my body had all evaporated; this was very rough on me.

With the lotus leaf on my head again, I scampered off with a whoop. I shouted even more hysterically than I had before, because the sunlight was particularly strong and I was afraid it would spell the end of me. I ran and ran, and finally got home. I plunged headfirst into the dark cave, and stuck my wrinkled skin tightly against the cold, wet earth. I nearly fainted. Not far from me, the earthworms were working systematically. These creatures of the moonlight in fact went their whole lives without seeing the moonlight, but they transmitted messages to me, telling me that they profoundly venerated the moonlight. And so, like me, they were looking into their ancestry. The earthworms' skin was even more fragile than mine. If they encountered sunlight, they would melt into water. It's said that this occurred many times in the past. Then why did they have to hide even from the moonlight? Why? They didn't tell me.

I recovered my strength, and began plunging down, down, into a deep spot in the ground. I wanted to till vertically. I had tried this earlier, but I had stopped each time I penetrated to the limestone. It wasn't that I didn't want to continue, but that I couldn't stand the smell. The strange thing was that no matter which direction I took in plunging down, in the end I always arrived at the layer of limestone. I couldn't detour around it. Perhaps it was only a thin layer, or perhaps it was a very deep mineral hell. Either was possible. This time, in desperation, I resolved to risk danger and explore one time. I thought there must be a way to get through this; otherwise, how had Grandfather and the others made their way down? I didn't believe that he had been born underground. I heard a slight noise behind me: it was the earthworm following me. He? Following me? This was suicidal! Just think about his skin. I was about to reach that place, and I already had a headache. My rigid eyeballs were also on the verge of softening. Following the course I had set, I circled toward the right. Circling for a long time, I put up with the odor. My eyeballs had already turned extremely turbid: I could see almost nothing.

What was this? A natural cave! A tunnel stretching down! This was unexpected. Naturally, I stuck my head inside. It happened that this cave could accommodate my body, so I went on for a while and then grew frightened. Was this a journey with no return? However, it was already too late to return. I had walked so far. If I turned around, I didn't know how many days it would take. It was great that the earthworm behind me kept making noise, as if to boost my courage; otherwise, I would have lost my nerve. Although there was also a limestone odor in the tunnel, it was better than outside. Bit by bit, as my vision was restored, I saw some strange decorative designs on the wall of the cave: they were everywhere. After observing enough of them, I concluded that this was a bunch of similar designs that were constantly changing places. They were dispatched and re-formed once and again, giving the eyes a constant sense of novelty. These simple, primitive designs took the edge off the dread I was feeling. How could there be this kind of tunnel? How had I happened to find it? Could it be that it was Grandfather's masterpiece? The moisture in my body began bubbling up, and I heard that fellow behind me excitedly grow even noisier. He was beating against the wall of the cave. Each time—in fact, he was rubbing the wall with his head—the wall of the cave made a strange sound, as if saying, "That's right, that's right. . . ." I felt comforted that he was there— my good friend. Otherwise, I probably would have fainted in dis- belief. I don't know how long I crept through the tunnel because underground there was no distinction between day and night. How- ever, I remember that in those moments, the distinctions between all things vanished. There was neither any sound nor any image: even the earthworm behind me didn't move. No matter how much energy I expended knocking my head against the wall of the cave, I couldn't make any sound nor could I see anything. Was it possible that this was "death"? But this situation didn't last long. When my ears made a rumbling sound, my feeling came back (was it simply a problem with my feeling?). With each passage I crept along, "death" repeated itself. Later on, I grew used to this. Not only was I no longer afraid, but I even looked forward to it a little. In moments like that, my brain was transformed into an endless ocean. The lion's incompara- bly huge silhouette appeared; he lay on the blue water. A nightingale flew over behind him. This scene appeared time after time, and I had the illusion that this trip wasn't to find Grandfather, but to find the lion. How could one go underground to find the lion? This was a question that would normally be raised, but now, in my thinking, I had already abandoned normal logic. I recognized that I was looking for the lion, and planned too to talk with him after I found him—even if it meant being eaten by him. I wouldn't mind.

How could I drop down? I thought back on this over and over, and I was still at a loss. At the time, it seemed I had come to the end of the tunnel, for I saw a vast expanse of white outside the tunnel. I couldn't grasp whether I had emerged from the ground or whether I was still underground. Even less could I figure out where up and down were ahead of me. By then, even the earthworm had vanished without a trace. Turning back had become even more impossible. I've already said that this tunnel was so narrow that it was really lucky it could accommodate my body, so there was no way I could turn around at the cave entrance. This was really dangerous, almost the same as finding a pretext to "drop down." Of course, after a long trip, I reached my goal. Was this place really my goal? Where was the lion? Now, even the lion didn't appear on the ocean. It had become a dead sea.

Time kept passing, and I was still in the same place. But how could I stay in the same place forever? I couldn't eat the earth here for it had a very strong limestone odor. I had never fasted for such a long time. Now, utterly weakened, I was about to faint. Maybe it was in that moment that I made up my mind that I was in for a penny, in for a pound, and I might as well drop down. Just as I was falling, the lion appeared. So large, and yet so agile, he filled my entire field of vision. His mane—ah, his mane . . . Whatever happened afterward, I don't remember. I seemed to be in a murky rocky hole. Something was swaying in the air—sometimes a foot, sometimes a skull. That was my last memory. Maybe I just couldn't bear to look back at what was happening, and so I forgot it. Sometimes I think that maybe what happened was truly death? Could that rocky hole have been Grandfather's tomb? What could be so unbearable to remember?

Anyhow, when I woke up, I was in my own field. There were earthworms above me and earthworms below me, earthworms to my left and earthworms to my right. They weren't tilling the land; they were quietly waiting for me to wake up. When I woke up and let out a sound, they slowly began their activity. I heard their excitement: their supple bodies were knocking the earth, making a "tili, tili, tili" sound, just like the falling rain. In that instant, I was intoxicated with the sound of rain purifying the soul. I really wanted to break through the layer of earth that separated us and embrace these viscous companions. I wouldn't care if their viscous fluid flowed all over my body. But I didn't, because I knew that neither they nor I was accustomed to expressing ourselves this way. We were introverted creatures, used to communicating our enthusiasm in solitude. How softly and comfortably the earth was clinging to my body! I roused myself to till more than ten meters away from here. My companions were following me. It was as if we were swimming freely in the ocean (naturally, I have to admit that I've never been to the ocean)! Ah, let me till deeper down; I wanted to double the size of my field! I tilled vertically again, and my companions kept following me. Some also tilled in front of me. Just as we were tilling enthusiastically, we heard the lion's roar. My companions and I all stopped. It seemed that the sound was coming from a grotto. It shook the soil until it wobbled a little. Had the lion gone underground? I recalled all the scenery I had glimpsed in the moment that I fell down from the entrance of the tunnel. Could it be that the lion had been underground then, and that the lion atop the wasteland had been merely a shadow—one of his many shadows? In the midst of the roaring, we were all hushed. We wanted to understand what the roar meant. But after roaring several times, he stopped: we hadn't had time to figure it out. We could only try our best to recall it. As we tried, our brains went blank. This kind of reasoning led to no outcome at all. Then, as if we had made an agreement, we began tilling the land together again. We were dead tired from our work. As I tilled the land, I dreamed about the lion in the grotto. Always, it was that incomparably large head, the silvery mane giving off light like the sun—so dazzling that I couldn't open my eyes. Someone whimpered in my ear: "I can't move." Who? Could it be the lion? Why couldn't the lion move? It was only my grandfather who couldn't move! Then was the lion my grandfather? Ah, my thinking was all mixed up. I couldn't go on thinking, but I still had my feelings, and I sensed that he was there, underground, holding his breath, about to explode. I dreamed for a really long time. In my dream, I ate a lot of earth. The "tili, tili, tili" sound enveloped me again. They were knocking again, and I was so moved that I thought I would cry.

When I emerged from the ground again, all the fireflies were dead, moonlight was spread across Mother Earth, and there was a strong funereal odor. I climbed to a limb of the old poplar tree and looked over at the plains. The whole area was deserted, except for the shadow of an occasional bird skimming past. Had the realm of lions lost its master? No. He was still present. It looked as if he were fused with the rock: he was absolutely still. His mane no longer shone; his entire body was tarnished. Had he died? The sound of thunder was gradually rolling closer, and the moon was hidden behind dark clouds. The lion's image was a little blurred. Suddenly, he melted into a bolt of lightning and shot out from behind the rock, breaking through the blackened night air. He illuminated heaven and earth, but he lost his own form. This made me doubt whether his body had ever been real. After the explosive thunder ended, there was another bolt of lightning . . . and another! Both shot out from the rock. Now there wasn't even the sound of thunder. These bolts of lightning turned the sky snow bright; the moon that now and then showed its face had lost its rays of light and was about to turn almost completely dark. How presumptuous this was. I couldn't bear to go on watching. I went under the ground. The snow-bright lightning jolted the earth. Really. It was willfully tossing the rocks on the earth, as well as the trees and hills, back and forth. I didn't dare look at it, for if I looked again, I would faint. I closed my eyes and felt my way home. Even though I was underground, I still faintly heard the turmoil on the ground.

I was so weary that I quickly went to sleep. In my sleep, I was plowing the familiar rich, black soil. The earthworms rapped politely toward me to transmit a message: Grandfather was alive again. Deep underground, he had regained life and was growing. In my dream, I was feverish all over. I couldn't hear Grandfather growing, but all of the earthworms did. They told me. This was the first time in my life that I felt profoundly that I—and also my companions— had become one with the grandfather at the earth's core. Was this because of the lion? I tried my best to imagine, but—no matter what—I couldn't call to mind the lion's face.

The Photographer Upstairs
Christopher Sorrentino

WE HAD IN THE PHOTOGRAPHER upstairs and his girlfriend for dinner last night. He is a recent émigré, having moved to the US from
Australia, where he lived in Melbourne. His arrival in this country
was coincident with his having moved in upstairs, though previously he had traveled extensively throughout the continental states (and
Hawaii), visiting most of our major cities on commercial and jour-
nalistic assignment. He and his girlfriend had grown tired of the
long-distance aspect of their relationship and, pursuant to a very
amusingly recounted bet, which he lost, he'd agreed to move here.
We shop carefully for the photographer upstairs and his girlfriend
because they are vegetarians. No, it's dairy that they can't or won't
eat. Carefully nevertheless.

I think, reflexively, of major cities as being those that are home to
major league baseball franchises. It is as valid a way as any of order-
ing things. Though surely Portland, Oregon, would disagree. Surely
Nashville, Tennessee, would disagree. Surely Salt Lake City, Utah,
would disagree. For years now I have heard that these are cities enjoying more significance, more *majority*, than (say) Cincinnati,
Ohio, or Pittsburgh, Pennsylvania. I will have to ask the photographer upstairs whether he has been to either and, if so, what his opinion is on the matter. It may be a photographic opinion. It's entirely
possible that Pittsburgh is the more photogenic city, with its smoky
foundries and ironwork silhouette. Names of cities flood my brain:
Memphis, Oklahoma City, Amarillo, Sante Fe. Cheyenne, Omaha,
Council Bluffs. Big skies and sulfurous clouds, prairie grasses and
mounds of native dead. The sweet song of America. I can imagine
myself in a jeep or a sporty coupe, wearing pants with extra pockets
stitched onto the thighs, lifting a heavy camera to my face to capture
an Elks Club sign or the neon of an old theater marquee. Waitresses
carrying steak and eggs, all my worldly possessions in a cordura bag
on the empty seat beside me.

It seems the photographer upstairs works at a model fabrication
shop. I offer him a glass of red wine, selected especially to go with

the grilled portobello mushrooms, and sit opposite him in the uncomfortable chair while listening to him describe his job, the dust, his wearing of a respirator. It seems that he works in an airlessly oppressive environment, some kind of sweatshop; that rather than traveling free throughout hill and range he fights to breathe amid deafening noise and fearsome equipment that might maim and disfigure him. Plus I have a slight problem with his accent. I think to myself, *But how unfortunate that he can't find work in his field, especially since he's so accomplished.* It may have something to do with immigration. I think. I begin to ask him is it true that if an American, a citizen, is capable, for example, of taking the photographs required for a given project, then that job necessarily must by law go to the American? He holds the red wineglass by the stem. No, I've served it to him in a fluted tumbler, as I've seen done in certain storefront bistros. Which would be the greater affectation? It—his lost stint at the dusty shop—seems inherently unfair, fails to take into account his unique ability and vision; I plan to ask him whether he feels at a disadvantage—being an Australian, that is, and a native speaker of English as well: does he sometimes feel he would be better off if, say, he were from   Mexico and could make a case that his photographs of the children of the East Los Angeles barrio could not have been obtained without his ability to converse with the kids in their native   tongue? But before I can ask the photographer upstairs about this thing, or these things, I am interrupted by my own lady friend as she brings in an attractive tray of kosher vegetarian hors d'oeuvres. I turn to his girlfriend: and how long has she been living here? From her slight accent I imagine that she is from Germany, or perhaps Austria or   Switzerland. She responds that she has been living in the neighborhood for twelve years, which is not what I, the answer I was seeking, at all, but then, before I have a chance to request clarification, to clarify my question, she responds animatedly to a passing remark I make about a minor neighborhood celebrity, *exclaiming* that she had attended high school with her, had been in the class two years behind her. The person in question is an American, definitely. An American or a Canadian. This fact, or probability, confuses me, but by now both the photographer upstairs and my lady friend are asking her, and me, who we're talking about and we both turn to face them and comically interrupt one another. For an instant it is a moment in a comedy of manners, a comedy involving mistaken or switched identities—as if the girlfriend and I are linked more closely than my lady

222

friend is with me and the photographer upstairs is with his girlfriend. In any case neither of them knows who the neighborhood celebrity, this actress in independent films or this performer of alternative music, this noteworthy person, neither of them knows the identity of this minor   icon, what I mean is like neither of them knows who we're talking about. Beloved of *BOMB* magazine and sometimes even *The New York Times.* Or is she just a minor neighborhood celebrity in the sense that one might intend when referring to the man always to be found sitting in a folding chair outside the bodega? The friendly one, with the red-rimmed eyes, whose life is a complete mystery? That may be what I meant when I first made, wrote that reference, more than seven months ago.

But I knew exactly who I meant then, and for my purposes I know it here, so I can go on: for a moment I feel how lonely it is for them, my lady friend and the photographer upstairs, skewered shrimp dangling from their limp fingers; their confusion has not given rise to the sort of fumbling fellowship that the photographer's girlfriend and I find in our small plot of common knowledge. They are simply united in their confusion, which has never really united anyone, as history has shown again and again.

There's a moment when the photographer upstairs places his wineglass on the coffee table. I can see the dirt embedded deeply, inaccessibly, under his fingernails, the dirt he carries with him from the model fabrication shop. The base of his glass simply breaks when it comes into contact with the table, and the wine spills. An inexpensive glass. Red wine on a white carpet: it's good luck, I say.

No, stepping in dog shit is good luck, says the photographer's girlfriend.

No, being shit on by a bird is good luck, says my lady friend.

What's good luck down under? I ask.

Coming up here, he says, and he actually looks relieved to be here.

When you're taking pictures, I ask—having thought of times when I was in a public place with a camera, usually in a strange city, and was seized with self-consciousness about raising the instrument to my face and snapping a photo—are you ever self-conscious? Or is that just something you lose? I'm pantomiming the act of taking a picture, burlesquing a kind of awkwardness. This is an entirely different flight of the imagination than the one having to do with rural waitresses, jeeps, restless creativity. This is pleated, relaxed-fit shorts, and a wheeled suitcase parked at the foot of a bed in some midrange hotel. Much closer to my actual experience. I mean there's an authoritativeness to the awkwardness I pantomime with my imaginary camera. It's that of a middle-class man more concerned about whether he will drop the camera or have it ripped from his hands by a street thief than about getting an excellent photo. I'm saying, what I'm saying is when I'm talking to a professional I always try to find some kind of common ground, thing. I might say something about teeth to a dentist. Say. I always try to find   I don't often stray outside my field. The other arts are a mystery to me. I finally drop my hands to my lap where they become hands, empty hands, again. Are you? He gazes at me blankly for a moment, his fork halfway to his mouth. I suppose I am, he replies. I've never thought about it. I can barely take a picture without putting my thumb before the lens, he says.

We serve the grilled portobellos with wild rice, cannelini in tomato sauce, and more of the red wine. It's a simple meal. That's how it's been described for several days running. "A simple meal." My lady friend and I sat down to discuss the preparations for this informal but anticipated dinner and agreed that we should serve an elegant yet simple meal. When the photographer's girlfriend had called to ask if she could bring anything she was met with the verbal shrug of being informed that it was a simple meal; as if she could bring either wine, dessert, or a handful of sod. Just bring yourselves, are the words I believe my lady friend used in response. And so they did; they arrived, empty-handed and coatless, from the apartment above. When the photographer upstairs had, finally, come downstairs, did he necessarily become simply "the photographer" upon entering our apartment? I'd shaken his hand and told him we had a simple meal planned. Then I immediately offered him smoked nuts, cheeses and crackers, cornichons; as if apologizing with this extravagance for the inadequacy of the simple meal. At the table I ask the photographer upstairs how it was having been a vegetarian in Australia, given that nation's renown for raising lamb. He tells me that in fact he is not a vegetarian, but quite a carnivore. He says these words, "quite a carnivore." His girlfriend places her hand gently on his and remarks that the two of them will eat anything except entrails. And snails, the photographer upstairs adds quickly. Don't worry, I say, We're not having snails. And he actually looks relieved. He is visibly relieved, as the newspapers say. I pour more wine. It is a fine dry white, perfect, really, for the veal. Furthermore, he says, it was New Zealand where he lived. I am embarrassed; I hadn't realized that Melbourne was in New Zealand. It seems increasingly silly and quixotic to dream of asking him questions about the American cities he's experienced. Clearly I'll exhaust him with my ignorance right from the start.

Melbourne, it seems, is in Australia.

Not only that, but he did not live in the city. He lived in the countryside. Where, coincidentally enough, he and his wife lived on what he describes as a hobby farm, raising about one hundred sheep.

"So you'll have no objection to eating veal then, I gather?"

There is silence.

There is the matter of this *wife*. It settles amid us, the matter, like the phantom woman herself. My lady friend and I look at one another, each daring the other to bring it up. I have a wife, I say. We didn't own a farm, though. Oh, says the photographer upstairs. Where is she then? I gesture to the northeast with my chin. She could be living behind the bookcase. She could be living in Greenland. About seven blocks from here, I say. Where's yours? He chews his food, nodding steadily, then swallows. In New Zealand. On the farm. We're divorced. Oh, I respond. I'm not. We're not. Actually, neither of us are. I gesture at my lady friend. We're both married to other people! I giggle. That sounds complicated, says the photographer upstairs.

I look at the photographer upstairs for a moment. He chews the simple meal smugly. I wonder about his simple divorce. How did they divide the sheep? I say, Did you have an even number of sheep? He looks startled. About a hundred, he says. So you divided them, fifty apiece? No, he laughs. She received the farm in the settlement. I got the apartment in Christchurch.

And this was before or after the bet?

Bet? What bet?

Hesitantly, uncertainly, I recount the bet as it was related to us, the amusing anecdote of the bet, as if I am trying to recall a difficult mathematical formula, pausing to look into his eyes for confirmation of the accuracy of individual details. I manage this theatrical business in a way that suggests my own inattention, not the obvious inability of the photographer upstairs to get the facts of his life straight, although my lady friend briefly rests her palm on her forehead and then leans over to the photographer's girlfriend to grip her wrist and whisper something. That wasn't a *bet*, says the photographer upstairs. It was an *agreement*. We *agreed* that whichever of us found a place to live in their home country—he pronounces this *ham cantray*—the other would move there.

Fruit and more cheese for dessert. The photographer's girlfriend happily lists the fruits on the plate to which she is allergic. The pears, the apples, the grapes. I rise to offer her a banana. It is intended as a comic maneuver but I am embarrassed by my failure to amuse, holding the banana arcing upward, in the form, roughly, of a male erection, or a Lorenz curve. Neither is funny. Nor is the banana itself, overripe, stippled and streaked with brown. There's port. Of course. I grab the port from the green furniture. The green furniture is a side-board that is not actually green. A can of green paint has been stowed inside it for two years awaiting the day that it will become green in fact, green outside of the system of private references my lady friend and I have developed. I take four small aperitif glasses from it as well and place them on the table. I *still* don't drink, says the photographer's girlfriend, in a friendly way. I apologize and put the bottle down on the table before me.

D'you know the bishop of Norwich? asks the photographer up-stairs. I do not.

Archimedes' New Light
Geometries of Excitable Species
Joan Retallack

> *Mortals are immortals and immortals mortals;
> the one living the other's death and dying the
> other's life.*
>
> —Heraclitus

bodies cleave space of   all the triangles in the prism :

one glimpse of cornered sky in   all the triangles in the sphere :

fleeing over cardboard mountain with   all the segments in the parabola :

gray morning blank aluminum   all the parabolas in the sphere :

their own cold love song breached   all the circles of the sphere :

abrupt start of rain   all the vertices of the prism :

clacking sticks
night barks
window blank

Reason is a daemon in its own right.

another song whose bird I do not know

.the.center.of.gravity.of.the.two.circles.combined.

around them in us we were very they

what comes to mind in this five second cove

.whose.diameters.are.and.when.their.position.is.

.changed.hence.will.in.its.present.position.be.

lacking usage equal to the noun she chose

.in.equilibrium.at.the.point.when.all.the.angles.

all different before he heft laughed defiled gravity lost again

.in.the.triangles.in.the.prism.all.the.triangles.in.the.cylinder.

interior angles exposed collapsed into each each

.section.and.the.prism.consists.of.the.triangles.in.

the terrible demonstration of fluid dynamics beginning again

.the.prism.hence.prism.hence.also.the.prism.and.the.

areas of distortion the burning vector fields

---

more mathematics of the unexpected:
the total curvature of all spheres
is exactly the same regardless of radius

Lacking experience equal to the adjective she chose
scratch abstract sky shape
hoping for more
.whole.prism.containing.four.times.the.size.of.the.
.other.prism.then.this.plane.will.cut.off.a.prism.from.

struggle to flee her altered nativity
repeat story of stilt accident now
no the drama has not abated
.the.whole.prism.to.circumscribe.another.composed.
.of.prisms.so.that.the.circumscribed.figure.exceeds.

exhausted boy soldier reads book numb
rag head taken by stiff light
fig one triumph of the we're
.the.inscribed.less.more.than.any.given.magnitude.
.but.it.has.been.shown.that.the.prism.cut.off.by.the.

empty listen ridge cold whistle
unison whipped wide awake
box of spook salt

.inclined.prism.the.plane.the.body.inscribed.now.in.
.the.cylinder-section.now.the.prism.cut.off.by.the.

not a coast but a horizon not a coast
blank seas soak grain senses demented
sense of thigh once now not yet juked

---

may deter may bruise
bequeath before death
green countdown bluebook

Joan Retallack

she said now that she thought about it
she thought it must have had something
to do with that feeling of self-possession in
the moment after the apostrophe took hold

One's   .inclined.plane.the.body.inscribed.in.the.cylinder.

a stock image
a rhetorical device
a dubious gesture
an obsolete hope

One's   .section.the.parallelograms.which.are.inscribed.in.

quadrant spoke motion
a prod to come to life
meddlesome meaning meaning tangent

One's   .the.segment.bounded.by.the.parabola.but.this.is.

sordid alignment of slippery parts
please hold that place stretch the we
jelly throat made good hold that note

One's   .impossible.and.all.prisms.in.the.prism.cut.off.by.the.

no such five illusions
no vowel exit mutters fruit
my no flute war
torque valley breath
gun cold air cont'd
night barks windows blank
gray morning's blank aluminum
its own long cold burst that kills
a look cornered sky

One's   .inclined.plane.all.prisms.in.the.figure.described.

geometry of the tragic spectrum
eye caught in grid
this thought empties itself in false déjà vu
the echo seen but not heard
the absence of x had been distracting all along

Rationalism born of terror turns to ecstasy.

.around.the.cylinder-section.all.parallelograms.in.the.
.parallelograms.all.parallelograms.in.the.figure.
.which.is.described.around.the.segment.bounded.
.by.the.parabola.and.the.straight.line.the.prism.cut.
.off.by.the.inclined.plane.the.figure.described.around.
.the.cylinder-section.the.parallelogram.the.figure.
.bounded.by.the.parabola.and.the.straight.line.
.the.prism.the.prism.cut.off.by.the.inclined.plane.

From Mother & Child
Carole Maso

ONCE A MONTH, when the moon was full and the weather was right she would invite the child out to the night garden. The garden at night scared the child, who was afraid of the dark, so she would always stay inside. It was time again for applying the fish emulsion: the ritual feeding of the roses with the bodies of liquidated bass and trout. It was a sight: her mother working through the night. When the child looked out the nursery window she saw fireflies plastered to the outline of her mother and she watched her like that for a long time. Small things seemed to attach themselves to her, to cling. When the raccoons came, as they always did, with their awful tiny human hands pressing, the child would be jealous and she would try to force herself out the door, but she could not.

And in the morning, stinking of fish and roses, and wiping away bits of fur and fin, the mother would bring the child out into the day-light world, dropping her off at school or camp or wherever it was the child was going that day, and the men would pant and swoon and grab the mother and the boys would hum and trip and fall, and this alarmed the child, for they lived in a household without boys who hummed or men. How laughable is mankind! The glittering mother laughed. How laughable is the human race! Mother, don't laugh like that, the child begged, and she reached out to try to hold something of the gleam.

The mother knew she would have to wait for the day when the men would at last leave her alone. The mother on that day will become invisible to them and she will at last be able to live unencumbered. And she will dance in the cities all night, and she will dance in the valleys, and in the night gardens. Until then she will have to bide her time.

*

Exiled from childhood but in the constant presence of it, the mother felt covetous of the child sometimes because the child still had child-

233

hood and to the mother childhood was no longer accessible. There was no going there again; she could only watch. She was walking, she knew, on thinning ice.

Even the mother's mother, the North Pole grandmother, was not young anymore. The light was bright in summer there late into the night. When the North Pole grandmother came with a platter of fish preserved in vodka and lingonberries, the fish had a face on it and the children ran and hid. In winter the candles were lit and there was juniper and holly.

The child is busy making sculptures out of apples in the corner. Next she is sculpting a boat. Even the child will one day die. It takes three cups of salt to cure a fish. The mother tries to remember being small, not as an adult remembers, but as a child, but it is hard. She would like to fit inside a thimble and someday she probably will. There is a casket the size of a walnut shell that waits in the garden. There is a husk. There is always the sorrow of the last morsel of fish to consider. Many of the children are still hiding in the garden. When she was little she remembers going into the sewing box and taking out her favorite thing: a pincushion encircled by Chinamen. When she was small she remembers the bright thimble and the way it looked like a castle on her thumb. The North Pole grandmother was in the next room, where the child could hear her preparing the fish. Lingonberries are something else she remembers. While the mother reaches to remember, the child wishes she had a picture phone so that while she talked to the North Pole grandmother she could see her face and watch her white hair blowing in the wind. The life span of a North Pole grandmother is eighty-three, the child reads.

*

The mother received a telephone call from her sister Inga. The sister had some bad news. The child had never seen her mother listen harder to anything than she listened then. The listening had a hard, smooth quality to it, like ice, only hot. After she hung up, the mother curled up into a ball and did not speak or move for a day and a night. The child watched her mother curled up like that and she thought about nests and she thought about shells. She felt so alone she did not know how she would bear it and so worn by the duration of time.

After a day and a night the mother finally uncurled, but the child saw the mother held something still clenched in her hand. When the mother saw the child she wept and opened her hand. Look, she said.

In her hand she was holding the left ventricle of a heart.

The child took the left ventricle of the heart from the mother. She walked down the hallway and she laid it in her bed. Although it had looked blurry and ruined on the X-ray, here it did not look bad at all. She was happy to have it on the pillow next to her. This way if anything went wrong with the heart she would know right away. It cast the room in ruby light. After pink, red was her favorite color. She thought of her aunt seven and a half states away.

After a while the child fell into dream. A kindle of kittens appeared under the bed. A clowder of cats soon came to join them outside under the sill. The mother came in to lick the kittens until they began to breathe. There was mother's milk for all. Then the mother went outside again with the others. Everything seemed contingent on this arrangement: the clowder under the sill, the kindle under the bed, the ventricle next to the sleeping child slowly repairing itself.

*

Snow falls and the roots call to the mother and the sleeping small-clawed animals in their burrows and tunnels and the winter vegetables that lie peacefully untouched under the earth. When she walks on the earth's crust she grows drowsy now, feeling their sleep. Magnified, so many sleeping creatures multiplied, she can barely lift a foot. What is wrong, the child says, and lies on the ground on her back, and helps the mother lift her feet one boot at a time.

The child has read that beneath the city of Paris there is another city. There you can find a home for abandoned children. I should like to see where the animals sleep in winter, says the child, watching her mother's eyes slowly begin to close.

The Man Who Spoke with His Hands
William H. Gass

THE MAN WHO SPOKE with his hands was not deaf nor did he speak
with his hands because he was communicating with deaf people.
The man who spoke with his hands was not noticeably shy, therefore unlikely to say much, or be inclined to wait for a passing noise
behind which to hide his remarks. He engaged in conversations with
average frequency and ordinary ease, and employed for these everyday purposes a voice that was mellow enough to spread on bread;
neither so low as to approach a whisper nor so high as to threaten
screech. It was a voice as brown as his eyes.

The man who spoke with his hands did not gesture expansively,
because he spoke with his hands, not his arms and/or eyebrows. His
hands tended to remain in close touch, mostly about midchest. His
hands were made almost entirely of fingers. These were long and
slim and supple. One thought of cigarette holders except for the
supple. A cigarette holder is not supple. It is a bamboo tube with a
coating of lacquer. Those who believe that smoke filtered through
the stem of such a holder is less likely to sicken them are probably
mistaken. According to authorities, they are being poisoned when
they breathe such drugs. Smoking is a bad habit but the man who
spoke with his hands did not appear to have any other habit than his
hands.

The man who spoke with his hands had cheeks that were tanned.
Except for those two places—the left and right cheeks at the lower
edge of the bone—his skin was pale. His fingers were exceptionally
white and consequently easy to see, which is possibly one reason
why he decided to speak with his hands, although nobody supposed
that he actually chose his gestures; what made them so graceful and
attractive was that they (his fingers for the most part) seemed to
dance outside the range of their owner's attention. It is no longer
fashionable to describe anything as "unconscious." The few who
still employ the concept have probably been smoking too much
Freud. Freud had a cigar habit, and we know it was bad because it
killed him.

The man who spoke with his hands would, while speaking, sometimes move the thumb of his right hand gently (one might say with circumspection) back and forth, in and out, of a hollow formed by a downward curl of the left hand's lengthy fingers, as if they were lightly gripping a pole where the thumb slid. Professors Rinse and Skizzen understood this to be a meditative moment; for instance, if he was saying that he hadn't taken any of the students in his History of Religious Music class to hear some famous organist who had come to Columbus yet again this year (it was the sixth occasion), they would take his hands to be indicating that he had debated long and hard about it. As Professor Skizzen saw the thumb glide gradually out again, he thought of the trombone. Freud would have ascribed this habit to another practice that was equally compulsive and otherwise unspeakable.

On the whole the man who spoke with his hands created movements that were slow, as if they were distant from his words, and reluctant to leap to conclusions. Only when his forefinger, seemingly held back by the pressure of the thumb, sprang forward in that snap one uses to flick a crumb from the dining cloth, did they call attention to themselves. This gesture meant—the professors believed— that whatever it was he was discussing—an event, a meeting, a class, an opinion—was over and done with, was no longer held by him, was not to be taken up again. When he said: I just couldn't face another long bus ride with a load of noisy kids, there was neither snick nor snip, but a gentle, almost imperceptible movement of the fingertips, the nails in full view, as if brushing something away or warding it off, pushing the imagined thing out of his purview. Then he might conclude: so I didn't. The snip would follow this.

A gentle brushing of a tabletop with the fingers will roll crumbs to the edge and over it onto a ready palm. There is no need to flick offending grains of salt or sugar into space where they will sand up something else—a chair seat or the floor beneath your feet. A table knife will scrape them to a corner and fancy folk or attentive waiters in high-toned restaurants employ a silver blade just for this purpose. So the flick is probably a bad habit too. The flick removes a problem from your presence but does not rid it from the world. Indeed, the cloth from which the crumbs have been so casually ushered remains stained and abused, and the gesture that removes these ashes and these cinders also signifies an intention to renew the table's use as if it were new and its covering not in need of removal. Germs are not thusly scraped away and remain to infect the éclair and its brood.

237

William H. Gass

The fingers of the man who spoke with his hands might mesh like the tines of forks, but gently and easily, for tines may jam. Then one could watch his fingers slide between his fingers like blending fans, again very gradually, so the hands were clasped, and almost immediately moved again, separating with the silence of cream, and thereby measuring degrees of commitment or withdrawal, of coolness or ardency, agreement or disavowal. His hands often assumed a prayerlike stance when he began to speak—pardon me, your humble servant, by your leave, sir—and then the right hand would withdraw, its fingers sliding very slowly down a calm left palm until the wrist was reached, when they would hesitate a moment before rising up again or continue to drop on down to the wristband of their owner's watch.

Yes, the man who spoke with his hands could be nervous and impatient too, the fingers of his right drumming on the back of his left, those tappings reminding Professors Skizzen and Rinse of the way his long slim white fingers flew on and off the holes of the flute, whereas if the left danced a bit on the back of the right, it meant, they calculated, expectation coupled with serene acceptance. Occasionally both hands would droop from their wrists like fresh wash hung from a rope, but this was not a feminine gesture, even though Professors Rinse and Skizzen judged it signified: you win, I give up, you don't say. Unless, of course, the hands suddenly flew up again, when it meant a very firm go away, take your topic elsewhere, little boy, run out and play.

When the man who spoke with his hands was confronting a knotty problem or trying to be clear about a complexity that had hold of him, he would revolve his hands around one another, slowly or quickly, quietly or forcefully, as the puzzle was pursued. The knot at last untied, the left hand, palm exposed, might fly gracefully away as if to say: there, you see, or, it consequently comes to this. I liked particularly the definite but brief pinches one pair of fingers might make on a lower arm or the upper skin of a hand, or all the subtle tweezer-style variations, since he seemed to have a special role for every digit, and Professor Skizzen particularly felt those fingers were very sincere about their business, well manicured and behaved, especially during geometric gestures, small circles mostly, as if one were twining one's hair, or unrolling an idea like a length of rug.

Occasionally, the man who spoke with his hands would add a little flutter or some zippy propulsion of the right indexical toward the object or person he was addressing (the way one adds "-ed" to a verb or tacks on "-ly" to an adverb or attaches an "-est" to an adjective or

238

"-ness" to a noun, of which "saintliness" could serve as an example, or "livelihood" be an attractive instance, or "implicational" at least representative), thereby altering the assumed character of a run of silent remarks.

Rarely did the man who spoke with his hands permit them to touch his head, ears, or face, though Professor Skizzen saw a forefinger brush his earlobe once in a gesture so expressive as to warrant applause. They never strayed below the belt or roamed far or widely from his torso or fell meekly like a coat sleeve to his sides. And despite all this nearly continuous motion, the professors hardly noticed them, took little heed of this habit, were not distracted as much by the fingers as by the light that rollicked from their owner's bald head, pale as paper. He was a man, compact and even slight, whom one could nevertheless pick out of a crowd as one would the most attractive piece of fruit from a bin. His hair would have been brown had he had any. The truth was, Rinse and Skizzen talked more about the man's dark curly eyebrows and his bald pate than his shiny nails or their scintillating moves.

When the man who spoke with his hands performed, his colleagues read his gestures as signs, and Rinse thought his fingers danced, but Skizzen heard an orchestra that the man conducted to accompany his words. Skizzen saw the pick, the drum, the strum, the tweak, the pluck, the rub, the damp, the trill, the run of the instruments, the strain of the strings, as the man's nails flickered, and loose fists were formed only to relax like petals leaning back into their blooms.

Arthur Devise was the man who spoke with his hands, and he played the flute, the piccolo, and the recorder. When the death of Clarence Carfagno created an opening in the music department, Arthur Devise arrived to fill it. Professors Morton Rinse and Joseph Skizzen held it against their new colleague that he had been chosen without consulting them; they held it against him that he was a friend of Howard Palfrey, the president who had hired Art (as they would later affectionately address him), and a president whom the male faculty to a man despised; they held it against him that he was almost as old as they were and so a failure for as long as they (though they didn't immediately put their animosity in such terms); they held it against him that, as a musician, he was quite accomplished; Professor Morton Rinse especially held it against him that he, like Rinse, played the flute, the piccolo, and the recorder; while both men held it against him that Palfrey had picked Arthur Devise because

239

the Department of Music had always—anyway in Palfrey's memory—had two members (there were three altogether) who professed the flute, the piccolo, and the recorder, and that it was proper to continue the tradition; the remainder held it against Arthur that he actually seemed a good sort and a wise choice, because they did not want to think the president ever acted wisely; Professor Joseph Skizzen held it against Devise in addition that he was a widower with an attractive daughter about to become a student of music in her parent's own college, in her parent's department, and might enroll in her parent's class; they jointly held it against him that Devise agreed to teach, lead, and pamper the choir and the chorus, and had them sounding splendid in no time; finally, they held it against him that he spoke with his hands, and that, at first, neither Rinse nor Skizzen liked what he said.

The man who spoke with his hands, because he spoke with his hands, was a quiet man, with a slow, warm, well-regulated smile, a smile hard to dislike, and he chuckled deeply in his chest to the point of an almost inaudible rumble, and the slow, well-regulated shaking of his ribs made his hands, so often positioned on what would have been his stomach had he had one, rise and fall lightly like a pair of drifting leaves—motions charming in their pacifying consequences.

It has been said that Saint Francis of Assisi used such gestures to charm birds, who would then perch upon his extended arm and eat grain strewn artfully along it, though some say they just flew in for the grub.

Dottie Devise was, in contrast, chipper, perky, cheeky, cheerful, and squeaky as a toy mouse; perhaps her voice could be better described as chirpy, high but thinly pitched, leaping from syllable to syllable almost as if it came from a clock. When she bounced, which was much of the time, her small breasts crossed the net like tennis balls, and reminded Professor Skizzen, unpleasantly, of the way his sister's rose and fell in a manner most disturbing when she had led cheers, her high school letter sweater leaping as if there were small animals bundled behind the cloth trying to burst free.

MOR ning PRO fes sor SKIZzzz en OW r u? The question was almost a relief. I am fine, Miss Devise, as you can see. TEE hee, I am HAP pee to no tha TT. And howw arr uuu, Professor Skizzen would particulate. FI ner than BE for. Holding books against her busy chest, Dottie (for that is what she chose to call herself) would flicker away at a half skip. Professor Skizzen would sigh like a dying inner tube, shake his head as he entered his office, and each time think how terrible poor Devise must feel, having raised such a giggly flibberti-gibbet almost from infancy, as the professor had been led to believe.

He remembered the way she seemed when Art had first arrived at the college: quiet, demure, in a frilly frock, her hair tied up like a restless dog, since Art apparently could not teach combing. She followed her father when he walked her to her school, precisely five paces behind. Dottie was untouched by her future nature then and didn't jiggle.

The sorrowful story that President Howard Palfrey so enjoyed re-telling about the tragedies their new colleague, Arthur Devise, had been honored by God to endure—the loss of his wife; the loss, during the war, of his power of speech; which might explain those expressive hands—was just one more thing to hold against him, and would have been held had it been necessary, but there was so much against him already that, at least in the early days of their acquaintance, Devise had to go about bent as if he were leaning into a persistent wind.

The man who spoke with his hands remained on the staff long enough to earn a sabbatical if Wittlebauer had granted them. Then he and his daughter disappeared without so much as a giggle of good-bye or an equivalent wave, though President Palfrey announced that Professor Devise was leaving for personal reasons. This was regrettable. The bags beneath President Palfrey's eyes swelled with something near tears. Professor Devise would be missed, especially his piccolo and his work with the chorus, which immediately fell out of tune. *Bon voyage et bon chance.* Don't forget us.

At the time of Art's departure, Joseph Skizzen not only held nothing against him, he considered Art his friend; he appreciated his trills, rests, riffs, roulades, and cadenzas, and understood what Art had to endure from his daughter whose birdsong Skizzen now heard as the cackle of starlings or the shriek of the shrike.

If one were thinking of the northern bird, this comparison would be inaccurate because its call is mellow when it isn't scolding. But the loggerhead's is as sharp and abrupt as a spill of tacks, and has a harsh complaining quality as well. Shrikes were not unheard of in this part of Ohio, so her appearance at the college was scarcely a miracle. They are predators, fierce to a fault, with bright white teeth often in a wide girlish grin.

Although she still lived in her father's protective shadow, Dottie was now a disturbing presence in Professor Skizzen's class, the

241

introductory Elements of Music, and she showed up for office hours more regularly than he had his lunch. She could play several instruments tolerably well and was far ahead of almost everyone else, a fact she let her questions prove. Skizzen had attempted to move her to a more advanced level but both Dottie and her father wanted her to stay where she was. Now, in his office, she was provocative, showing leg, showing smile, standing close, tossing her hair as she'd no doubt seen in the movies, and asking increasingly personal questions.

On a day no more dismal than most others, Joseph Skizzen was approached, while reading in the faculty lounge (a large closet-sized space with a coffee pot, scarred wooden table, and few chairs, where he liked to hide out and study scores because everyone else hated the ratty little room and found that it reminded them of Wittlebauer's tightwad president and their benighted condition), by Arthur Devise, who had entered with his hands wrapped around a steaming mug in order that they should enjoy its warmth since the day was sleety, gray, and cold, although no more dismal than most others.

Devise placed the mug rather emphatically in the middle of the table where some chiseler had scratched "teachers love the igno-rant" with a flinty pointed pencil, its carbon darkening the line, and then he pulled up a chair near Skizzen as a conspirator might, and allowed his hands to make his apologies.

Skizzen shrugged his "no matter" shrug. Devise pursed his right thumb and forefinger, and snapped the clasp. I understand, he said in a tone level enough to encourage planting, my daughter Dorothy has been making a nuisance of herself. Devise's left thumb wiggled as if to say, I don't mean that. Instead, maybe the pursed thumb meant, she is my dear girl who has never had an unclean thought. Perhaps the wiggled thumb meant that an innocent batting of her lashes had led to a misunderstanding. Skizzen wondered how to approach such a confession.

Dottie had, of course, been making eyes at Skizzen, embarrassing him past pink, but he naturally said, of course not, why would you think that? Both of Devise's palms slowly showed themselves as if they were aces peeking from a poker hand. Well, she has predilec-tions . . . she . . . in the past . . . From a binocular position, the fingers tentatively disclosed the inner hand, then exhibited one apologetic spasm like tossing a toad from their grasp.

Ah, Skizzen exclaimed, genuinely surprised, that's why you put her in my class. You thought I'd understand.

I thought you'd know I wouldn't do so otherwise.

Yes, otherwise it would be a poor practice.

I had to keep her near me.

A class with you, a class with me—that's near.

The hands of the man who spoke with his hands slid into a tangle of shame.

I think it's because she misses her mother. Well, not misses exactly. Because she has no mother. She's decided to be the mother she needs.

She doesn't act like a mother with me.

Ah . . . she . . . I'm afraid she wants you to make her a mother.

But anyone . . . nearly anyone . . . will do, I presume.

She has gone rather far in other . . . schools.

High school even?

Yes . . . well, other places . . . community colleges. . . . She's gone rather far. Since she was thirteen.

Surely she would not promote such things with me?

Possibly. It's likely.

She has accused me of . . . you know . . . looking at her.

I am terribly sorry. She is playing the coquette. It's her subject.

But her speech . . .

Oh yes, I know, her speech is mechanical. It's made up. It is a complaint about mine . . . my hands. His hands were stitching cloth. She . . . you see . . . squeaks in protest.

I've noticed you do move your hands about.

I don't do it. God does. God moves my hands. I speak that way on his behalf.

This conversation had been so painful for Skizzen that each previous word had felt pulled from him like an embedded cork, but now almost every function ceased: his throat clogged, his face burned, so his blood must have rushed into his cheeks. They are both mad, he thought. Since he was able to make such a judgment, his mind must be operating. But he wasn't breathing. Never had he heard anything so preposterous, but such a statement, made to his face and meant for him, was like a blow to his chest.

I know that what I say must seem surprising, although our good president Palfrey was ready to entertain it. However, I have become merely an instrument of God's, or rather, not I, but my hands have become an instrument of God's. They do his bidding and, when he's speaking, will not mind me. Since they often make their moves while I am speaking as I am speaking now to you, some people have concluded that they are accompanying me. Two fingers pinched and lifted the loose skin about the knuckles of his left hand. I have thought you might be one of those. The musical connection, you know.

Devise's pause made his statement a question. Skizzen could not answer. He began to think, though, of what he might possibly say to this man who had become a threatening stranger—humor him, deny him, sympathize, chastise him, return the subject to his daughter's wayward ways? say I don't want to hear another word, bolt the room? Skizzen's weight shifted. This was sensed. One of those hands touched his arm.

As if released, Skizzen stood up. He thanked God he had grown a beard, and in that moment realized who it was he had invoked—already a ghostly presence if this testimony could be believed. Always a presence according to doctrine. He might perhaps ask how Professor Devise presumed to know that the gestures he involuntarily made were those of some other spirit than his own unconscious, but this would prolong a conversation he wished had never begun. Well, there was no conversation since he hadn't said a word. Maybe he shouldn't aid or abet it. He would just go.

I can't make out the signs they are sending; I cannot read their code; I just know; and I was never a believer either, before my wife was so terribly killed. Devise's smooth, firm features looked to be dissolving into a solution of sorrow. He was swimming in tears, that was it. When I told Dorothy what had happened to my hands, she became hysterical. She accused me of leaving her as her mother had, though, of course, I hadn't, and I assured her that my mind was clear, sane through and through like—you know—paper that's one hundred percent cotton.

Skizzen found this comparison almost as unsettling as his colleague's revelation about his hands. The man was mad. Did his hands heal? He had been touched but was it a king's touch? He had some warts . . . perhaps if . . . He had shaken this man's hands. What happened then? The man was mad. I shall wash my hands of him, Skizzen thought. He has the whole world in those hands. They certainly were idle, but why was it only his hands? If he were a puppet, his legs should move too. When his head tilts, his eyes should roll. The madman . . . Why was he—Joseph Skizzen—a person who endeavored to stay in the background—why was he always the accosted one? the falsely accused? the rudely confronted? After all, he had only backed around his office desk, keeping his moral distance, with

Dottie in salacious pursuit, and then, rid of her one more time, all he had done . . . well, he had locked up all his temptations in a steel cabinet and fled to this squatters' hole, a place forsaken by all until now when a crowd seemed to have assembled. The chairs were standing guard, the coffee pot was listening. No comment from the mug but steam. Skizzen noticed that there were only six checkers left. Mostly reds.

I've endured the shame of her nymphomaniacal imposture; I've put up with all the jokes—

Jokes?

That I'm only going through the motions.

I—. Ah . . . Oh.

Professor Skizzen, my friend, if you complain of her, we shall have to move on again, and we are running out of places to land.

I despise imposture, Skizzen found himself saying.

I thought you might understand imposture very well.

Skizzen did not reply because he was suddenly frightened. What was meant by that? Was there a threat? what sort? from what quarter? Devise had been last seen smothering his mug with both hands. Perhaps he was making a joke about the quality of its—what did one say?—mud. Led by his beard, Skizzen retreated toward the door. Keep your eye on the hands, he implored himself. Keep an eye on.

I mean it is very hard to be honestly what we are. A finger, rooted in a fist, popped free.

Well, she better not. Dottie. Dottie better not imposture me. She crowds me, even in corridors. Where everyone can see. Skizzen cracked the door and slid through. And from the building, he ran out.

Perhaps, after this, the man who spoke with his hands said less with his hands than before. Perhaps he kept his arms loaded with books. Perhaps he chose to participate in fewer social gatherings or to plan fewer accidental encounters. It was hard to tell. But for a time, at least, Dottie did nothing in class but cross her legs, and nothing after class but bob when—by circumstance—he was carried close.

Professor Skizzen said nothing with his eyes or mouth, or evidenced anything in the way he walked, or gave his own hands leave to stray into oratory. He kept mum about God and God's signals; he kept mum about Dottie's—well—devices; he kept mum about his fears. Before the morning mirror he made certain to be clothed.

But he did practice flicking crumbs from the dinner table. Flick, that's gone, he would say his hands said. Get thee to a nunnery.

Flick. As if it were a picnic and there were ants on the cloth. Flick. Let the air eat you.

If it is possible for a member of the faculty to drop out of school that is what Arthur and his daughter did. He disappeared and left his colleagues with four classes adrift like bottles in midocean. Rinse decided to bus one bunch to Oberlin for the Fauré *Requiem* and regretted the ride. Buses, when every seat is occupied by a stranger, can be cheap, convenient, and restful ways to travel. Unless the bus careens over an embankment and tips, it gives the hits, it does not receive them. But when a bus is transporting what is called a group, there are likely to be singing and other forms of merriment—jokes, nips, make outs, disorderly glee—and a weakening of the leader's position. It was unlikely that the man who spoke with his hands left by car because he didn't seem to drive. Perhaps his hands were too busy with their obedience to God's will. Perhaps he took a bus to Uhrichsville and the train from there. Perhaps he had his goods shipped, whatever they were. His flute. His piccolo. His recorder. Dottie's clarinet.

The last time Professor Skizzen saw Professor Arthur Devise the man was sitting on a campus bench like an ampersand. Skizzen studied, from a safe distance, those hands, but what he saw was a very ordinary clench.

From The Prague Sonatas
Bradford Morrow

*. . . we are in the situation of travelers in a train
that has met with an accident in a tunnel, and
this at a place where the light at the beginning
can no longer be seen, and the light at the end is
so very small a glimmer that the gaze must continually search for it and is always losing it again,
and furthermore, both the beginning and the end
are not even certainties.*

—Franz Kafka
The Blue Octavo Notebooks, 1917

ALL WARS BEGIN WITH music. Her father told her that when she was
nine years old. The fife and drum. The marching songs, sung to the
rhythm of boots tramping their way to battle. The bugle's call for
an infantry to charge. Even the wailing bassoon sirens that precede
bombardment and the piccolo whistles of falling bombs themselves.
War is music and music is war, he said, his breath sharp with garlic
from their evening stew and mulled wine. He was frantic with the
truth of his idea.

The girl looked up from her pillow and said nothing. She had no
siblings, and her mother was already dead of the influenza that was
sweeping across Europe like a scythe. This soldier father of hers, in
peacetime a devoted piano teacher at the local conservatory, was all
she had left. She knew she needed to remember what he said even if
she didn't really understand. She did her best to focus on him, a rav-
ing blur in her candlelit room, more a mad dream than a man, his
voice melodic if a little slurred. Not just the outset but the end of
war is music, too. Dirges of the defeated will always be played in
counterpoint with the fanfare of victors. The screams of the fallen
are the second measure in the symphony opened by the crack of gun-
shots. Think of it as God's duet of tears and triumph, from the day
war is declared to the day the surrenders are signed.

Why do people fight wars? the girl asked.

Because God lets them, he answered, suddenly quieter.

But why does he let them?

He thought for a moment, tucking the wool blanket under her chin, before saying, Because God loves music and so he must abide war.

Don't go back, she pleaded in a voice so faint she herself hardly heard the words. He traced his fingers over her forehead, moving her fine brown hair away from her face so that he could see his daughter better. When he kissed her forehead, she could smell the vanilla and cinnamon she'd mixed in with his wine. And that was how she would always remember him, there where he stood by her bed, her papa, whispering his good nights, this wisp of a man in his tattered uniform and thin boots, with coal-bright eyes and a deep tenor voice that never failed to convince the girl of whatever puddings came into his head. She fell asleep lullabyed in the arms of a song she had heard some men singing on the village road in a language she could not understand. *It's a long way to Berlin, but we'll get there, boys.* The following day, her father's furlough was up and he was gone before she woke, leaving her in the care of a widow neighbor.

Within a week of his drunken evening rhapsody he was dead, one of the unfortunate last to fall in that war that was supposed to end all wars. Barraged in some desperate muddy trench as the tanks rolled through and mustard gas settled over the ruined land like clouds of ghosts, leaving her another orphan of the Great War. She was packed off to live with a French-Bohemian aunt in the Vyšehrad district of Prague, capital of what was now to become the independent state of Czechoslovakia. On the crowded train, clutching a valise containing her few clothes, a wedding silver print of her parents, and an antique musical manuscript her father had inherited from her grandfather, and before that from her grandfather's grandfather, Otýlie made a pact with herself. She would never again listen to men who talked war. And she would never sing or play music as long as she lived.

When war came raging once more into her life on a gray morning, the fifteenth of March, 1939, she thought of her father's last words to her. She didn't hear his fife and drum. No bugle blared. The tympani of gunfire didn't shatter the air. But music was there on the first day just as he had promised. Voices rose up together as masses of Czechs crowded Wenceslas Square to protest the German troops marching into Prague. Otýlie, now thirty, saw the unfolding nightmare from behind the sheer curtains of her third-floor apartment window as a wan sun struggled to peek through the blustery clouds. Another mad dream. Many thousands of men and women bundled in overcoats and shawls were pushed aside by the advancing soldiers, shoved against the facades of buildings as they defiantly sang the Czech national anthem. A wintry wind blew across the cobblestones under the sky dim as an eclipse. Crisp snow fell over the spires and statuary while the crowds sang with patriotic anger in the faces of the occupiers, *Kde domov můj . . . where is my homeland?* The opening line of the anthem had never before made such poignant sense, Otýlie thought. A keening requiem for the dead had begun and, look, the first shot hadn't even been fired.

Her immediate concern was for her husband, Jakub. He had gone to work early that day. Would he get back home before the inevitable violence broke out? So many of Prague's narrow, serpentine streets would be dangerous to negotiate if a throng were to stampede or the troops begin making sweeps. His shop was by the river near the university, in Josefov. Antiquarian artifacts, religious objects, some musical instruments, a miscellany of antique things. If he had any knowledge of what was happening, he would right now be spiriting the most precious items to his backroom safe so he could lock up shop and return to Wenceslas. He would move the finger-polished ivory mezuzot and old siddurim, the silver Torah ornaments and havdalah sets, the porcelain seder plates and ornate menorahs out of the display window. A virginal with a cracked soundboard that dated back to the year Mozart completed *Don Giovanni* in Prague and conducted the opera at the Estates Theater here, he would hide under an old packing blanket. Some manuscripts by lesser composers, Franz Christoph Neubauer, for one, or Anton Kraft, whose best-known Cello Concerto in D major had actually been composed by Haydn, would be locked in the bottom drawer of his desk along with a clutch of letters from Čapek, the Czech writer who coined the word *robot*. His shop was a mishmash of culture. It wouldn't be so much a matter of salvaging inventory, she knew, as protecting heritage.

Whispers and shouts echoed in the hallway of the apartment building. Someone asked what in the world was happening and another answered, You didn't hear the announcement on the radio this morning? What announcement? President Hácha was summoned to an emergency meeting with Hitler last night, the first woman rasped as Otýlie pressed her ear to the door, eavesdropping. Dragged him up to Berlin on no notice, sick as he is. Berlin, she thought with a scowl. The same crazy Berlin those johnnies sang about two decades earlier. They're saying the Führer threatened to bomb Prague into rubble if

249

Hácha didn't put us under the Reich's protection. So he knuckled under and signed in the middle of the night. Doesn't sound like he had much of a choice, the other voice responded. No, and besides, the first SS troops, Leibstandarte Adolf Hitler they're called, had already crossed into Moravská Ostrava and overrun the fortifications there. They said on the radio that Prague would be occupied this morning, but I didn't believe it until I saw it with my own eyes. Our army's under German command now. The police, the government. Everything's just turned upside down overnight. Hitler promised if we resist in any way we'll be crushed. Prague will cease to exist, is what he said. *Ježišmarja*, what are we supposed to do? Stay calm, the radio told us, and go about our business as if today were any other day of the week. Madness!

She heard more shouting, and the conversation abruptly came to a halt. Otýlie, hands quaking, sat at the kitchen table and tried to gather her wits. They needed to escape. Jakub was too well known in intellectual and Jewish circles here to hope they would ignore him. She and her husband had read about the bloody pogroms in Vienna just the year before and understood what Hitler had in mind, despite any initial assurances he might make to the contrary. Maybe the train station hadn't been secured yet. Perhaps they could somehow get to Paris, to London, and from there, with luck, to America. She knew her husband would scoff at such a plan. I may not be the most courageous man, he would say, but I'm no runner. The problem was, as she well understood, there was an important difference between her and Jakub. She had been touched by war once, and he hadn't. *Kubíčku*, my Jakub, she thought, panic rising like some flaring ember caught in her chest.

Another neighbor, an émigré named Franz Bittner who had recently moved into the next flat, knocked on her door to see if she was all right. No one in Prague was all right, she managed to say. He shook his head and handed her his cat, asking if she wouldn't mind taking care of it until he came back. He'd been outside and said they were marching in endless columns of three across the Charles Bridge, their rifles bayoneted, past the statues of the Madonna and John the Baptist and the rest. Shaven, grim, disciplined boys in uniforms and helmets, each with a jaw set square as some marionette with a fixed mouth. Not one of them glanced up at the sculpted figures mounted on the bridge pillars, he said, but stared dead ahead toward the Týn Cathedral towers as if they already owned the city. Where are you going? she asked, holding the poor squirming beast in her arms. No

250

time to explain other than that he'd been a Social Democrat before he fled Sudetenland, was known to the Gestapo as an anti-Nazi, and was going to seek asylum at the American Legation. She wished him luck and, after locking the door behind him, set out a bowl of milk for his marmalade kitty, realizing that in the confusion of the moment she'd forgotten to ask him its name. Later that same day she would learn he had committed suicide after being turned away by the Americans.

The world was about to change, radically and forever. Her eyes darted around the room before settling on the wedding photograph of her father and mother with their confident faces almost stolidly serene. She took the photograph down from where it hung on the wall and sat at the kitchen table, studying their faces. So many different tones of fear, she thought. Chromatic scales of terror, semitones of horror. Her parents' was the simple newlywed fear of somehow failing to make life work out perfectly, to draw the dream toward them as if it were tethered on a golden string and all they needed to do was gently, tenderly pull. She too had felt that newlywed fear, and she and Jakub had lived a golden-dream life, despite not having had any children. Love's early fears now seemed so innocent. For the first time in her life she could comprehend her father's terror at returning to the deadly fields of battle; his fond, drunken lecture about music and war was a heroic, misguided attempt to mitigate what he most loved and hated. Her own terror, here, now, like his had been, arose from the deep certainty of being cornered, trapped, doomed. Her end might wait until tomorrow, it might be delayed for a month or even a year. It might coil itself like a viper around her this very day. But whether today or some other day, she knew for a visceral fact that Otýlie Bartošová was not going to escape this new specter that had just entered her life.

She rose and peered out the tall window that overlooked the square. More Germans down there now than Czechs, some long open-air staff cars carrying officers, flanked by SS Guard Battalions armed to the hilt, and motorcycle troops. Men hoisting banners emblazoned with the swastika. Maybe Emil Hácha knew what was best for his country, Otýlie thought for one thinly hopeful moment. Perhaps this wasn't the aggressors' invasion it appeared to be, but instead a way of defending Prague against the depravities of other forces. As she watched the surging masses, she couldn't help but wonder about those soldiers marching in tight ranks down alien streets, hearing outraged mobs sing words that clearly were not welcoming. Were they, too, frightened behind all their fresh pink-cheeked military reserve? She saw some tussling between day laborers and the columns of soldiers along the periphery, beneath the unleafed trees. Several heavy pounding sounds in the distance and a roar went up from the crowd. A drumbeat, also far away. And was it possible she heard the strains of a brass band or was it just the cat crying?

Jakub would surely have left the shop in Josefov by now. Two hours had passed since the first troops made their appearance. The *antikva* was small, just a narrow cavern with high ornate ceilings, its facade a door and display window. Otýlie had to believe he'd finished hiding the valuables, shut off the lights, closed, and locked up. This meant he was either delayed by the growing crowds of townspeople and Nazis flooding the squares and streets or that he had been arrested. Numb, without giving matters further thought, she pulled out a suitcase from the back of their bedroom closet and began to pack. Some shirts of his, underclothing, an extra pair of flannel trousers, and a jacket. His favorite cravat, the black silk one he wore for graduation exercises at the engineering school, before he left that trade for the shop he inherited from his father. His grandfather's worn tefillin and wool tallit woven with gold threads. For herself, she folded some dresses, toiletries, hose, a pair of lace gloves her mother had passed down to her. Lace gloves, she smirked, the silly things we cherish. Just like the last time she was displaced by war, she also packed the photograph of her parents. Her chest was heaving although no tears filled her eyes. She used to be a weeper when she was a little girl but that was centuries ago. With effort, she got the overstuffed suitcase closed and buckled its leather straps in place.

Then there was the matter of the manuscript. Both her birthright and burden for these two decades since her father's death. Her birthright because its fragile pages, whose staves were scored with musical notes in sepia ink by a furious, impassioned, anonymous hand sometime in the late eighteenth or early nineteenth century, had been passed down through seven generations of her family, gaining an air of mystery and hieratic status with every decade. Her burden because the sheaf never failed to remind Otýlie of how that last war stranded her in the world. Left her with a girl's memories and little else of value besides that studio portrait of her mother and father and this piece of unidentified music, a sonata in three movements entrusted to her by a man whose mad and maddening words on their last night together had turned her against the thing. Guard it as if it were your own child, he told her when she was still a child herself, and indeed, she'd more than once cradled it in her young arms. She could almost hear her father telling her, Get it away from them, don't let them take it from you at any cost. Over the years there had been times, melancholy moments, when she wondered if this handwritten manuscript with its watermarked paper and haunted history—like some bad-luck talisman—ought best be destroyed. But reason, or perhaps sentiment, got the better of her always and it still lay protected in the deerskin satchel where it had survived for lifetimes on end.

She knew the manuscript was more important than she cared to admit. Jakub himself had done some research into it, once she finally told him about its existence. He had shown it to a musicologist friend who expressed great excitement about the possibilities of its origins. This was several years into their marriage. One would have thought it was a skeleton in her closet, a dirty secret, the way she had kept its very existence hidden from him for so long. He even asked her if it had been stolen, perhaps, by some great-grandfather whose moldering memory she wanted to protect. But when he realized the connection between the document and her father's death, he never delved into her ambiguous feelings about it again.

He did delve as deeply as he could into the manuscript itself, though. It fascinated him, even obsessed him a little. The three moons and letters *AV* in the watermark, he told Otýlie, suggested that the paper was fabricated in Austria during the late seventeen hundreds. The brown ink, the holograph style of the score, the stitching holes down the left side of the leaves that indicated it once had been bound, even the pagination in a dark russet crayon from a later period—the more he learned, the more everything about the object only underscored its authenticity. Questions about it chased around in his mind. How did it come to be in the possession of his wife's family? Was this a copyist's hand or the composer's own? Who had written it? Would it be possible someday to unravel its story?

What an unforgettable evening it had been the summer before last, when Jakub finally convinced Otýlie to allow the piece to be performed by a pianist who was friends with the couple, in his atelier in Malá Strana, on an honest if defective Bösendorfer grand piano, sight-reading the score before an audience of a dozen acquaintances, including Otýlie's best friend, Irena Svobodová, who had long urged her to make peace with the manuscript and what it represented. Three sonatas were performed that night. The private evening concert began with the crown of Haydn's piano works, the Sonata in

E-flat major, followed by Beethoven's F minor, his audacious first, a work the younger composer dedicated to Haydn, who had been his teacher in Vienna. After these came the Prague sonata, as Otýlie had come to call it since much of its nameless, mute existence, so far as she could determine, had been spent here.

The reaction to this performance was spontaneous and overwhelming. When the final notes died away, there was a collective gasp and sudden burst of applause in the small room. Hobbled as the sonata had been by the fact that its performer was playing the work for the first time, without benefit of rehearsal or more than an hour's study of its pages, not to mention the unsympathetic acoustics of the room, it was clear even to the most unmusical ear in attendance that this was something important. A critical moment in the life of music. Its rich polyphonies, harmonic poignancies, expansions, recapitulations, and sophisticated figurations reminded Tomáš, the pianist that evening, so much of Mozart's final sonata that he had to wonder if this wasn't a treasure that had been dropped onto the planet by some Mozartian genius from another galaxy. It combined joyous esprit with passages of unsettling, unspeakable darkness. Torrential cascades of scales were set against lyrical eddyings that seemed to defy all laws of spiritual gravity. You absolutely must allow this to be published, Tomáš exclaimed. But Otýlie wouldn't hear of it. Even Irena was unable to persuade her friend to listen to reason. She carefully slid the manuscript back into its satchel and there it had remained ever since.

Now she could do nothing but wait. Though the sky hadn't grown brighter she didn't turn on any lights and left the curtains mostly drawn. The passageway outside her door had fallen quiet. Others had taken to the streets to watch the spectacle or else were cowering in their caves just like she was. Of course she would never leave without Jakub. At this oddest moment she remembered a joke of her father's about two barristers who walk into a pub carrying baguettes. When they order their beers, the waiter warns them they're not permitted to eat their own food here. The barristers shrug, then trade baguettes and calmly begin to eat. The thing was, Hitler had pulled a sleight of hand on Hácha. He now held both baguettes and even usurped the pub. Otýlie frowned, wondering if she wasn't losing her sanity.

Not until some time past noon did her husband manage to send word to her through an emissary. A young man named Marek appeared at her door, a first-year student at the university who swept the floor, made deliveries, did odd jobs at the shop in his spare time. She let him in, stood back away from the boy with her fists clenched together against her mouth, not able to say a word, believing she was about to learn her husband had been arrested or killed. But he wasn't dead. He had agreed to join the fledgling underground of resistance fighters that had begun organizing even as the first rumors of a possible invasion circulated, and was making arrangements for Otýlie to leave Prague. She glared at this kid with his curly brown hair and large soft eyes, exhibiting such rage that he took a couple of awkward steps back toward the door. You tell my husband, she said, her voice quiet but firm, that I'll do nothing of the kind and that he should come home. *Hned, hned ted'!* she suddenly shouted, startling both of them. *Immediately, now!*

I can tell him, Marek said. But I'm not sure he'll listen.

Do your mother and father live in Prague?

Marek nodded, a little sheepish for one his age.

Once you've told my husband what I said, go to them, see if they're all right. Take care of them. Leave the underground to grave diggers.

Somebody's got to fight these jackals.

Only fools fight the inevitable, she said, hearing the crazed edge in her voice. Even as these words came out of her mouth she felt the stinging shame of them, the embarrassment of defeat without a struggle. Not quite thirty years from that day, long after the Germans were gone, when Soviet tanks would roll into Prague in 1968, and her glorious city, already under Moscow's influence, was yet again invaded and occupied by foreign military forces, Otýlie would remember her words with such deep disgust that she would be tempted to go and throw herself under the grinding treads of one of those tanks, put an end to her lifelong dance with war.

After Marek left, she passed an excruciating hour stealing back and forth from chair to window like some hapless spy before finally putting on her coat and scarf and going outside into the mayhem to search for her husband. Things were more desperate in the streets than they had appeared to be from her aerie. Men and women freely wept, many of them shouting obscenities at the Germans, who either couldn't understand them or were indifferent to what they were saying. Pitiful, dejected Czech soldiers dressed in drab khaki uniforms looked on in disbelief. Several people suicided themselves from windows, which put Otýlie in mind of some new defenestration of Prague. A couple of boys from the farmers' market who were both brave and ignorant of their situation threw snowballs at an armored truck and then ducked away into the swarm of protesters; otherwise the occupation proceeded almost entirely without resistance. Yet everyone continued to sing. Singing was their sole weapon, their salvo against this tyranny. They sang as if music were a kind of fusillade, as if their voices rising together could meet in battle the loud clatter of tank treads and jackboots on the stone streets.

While she threaded her way toward Josefov across the city gone insane and riotous, a strange feeling came over Otýlie. She gazed at the Old Town Hall clock and the cathedral spires, the pastel facades of the buildings lining Staroměstské náměstí, and glimpsed the fairytale castle atop the hill in Hradčany that had towered over the city for many centuries years, and she realized that all this would survive. Had to survive long after every soldier and citizen in the streets was dead. The people and politics of any given day eventually fade into a dust of unreality, but the best of what men forge with their imaginations survives. Hers was a simple enough epiphany, but the extremity of the moment made the idea seem monumental. When she reached the shop and saw that the lights were off, the curtain on the door was drawn, the door locked, she stood staring for a moment at the handwritten sign he had affixed to the display window.

Odmítám, it read. *I refuse.*

Simple, firm, dignified.

At that moment Otýlie realized two more things. She understood Jakub's impulses were right. And she knew she might never see her husband again.

Not that she didn't spend the rest of that freezing, frenetic day looking for him. She knocked on the doors of every friend they had, forced her way through the surging, hysteric multitudes past the ranks of soldiers and more soldiers, questioning whether the Reich really needed to send so many to secure the peace among an already defeated people. After spending an hour with Irena, who rued the fact that she was pregnant and her husband was off in Brno on business in the midst of all this chaos, she arrived back home just as the first curfews were announced, in Czech and German, on wall posters and traffic boxes. Loudspeakers blared in the dusk, demanding people clear the squares and curbs. That night, alone in bed for the first time since she had been married, she who'd believed she would never weep again cried herself to sleep. It gave Otýlie no solace to know that hundreds of thousands of others were doing the same.

More quickly than she or anyone else might have imagined it possible, the Germans reinvented Prague. They recast every street and square with their former Germanic names. The river Vltava, which flowed through the center of the city, became the Moldau for the first time since the Czech parliament banned German in the last century. Whereas before Czechs drove on the left-hand side of the road, now they were immediately forced to drive on the right in accordance with German custom. *In Prag wird Rechts gefahren!* Political parties were abolished, radio and newspapers were censored. A torture chamber, very medieval in this medieval place, was soon to be established by the Gestapo at Petschek Palace. Jewish businesses were Aryanized even before the deportations to death camps began. Small things changed, too, as the new order crystallized. Concealing weapons was strictly unlawful. Possessing a broadcasting set would assure an appearance before a firing squad. Whenever SS troops paraded down streets, passers-by were expected to halt, remove their hats, stand at attention as a sign of respect for the swastika banners or marching band playing "Deutschland über Alles" and the "Horst Wessel Song," anthem of the Nazi Party. The world Otýlie had known since she was nine years old was being annihilated before her very eyes. Czechmate, one of her English-speaking friends said, a pale attempt at levity. Neither woman laughed.

Every day, as the eerie, seething quiet of vanquishment settled over Prague, Otýlie made her way to Josefov to see what if anything was happening at the shop. She of course didn't expect to find Jakub there sitting on the stool behind his counter reading, as had been his habit before all this horror came down on their heads. She had no idea what to expect. More than once she'd taken the key to the *antikva* with her, intending at least to remove the provocative sign he had left in the window. But sentries were posted on every corner of the Jewish quarter and she knew she dared not expose herself as being in any way affiliated with the place. Intuition told her not even to pause in front of the store lest her interest be noticed and she be taken in for questioning. When, on the fifth day of the Protectorate's occupation, she side-glanced the shop facade and saw that the door window had been smashed and then boarded up, the *Odmítám* sign removed and replaced with a poster printed in red and black stating that this establishment was closed until further notice, she knew that it wouldn't be long before they came knocking on the apartment door on Wenceslas. She hastily walked home, fully anticipating the rooms to be ransacked. When she unlocked the door and found everything undisturbed, Otýlie grabbed her suitcase and satchel. Tucking the nameless cat inside her coat, she left the building hoping to make it to Irena's without being accosted. It was a preposterous idea, she knew, to try to walk in the streets with a suitcase and cat in tow, but staying home was impossible. Otýlie was welcomed by Irena inside her house on a narrow winding street in the same quarter where the sonata had been performed that time years ago, having made a daring dash across one of the smaller bridges upriver from the Charles, which was totally blocked by the Germans. She had been stopped once, asked a few questions, then allowed to move on in part because she had lied that the cat was sick and she needed to take it to the home of her sister, whose husband was a veterinarian. These were the days before identity cards and martial law. Chance miracles still played out now and again.

Otýlie left no note for her husband that would lead the Gestapo to Irena's door. She knew he would figure out her hiding place without her leaving behind a trail of bread crumbs for the rats to follow.

Within a week of sleepless nights and interminable days her guess was proven right. But it wasn't Jakub who knocked tentatively on Irena's door. Marek turned up, bearing news, bringing her letters and money. He became her go-between and the one left to plead with her on Jakub's behalf to emigrate immediately, before the noose was entirely closed, and take Irena with her. No longer in Prague himself, but in hiding on its outskirts with a small but growing group of resisters discussing ways to mount an armed insurrection, Jakub had a plan in place for her, for both of them. He even had work for her to do on behalf of the Czech resistance once she was safely resettled abroad. Overnight, it would seem, her husband had been galvanized. Her sedate, educated, religious, humble, adoring Jakub, who loved nothing better than to hike with her to the top of Petřín Hill to picnic on Sundays, or go to the Rudolfinum in the evening to hear the symphony, was now a conspirator against the Reich.

Bitterness and uneasy pride was what she felt. The maddening part was that her pride made her unhappy with herself and her bitterness left her feeling hollow as a bone. Life had become an impossible tangle, and the anger she'd always harbored against her father for not having listened to his daughter's wishes on that final night together now began to form like a wicked storm cloud against Jakub. What was he possibly thinking? Not of her. Not of them. As heroic as his acts might seem to others, to Otýlie they were nothing more than a selfish death wish born of ignorance. She felt her heart turning on itself, felt it growing black and ugly. The old saying about how love and hate were kith and kin had always seemed a bit of foolish fluff, but Otýlie now began to understand the depths of experience and wisdom that lay behind these words. Irena reminded her that Jakub had exiled himself from Prague, his birthplace, sending an emissary rather than coming to her himself, because he was trying to protect her from guilt by association. She knew her friend was right.

Otýlie Bartošová fled occupied Prague in mid-August that year, not two weeks before Hitler invaded Poland, and Britain and France declared war on Germany. Irena had given birth to a baby girl earlier that month and the apartment was too small to accommodate four, Otýlie believed. Irena's husband had returned from Brno, and although he was a decent and generous man, Otýlie could see that their harboring the wife of a fugitive—for by then the Gestapo was looking for Jakub—made him sick with worry. Marek brought her rumors that summer of England and France's impending clash with Germany from Jakub, whose colleagues monitored the situation on their contraband radios in safehouses dotting the forests and farmlands surrounding Prague. It was now or never, he told his wife. Marek was to escort her to an abandoned house in the woods south of the city, where, if things worked out, they could say goodbye. Travel light, bring little or nothing with you, Jakub instructed. And be prepared to abandon the plan to see each other if the situation becomes too risky. More lives than just theirs were now at stake.

Otýlie was beside herself with excitement at the chance to see him again. Her own life was largely spent indoors, off the streets, out of sight. If she didn't have Irena's baby to help feed and change, she would have gone crazy by now. She traded her valise with Irena for a small traveling bag that was just large enough to carry some clean clothes for Jakub, her parents' wedding photograph, which she'd removed from its frame, and her winter coat.

What to do with the manuscript had preoccupied her for months. The Germans had already decreed in June that Jews were forbidden to participate in the economic life of the Protectorate. All assets were to be registered and valuables confiscated. She could only imagine how emptied the *antikva* must now be. Although she didn't yet know it, every last precious object in it would either be sold to help finance the deportation of Jews to Dachau and elsewhere, or set aside for the proposed museum of Jewish culture that was envisioned as part of the Final Solution. A natural history museum for an endangered species soon to be made extinct. Herr Eichmann, the so-called Jewish expert, had already established headquarters in an expropriated mansion near town and was hard at work preparing the mass expulsion and cultural rape of Otýlie's community. Even though she herself was a fallen Catholic married to a Jew, the Nazis would not see their way clear to such nice distinctions were they to find her. Her heirloom, her troubling Prague sonata, if seen for what it surely was, would be a great prize for the Treuhänder, the Reich's ministry of exemplary thieves. What if it proved to be a late lost manuscript of the prolific Mozart or midcareer Haydn? Or even, as their pianist friend Tomáš improbably but repeatedly theorized, a juvenile manuscript that Beethoven had dashed off for Mozart to review when the young prodigy had hopes of studying with the master, who unfortunately died before that dream could be realized? To Otýlie it was of little or no consequence who wrote the sonata. But it did matter to her that the SS not confiscate it, or if they did, that they didn't have the work in its entirety.

No, she would save it by ruining it. That is, she would break it up into three parts, giving the first movement to Jakub, either directly if she managed to reach him or through Marek if not. The second movement she entrusted to Irena with instructions that if Eichmann's SS larcenists got anywhere near the thing she should destroy it. The third she would take with her abroad, if she was able to get that far.

If and if and if, she thought. Still, the heirloom her father had transferred into her care would have no more value broken into pieces than some shattered Grecian urn whose mythic narrative could only be rightly read by turning it all the way around in one's hands. If the war destroyed her or her husband or her dearest friend, then it would destroy the celestial music the manuscript mapped as well. She didn't like to keep secrets from her husband or her friend. Truth had always been something Otýlie, who was otherwise not particularly religious or concerned about the science of human ethics, held in the highest esteem. Being truthful was as close as she got to being pious. But her supposed indifference to the music she heard that night in Malá Strana and her refusal to allow the manuscript to be circulated further were acts of prodigious falsity. Perhaps the greatest lies of her life. While professing to Jakub and Irena the night of the performance that she'd thought the Prague sonata was unfocused, derivative, a mediocrity finally, she knew it was anything but. An exquisite act of human imagination was what it was, nothing less. But the thing was also bad luck and like a sleeping tiger best kept in its suede cage. It had terrified her from the night her father had given it to her and marched off to his early demise. Now it would rest, at least in part, in the hands of others.

She never did manage to speak with Jakub, but was able at least to see him standing alone at the far end of a field in a copse of trees flooded with morning mist. He was looking intently at her. She saw him place his palm over his heart, and even very guardedly wave once before disappearing again, unable to cross the empty expanse that lay between them for fear of being seen. He looked gaunt and exhausted, and she herself would have run across the fallow ground to embrace him but for Marek's warning that by doing so she would jeopardize everything he was doing, and likely forfeit both their lives as well as the envoy's. Their reunion, such as it was, lasted all of a quarter minute but would sustain itself in Otýlie's memory for the rest of her life.

At the end of a dizzying subterranean journey that lasted nearly a month, hidden in wagons, trunks of cars, in the closed compartment of a train and steerage of a boat in rough waters, she did arrive in London, where she began work with the exile government of Edvard Beneš, the true president of her homeland. That fall, the great vortex began to swallow Prague whole. Many thousands were carried off, never to be seen again. After the allies' triumph, Otýlie returned to look for Jakub and Irena. She was certain she would not find them, and she was right. For months she searched in vain before booking passage to America. She arrived at Ellis Island on a brisk day in October 1946. Her second impression of this new country was that she was surprised to see in Manhattan's harbor Lady Liberty bearing not a sword, as Franz Kafka had written, but a torch. Her first was that she heard no music.

Because His Youth
Or
The Parrot's Spanish
Rikki Ducornet

HE HAS ALWAYS DEPENDED on his boundless, one might say *uncanny,* vitality to keep his head above water. Because his youth sustains him, he cannot grow old without it. His hands, once so elegant, are now reduced to paws. His entire body like some great damaged paw. Already he can see it fallen to the pavement, its contours marked with chalk. An hour does not pass without his cursing the Fate of Man. His own fate in particular. When he sups, he sups on clay.

At lunchtime he had passed his daughter in the street. She introduced him to a raven-haired beauty in vermilion sandals who treated him to instinctive apathy. The memory of that, the girl's impeccable feet, her scent of freshly steamed rice, compounds his torment.

These days any disagreeable encounter, even with lesser creatures such as salesgirls, mortifies him. He takes care to shop in familiar places where he is respected and well known. In the precipitously receding, yet palpable past, he had purchased a Panama hat from a woman his daughter's age and with whom he flirted so successfully she called the house—the risks of his duplicity are immense—*just wondering,* she had whispered, her voice pleasantly unhinged, *just wondering if . . .*

But already unlike his former self, he had put her off. His prostate, for God's sake, gave him pause. His marvelous sperm was thicker now, unfamiliarly so—as if he had changed species. And he has! He is become a member of an endangered species.

"You are fascinating," he had said to her, wondering as he spoke how many such as she he had possessed. But his past was littered with conquests and he had lost count. "Fascinating . . . ," he breathed it, "but I am about to go on vacation with my wife." He sighed and when the salesgirl laughed knowingly, he laughed along although the wife in question was relatively new and a hottie with a mane of magenta hair and a lapis lazuli navel stud. She was a successful therapist; he took wives who were independent: an actress, a scholar, a neurologist—the better to conceal his own mysteries.

"We'll leave it to your return," the girl offered with all the cheek of youth, "but when you wear the Panama, think of me."

He liked to say that to assess a woman's erotic capacities was a form of ecstatic divination. His clairvoyance, the ease of his seductions, establish him in his own eyes as a prince of erotic practice. And the many brief encounters, the extended affairs, demand ingenuity and diligence, a cautious crafting of the hours. (He had once loved to sail and had prided himself on his skills with charts and compass; he handled his daily agenda with equal caution.)

The women assured that he never had time on his hands—a thing he abhorred above all else. As his wives faded into insignificance, the women in their variety provided for fresh forms and a sense that his life—in fact mundane—was significant. The world carried little meaning for him, and the women functioned as semaphores. When he fucked he was alive among the living. When he fucked he was hatched of his shell like any new thing.

Weeks passed and when he did not call, the salesgirl wondered if, in fact, they had been laughing together at his easy duplicity and the promise it implied, or if she had simply been jacked around.

She called again. She was bored and she was broke; she wanted an older man to treat her to a good dinner at the very least. She imagined receiving presents. She entertained this fantasy: they would meet at Victoria's Secret when his wife was out of town and he would look on with admiration as she modeled underwear. She did not know that he was too much a narcissist to consider spending time and money on a shopgirl. A few hours of illicit sex was all he planned to give her, although illicit sex was a thing he liked above all to give himself. Also, he was putting money aside for retirement and dental work—those inevitable indecencies. (There was a brief period when he did enjoy helping out a certain very pretty Vietnamese waitress whose exoticism and infant daughter—so full of promise—inspired unprecedented acts of selflessness.)

The salesgirl was his first and last experience with Viagra. Initially impressed, she soon became dubious, even skeptical. An hour into it she wondered what was wrong with him. Was he overcome with guilt, unable to forget his wife and so incapable of orgasm? Something of a sexual athlete herself, she grew irritated. And he, exhausted, looked at this woman who was gasping with irritation beneath him and, for the first time in a lifetime of fucking, feared for his sanity. Fucking the shopgirl was like fucking in the underworld, airless and interminable. He imagined he was an old bull about to be sacrificed to a bankrupt god; he imagined his throat was about to be cut. Hers was the last Panama he'd buy.

That night as he slept beside his wife he awakened from a nightmare, shouting.

In his recent youth, a mere decade or so ago, and at the height of his powers, he was a magnificent animal with an uncanny capacity to shimmer with sexual heat whenever he entered a crowded room. He thought of himself as a minotaur, his world mazed with cunts. But now he can feel himself cooling down. He considers fish oil and a personal trainer. Terrible thoughts come to him at his most intimate moments—when flossing his teeth or sitting on the can. These physical acts remind him of death, stampeding. His mood is abrasive, the minutes pernicious, his guts tied in knots. Advancing age is torture! Torture! It is like having one's knuckles fractured with screws! He thinks of the photographs taken at Abu Ghraib—those unfathomable mortifications. He thinks his own predicament is somehow this terrible. Hell. He might as well be shitting fossils. Pissing thorns! Like the codgers he despises precariously nursing their old bones down the sidewalk, he too is reduced to taking powders in order to function like a normal human being. In other words, it is evident that old age is a monstrosity of nature. There is no room left on the planet for a man trundling toward seventy at twenty miles an hour! If only he had the sexual energy he'd lost just yesterday, he'd go out like a firecracker. He'd go up in flames! Fuck his wife's solicitous blow jobs; fuck his doctor's cautious inquiries! Fuck his wife's twenty years' leg up on him!

One early evening he finds himself alone, his wife detained in city traffic. It is the end of summer and the light in the living room is dim. Another summer gone, goddamn it! Even the seasons betray him. He catches himself before he can doze off. Five years more of this shit and he'll drown in his own bloody tears.

He thinks that to have lived in the present was a gift of real beauty. He thinks that those who have the gift of the present are the ones lively women like to be near. He considers that what he had offered was both indecipherable and indescribable, something manic but not exactly scary: his own brand of super-attenuated joy. Unsustainable, clearly. Risky—God how it had *cost* him! But absolutely essential.

And irresistible. Not only to women, but small children, girls above all (!); sometimes little boys. When on the rare occasion he would accompany a wife to the supermarket, a little boy might offer him a gumball or a rubber worm. His current wife likes to tell how she had seen an unknown toddler dash down the canned soup aisle to hug her husband's knees. Other people's household pets adore him. Cats that habitually despise visitors leap onto his lap. Once when they walked into a café together in Mérida, a dejected parrot surged to life, pressing its face against the bars of its cage to cry out with such passion all conversation stilled and everyone turned to look. And although he had only just assured his wife he would not abandon her in public places in his quest for attention—a thing that had begun to seriously test her temper—he responded to the parrot's solicitation without hesitation. His Panama balanced jauntily on a head of hair that at the time was barely threaded with gray, he walked to the cage and leaned close. The parrot's little black tongue, its eager eye and urgency, caused his pulse to quicken. If the attention was anomalous and uncanny, it was also flattering. As his wife stood by impatiently tapping her foot, her bottom appealing to the local crowd, he engaged the parrot with impudent good humor. The parrot's Spanish was far more extensive than his own, yet this did not appear to faze either of them. They kept it up, his wife remarked, beyond the bounds of sense or decency.

Trestle
Andrew Mossin

And every ark awaits its raven,
Its vesper dove with an olive leaf,
Its rainbow over Ararat.

—Melvin Tolson
Libretto for the Republic of Liberia

One ought to speak of events that reach us like an
echo awakened by a call.

—Walter Benjamin
A Berlin Chronicle

1.

Is it paradise to know the end
is coming by water the ending and the water
as they come are there in dry eastern banks
likeness without form the bright innocent
tasks undone undoing the wintry onslaught.

What are acts
how do they define who we are where we
may yet go undone becomings
unsituated alternative selves whose limits
cannot yet be determined.
A decade is not so long to utter one true sentence.
Knots lying on the floor and the hands
supple to the touch as a woman's hair
divides one part of her face from the other

Reading how he wept
how he stays weeping after the event
in a text of Avrils unfurling April-like in a rush
of bitten-off leaves. . . .

"He wept he weeps on my breast
a womanlike man is crying for his life and I—
what should I say?"

The dusty trees, the elongated arms that stretch
out to receive the rain that comes in bands
down the hills where one goes
as another breaks open the Gospel
"No man trespasses without water at his side"
in idioms of faith
dispensed almost as an afterthought
over blanched bones of the
unburied dead.

2.

And if you
put your body in place
of others memorialized the positions
again of bodies in death as they lie
under earth no salient record of their having died but these:
The soldiers and their prisoners entered the Katyn Forest at
     sundown.
It was April they wore their summer uniforms.
Hands tied behind their backs they were led to the graves and shot
     once in the neck.
The rope used to tie their hands was Russian.
The bullets used to kill them were German.
Most were found with indecipherable documents in their pockets.
They had been wearing their summer uniforms.
It was April their hands were roped together.
One by one they were led into the forest on the banks of the
     Dnieper and forced to dig
their own graves and were shot once in the back of the head.

Three iron crosses now mark
the ground where corpses lay indistinguishable from
each other . . . *so perfect does a thing become*
it cannot live out its time on earth. . . .

Ideas that turn into words & back again.
"The way of killing men and beasts is the same . . .

267

truckfuls of chopped-up men
who will not be saved."

Alter the language the bodies remain out in the open for all to see.
"When the graves were opened some were still
holding their rosaries. Their hands were tied behind
their backs, a single bullet to the back of the
head at close range. The rope looped through
their hands and around their necks to choke
them if they offered resistance."

There is this record between us. We saw
them once in a photograph. Passed
and passing. A ritual
of reenactment that leads ineluctably
elsewhere. Away from where they lie in an embankment
still covered in snow.

What we hold in common
are those we have killed. "Black
entrance, white shrouded
figure of far-flung familiarity."
I cannot redeem your voice
sadly can neither remember the last
time we heard you or saw
your shadow, there.

3.

There's no end to the giving of names.
Alleged blankness. Blind allegiance. *"I saw you . . .*
terrible . . . light built a shrine in place of
your presence."

What obliterates suspends belief.
Some toughness some illogic that can't accept
degradation terror inhumanity
as the only proper subject.
Posthumous debt. Posthumanist drift.
"One cannot speak of inhumanity . . . protection . . .
by contrast the international community . . . ineffectual . . ."

When Jan Karski said to us, "Never
let others know how smart you are"
he meant: *recognize your own complicity*
intellectual prowess that cannot prevail if seen
by others as they will surely recognize it
and kill all sign of "you."

To get to the other side
we must build arable rivers, wide avenues
of grass and trees. There must be
a motive for return, as if the very spirits
were called forth again, the dead
arrayed before us: "drink black
waters, there too will humanity go."

Or else an accord reached within oneself
that to survive means to mask oneself to undo
identity *spiritual theft* forging selves
foraging leftover speech spiraling
out of control as if one's body
were witness to itself
in perpetual freefall.

Blood slickens the palms.
Moving with the rhythmic depressions
of dystopic suffering
time slides backward and forward
across the grain of encounters
too numerous to name—

> *you are reading me right* a friend writes *I was pushed
> down on the ground they handcuffed me & said here's something
> for your book you fucking faggot here's something
> you can tell your folks at home*

So that when he stood in the sunlight
they brought him upward until his elbows and forearms were
parallel with his chest and pushed him into the
waiting car one of them making sure to
grab his crotch as he did so.

269

4.

At random
what can it be that strips volition
compels us each in our own way to a
politics of silence. Why should the
tragic facts come back at all. A man
stoops over bends down hears
the voices inside when they come to take him away.
Hears nothing but the wind against his home.
"And what I carry in the bag on my back
wherever I'm exiled, to whatever prison . . ."
Abandoned city, its population center held in an image
that will not settle will not sharpen
with time's passage.

In the forest there is
nothing noble, the deer stand apart
from us, go off, blackness of their departure.
We cannot see past where they have gone
into the trees the human inhuman
shelter where the animals stare back
at us, not noble, not suffering, simply
present.

And the burden . . . on whose
legs when they stop running the bodies
stopped in place:
　　　　　　memory can't suture the fragments
back into place the bodies can't be summoned
back from their hiding places: loam seventh octave
supple hinge of breastbone cartilage
fleshy cadavers arranged
for burial.

I remember my father (reading from Oppen) *as a younger man than I am now*
My mother was a tragic girl
Long ago, the autonomous figures are gone. . . .

Or the deaths are merely fantasies the holes
cut through the box and light seeping through until

you can break the spell *memorabilia*
of the fortunate
   Its war their war the same war
is never the same war we fought here is salvage stricken from the record
they kept so little there is what remains in this son's blackened hands.

  His own shadow
was more than he could bear the war

And yet fugitive traces
emblems stitched together . . .
the young face of a soldier in Palestine 1941
reunited with the Polish Home Army
football played against the Iraqi team until late afternoon
in blinding desert heat. . . .

5.

Fatal to recall
in human time the end of
our ability to record what we did.
The surface brittle, even the script
mottled and illegible. "Looking
for you, smoke trail above me,
you, in the shape of a woman . . ."
What stills existence when it shuts
down before the camera. No hunt
no privy or intimacy. Mordant
regret? Sanguine policing of the last
quadrant of memory? There is no building
left standing, no ditch we can
stand in where we might find again
those present at the scene.

"You are the last who will see him. . . ."

Undefinable indeterminate gesture of one passing between.

And held in one hand
a bag of red stones its archive of
suffering blown open.

6.

If one can look
one can look away
the distance can be covered in a
second: appeal of hands
smothering grafted pieces of wood
fingers caught on wire that
miss their spacing in the frame.
What is the burden
when it is encapsulated as bulletins
jagged marks that weave through air in solitary
intimacy paralyzed almost
before the subject has emerged.

Does will mask
the authoritative record, the unfurling
of a narrative almost remote enough to
converge in myth. Acts and actors
spilled onto the landscape, there were
so many at first you couldn't undo the layers
as they lay within touch. You can kneel
beside the forms of them, you can
almost ascertain their textured delicate flesh.
And if one sang these songs
before they were written he would still
smell the burnt gasoline
the dead who lie underground and rot
like black branches under the earth.

7.

When it comes it comes to us it comes back to us it
comes little by little the humiliation shame severed from
discourse the exilic figure his face chagrined near tears
manhood in tatters or obliquely attending errant strains of
knowledge dependent upon erasure ellipsis the radical
plasticity of language that conceals as much as it reveals.

I walked where he is walking now gnomic father partner
to none recognizing only "it is terrible to see the children"

their faces delivered to us again & again in some
paralysis of image formation we cannot abjure what is
seen the images of their eyes as they look dead
straight into ours a complexity immutable bound
as real happenings that repeatedly fall to silence
one is carrying a plastic gallon jug of water and behind
the tree another looks through cut glass her eyes small
and black like stones or stars from which light has gone out
and if one begins there one ends there for our pity is
exigent our own complicity in survival remains
and what can we do when (we fear) we can do nothing
but get down on our knees and in the saffron light
of evening help bury the dead.

8.

To offer: hidden bread, stolen lace.
To offer: dirt smudge, fingertip, rusted blade.
The hands submerged in mire, the arms
dissolving like pins in a smoky clearing.

We may carry nothing less
    canteens tossed onto a road in Basra
        nets thrown over children's bodies in a camp

       to protect them. There is little
    protection. The word is ugly
        even if it means what it says.

Only a tree only if
a woman kneeling her hands
caked in mud her white
tunic ripped to the breastbone
only if the wail
is banished only if their enmeshed
faces appear when soldiers enter the rooms
at sundown & search each one for weapons.
Only if one comes between
the girl and the soldier
her mother holding out
a plate of olives some bread

273

and lays it on the ground before them
and doesn't move until an
arras of silence barricades them
"with these near ones made afar."

9.

When what is evident
testimony that leads toward the gap
fissure silent partner of witness
so that there is the history written
in the gap of history
"I started to flee . . . how many times . . . in the woods
the soldiers . . . our own companions . . . one by one . . . how many . . ."
"I can only stammer"
when asked how she felt
now that the worst had happened
the possibility of the worst happening is always
that it never happened
she said, *"I stopped where it ended . . . a voice*
inside me tells me there is no one left. . . ."

Avowals—or is it aversions?—that lead
back to the erased facts
erased person one was once
"a crystal of breath"
chrysalis of faith
the burden of which is to testify
of no one. Again.

10.

Evident as toil task tertiary meaning. *Nicht* becomes night. Plenum of voices
too many to believe.

In a day (say this is evident) you will no longer exist.
Can we archive
what was never present? Or do we
become like memory considered after the facts
a locale impressive
readily repeated?

Is it reclamation we're after? reversals too numerous to count.
Story is slippery, the facts' illogic imperils easy canonization. "I was leaning
out my window, the day like this day, when I saw the man below
explode into a ball of flame. . . ."

Invention? phantasmagoria? Blood blots out
the rest. "this day . . . a man . . . exploded from within . . . flaming up . . ."

Let it enter. Failures of spirit, guerdon of loss. Encircling our torso
the arms of those no longer present.

11.

*"In the evening the convoy pulled onto the road and suspended in the
distance the men could see coming from behind them civilians who'd
hidden from snipers now coming toward them the candy truck moving
slowly behind then merging with the column when it was suddenly run
over and smashed the occupants inside smashed beyond recognition.
Our first sight of death the only one from the way they lay there was of
a husband and wife ripped open dismembered their intestines strewn
across shattered boxes of candy bars that lay around them on the
ground. The entire platoon hadn't eaten for 24 hours and as we stood
there one by one we began to pick up the candy bars and wiped the
blood and fuel from the wrappers and ate them standing in a circle
around the bodies and the empty van."*

12.

Each round
nothing more desolate

hindrance captive sign
worn linguistic creation

a doll
suspended on wire

futile to speak of it
some say it comes

Andrew Mossin

without effort
stripped art of bread and sinew held above

a denuded head
widening its cavity opening

yellowed hands built to this conclusion
of paper and sand

"give us this day"
what we are not worthy of

no rite no pledge
only these foreign signs

passed hand to hand. . . .

—To Catherine Taylor

NOTES. The writing of this poem arose from a reading of multiple documents, testimonies, and archival materials related to the Iraq War (2003–), including *The Torture Papers: The Road to Abu Ghraib* (eds. Karen A. Greenberg and Joshua A. Dratel) and commentary by Michael Massing in *The New York Review of Books*. Sources for certain lines and phrases in the poem are as follows: Jan Karski, Polish Catholic who traveled at great risk to his own life into the Warsaw Ghetto and brought back to the Allies news of the German liquidation of the Jewish population. He made this comment during a private conversation with my father and me in 1989 in Washington, DC. Information in Section 2 on the Katyn massacre has been drawn primarily from Norman Davies's *God's Playground: A History of Poland, Volume II 1795–Present*. The historical and cultural significance of this event for Poles in the postwar period cannot be overstated. As Davies suggests, "In Polish eyes, this one concealed crime became the symbol for countless other recorded atrocities committed by the USSR against the Polish nation." "The way of killing men and beasts . . ." appears in Tadeusz Rosewicz's "The Survivor" (tr. Adam Czerniawski). "No man trespasses without water at his side" and "Drink black waters" are from Hölderlin (tr. Michael Hamburger, *Hyperion and Selected Poems*), as is the adapted text that begins "In the forest there is nothing noble" (tr. Richard Sieburth, *Hymns and Fragments*). "His own shadow . . ." is from Jerome Rothenberg, *Poland / 1931*. Paul Celan is the source for "Looking / for you, smoke trail above me" and "with these near ones made afar" (tr. Michael Hamburger, *Poems of Paul Celan*). "Like black branches under the dead earth" is from Nazim Hikmet's "Last Will and Testament" (tr. Randy Blasing and Mutlu Konuk, *Poems of Nazim Hikmet*). "It is terrible to see the children" is from George Oppen. The prose of Section 11 has been adapted from David Bellavia's *House to House: An Epic Memoir of War*, reviewed by Massing in *The New York Review of Books* (December 20, 2007). Shoshana Felman's extremely useful "Benjamin's Silence" (*Critical Inquiry* 25, Winter 1999) is the direct source for language in the second stanza of Section 6, as well as insights into Benjamin's theory of history as trauma that inform my work here.

276

Women
Eduardo Galeano

—Translated from Spanish by Mark Fried

SUN VICTORIOUS, MOON VANQUISHED

THE MOON LOST HER FIRST battle against the sun when he spread word that it wasn't the wind who was impregnating women.

Then history brought more sad news:

the division of labor assigned nearly all tasks to the females so that we males could dedicate ourselves to mutual extermination;

the right to property and the right to inheritance allowed women to be owners of nothing;

the organization of the family enclosed them in the cage of father, husband, and son;

and along came the state, which was like the family, only bigger.

The moon shared in her daughters' downfall.

Left far behind were the times when the Egyptian moon would devour the sun at dusk and at dawn would sire him,

when the Irish moon kept the sun in line by threatening him with perpetual night,

and when the kings of Greece and Crete would dress up as queens with taffeta tits, and in sacred ceremonies unfurl the moon as their standard.

In the Yucatan, moon and sun lived in matrimony. When they fought, there was an eclipse. The moon was lady of the seas and the springs, and goddess of the earth. With the passing of time, she lost her powers. Now she only reigns over births and illnesses.

On the coasts of Peru, we can date her humiliation. Shortly before the Spanish invasion, in the year 1463, the moon of the Chimú kingdom, the most powerful of moons, surrendered to the army of the Incan sun.

Eduardo Galeano

MEXICANS

Tlazoltéotl, Mexico's moon, goddess of the Huasteca night, managed to elbow her way into the macho pantheon of the Aztecs.

She was the most mothering of mothers, who protected women in labor and their midwives, and guided seeds on their voyage to becoming plants. Goddess of love and also of garbage, condemned to eat shit, she embodied fertility and lust.

Like Eve, like Pandora, Tlazoltéotl bore the guilt for men's perdition; women born in her times lived condemned to pleasure.

And when the earth trembled in soft vibrations or devastating earthquakes, no one doubted: "It is she."

EGYPTIANS

Herodotus the Greek proved that the river and the sky of Egypt were unlike any other river or any other sky, and the same was true of its customs. Funny people, the Egyptians: they kneaded dough with their feet, and clay with their hands, and they mummified their dead cats and kept them in sacred chests.

But most remarkable was the place women held among men. Whether nobles or plebeians, they married freely without surrendering their names or their possessions. Education, property, work, and inheritance were theirs by right, not only for men, and women were the ones who shopped in the market while men stayed home weaving. According to Herodotus, who was not entirely trustworthy, women pissed standing up and men on their knees.

HEBREWS

According to the Old Testament, the daughters of Eve were to suffer divine punishment forever.

Stoning could be the fate of adulteresses and witches and brides who were not virgins,

to the stake marched the daughters of priests who became prostitutes,

and off with the hand of any woman who grabbed a man by the balls, even in self-defense or in defense of her husband.

For forty days a woman giving birth to a son remained impure.

278

Eighty days of filth if the child was a girl. Impure was the menstruating woman for seven days and nights, and her impurity infected all who touched her or touched the chair on which she sat or the bed in which she slept.

HINDUS

Mitra, mother of the sun and the water and of all sources of life, was a goddess from birth. When she arrived in India from Babylonia or Persia the goddess had to become a god.

A number of years have passed since Mitra's arrival, and women are still not very welcome in India. There are fewer women than men, in some regions eight for every ten. Many are those who never arrive because they die in their mothers' wombs, and countless more are smothered at birth.

Prevention is the best medicine, since some women are very dangerous. As a sacred text of the Hindu tradition warns: "A lascivious woman is poison, serpent, and death, all in one."

Others are virtuous, though proper habits are being lost. Tradition orders widows to throw themselves into the fire where the dead husband's body burns, but today few if any are willing to obey that command.

For centuries or millennia they were willing, and they were many. In contrast, there is no instance ever in the whole history of India of a husband leaping into the pyre of his deceased wife.

CHINESE

About a thousand years ago, Chinese goddesses stopped being goddesses.

Male power, which by then had taken over the earth, was also aligning the heavens. The goddess Xi He was split in two and the goddess Nu Gua was relegated to the status of mere woman.

Xi He had been mother of the suns and the moons. She gave comfort and succor to her sons and daughters at the end of their exhausting voyages through day and night. When she was divided into Xi and He, each of them a he-god, she was no longer a she and she disappeared.

Nu Gua did not disappear but she was reduced to a woman.

In other times she had been the founder of all that lives:
she had cut off the legs of the great cosmic tortoise to give the
world and the sky columns to rest on,
she had invented love, lying with her brother behind a tall screen
of grasses,
and she had created nobles and plebeians by modeling the higher
ones of yellow clay and the lower ones of mud from the river.

GREEKS

A headache may give birth to a goddess. Athena sprouted from the
throbbing head of her father, Zeus, whose temples split open to deliver her. She was born without a mother.

Sometime later she cast the deciding vote when the tribunal of the
gods on Olympus had to judge a difficult case: to avenge their father,
Electra and her brother Orestes had chopped off their mother's head
with an ax.

The Furies prosecuted. They demanded the murderers be stoned to
death because the life of a queen is sacred, and killing one's mother
cannot be forgiven.

Apollo took up the defense. He maintained that the accused were
children of an unworthy mother and that maternity did not matter
in the least. A mother, argued Apollo, is nothing more than an inert
furrow where the man throws his seed.

Of the thirteen gods of the jury, six voted to condemn and six to
absolve.

Athena would break the tie. She voted against the mother she
never had and gave eternal life to the power of men in Athens.

ROMANS

Cicero explained that women ought to be ruled by male guardians
"due to the weakness of their intellect."

Roman women went from one pair of male hands to another. The
father who married off his daughter could cede her to her husband as
property or tender her to him as a loan. In either case what counted
was the dowry, the patrimony, the inheritance. For pleasure there
were slave women.

Like Aristotle, Roman physicians believed that women, all of them, patricians, plebeians, or slaves, had fewer teeth and smaller brains than men, and that on the days they menstruated their mirrors darkened with a reddish tinge.

Pliny the Elder, the empire's greatest scientific authority, demonstrated that a menstruating woman soured new wine, sterilized crops, caused seeds and fruits to wither, killed grafted plants and swarms of bees, tarnished bronze, and made dogs go crazy.

From The Philosopher's Apprentice
James Morrow

Vain is the word of a philosopher by whom no suffering is cured.

—Epicurus
341–270 BCE

THIS BEGINS WITH a butterfly. The insect in question, a monarch, was flitting along a strand of morning glories threaded through the chain-link fence outside my apartment window, systematically dipping its proboscis into the powder blue cones. It was a warm, fecund morning in August, and I was twenty-seven years old. The butterfly mesmerized me, this *Danaus plexippus* with its ethereal antennae and magnificent orange wings limned by black stripes as bold and stark as the leading in a stained-glass window. How numinous it must have appeared to a lesser insect: a cricket's epiphany.

Inevitably Lao-tzu's famous riddle crossed my mind—"Am I a man dreaming he is a butterfly, or a butterfly dreaming he is a man?"—and I performed a thought experiment, mentally trading places with the monarch. I don't know whether the butterfly enjoyed being an impoverished philosophy student with a particular interest in ethics, but my lepidopterous condition delighted me. The sun warmed my wings, the nectar sated my hunger, and the perfume gratified my olfactory organs, located in, of all places, my feet.

The telephone rang: a representative from my bank, recommending that I go further into debt. I slammed down the receiver and attempted to reenter my Taoist reverie, but it had evaporated. No matter. The butterfly had served its purpose. Thanks to that fragile creature I'd finally acquired the hook on which to hang my doctoral dissertation. Mason Ambrose, embryonic ethicist, would write about the imperatives entailed in humankind's connection to *Danaus plexippus*, and to insects in general, and to everything else in the world boasting wings, legs, tentacles, talons, tusks, claws, scales, feathers, fins, fur, flesh, or feet. With a rush of joy I realized that this Darwinist stance would appeal neither to secular Marxists, for whom moral lessons lay exclusively within history's brute curriculum, nor to evangelical Christians, for whom a naturalist ethics was a contradiction in terms, nor to middle-class mystics, who detested any argument smacking of biological determinism. A philosophical position that could simultaneously antagonize the collectivist left, the God-besotted right, and the Aquarian fringe must, I decided, have a lot going for it.

"I've even thought of a title," I told my long-suffering adviser, Tracy Blasko, as we shared a pitcher of sangria in the Pettifog Café that afternoon.

"That's half the battle," Tracy said. In recent months she'd begun to despair that I would ever find what she called, not unfairly, "a topic sufficiently pretentious to hold your interest during the writing phase."

"I want to call it *Toward a Materialist Deontology*," I said.

"Sounds like a goddamn doctoral dissertation," Tracy replied, unsheathing her wickedest grin. She had a round melodic face whose softness belied her grisly intellect. When the renowned deconstructionist Benoit Tourneur had visited our campus earlier in the year, Tracy alone had summoned the gumption to dismantle, publicly and definitively, his ingenious apologia for Heidegger's Nazi affiliations. "But whatever you call it," she added, looking me in the eye, "the topic is eminently worth wrestling to the ground."

"Will the committee agree?" I said, all aglow.

She nodded. "I'll call in a few favors. Congratulations, Mason. You've cracked the first nut. The fruitcake can't be far behind. Shall we order another pitcher?"

"Love to, but I'm late for a class." I rose abruptly, kissed her on each cheek, and explained that in prelude to my Darwinian explorations I was auditing Ben Glockman's legendary Biology 412, *Monkey Business: Sexuoeconomic Transactions in African Primate Communities.*

"One more thing," Tracy said as I started out of the café. "You should call it *Ethics from the Earth.*"

For the next two years I taught English at Watertown High School by day and wrote *Ethics from the Earth* by night, laboring to convert my status at Hawthorne University from ABD—which at most schools stood for "All But Dissertation," though Tracy preferred "Aristotle Be Damned"—to genuine doctor of philosophy, and so it was that raisin by raisin, currant by currant, the fruitcake took form, until 382 manuscript pages lay in my hard drive. And then disaster struck.

Tracy Blasko, dear Tracy who was half in love with me and I with her, poor Tracy went to pieces, checking herself into the Boston Psychiatric Center for clinical depression and alcoholism. The task of shepherding me through the final revisions fell to the innocuous Carol Eberling, a glum Hegelian who had none of Tracy's acid humor or affection for audacity. But for me the real catastrophe—and I'm afraid this is how graduate students construct these matters—was that the person selected to round out my committee was certain to cause me trouble. The nemesis in question was the celebrated post-rationalist theologian Felix Pielmeister, newly arrived from Notre Dame.

There are certain coordinates on this planet, spatial and temporal, where one is well advised to avoid antagonizing the locals. The Lower East Side of Manhattan at three o'clock in the morning, for example, or Fenway Park during the bottom of the ninth with the Sox trailing the Yankees by seven runs, or the philosophy department of a major university any day of the week. I never found out how Felix Pielmeister came to visit my Web site. This scholar who'd once delivered the Gifford Lectures, published eighteen books, and routinely communed with Saint Augustine's shade—why would such a man waste his time picking through the dregs and dross of cyberspace? I suppose he went slumming one day, telling his search engine to display all notices of his newest book, an anti-Darwinist screed called *The Algorithms of Immortality*, and suddenly, voilà: the blistering review I'd composed to amuse myself during the gestation of *Ethics from the Earth*.

It was Dr. Eberling who alerted me to Pielmeister's displeasure. "He's livid, you know," she said. "Really, Mason, you ought to send him an apology."

"I will not eat crow," I replied. "Nor any other bird that Pielmeister would put on my platter."

What most infuriated the Augustinian, I suspected, was not my essay's sarcastic tone, savage rhetoric, or unkind cuts. My sin was that I'd caught him in a logical error. Pielmeister's argument reduced to an assertion that the acknowledged incompleteness of the evolutionary model (paradigm A) meant that divine creationism (paradigm B) must be the case. In other words, he was telling his readers that *not A* equals *B*, a lapse in rationality of a sort normally granted only to incoming freshmen and aging department heads.

It's a particularly bad idea to make academic enemies when the school in question is Hawthorne. At the turn of the millennium our eccentric president, Gaylord Boynton, since retired, inaugurated a forum that endures to this day: dissertation defenses staged in a large auditorium and open to the general campus community. Boynton believed that such a practice would increase both the quality of the dissertations and the intellectual vigilance of the sponsoring faculty. Did this in fact occur? Hard to say. I know only that the innovation makes the average Hawthorne PhD candidate feel less like he's explicating a thesis in early twenty-first-century Boston than answering the charge of necromancy in late seventeenth-century Salem.

So there I was, striding down the aisle of Schneider Auditorium in prelude to mounting the stage and holding forth on my *Ethics* while several dozen students and professors stared and salivated. Perhaps a heated argument would break out, complete with red faces and projectile epithets. Maybe Dr. Pielmeister would ask a question so devastating that the candidate would faint dead away. Conceivably the event would turn physical, the professors assailing each other with half-eaten doughnuts. You never knew.

My abdomen spasmed. My bowels went slack. I gritted my teeth, decorated my face with a grin, and entered the arena.

My passion for philosophy traces to an unlikely source. When I was ten years old, a subversive babysitter allowed me to stay up till midnight watching *The Egyptian* on American Movie Classics. This 1954 Cinemascope spectacle stars stolid Edmund Purdom as Sinuhe, an abandoned infant who rises to become the most famous healer of his generation, physician to the Pharaoh Akhenaton. It's not a very good movie, being overlong, ponderous, and badly acted. I love it to this day.

Early in *The Egyptian,* Sinuhe's adoptive father, a master of the trepanner's art, opens up a patient's skull. "Look, this tiny splinter of bone pressing on the brain," the old man tells his son. "When I remove it, he will speak again, and walk, and live."

Young Sinuhe asks, "Why, Father? Why?"

"No one knows."

Cut to our hero, still a boy, walking beside the ancient world's most philosophical river, meditating on the mystery of it all. "From the beginning I kept to myself," Sinuhe tells us in voice-over. "I used to wander alone on the banks of the Nile, until the day came when

I was ready to enter the School of Life."

Cut to civilization's would-be elite prostrating themselves before a basalt idol, among them Sinuhe, now a handsome adolescent.

"In the School of Life were trained the chosen young men of Egypt, her future scientists and philosophers, statesmen and generals," Sinuhe continues. "All the learning of Egypt lay in the keeping of the gods. For ten years I served them in the school that I might earn the right to call myself a physician. I learned to bend my body to them, but that was all. My mind still asked a question, 'Why?'"

From the moment I saw Edmund Purdom impersonating piety in that Egyptian academy, I was hooked. The inquiring and defiant mind thriving within a begrudgingly reverent posture—it all made sense. Bow before Isis and Horus and Thoth, perhaps even believe in them, but give them no sovereignty over your thoughts—that was the way to be in the world. Sign me up. Call me Sinuhe.

At Villanova I took every undergraduate philosophy course I could squeeze into my schedule, and soon I'd set my sights on the doctoral program at Hawthorne. Late in my senior year I went through a crisis of doubt when my provisional girlfriend, a willowy physics major named Morgan Piziks, informed me at the end of our fourth date that anybody seriously interested in the question "Why?" should look not to philosophy but to the physical sciences—to cosmology, quantum mechanics, molecular biology, and the periodic table of the elements.

My mind went blank. Try as I might, I could contrive no riposte. I felt instinctively that Morgan's claim enjoyed the nontrivial virtue of being true. What could I say? What counterblast was possible? By what conceivable stratagem might I send her worldview tumbling down when I couldn't even get her to sleep with me?

A few weeks later I chanced upon a quote from Wittgenstein that renewed my faith in philosophy. "At the basis of our contemporary picture of the universe lies the illusion that the so-called laws of nature are the explanations of natural phenomena." Today that assertion strikes me as glib at best, but at the time it saved my sanity. Science could merely *describe* a phenomenon; it could never tell us the *purpose* of that phenomenon. The seminal question "Why?" still sat squarely within philosophy's domain. So I continued to think of myself as the post-Aristotelian Sinuhe, exploring the banks of the Nile, wandering and wondering and idly tossing stones in the water.

A long table, draped in white, and five folding chairs occupied the center of the Schneider Auditorium stage, as if the audience were about to endure an avant-garde play in which the characters spent two hours sitting down and standing up and doing other minimalist things. Clutching a fresh printout of *Ethics from the Earth* to my breast, I trod across the boards, assumed my place at the table, and locked my anxious gaze on a plate of frosted doughnuts and a dewy carafe of ice water.

My committee entered from the wings, each member carrying a copy of my dissertation. One by one they shook my hand, beginning with Dr. Eberling, wearing the pessimistic countenance of a deer who knows about prions and hunting season. Then came Desmond Girard, last of the Medieval Scholastics, stocky, grim, reportedly in possession of a steel-trap mind, though these days he baited it not for bear but merely for the occasional logical positivist who found his way to Hawthorne. Next to greet me was Joseph Schwendeman, our Nietzschean department chair, exuding his usual air of exultant nihilism. And finally I stood face to face with Pielmeister, a hulking, densely bearded figure who looked prepared to defend his views through whatever forum might present itself, from philosophical colloquium to pie-eating contest.

A palpable hush settled over the auditorium as the committee, seated now, passed the carafe around and filled their tumblers. Dr. Girard asked if I too would like some water. I accepted his offer, lest I appear diffident on a day I was expected to exhibit tough-mindedness.

Dr. Eberling said, "Mr. Ambrose, please begin by telling us what you feel you've accomplished in *Ethics from the Earth*."

"Be happy to," I said, cringing to hear such a dumb folksy locution escape my lips, then launched into my well-rehearsed précis. The fact that humankind now finds itself in a post-Darwinian epistemological condition, I explained, need not trouble us from an ethical perspective. Indeed, by problematizing our tendency to view ourselves as creatures apart—God's chosen species, discontinuous with the rest of nature—the evolutionary paradigm obliges us to address the assorted evils, from overpopulation to climate disruption to habitat destruction, that we have visited upon this, our only planet. By means of a Darwinian deontology we might at last come to know the true character of our sins, a catalog of transgressions not against heaven but against the earth and its life-forms.

Throughout the auditorium there arose mutterings of approval mingled with bursts of applause, a smattering of jeers, and several sustained moans.

"Mr. Ambrose, are you saying that your naturalist ethics supplants the other moral systems surveyed in these pages?" Dr. Girard removed his glasses and rubbed his aquiline nose. "Are you telling us to forget about Platonism, Aristotelianism, Stoicism, Epicureanism, Thomism, Kantianism, and utilitarianism?"

Although I was prepared in principle for Girard's question, a nugget of dread congealed in my stomach. I took a slow breath, swallowed a mouthful of now tepid water, and assumed a swaggering smile that immediately degenerated into a grimace. For the next ten minutes I spouted convoluted and uniformly incoherent sentences, many turning to vapor before their subjects could enjoy intimacy with their verbs. Phrase by awkward phrase, I endeavored to explain why the admitted materialism underlying my dissertation was perfectly in step with the parade of ethical discourse that had marched through human history, from the ancient Greeks to the early Christians to the twentieth-century Rawlsians.

The audience grew restless. They'd come for blood, not dialectic. Only in my concluding remarks did I manage to articulate a reasonably feisty thought.

"Rather than eclipsing Kantianism or utilitarianism," I said, "Darwinian deontology adds yet another pigment to the palette of moral philosophy."

At this juncture Felix Pielmeister slammed his copy of my *Ethics* on the table—violently, righteously, as if to crush a cockroach. From his throat came a sound suggesting a wild boar simultaneously enjoying a good joke and an important orgasm.

"As I'm sure you're aware, Mr. Ambrose," Pielmeister said, "post-rationalist thought is not ipso facto at odds with the arguments of Charles Darwin. And yet I find that these fulminations of yours carry the reader far beyond the theory of natural selection, depositing him in a place devoid of all hope, meaning, and teleology. Is that in fact your position? Is transcendence an illusion? Is God dead?"

Excited murmurings wafted through the hall. This was why our audience had gotten up at nine o'clock on a Saturday morning—to watch state-of-the-art Augustinian theology stomp Mason Ambrose into the dirt.

"It depends on what you mean by transcendence," I said.

"I believe you know what I mean by transcendence," Pielmeister replied.

"Honestly, sir, I can't unpack your question."

"Stop temporizing, Mason," Dr. Schwendeman said.

I fixed on the uneaten doughnuts. A solitary fly hovered above the pile, wondering what it had done to merit such sugary grace. My dilemma was elegant in its simplicity. I needed merely to assert that evolutionary biology, like the other physical sciences, had nothing to say about God, and I was home free. I had only to insist that I had no fundamental quarrel with either Jesus Christ or Felix Pielmeister, and I could pick up my union card.

With an impertinent flourish I seized the carafe and filled my tumbler to the brim. I sipped. The fluid that entered my mouth, however, was not Hawthorne tap water but some metaphysical beverage drawn from the Nile by Sinuhe himself. It tasted sweet. I savored the sensation, then took another swallow. Why did I want to be a doctor of philosophy anyway? Would I jump through any conceivable hoop to join that dubious fellowship whose attention I had momentarily claimed? What quantity of self-respect was I willing to lose in acquiring this most conventional of prizes?

"I believe I can best answer Dr. Pielmeister's question with a few questions of my own," I said at last. "They all begin with Sinuhe's favorite word, *why.*"

"Sinuhe?" Dr. Girard said. "You mean from *The Egyptian?*"

"Correct," I said.

"That's not a very good movie," Dr. Girard said.

"The book was better," Dr. Schwendeman said.

"Why," I said, "do our postrationalist theologians, Dr. Pielmeister among them, expect us to prostrate ourselves before a deity who, by the Darwinian insight he claims to endorse, stands exposed as a kind of cosmic dilettante—"

"That is not the language of philosophy," interrupted Pielmeister, wagging his finger.

"—a kind of cosmic dilettante, idly tinkering plants and animals into existence only to have them go extinct from the very environmental conditions he provided for them?"

Delicate but palpable vibrations filled the stuffy air of Schneider Auditorium. The attendees shifted in their seats, delighted that the gladiator had mysteriously elected to insert his head into the lion's mouth. My committee was likewise astir, wondering what sort of demon had possessed this outwardly rational candidate.

"Why," I continued, "was Dr. Pielmeister's presumably competent God unable to produce the contemporary biosphere through any process other than the systematic creation and equally systematic obliteration of countless species?"

Nervous laughter emerged here and there throughout the audience.

"Why," I persisted, "would this same divine serial killer have begun his career spending thirteen billion years fashioning quadrillions of needless galaxies before finally starting on his pet project: singling out a minor planet in an obscure precinct of the Milky Way and seeding it with vain bipedal vertebrates condemned to wait indefinitely for the deity in question to reveal himself?"

"Mason, this isn't going anywhere," Carol Eberling asserted.

"Right you are," I said. "The show is over. Time to close the concession stand and sweep up the peanut shells. I would rather teach front-end alignment at an auto mechanics school in Framingham than continue to cast my lot with higher education. And so, with all humility and a deep appreciation for the effort you've expended in reading my dissertation, I withdraw my candidacy."

"Mason, no," Dr. Eberling said through gritted teeth.

"That is a terrible idea," said Dr. Girard.

"Most Nietzschean," said Dr. Schwendeman.

"Withdrawal accepted," said Dr. Pielmeister.

"Go back to your offices, good professors," I concluded. "Pick up your paychecks. See who's reviewed your latest books in *The Journal of Astonishingly Articulate Academic Discourse*. But from this moment on, Sinuhe is his own man."

I rose and, stepping toward the footlights, dipped my head in a theatrical bow. The audience members variously clapped, booed, hissed, and cheered. As I rushed down the aisle and into the foyer, a young man drew abreast of me and asked if I wanted to star in his student film about Sigmund Freud's first sexual encounter. I gave him my e-mail address, then hurried into the street.

Every college campus has its beer hall, its rathskeller, its underground den of inconsequential iniquity—someplace where the philosophy majors can huddle in the corners hashing over eros and mortality while the athletes sit at the bar discussing fucking and sudden-death overtime. At Hawthorne this favored hangout was the Shepherd's Pie, a convivial Commonwealth Avenue grotto where, according to rumor, H. P. Lovecraft had once sat composing what is probably his worst piece of fiction, *Re-animator: Tales of Herbert West*, but the theory is dubious at best, as that hidebound recluse rarely left Providence.

I skipped dinner and headed straight for the Pie, where I ordered a pitcher of Guinness, then sidled toward my favorite alcove, the very niche in which I'd once gotten my fellow PhD candidate Matthew Forstchen, a card-carrying pragmatist, to admit the logical flaw in William James's assertion that refusing to believe something is itself a kind of faith. (Do I have *faith* that the moon is not made of green cheese? Must I experience a divine revelation before rejecting Ouija boards?) Although my intention was to celebrate my escape from academe, I could not summon the requisite jollity. My position at Watertown High was about to evaporate, and since I wasn't remotely qualified to teach front-end alignment in Framingham or anywhere else, I would soon be staring privation in the face. Returning to my parents in Philadelphia wasn't an option, as the law of self-preservation required me to distance myself from the slow-motion train wreck that was their marriage, nor could I imagine moving in with my sister Gwen, who was barely surviving through a combination of waitressing and off-Broadway acting gigs and didn't need a grumpy unemployed little brother in her life.

I was also enduring the emotional aftermath of my meltdown in Schneider. Holding forth on the stage, I'd imagined I was participating in a venerable heroic tradition—the individual versus the system—but now I simply felt like a screwup. I vowed to send apologetic e-mails to Eberling, Schwendeman, Girard, and perhaps even Pielmeister. Tracy Blasko also deserved a letter, a real one, the kind that reposes on paper and arrives in an envelope. I would thank her for tolerating my eccentricities during the past five years, then attempt to explain why I'd jumped ship.

"Mind if I join you?" a sonorous voice inquired.

I looked up. My visitor was an owlish black man in his late forties, with a salt-and-pepper beard and eyes as dark and soft as plums.

"I'm not in a very good mood," I told him. "Have a seat."

We shook hands.

"Dawson Wilcox, Paleontology Department," he said. "Your notoriety precedes you. Mason Ambrose, late of the Philosophy Department, author of a quirky dissertation called *Ethics from the Earth.*" On the nearest empty chair he deposited a leather satchel, brown and scuffed and also bulging, as if perhaps it contained a fossil mandible. "May I buy you a beer?"

I gestured toward my pitcher of stout. "I'm fixed for the evening. Here's a question for you, Dr. Wilcox. Does this pitcher truly hold four beers, or merely four *potential* beers, each awaiting the reification that will occur upon being poured?"

Wilcox gave me a blank look. "No wonder philosophers can't get funded."

I filled my glass with stout. An ivory wave of foam frothed over the rim and cascaded onto the table. "Will you help me get to the bottom of this? The pitcher, I mean, not the ontological mystery."

Wilcox fetched a second glass from the bar, along with a bowl of miniature pretzels. I poured him a beer, grabbed a pretzel, and took a gulp of Guinness.

"I followed you here from Schneider," my drinking companion said. "Let me congratulate you on what was perhaps the liveliest dissertation defense in Hawthorne history."

"Seppuka makes a great spectator sport," I said, munching.

"I'm here to offer you a job."

"I never even played with plastic dinosaurs."

"Oh, no, not in my department, though I appreciate the kind words you put in for Mr. Darwin this afternoon."

"Let me guess. You decided to become a paleontologist when you fell madly in love with *Tyrannosaurus rex* in fourth grade."

Wilcox issued a cryptic laugh and downed some Guinness, embroidering his upper lip with a second mustache. "Ever hear of Isla de Sangre?"

"Blood Island?"

"Ringed by a rare species of red coral," he replied, nodding. "The coccyx of the Florida Keys, so far south it nudges the Tropic of Cancer. The owner's a former colleague of mine, Edwina Sabacthani, a molecular geneticist. Eccentric, capricious, smart as God—the sort of person who'll show up on the last day of an academic conference, sniff out whoever's been a particularly pompous boor all week, and start hinting that she's noticed a major methodological flaw in his latest published results."

I drained my glass. The Guinness started doing what it was designed to do. "Three cheers for academic conferences," I said. The one time I'd delivered a paper at a conference, "The *Geist* in the Machine," a précis of my master's thesis on Schelling, I didn't meet any minds of Edwina Sabacthani caliber, but I was memorably seduced by a tenured utilitarian from Toronto named Frédérique Wintrebert, who said she'd become aroused by my use of the word *praxis*.

"Here's the deal," Wilcox said. "Edwina has asked me to find a tutor for her adolescent daughter. I think you're our man."

"I'm a neo-Darwinian atheist, Dr. Wilcox. The average American mother would rather fill the position with Humbert Humbert."

"It's not your Darwinism that caught my attention," Wilcox said. "What impressed me was your rambling but nonetheless astute overview of Western ethics. I've never met the young woman in question, but evidently she has a handicap. In Edwina's words, Londa Sabacthani 'lacks a moral center.' You're supposed to give her one."

I poured myself a second glass. "Maybe I should print up a business card. *Mason Ambrose. Failed Philosopher. Superegos Installed While You Wait.*"

"This is a sad and serious case," Wilcox said in a mildly reproving tone.

I gulped some stout and picked up a pretzel, orienting it so the parabolas suggested laudable breasts viewed from above. "There's a whole science to pretzels," I said as still more Guinness washed through my brain's aching capillaries. "Mathematicians can plot the twists and curves. Wittgenstein would not be impressed. Actually I don't think anything impressed Wittgenstein, with the possible exception of Wittgenstein."

"The position pays one hundred thousand dollars for the first year. After that, you and Edwina can negotiate."

I sucked on the pretzel, enjoying the sensation of the salt crystals copulating with my taste buds. One hundred thousand dollars? Pielmeister probably made more than a hundred thousand a year, but certainly not per *student*.

"You have to realize, this is an extremely difficult decision for me. I'm broke. I'm about to lose my job. I just threw away my future. And yet, sir—and yet you have the *audacity* to imagine I would accept a small fortune for taking an undemanding sinecure in a tropical paradise."

Wilcox patted his battered satchel. "I've got the paperwork with me."

"I think I should meet the girl before I sign anything."

"A sensible precaution, but Edwina and sensible precautions haven't been on speaking terms in years." Wilcox unzipped his satchel, rooted around, and pulled out a file folder labeled *Sabacthani.* "I'm afraid you must either accept the job right now or send me off in search of another ethicist."

"One hundred thousand dollars? No fine print?"

"None required—the bold print is outrageous enough. Edwina expects you to drop everything, fly to Key West on Friday, and be prepared to give Londa her first lesson starting at ten o'clock Monday morning. On my way over here I made your plane reservations, and my graduate assistant will sublet your apartment and forward your mail. Don't worry about your worldly possessions. We'll crate everything up and ship it to you."

"No moral center," I said. "What could that possibly mean?"

Wilcox shrugged, then set the contract on the table, taking care to avoid the liquid rings stamped by our beer glasses. "Your liaison in Key West will be Edwina's colleague Vincent Charnock, another biologist. Maybe he can answer your questions."

I retrieved a ballpoint pen from my jacket and clicked the cartridge into place. "One hundred thousand?"

"Plus room, board, and travel expenses." Wilcox ate a pretzel. "By the way, it was third grade, and it was the ankylosaur, so here I am at Hawthorne, working it all out."

A Helpful Story, a Devious Storm, the Weird Directions, the Difficult Wait, the Risky Wait, the Happy Appointment, the Familiar Property, the Safety Sign, the Frightened Enemy

Diane Williams

THERE WAS SOMETHING legendary about the bird and also about the gloom that had set in. The sky twisted up again and the sun was produced.

I thought this is not going to end well and I saw the unremarkable sparrow until it did this one thing—this, this is not going to turn out the way I want it to end. It flew full speed toward the fence. Just inches in front of the fence, the bird folds its wings out—then stretches its body into a dart shape, inhales deeply, passes through the slats at top speed.

I can't think what else I am interested in. I dragged myself in the summer of that year. I had just finished monkeying with my lips with a moisturizing stick, while through habit, I kept up with all my basic dreams. My gingery eyebrows are thoroughly redrawn.

I had left my orange date-book planner at the Grogg house—Angus and Barb's.

One of the doors inside their house led to a table and chairs. I couldn't step into, say, the dining room and look around.

"What's this?" I said. "I can't say I like that." Mrs. Grogg stuck the tips of her fingers against my breast to push me back.

"She's still here, Angus!" she called. Barb said, "Come, I'll give you a brownie if you go this way. Here, darling, look what I have."

My friend provided food. It's like a personal relationship. But what if Barb Grogg is a better person than I am? I love her mind so much.

I left a sack with presents at their house too, so I had to walk all the way back there again.

I went there to have Mrs. Grogg hold my hand or rub my back. The rain made everything indoors wicked and weak except for the jug on her table that was cold and full because anyone can drink while repeating inner honest answers—fickle heart, broken heart, lion heart, heart of flame, proud heart.

And how does one get to more heart-to-hearts?

"I've never been happier. Haven't you been happier?" Angus Grogg said. "Milka, come and sit next to me. I am not watching out for you anymore," he said.

The rain was white. It came in this way through the window. One of the drops directly touched me. I closed the window and Barb gave me rags to get the bottom of the puddles. In fact, in real life no human being can be struck for the first time by surprise.

I had been able each time to recognize being surrounded with some hesitation that had to be gotten rid of.

Why else would my neck hurt, where it connects with my back?—and there's the headache—so that I felt called upon to take care.

A carafe of water, a choice between fruits. The fruits were almost the same fruit. The red globes, the ruby seedless—they were a color of red. Angus ate his food. His skin was soaked and bluish. They had fed me, carried chairs to the table, had taken breaths, panted. "Stop it, Angus!" Barbara said. "I guess you don't know when to stop it."

Barbara wears a large ring with a carbuncle in it. This time there was something legendary about the normal skin on her finger with the patches of discoloration and there were intertwining patterns of veins on her hand, each newly charged with a small quantity of blood. This matter of the blood is routine, so tragic, so shattering and I saw birds shooting their heads forward with every step they could take—out on the pounded earth, after the rain—and it worries me how painful for all of their bird necks that this must be.

Hmmm, I felt also that the conquest of happiness, if anything, includes ample room to move about, to make an incident die down a little. I *oohed* as if I had pulled my skirt up, bent over, lifted my skirt on over my head, so that my head could be slid through. When I started to gasp, I sighed because an experienced person like me—Milka Grogg!—she can reach a lovely large clearing too.

Although I am not like other people who can go there whenever they please and I'd like some leadership training.

I gave consideration to the green scum in shallow water as I left and realized there was something amateurish about my breathing just then.

I heard Angus say, "Is she bad?" and then music went on inside.

You'd think that I had been out of bounds the way I scrambled to get back to where I was and I started out on my course outside. I curved back and landed, with a side spin like that! Impossible. I can't imagine a more sophisticated and powerful maneuver and I looked at my arms. Wow.

The Boat

Nam Le

THE STORM CAME ON QUICKLY. The crosswind surged in, filtering through the apertures in the rotten wood, sounding like a chorus of low moans. The boat began to rock. Hugging a beam at the top of the hatch, Mai looked out and her breath stopped: the boat had heeled so steeply that all she saw was an enormous wall of black-green water bearing down; she shut her eyes, opened them again—now the gunwale had crested the water—the ocean completely vanished—and it was as though they were soaring through the air, the sky around them dark and inky and shifting.

A body collided into hers, slammed her against the side of the hatch door. The boat righted and she slipped again, skidding in jets of water down the companionway. The hatch banged shut. Other bodies—she was on top of them—thighs and ribs and arms and heads—jammed this way and that with each groaning tilt, writhing toward space as though impelling the boat to heave to, back into the wind. The rocking got worse. Light was falling fast now and inside the hold it had become uncannily dim.

Inches away from Mai's face, a cross-legged man tipped forward, coughed once into his hands, then keeled back onto his elbows. His face was expressionless. When the smell arrived she realized he had vomited. In the swaying half dark, people pitched forward and back, one by one, adding to the slosh of saltwater and urine in the bilge. People threw up in plastic bags, which they then passed on, hand to hand, until the parcel reached someone next to a scupper.

"Here."

Mai pinched the bag, tried to squeeze it out through the draining slit, but her fingers lost their hold as the boat bucked. The thin yellow juice sprayed into her lap.

On the steps below her, an infant started crying: short choking bursts.

Instantly she looked for Truong—there he was, knees drawn up to his chin, face as smooth and impassive as that of a ceramic toy soldier. Their eyes met. Nothing she could do. He was wedged between an older couple at the bottom of the steps. Where was Quyen? She shook off the automatic anxiety.

Finally the storm arrived in force. The remaining light drained out of the hold. Wind screamed through the cracks. She felt the panicked limbs, people clawing for direction, sudden slaps of ice-cold water, the banging and shapeless shouts from the deck above. The whole world reeled. Everywhere the stink of vomit. Her stomach forced up, squashed through her throat. So this was what it was like, she thought, the moment before death.

She closed her eyes, swallowed compulsively, tried to close out the crawling blackness, the howl of the wind. She tried to recall her father's stories—storms at sea, waves ten, fifteen meters high!—but they rang shallow against what she'd just seen: those dense roaring slabs of water, sky churning overhead like a puddle being mucked with a stick. She was crammed in by a boatload of human bodies, thinking of her father and becoming overwhelmed, slowly, with loneliness. As much loneliness as fear. Concentrate, she told herself. And she did—forcing herself to concentrate, if not—if she was unable to—on the thought of her family, then on the contact of flesh pressed against her on every side, the human warmth, feeling every square inch of skin against her body and through it the shared consciousness of—what? Death? Fear? Surrender? She stayed in that human cocoon, heaving and rolling, concentrating, until it was over.

She opened her eyes. A procession of people stepping over her, measuredly, as though hypnotized, up the companionway and onto the deck. She got up and followed them.

The night sky was starless. Only moonlight illuminated everything, emanating from a moon low and yellow and pocked, larger than she had ever seen it before. Its surface appeared to her as clear and as close as the ridges of a mountain from a valley. Pearly light bathed the stunned and salt-specked faces of the hundred people on deck, all of whom had expected to die but were instead granted this eerie reprieve.

Nobody talked. Night, empty of sound, held every soul in thrall—the retching, the complaint of babies, the nervous breathings, now all muted. The world seemed alien, somehow beyond the reach of Mai's mind—to be beneath the giant moon, and have nothing but space, and silence, all around.

A fog rolled over the water.

Mai looked sternward and saw Quyen slumped, arms outstretched, collapsed to one knee. Her head lolled against her left shoulder. Her forearms were bleeding from rope burn—she must have been stranded on deck when the storm came in; someone had strapped her, spread-eagled, to a low horizontal spar, and saved her life.

Mai searched for Truong.

From below deck there now came a humming of prayer. Then someone gasped—Mai swung to find a face, then several, turning pale, hands to mouths beneath stupefied eyes.

"Do you hear?"

"What is it?"

"Be quiet! Be quiet!" an urgent voice commanded. "Listen."

But when the noise on the boat ceased, there still came from every direction the sound of people whispering, hundreds of people, thousands, the musical fall and rise of their native tongue. Barely intelligible. Sometimes right next to Mai's ear and she would whip around—but there would be nothing except the close, gray fog.

In a whisper, "It's nothing—the wind, that's all."

"Who's there?" someone demanded loudly, unsteadily, from the prow.

No answer, just the lapping of low murmurs.

On the foredeck, a man turned to his companion.

"Here?"

The second man nodded. Beneath the moonlight Mai recognized him. It was Anh Phuoc, the leader of the boat. He was, Quyen had told her, one of those mythic figures who'd already made his escape and yet returned, again and again, to help others.

He nodded and looked out into the haze.

And now she realized where they were—where they must be. Everyone had heard about these places. They had ventured into the fields of the dead, those plots of ocean where thousands had capsized with their scows and drowned. They stared into the fog. All drawn into a shared imagination, each in some space of unthinking as though they had leapt overboard, some madness possessing them, puncturing the glassy surface of the water and then plunged into black syrup, coming up into breath but panicked, disoriented, flailing in a viscid space without reference or light or sound.

"Try to sleep."

It was Quyen; she had untangled herself from her station and crawled forward. Mai turned to her, then looked away. There was a sort of death in her face.

"I saw Truong, down—," Mai began, then saw that he had appeared silently behind his mother. He stood close by Quyen without touching her. For a moment Mai was seized with a desire to take the boy up and press him hard against her chest, to keep him—his stillness, self-containment, whatever it was about him—close to her. But she too was contained, and didn't move. She began to smell incense from the hold. People praying to their ancestors. It lightened her head. A dim thought struggled, stabilized, in her mind—maybe the voices on the water were those of their ancestors. Maybe, she thought, they were answering their prayers. What did they know? What were they so desperate to communicate?

"It's over now."

She let herself pretend Quyen was speaking to her and not to Truong.

"The storm's over, Child. Try to sleep."

Mai submitted, and when she closed her eyes, knowing they were both beside her, she found the hum of the phantom voices almost lulling—almost like the wash, when she dozed off, of a monsoon starting, or a wedding, dim sounding on distant midday streets. A sea wind bearing men's voices up from the wharf. At times she thought she almost recognized a voice. When her eyes opened a second later it was morning: the moon had disappeared and the cloud streaks were already blue bruised against a sky the color of skin.

The first five days they'd traveled on flat seas. It had been hot, and Mai had faced the choice of being on deck and burnt by the sun or being below in the oven-heated hold. In the beginning people swam in the ocean, trailing ropes off the slow-moving junk, but afterward the salt on their bodies cooked their skin like crispy pork.

She spent as much time as she could bear out of the hold, which simmered the excrement of a hundred people. Their boat was especially crowded, Quyen had explained, because it carried two human loads: another boat organized by the same guide had at the last minute been confiscated by the Communists.

Each family kept mostly to itself. Mai was alone. She stayed close to Quyen and Quyen's six-year-old son, Truong. He was a skinny child with an unusually bony frame and a head too big for his body. His eyes, black and preternaturally calm, were too big for his head. He spoke in a watery voice—rarely—and, as far as Mai could tell, never smiled. He was like an old man crushed into the rude shape of

301

a boy. It was strange, she thought, that such a child could have issued from Quyen—warm and mischievous Quyen.

When Mai first met him they'd been gliding—silently, under cover of night—through a port full of enemies. Even then his demeanor had been improbably blank. The war had that to answer for too, she'd thought—the stone-hard face of a child barely six years old. Only when the boat shifted and his body leaned into hers had she felt, astonishingly, his heartbeat through his trunk—an electric flurry racing through the concavities of his back, stomach, and chest. His body furious with life. He was engaged in some inward working out, she realized, and in that instant she'd grasped that nothing—nothing— was more important than her trying to see whatever it was he was seeing behind his dark, flat eyes.

Two nights later, as Mai had been trying to sleep on deck, the song began. The faint voice drifted out of the hold with a familiar undertow. It was an old Vietnamese folk song:

> I never thought to be a soldier's wife,
> You were not born to foreign lands preside;
> Why do the streams and hills our love divide?
> Why are we destined for this faithless life?

In the shade of the hibiscus hedge her mother had once sung the same words to her during the years her father was away at war. The hibiscus flowers outside their kitchen in Phu Vinh, which bloomed only for a single day. And though dusk came, her mother would keep singing the soldier's wife's lament, her long black hair falling over Mai's face soft as a mosquito net, and Mai would trace the darkening red of the flowers through that curtain of hair.

Mai followed the song into the hold. She stopped at the bottom of the companionway steps; in the darkness she could just make out Quyen's form, lying on her side behind Truong as though shielding him. Her voice was thin, attenuated in some way, stripped of vibrato. It didn't slide up to notes the way traditional singers' did. Mai stood on the dark steps and listened:

> The path of wind and rain is yours to take,
> While mine does mourn an empty room and bed;
> We reach to touch each other, but instead . . .

Her mother, who had waited each time her husband went to sea, again when he left to fight the Communists, and then—five years later—when he left once more, to report for reeducation camp. That was supposed to have been the last time. He was supposed to have been gone for ten days—the prescribed sentence for low-ranked soldiers. Mai remembered: on the eleventh day the streets were swept, washed, festooned with lanterns—women in their best and brightest outfits. The war had been lost, their husbands and fathers were coming home. Mai and Loc wore clothes their mother had borrowed. All through the afternoon they'd waited, through the night too, the lanterns growing more and more dazzling, the congee and suckling pig cold, congealed. The next morning Mai's mother sent for word but received none. What could she—could any of them—do?

Overcome with feeling, Mai wanted to ask Quyen to stop singing—not to stop singing. Never to stop. How could she explain it all? Afterward, she had seen her mother caught on that cruel grade of time, growing old, aging more in months than she had in years—and yet she had given no comfort to her. She had been a daughter selfish with her own loss. From that day on, she never again heard her mother sing.

Squatting down, Mai dried her eyes with her sleeves. The song continued. With a shock, Mai realized Quyen's mouth was not moving. She was asleep. The singing cut off as Truong lifted, turned his head, staring at Mai with large obsidian eyes. Stunned, she said nothing. She looked back at his pale face, the slight, girlish curve beneath his nose to his lips. The intentness of his gaze. Then, slowly, she felt whatever turmoil broke and banked inside her becoming still. Watching her the whole time, Truong opened his mouth and took a deep breath:

> You took my love southeast before I asked
> Whereto you went, and when you should return;
> Oh warring soul! through bitter years you learned
> To treat your sacred life like leaves of grass.

Quyen stirred. Her eyelids still closed, she murmured, "Yes, you miss your father too. Don't you, my prince?"

He stopped singing. Shadows shifted in the darkness.

Here was how it began: her mother brought her through the dim kitchen into the yard. Her father had been released, three months

303

prior, from reeducation camp, and immediately admitted into the hospital in Vinh Long. He had gone blind. The doctors were baffled because they could identify no physical abnormality, no root cause. His reeducation had blinded him. Mai, in the meantime, continued trundling every day from corner to corner, selling cut tobacco to supplement their family income. Her father's sickness was not unlike the war: something always happening elsewhere while she was forced on with her daily routine.

That day had been a slow one and she'd come home early. In the yard, beneath branches of mastic and white storax flowers, next to the deciduated hibiscus hedge, her mother had hooked her fingers under her waistband and handed her a damp bundle of money. The ink faded from the sweat of counting and recounting.

"Child can spend it however Child likes but try to keep, *nha?*"

Knowing her mother's usual frugality, Mai struggled to respond but her mother said nothing more, wiping her hands stiffly on her pajama pants and turning back into the house.

Two days later she told Mai to go visit her father at the hospital.

"Child is a good child," he told her after a long silence, his eyes fixed on some invisible locus in the air. He'd barely reacted when she came in and greeted him—it was only her second visit since he'd returned from reeducation camp. What had they done to him there? She remembered him being gaunt three months ago, when he'd first returned, but now his whole face was sunken—as though its foundation had finally disintegrated, leaving his features to their low inward collapse. His eyes extruded from their deep-set sockets like black stones.

"How is Ba?"

"Ba is unwell," he said, rubbing his stubbled chin. He spoke to her as if to a servant. He didn't even look in her direction.

Mai hesitated. "Can Ba see?"

He didn't seem blind to her. She'd always imagined blindness to be a blacking out—but what if it wasn't? What if he *could* see—his eyes seemed outwardly unchanged—but had now chosen not to? What if his eyes were already looking elsewhere?

She said, "Ba will get better."

"Child is a big girl now. How old is Child now?"

"Sixteen."

"Heavens," he cried. Then jokingly, "So Child has a boyfriend, *ha?*"

Mai blushed and her father's hand searched for her head, patted it.

Instinctively she twisted her cheek up into his rough palm. She'd come with so much to say—so much to ask—but he might as well have been deaf as blind. He laughed humorlessly. "At sixteen, Ba had to look after Ba's whole family."

Mai didn't reply. She felt insolent looking at his face when he didn't look back.

"Look after your mother," he said.

Look at me, she wanted to say. She considered moving into his fixed line of sight but didn't dare. Just once, she thought. Just look at me once, Ba, and I'll do anything you say.

"And obey her, *nha?*"

"Yes, Ba."

He gave a single nod, then smiled, but it was nothing more than a flexing of his lips.

"Obey your mother. Promise, *nha?*"

"Yes, Ba."

"Child." His voice lowered conspiratorially and, her breath quickening, Mai stooped down closer to him. He was going to talk to her. Once, that had been her whole life. He smelled like rusted pipes. "Stop it," he whispered. She held her breath, watching his eyes. They were still locked in midair. "Stop crying, Child."

She held herself still as he patted her head again.

"Good girl," he said.

The next day her mother put her on a bus to Rach Gia. It was a five-hour trip, she was told. Here was a plastic bag for motion sickness. In the market she would be picked up by an uncle she had never met. "Give this to him," her mother said, and pressed a fold of paper, torn from an exercise book, into her confused hands. Just before she got on the bus, her little brother, Loc, tugged at her shirt and asked if she minded if he used her bicycle.

"Use your own bicycle."

She boarded. Watched the two of them through the scuffed, stained window. Then, on the street, her mother raised one hand from her thigh in a hesitant motion, as though halfway hailing a cyclo.

"Ma?"

Mai pushed through the scree of indifferent bodies and rushed out to her mother. She stood there, breathing hard, sensing the larger finality in their parting. Her mother asked if she still had the money. Yes. Remember not to let anybody see it. Yes. Her mother smiled abstractedly, then brought her hand onto Mai's head and eased down, combing hair between her fingers.

Nam Le

"Child," she said softly, "remember, *nha?* Put your hat on when Child gets off."

Mai stammered, "Child hasn't said good-bye to Ba."

Her mother's hand followed the contours of her skull down into the inlet of her neck, a single motion. "Don't worry," she said. "Ma will say. For Child."

As the bus pulled out, a residue of memory surfaced in Mai's mind. Seeing her father off the first time—seven years ago, when he left for the war—her mother had clung fast to his elbow, her body turned completely into his, her face creased as though it were having trouble holding together a coherent emotion. But the second time—five years later, at the end of the war—her face had completely smoothed itself over. It had learned how to be expressionless.

Mai looked out of the back window—searching for her mother's face—but the street, like a wound, had closed over the space where it had been.

After hearing him sing, Mai caught herself, time and time again, searching for Truong. She was most at ease sitting in the shade of the hatch door, facing the prow, watching him with the other children. The only structure on the foredeck was the pilothouse, and the children played in a small clearing behind it—a concession of territory from the adults teeming all around. Many of the children were twice Truong's age. He played with them laconically, indifferently, often leaving a game halfway through when he was bored, inevitably pulling a small group along—eager for him to dictate a new game.

Unlike the others, he didn't constantly look around to find his family. He lived in a space of his own absorption. Quyen too seemed content to let him be. Hemmed in always by dozens of other sweaty, salt-gritted bodies, Mai watched him, stealing solace, marveling at how he could be in the sun all day and remain so pale.

It seemed impossible she'd known him only a few days.

According to Quyen, Truong's father—her husband—had already made his escape. She told Mai that he had arrived safely in Pulau Bidong, one of the larger Malaysian refugee camps, eight months ago. He was waiting for them there.

Why hadn't they traveled together?

"We are going to America," Quyen continued, passing over Mai's question. "My husband has already rejected one offer from Canada. He says he has made friends in the Red Crescent."

306

"Red Crescent?"

"Do you have any family there?"

After a while, Quyen, misreading Mai's silence, continued, "You are probably going to Australia, no? Many people are going there now."

"No. I don't know."

"You don't know?" She pursed her lips in mock decision: "Then Mai will come with us."

"*Thoi*," started Mai uncertainly.

"You must come. That one likes you," Quyen said, gesturing at Truong. "He talks about you all the time."

Mai flushed with pleasure, not fully understanding why—as she knew Quyen was lying. "He is very good," she said. "Very patient."

"Yes," Quyen replied. She reflected for a moment. "Like his father."

"And who has ever heard of a young boy who can sing like that? It's a miracle. He will make you rich one day."

"*Thoi*, don't joke."

She looked at her friend, surprised. "I am not joking."

Together they turned toward him. He stood skinny and erect, his clothes hanging from his limbs as though from a denuded tree's branches. His hands directing the ragtag crew to throw their sandals into a pile. Mai wondered briefly if it made Quyen proud—seeing all those children scrambling to obey her son. The game was one her brother used to play. Relaxing her mind, Mai could almost fool herself into thinking he was there, little Loc, springing away as the designated dragon swung around to protect his treasure hoard. He was about the same age as Truong. Her thoughts started to drift back to her last meeting with her father, at the hospital, when Quyen interrupted: "That one was an accident."

Mai immediately blushed, said nothing.

"He slid out in the middle of the war."

How could she joke about such a thing? Mai still remembered her father's photo on the altar those five years, the incense and prayer, the hurt daily refreshing in her mother.

"You must miss him," said Mai. "Truong's father."

Quyen nodded.

"When were you married?"

"Nineteen seventy-two," Quyen answered, "in the middle of everything." For a moment her expression emptied out, making her seem younger. "I was your age then."

307

"Maybe more accidents will happen," Mai said, swallowing quickly through her words, "when you see him again. When we reach land."

Quyen snorted, then started laughing. Her face had recomposed itself now—was again knowing, shrewd, self-aware. She was pretty when she laughed. "Maybe," she said. She prodded Mai. "And what about you?"

But the mention of land—coming even from her own mouth—canceled out any joke for Mai. She had been trying not to think about it. From every quarter everyone now discussed, obsessively, their situation: they were on a broken-down junk, stranded in the Eastern Sea—here, or maybe here—an easy target for pirates—everyone knew about the pirates, had heard stories of boats being robbed and then rammed, of women being taken, used, dumped. On top of that they were starving, some of them beginning to get sick. No one, however, gave voice to the main fear: that they might not make it.

Mai pushed the dread down. Desperate to change the subject, she said the first thing that came to mind. "Wasn't it dangerous to escape," she asked, "with Truong so young?"

Her laughter subsiding, Quyen settled into a smile. "It was because of him," she said at last, "that I decided to escape." The smile hardened on her mouth.

They both turned toward him again. It had been three days. Watching him—letting in the thought of another day, and after that, another—Mai realized that Quyen's determination, as much as she tried to take part in it, felt increasingly superficial to her. She studied the boy's face. Above his awkward body it remained as stony and impassive as ever.

In Rach Gia, in the milling market, Mai had been met by a man with a skewed look who talked to a spot behind her shoulder. He called her name by the coriander-selling place. She was waiting for him, her hat on, next to a grease stand, petrols and oils and lubricants spread out like lunch condiments.

"Mai," she heard, "Mai, *ha?*" and, still sick from the lurching trip—it had been her first ride in a bus—she was swept up by this man, who hugged her, turning her this way and that.

"Child has the letter?" he grunted into her ear.

She was confused. He said it again, thrust her out at arm's length, and glared straight at her for the first time. She tried hard not to cry.

"Heavens," he said, hastily letting go of her and stepping back. His face spread in an open, unnatural smile before he walked away. All at once Mai remembered her mother's instructions. The folded paper. She ran after him and pressed it into his hand. He read it furtively, refolded it into a tiny square, and then he was Uncle again.

The first hiding place was behind a house by the river. Uncle told her to climb to the top of a plank bed and stay there, don't go anywhere. She lay with the corrugated aluminum roof just a few thumbs above her head, and in the middle of the day the heat was unbearable. The wooden boards beneath her became darkened and tender with her sweat.

A few days later Uncle came to get her—it was after the worst of the afternoon heat—and made her memorize a name and address in Rach Gia in case anyone asked her questions. She felt light-headed standing up.

"When Child reaches land," he told her, "write to Child's mother. She will say what to do next." She nodded dumbly. It was the first and final confirmation of her life's new plan: she was leaving on a boat. He looked at her and sighed. "She said nothing for Child's own protection." He gave her another abbreviated hug. "Does Child understand?" He wasn't, in all likelihood, her real uncle—she knew that now—but still, when he left, she felt in her stomach a deep-seated fluster. It was the last she saw of him.

The second hiding place was a boat anchored beneath a bridge on the Loc Thang River. Mai stayed down below deck for days and days, with sixty people maybe, among cargo sacks of sweet potatoes. No one talked; every sound in the dark was rat made. She caught herself whimpering and covered her mouth. Once in a while the owner brought a few kilos of rice and they cooked it with potatoes over low kerosene flames and ate, salting their bits, chewing quietly. People coughed into their sleeves to muffle the sound. Parents fed their babies sleeping pills.

One night the owner appeared with another man, who came in and tapped her on the shoulder. He tapped five other people as well. They all followed him out of the boat into the hot, dark, strange openness. A rower waited nearby and after some hesitation and muted dissent they climbed into his canoe, sitting one behind the other, Mai in the middle. The new man—the guide—instructed the rower to cross to the other side of the river. But he didn't, he kept on paddling downstream for what seemed to Mai like hours and hours. At one point she found herself falling asleep. She woke to the sound of wood tapping hollowly against wood. They were pushing into the midst of a dark cluster of houseboats. The rower stopped, secured a lanyard to one of the boats, and leapt aboard. He lit a small lantern and began passing large drums reeking of diesel into the canoe. Moments later they moored against the riverbank. The rower crept onshore with a hoe and exhumed something long and gray from beneath a coconut grove.

"Detachable sail," someone whispered.

Mai turned around. The speaker was a young woman. She sounded as though she might have been pointing out bad produce at a market stall.

"It's a detachable sail," the woman repeated.

Mai began asking her what that was when the rower turned, silencing them both with a glare. A moment later Mai felt a cupped hand against her ear.

"My name is Chi Quyen." The woman used the word *chi*, for "older sister." She reclined, smiling grimly but not unkindly, then leaned forward again. "Chi too is by herself."

Mai nodded. Shyly, she lifted a finger and crossed her lips.

For a long time they glided soundlessly, close to shore, and then they entered a thick bed of reeds. They stopped. The rower turned around, shook his heavy head, and made the sign for no talking. It was dark. He struck a match and lit an incense stick and planted it in the front tip of the canoe. After a while Mai became confused. No one else seemed to be praying. When the stick burned down, the guide asked the rower, in a low voice, to light another one. At least an hour passed. Occasionally Mai made out the rower's profile, hard and somber. She took the dark smell of sandalwood into her body.

The canoe swayed. "Maybe they're waiting," a new voice whispered gruffly. "Move out of the reeds so they can see the signal."

"Keep your head down!" the rower spat.

At that moment Mai realized the incense stick—its dim glow, its smoke, perhaps—was their signal.

Someone else said, "They won't wait."

"Move out of the reeds," the man repeated.

Mai felt a hot breath in her ear: "If they come, follow Chi, *nha?* Jump out and swim into the reeds. You can swim, no?"

"If who comes?"

"Fuck your mother, I said keep your head down!"

Someone behind her hissed and the canoe rocked wildly from side to side. The rower whirled around. Then, through the reeds, a light like a car beam flashed on and off. Fumbling, the rower lit a new incense stick, planted it at the canoe tip, and paddled, swiftly and silently, back out. They saw it ahead, barely visible in the weird, weakly thrown light from the banks. An old fishing trawler, smaller than she'd imagined—maybe fifteen meters long—sitting low in the water. It inched forward with a diesel growl. A square pilothouse rose up from the foredeck, a large derrick crane straddling its back deck, and the boat's midsection congested with short masts and cable rigs. Two big eyes painted on the bow. The canoe drew along-side and three men leaned over the gunwale above them and pulled them up, wrist by wrist. Everyone was aboard within a minute. Before being ushered down the hatch, Mai looked back and saw the canoe, abandoned in the boat's wake, rocking on the dark river.

Inside the hold, the stench was incredible, almost eye watering. The smell of urine and human waste, sweat and vomit. The black space full of people, bodies upon bodies, eyes and eyes and eyes and if she'd thought the first boat was crowded, here she could hardly breathe, let alone move. Later she counted at least two hundred peo-ple, squashed into a space meant for fifteen. No place to sit, nor even put a foot down; she found a crossbeam near the hatchway and hooked her arm over it. Luckily it was next to a scupper where the air came through.

Quyen settled on the step below her, whispering to a young boy. She caught Mai's eye and smiled firmly.

The boat continued its creeping pace. People padded the engines with their clothes to reduce the noise.

"Quiet," an angry voice shushed downward. "We're near the gate."

But no one had been speaking. Through the scupper Mai peered into the night: their boat was gliding into a busy port. Pressed hard beneath her was the body of the boy Quyen had been talking to.

"Natural gate a hundred meters long," she heard suddenly. The water carried the low sound clearly. Then she realized the voice came from above deck, so subdued the person might have been talking to himself. "About ten meters wide. On the rising tide."

Then another voice under the wind: "Vietcong . . . manned with two M30s—"

"Automatic, no?"

"Machine guns."

"What did Phuoc say about the permit?"

In the darkness, thought Mai, to feel against you the urgent flutter of a child's heart. The hopped-up fragility of it.

A tense sigh. "Even with the permit."

"Leave at night and they shoot. They shoot anything."

The speakers paused for a short while. Then a voice said, "We'll find out soon enough."

She settled forward against the young boy, not wanting to hear any more. Trying to block it all out: the voices, the smell. It was unnerving to think of all those other bodies in the darkness. Black shapes in the blackness, merging like shadows on the surface of oil. She crouched there, in the silence, beneath the hatchway. Spying on the bay through the scupper. Gradually, inevitably, the dark thoughts came. Here, in the dead of night, contorted inside the black underbelly of a junk—she was being drawn out into an endless waste. What did she know about the sea? She was the daughter of a fisherman and yet it terrified her. She watched as Quyen reached back and, with a surprisingly practiced gesture, pressed her palm against the boy's forehead. From above, watching the set of his grim face, Mai thought of her father. Their last meeting. His blindness. He'd taught her not to blame the war but how could she not?—all the power of his own sight seemed still intent on it.

Through the crack of the scupper the land lights, like mere tricks of her eyes, were extinguished one by one. Someone cut the engines.

She pulled the young boy's body closer to her; it squirmed like a restless animal's.

"Truong," a voice whispered sharply from beneath them.

She peered down. It was Quyen.

"Don't be a nuisance, Child." Quyen looked up at Mai, then said ruefully, "This is my little brat. Truong."

"Yours?" Mai frowned. "But—"

From the deepest part of the hold, several voices shushed them. In the silence that followed, even the tidal backwash seemed loud against the hull. Then a grind of something against the boat. Mai had never heard a sound so sudden and hideous.

"What is it?"

"A mine? I heard they put mines—"

The metal shrieked each minute movement of the boat.

"Heavens!"

"But boats pass here, must pass here every day—"

Fiercely: "Quiet!"

The sound sheared off—leaving behind a deep, capacious silence. Mai stiffening at every creak of the boat, every dash of water against its rotten sidewood. Then, without warning, the call and fade of a faraway voice. She crushed her cheek against the crown of the young boy's head and for the first time felt him respond—both of his small fists clamping her forearm. She shut her eyes and trained herself to his frenzied heartbeat, as though its pulse—its fine-knitting rhythm—carried the only possible thread of their escape. Long minutes passed. The boat glided on, pointed headway into the swell. Finally the fierce voice coughed: "We're safe for now."

Murmurs rose up. The hatch was lifted. Under the sudden starlight Mai could see the whole of the boy's face, arching up to meet the fresh air.

"Child," said Quyen, "greet Chi. Properly."

He looked up at Mai—his eyes black and clear and unblinking. "*Chao* Chi," he said in his reed-thin voice.

All around them people's faces were untensing, bodies and voices stirring in restless relief. But Mai, clutching this strange young boy, found herself shivering in the warm night, relief only a sharp and unexpected condensation in her eyes.

Once the storm passed, six days out, everything changed.

Fishermen on the boat agreed that this storm had come on faster than any they'd ever experienced. It destroyed the caulking and much of the planking on the hull. The inboard was flooded, and soon afterward, both engines cut out completely.

What food had been left was spoiled. Water was short. Anh Phuoc, whose authority was never questioned, took charge of rationing the remaining supply, doling it out first to children, then the infirm, then everyone else. It amounted to a couple of wet mouthfuls a day.

The heat was unbearable. Before long the first body was cast overboard. Already a handful of people had been lost during the storm, but this was the first casualty witnessed by the entire boat. To the terrible drawn-out note of a woman's keening, the bundle was tossed, a meek splash, into the water.

Like everyone else, Mai looked away.

After the storm it seemed to Mai that a film had been stripped from the world. Everything became more intense—the sun hotter, the light more vivid, the sea darker, every word a discordant affront to the new silence. The storm had forced people into their privacies:

313

the presence of others now assailed each person's solitude in facing up to the experience of it. Children turned introverted, playing as though conducting conversations with themselves.

Even time took on a false depth: the six days before the storm stretched out, merged with memory, until it seemed as though everything that had ever happened had happened on the boat.

A man burned his clothes to let up smoke. He was quickly set upon, the fire smothered—the longer they drifted, the more fearful they became of pirates. That night another bundle was thrown overboard. Minutes later they heard a thrashing in the water. It was too dark to see anything, yet, still, everyone averted their gaze.

Thirst set in. Some people trapped their own urine. Some, desperate for drinkable water, even allowed themselves the quick amnesia and prayed for another storm. It was fantastic to be surrounded by so much water and yet be dehydrated. Mai soon realized she wouldn't make it. The day following the storm she imitated some of the other youth, hauling up a bucket tied to the bowline. Under the noon sun the seawater was the color of amethyst and looked delicious and refreshing.

She drank it. It was all right at first. It was bliss. Then her throat started scalding and she wanted to claw it out.

"You stupid girl," Quyen reproached her, demonstrating how to use her fingers to induce vomiting. She hugged her fiercely. "Heavens, you can't wait? We're almost there."

But what did Quyen know? Mai had heard—how could she possibly have not?—that other boats had successfully made the crossing in two days. She tried to sleep, to slide beneath the raw scour of pain in her throat. They'd been out seven days. How much longer? Her father was persistent in her thoughts now—all those weeks, even months, he'd spent on this same sea, in trawlers much like this one. He'd been here before her.

That afternoon, when she awoke, her muscles felt as though they had turned to liquid. She could feel her heart beating slurpily. She followed the weakening palpitations, counterpointing them to the creak and strain of the boat, the occasional luff of the sail. The sun brilliant but without heat. She was even thirstier than before.

"I'm not going to make it," she said. Saying it touched the panic, brought it alive.

"Don't speak," said Quyen. "Go back to sleep."

Mai struggled into a half-upright position. She made out a small group of children next to the bulwark, then pressed her imagination to find him again, little Loc, turning with a snarl as he growled, "Dragon!" She smiled, bit back tears. Behind him, her old school friend Huong was selling beef noodles in front of the damp, stink-shaded fish market. Straight through the market she followed her daily route, picking up speed, past fabric stalls and coffee yards, the dusty soccer field where sons of fishermen and truck drivers broke off from the game to buy cigarettes, and then to the wharf, her main place of business, among the taut, hard bodies crating boxes, the smell of fish sauce, the rattling talk of men and the gleaming blue backs of silver fish, ice pallets, copper weighing scales bright in the sun, the bustle of docking and undocking, loading and unloading—

A bare-chested man turned around and looked directly at her.

"Ba?"

It filled her with joy to see him like that again: young and strong, his eyes clear and dead straight. He looked like he did in the altar photograph. It was her father before the war, before reeducation, hospitalization. Back when to be seen by him was to be hoisted onto his shoulders, gripped by the ankles. His hands tough, saltish with the smell of wet rope. She moved toward him; she was smiling, but he was stern.

"Child promised," he said.

During his long absences at sea she had lived incompletely, waiting for him to come back so they could tell to each other each moment of their time apart. He spoiled her, her mother said. Her mother was right and yet it changed nothing: still he went away and still, each time, Mai waited.

Her sudden, fervent anger startled her.

"Why send Child away? Child obeyed Ba." Her mind sparked off the words in terrific directions. "Child could have waited for Ba to get better." They had promised each other. He had left for ten days and returned, strange and newly blind, after two years. A thought connected with another: "It was Ba who left Child."

He stood there, tar faced, empty eyed, looking straight at her. She lifted her hands to her mouth, unable to believe what she had just said. The words still searing the length of her throat.

"Child is sorry," she whispered. "Ba and Ma sacrificed everything for Child. Child knows. Child is stupid."

He would leap off the boat and swing her into the crook of his arm, up onto his shoulders. Her mother fretting, her hands dry on her silken pants, smiling nervously. I can't get it off me, he would say. His hands quivering on either side of Mai's rib cage—It's stuck, I

315

can't get this little beetle off me!

She missed him with an ache that was worse, even, than the thirst had been. All she'd ever known to want was his return. So she would enjoy the gift of his returning, and not be stupid.

"Child is sorry."

He didn't respond.

"Child is sorry, Ba."

"Mai."

He was shaking her. She said again, "Child is sorry," then she felt fingers groping around in her mouth, a polluting smell, and then her eyes refocused and she realized it was not her father she saw but Truong, standing gaunt over her.

"Thank heavens," came Quyen's murmur.

Looking at him, she finally understood, with a deep internal tremor, what it was that had drawn her to the boy all this time. It was not, as she had first assumed, his age, his awkward build. Nothing at all to do with Loc. It was his face. The expression on his face was the same expression she had seen on her father's face every day since he'd returned from reeducation. It was a face dead of surprise.

She gasped as the pain flooded back into her body. She was awake again, cold.

"Mai's fever is gone," Quyen said. She smiled at Mai, a smile of bright industry—such a smile as Mai had never hoped to see again. Unexpectedly she was reminded of her mother, and, to her even greater surprise, she found herself breaking into tears.

"Good," whispered Quyen. "That's good."

Mai wiped her eyes, her mouth, with the hem of her shirt. "I'm thirsty," she said. She looked around for Truong but he seemed to have slipped away.

"You should be. You slept almost two days."

It was evening. She stood up, Quyen helping her. Her legs giving at first. Slowly she climbed up the hatch. On deck she shielded her eyes against the sunset. An incandescent red sky veered into the dark ocean. Rows and rows of the same sun-blotched, peeling faces looked out at nothing.

"Everyone's up here," Quyen whispered, "because down there are all the sick people."

"Sick people?"

Mai checked the deck, then searched it again with growing unease. He'd been standing over her. Keeping her voice even, she asked, "Where is Truong?"

"Truong? I don't know."

"But I saw him—when I woke up."

Quyen considered her carefully. "He was very worried about you, you know."

He wasn't in the clearing with the other children. Mai shuffled into the morass of arms and legs, heading for the pilothouse. Nobody made way for her. At that moment Truong emerged from the companionway. She almost cried out aloud when she saw him—gone was the pale, delicate-faced boy she'd remembered: now his lips were bloated, the skin of his cheeks brown, chapped in the pattern of bruised glass. An awful new wateriness in his gaze. He stood there warily as though summoned for punishment. Mai mustered her voice: "Is Child well?"

"Yes. Are you better?"

"Truong, speak properly!" scolded Quyen.

"How is Chi Mai?"

"Well. Better." She leaned toward him, probing the viscosity of his eyes. His face's swollenness gave it a sleepy aspect.

"Ma said Chi Mai was very sick."

"Chi is better now."

"Tan and An were more sick than Chi," he said. "But Ma says they were lucky."

Mai smiled at Quyen; she hadn't heard him talk so much before. His voice came out scratchy but steady. He stood before them in a waiting stance: legs together, hands by his sides.

"Chi is glad for them."

"They died," he said. When Mai didn't respond he went on: "I saw the shark. All the uncles tried to catch it with that"—he pointed to a cable hanging off the derrick crane—"but it was too fast."

"Truong!"

His eyes flicked to his mother. Then he said: "Fourteen people died while Chi Mai was sleeping."

"Child!"

He balled up his hands by his sides, then opened them again. "Chi Mai isn't sick anymore, *ha?*"

"That's right," Mai and Quyen said together.

It was difficult to reconcile him with his frail, wasting body. Seeing him, Mai's own body felt its full exhaustion. "Now . . . let's see . . ." She lifted one hand until it hovered between them, palm down. "Child wants to play slaps?"

His black eyes stared at her with something akin to pity.

317

"Pretend this is the shark," she exclaimed. Quyen glanced up at her. Immediately—horrified, shocked by herself—Mai pulled back her hand. "Chi is just joking."

Later that evening, a young teenage girl with chicken legs wandered over to the gunwale and in a motion like a bow that didn't stop, toppled gracefully over the side.

"Wait!" someone cried.

"Let her be," another person said. "If she wants to, let her be."

"Heavens, someone save her. Someone!" The first man stumbled to his feet, wild eyed.

"You do it. Go on. Jump."

He stood like a scarecrow, frozen. Everyone watched him. He walked to the side and looked down at the shiny, dusk-reflecting water.

"I can't see her," he said.

"She must not have any family," Quyen whispered to Mai.

"She has the right idea," another low voice said. "Is there any better way to go?"

"*Thoi,*" Anh Phuoc said, coming over. "*Thoi,* that's enough."

Reeducation camp. For two years those two words had framed the entirety of her imaginative life. Her father, of course, hadn't talked about it when he returned—nor her mother. Now, for the first time, someone talked to her about it. Anh Phuoc had fought in the same regiment as her father—had been sentenced to a camp in the same district. No, he hadn't known him. By the time the Communists took Ban Me Thuot in March 1975, the Americans were long gone and the southern regiments in tatters—soldiers deserting, taking cover as civilians, fleeing into the jungles. Escape on every man's mind. Soon they all learned there was no escaping the Communists: not in the country they now controlled. They were skilled, he said, at turning north against south, village against village. He fell quiet.

Mai waited. She watched him remembering. Nine days had passed and now she noticed how severely he had aged: his eyes gone saggy, his skin mottled with dark sun spots.

"In the camps," he said, "they do what they do best. They take a man—and then they turn him against things."

From the back deck a middle-aged woman started wading in their direction through the sprawl of bodies. She held the port gunwale with both hands for balance.

"Husbands against wives," he went on. "Children against parents. Your only chance is to denounce everyone, and everything, they tell you to."

The woman reached them. She made her complaint in a hoarse voice. She was owed water. She had tendered hers to another child who had collapsed, she said, and pointed aft. Anh Phuoc held Mai's eyes for a second, then followed the woman.

Her father wouldn't have denounced her—she was sure of that. Not in his own heart. But again she understood how necessary it was to stay on the surface of things. Because beneath the surface was either dread or delirium. As more and more bundles were thrown overboard she taught herself not to look—not to think of the bundles as human—she resisted the impulse to identify which families had been depleted. She seized distraction from the immediate things: the weather, the next swallow of water, the ever-forward draw of time.

"Mai!"

It was Anh Phuoc. She stood up, hauled herself on weak legs along the gunwale, toward the rear of the boat. Past the hatch she suddenly saw Truong—propped up against the rusty mast of the derrick crane, his chin drooping onto his chest, arms bony and limp by his sides.

Mai leapt forward, swiping her elbows and knees from side to side to clear space. The surrounding people watched listlessly.

"Water!"

No one reacted. She looked around and spotted an army flask— grabbed it, swiveled the cap open, held it to his mouth. A thin trickle ran over his rubbery lips before the flask was snatched away. She looked up and saw a man's face, twisted in hate the moment he struck her, his knuckles hard as a bottle against her cheek. She fell over and covered Truong's body.

"She stole water."

"I'll pay it back," said Anh Phuoc roughly.

Truong started coughing. Mai sat back, her cheek burning, and mumbled apology in the direction of the man. He was picking the flask up from the ground. People glanced over, disturbed by the waste. There had been a minor outcry the previous evening when a woman—an actress, people said—had used the last of her ration to wash her face.

Truong squinted up at Mai. Everything about him—the dark sore of his face, his disproportioned, skeletal limbs—seemed to be ceding its sense of solidity. She touched his blistered cheek with her fingers—

319

was reminded of the sting on her own cheek from the man's blow.

"Ma," he wheezed.

"It's all right," she said. "Ma is coming. Chi is here."

"Where's Quyen?" asked Anh Phuoc. He stood up quickly and walked off.

Truong said, "Child wanted to count the people."

He coughed again, the air scraping through his throat. Watching him, a helpless feeling welled up within Mai and started to coalesce at the front of her skull. "Child," she whispered.

Quyen arrived. She seemed to be moving within a slower state, her face drawn, hair tangled. She saw Truong and bent down to him. "Look," she murmured, "you hurt yourself."

"He fainted," said Mai.

"Why didn't Child stay with Ma?"

"I don't like it down there," he said.

"Oh, Mai," Quyen exclaimed, turning to her. "Are you all right?"

"He shouldn't be in the sun. He needs more water."

"It's too dark to count down there," Truong said. He brought up his arms, dangled them loosely over his knees. An old man's pose. Quyen squatted down and enfolded him, clamping him between her elbows, raking one hand through his hair and cupping his forehead with the other.

"I was so tired," said Quyen. "Thank you."

"He needs more water."

"Does Child know?" She was speaking to Truong. "Does Child know how lucky he is? To have Chi Mai look after him?"

Anh Phuoc leaned down close to both of them. "Come with me," he muttered. They followed him forward to the pilothouse, everyone watching as they passed. Once inside he closed the door. Carefully, he measured out a capful of water from a plastic carton and administered it into Truong's mouth.

The sight—even the smell—of the water roused an appalling ache in Mai's stomach, but she said nothing.

"Good boy," said Anh Phuoc.

Quyen's eyes followed the carton. "Is that all there is?"

Holding the tiller with one hand, he reached down and opened the cupboard beneath it. Three plastic white cartons.

"That's all," he said, "unless it rains."

"How long will it last?"

"Another day. Two at the most."

Her temple still aching, Mai looked out the pilothouse windows.

From up here she could see the full length and breadth of the boat: every inch of it clogged with rags and black-tufted heads and sunburned flesh. Up here would be the best place to count people. She wrenched her eyes away from the water carton and looked out instead at the sky. Not a cloud in sight. But the sky was full of deceit—it looked the same everywhere. She looked at the horizon, long and pale and eye level all around them. Whatever direction she looked, it fell away into more water.

The tenth day dawned. Engines dead, the boat drifted on. Gray shadows strafing the water behind it. The detachable sail hoisted onto a short mast's yard and men taking turns, croaking directions to each other as they tried to steer the boat, as best they could, to the south.

Mai watched Truong with renewed intensity. Since Mai's recovery Quyen had kept to herself, remaining huddled, during the day as well as night, underneath the companionway stairs where they all slept. That morning Mai had found her sitting in the slatted light, staring vacantly into the dark hold. Squeezed between two old women.

"How is Truong?" Quyen asked her quietly.

Mai said, "I keep telling him to come down."

"He doesn't like it down here."

Mai nodded, not knowing what to say.

Quyen dropped her chin and closed her eyes. Mai looked her over. She didn't look sick.

"Is Chi all right?"

Quyen nodded almost impatiently. One of the women beside her spat into her hands. When Quyen looked up her face was distant, drawn in unsparing lines.

"Look after him, *nha?* Please."

Above deck, each hour stretched out its hot minutes. Mai lay on her back under the derrick crane, her head against someone's shin, limbs interwoven with her neighbors'. Truong wedged beside her. The crane cast a shadow that inched up their bodies. She threw her sleeve over her face to ward off the sweltering sun. At one point a wind blew in and the boat began to sway lightly in the water. She was riding her father's shoulders. Her mother watching them happily. Whenever he was home he brought with him some quality that filled her mother so there was enough left, sometimes, for her to be happy.

Truong started singing. Softly—to himself—so softly she wouldn't have heard him if her ear hadn't been inches from his mouth. She gradually shifted her arm down so she could hear better. He sang the ballad from the third night. She listened, hardly daring to breathe, watching the now-darkening sky knitting together the rigs and cables of the crane above them as though they were the branches of trees.

When he finished, the silence that surged in afterward was unbearable. Mai reached across her body and gently took hold of his arm.

"Who taught Child how to sing like that?"

He didn't answer.

The next morning, back below deck, she woke up to find a puddle of vomit next to his curled-up, sleeping body. It gleamed gray in the early light of dawn.

"The child has the sickness," a voice said without a second thought. It was one of the old women who had camped with them beneath the companionway stairs. The hatch was open and light flowed in like a mist, dimly illumining the three other bodies entangled in their nook. The deeper recess of the hold remained black.

"No, he doesn't," said Mai.

"Poor child. He is not the last. Such a pity."

"Be quiet!" Mai covered her mouth, abashed, but no one reproached her. Several bodies stirred on the other side of the stairs.

Barely awake, Quyen rolled over to her son and propped herself up on an elbow. She brushed his cheek with her knuckles. For a second, in the half-light, Mai thought she saw an expression of horror move across her friend's face.

"Child is sorry," Mai murmured to the old woman.

Truong's eyes were glazed when he opened them. He looked like a burned ghost. He leaned over, away from his mother, and dry-retched. There was nothing left in him to expel. Another of their neighbors, a man who smelled of stale tobacco, averted his legs casually.

"What it can do to you," the old woman said, her gums stained crimson from chewing betel leaves. "The ocean."

"Does Child's stomach hurt?" asked Mai.

"Yes."

"What it can steal from you and never give back. My husband, both my daughters."

"It's just a stomachache," said Quyen, then looked up as though daring the old woman—or anyone—to disagree. A gang of eyes, unmoving, inexpressive, watched them from the shadows.

That evening, Anh Phuoc ladled out the last rations of water. He shuffled wearily through the boat, repeating the same account to anyone who stopped him, intoning his interlocutors' names as though that were the only consolation left him to offer them. Weak moans and thick silences trailed him.

When Mai poured her ration into Truong's cup, Quyen frowned, and then flinched away. "Thank you," she said at last. For the first time she used the word for "younger sister."

"It's nothing. I already took a sip."

"Poor child," repeated the old woman, shaking her head.

Truong took some water in, then coughed some of it out. People looked over. In the dusk light his face was pallid and shiny.

He opened his mouth. "Ma," he said.

"I'm here," said Quyen.

"Ma."

Quyen bit her lips, wiped the sweat from Truong's brow with a corner of her shirt. Finally his eyes focused and he seemed to look straight at Mai.

"It's so hot," he said.

"*Thoi,*" said Quyen, dabbing above his eyes, around his hairline.

"I want to go up."

"Sleep, my beloved. My little prince. Sleep."

Mai wanted desperately to say something to him—something useful, or comforting—but no words came. She got up to close the hatch door.

The old woman took out a betel leaf and inserted it into the slit of her toothless mouth.

His sickness followed the usual course. Muscle soreness and nausea in the early stages. That evening his blisters began to rise, some of them bleeding pus. He became too weak to swallow water.

In the middle of the night, Mai woke to find Truong half draped over her stomach. His weight on her so light as to be almost imperceptible, as though his body were already nothing more than bones and air. "Everything will be fine," she whispered into the darkness, her thoughts still interlaced with dream, scattered remotely across space and gray sea. Back home she'd slept on the same mat as Loc. Her mother by the opposite wall. She reached down and touched Truong's brow.

He stirred awake.

"Is Child all right?"

"I want to go up."

The skin on his face was hot and moist. Mai lifted her eyes and noticed Quyen, mashed in the shadow of the companionway steps, staring at both of them.

"Take him," she said dully.

Mai found a spot for them by the pilothouse, surrounded by sleeping families. When dawn came, Truong's head slid with a slight thud onto the planking. Half asleep, Mai sought his shoulder, shook it. His body gave no response. She sat up and shook him again. His clothes stiff with dried sweat. Nothing.

"Truong," whispered Mai, feeling the worry build within her. She poked his cheek. It was still warm—thank heavens!—it was still warm. She checked his forehead: hotter than it had been last night. He was boiling up. His breath shallow and short. With agonizing effort she cradled his slight, inert body and bore him up the stairs into the pilothouse.

Anh Phuoc was slumped underneath the tiller, sleeping. Three infants were laid out side by side on the floor, swaddled in rags.

He woke up. "What is it?" He saw Truong in her arms. "Where's Quyen?"

She laid him down. Then she turned to find Quyen.

"Wait." Anh Phuoc got up, surveilled the boat through the windows, then retrieved a flask from behind the bank of gauges. He unscrewed the cap and poured a tiny trickle of water into a cup. "This was for them," he said, gesturing at the motionless babies. "How they've lasted twelve days I don't know." He screwed the flask cap back on and then, with tremendous care, handed her the cup. "But they won't make it either." He paused. "Let me find Quyen."

Truong wouldn't wake up. Mai dipped one finger into the cup, traced it along the inner line of his lips. Once it dried she dipped her finger again, ran it across his lips again. She did this over and over. One time she thought she saw his throat twitch. His face— the burned, blistered skin, its spots and scabs—the deeper she looked, the more his features dissociated from one another until what she looked into, as she tended him, was not a face, but a brown and blasted landscape. Like a slow fire it drew the air from her lungs.

Commotion on deck. Someone shouting. She jolted awake, checked Truong—he was still unconscious, his fever holding. A weird tension suffusing the air. Another death? Mai opened the pilothouse door and asked a nearby woman what was happening.

"They saw whales," the woman said.

"Whales?"

"And then land birds."

It was as though she were sick again, her heart shocked out of its usual rhythm. "Land? They saw land?"

The woman shrugged.

All at once Quyen burst out of the hold, her hair disheveled and her eyes watery and red. She spotted Mai.

"Here!" Mai called out excitedly. "Chi Quyen, here!" She stood on tiptoe and scanned all the horizon she could see. Nothing. She looked again. "Someone said they saw land," she announced aloud. Realizing people were scowling at her, she turned toward Quyen. Too late she caught a new, rough aspect in her eyes. Quyen strode up into Mai's face.

"Where's my son?"

She pushed into the pilothouse. Mai stumbled back, tripping over the doorsill.

Inside, Quyen saw Truong and rushed toward him, lowering her head to his. She emitted a throaty cry and twisted around to face Mai.

"Stay away," she declared. "You've done enough!" Her voice was strained, on the verge of shrillness.

"Chi," gasped Mai.

"I've changed my mind," Quyen went on, the pitch of her words wavering. Her expression was wild, now—cunning. "He's my son! Not yours—mine!"

"*Thoi,*" a man's voice interjected.

Mai spun and saw Anh Phuoc in the doorway.

"What's the matter?"

Quyen glared at him. He waited for her to speak. Finally, her tone gone sullen, she said, "She took my son."

He sighed. "Mai was looking after him."

Quyen stared at him, incredulous, then started laughing. She clamped both hands over her mouth. Then, as though in embarrassment, she dipped her head, nuzzling Truong's chest like an animal. Mai watched it all. The thick, dense knot back behind her temple. Quyen's body shuddered in tight bursts a while, then slowly, hitchingly, it began to calm. It seemed for a moment as though Quyen might never look up again. When she did, her face was utterly blanched of expression.

"Mai wouldn't hurt Truong," said Anh Phuoc tiredly. "She loves him."

Quyen threw him a spent smile. "I know." But she didn't look at Mai. Instead, she turned and again bent over the unconscious shape of her son. That was when she began to cry—silently at first, inside her body, but then, breath by breath, letting out her wail until the whole boat could hear.

He was her shame and yet she loved him. What did that make her? She had conceived him when she was young, and passed him off to her aunt in Da Lat to raise, and then she had gotten married. With the war and all its disturbances, she had never gone back to visit him. Worse, she had never told her husband.

"He would leave me," she told Mai. "He will."

But she couldn't abandon her only son—not to the Communists—not if she could find a way out of the country. Even if he didn't want to leave, and even if he didn't know her. Her aunt had balked and Quyen had been forced to abduct him. She'd been wrong to have him—she knew that—but she'd been even more wrong to give him away. Surely, she thought, she was right to take him with her. Then, when she saw him weakening—then falling sick—she realized that perhaps he was being punished for her shame. Whether he lived or died—perhaps it wasn't for her to decide.

She begged Mai to forgive her.

Mai didn't say anything.

"He doesn't love his own mother," said Quyen.

"That's not true."

Quyen leaned down and unstuck his hair from his forehead, and parted it. They'd moved him back down into the hold, under the companionway stairs, for shade.

Quyen sniffed. "It's fair. What kind of mother watches that happen to her only son—and does nothing?"

"You were sick."

Quyen turned to her with a strange, shy expression, then lowered her gaze.

"I knew you would take care of him," she said.

"Of course."

"No." She looked down at her son's fevered face. "Forgive me. It was more than that. My thoughts were mad." She gave out a noise like a hollow chuckle. "I thought of asking you . . . ," she said. "I

was going to ask you to take him in—to pretend he was your son."
She shook her head in wonderment. "He likes you so much. Yes.
I thought—just until I could tell my husband the truth."

Mai remained quiet, her mind turbulent.

Quyen sniffed again. "*Thoi,*" she declared. "Enough!" Caressing
her forearm—still scored with rope marks from the storm six days
ago—she smiled into the air. "It's my fault."

"Chi."

"Whatever happens to him."

Mai stared down, unsteadily, at the marred, exposed field of
Truong's face.

"You don't have to answer," Quyen continued in her bright voice.
"Whatever happens, I deserve it."

He entered into the worst of it that afternoon, moving fitfully into
and out of sleep. His breath short, irregular. Their neighbors kindly
made some space for him to lie down. When some children came to
visit, Quyen rebuffed them without even looking. Mai sat silently
opposite them, next to the old betel-gummed woman, transfixed by
her friend's intensity.

Then, at the end of the afternoon—after five long hours—Truong's
small body suddenly unclenched and his breath eased. The lines on
his forehead cleared. It seemed, unbelievably, that he had prevailed.

"It's over," Mai said joyfully. "Chi, the fever has broken."

Quyen cradled him in her lap, rocking him lightly. "Yes, yes, yes,
yes," she sighed, "Sleep, my beloved."

His clothes were soaked with sweat. For a fleeting moment, as
Mai saw his face unfastened from its distress, the fantasy crossed
her mind that he was dead. She shook it off. Quyen's hair fell over her
son's face. They both appeared to her strangely now, as if at an increasing remove, as if she were trying to hold them in view through
the stained, swaying window of a bus.

Truong hiccuped, opened his eyes, and rasped, "Ma has some
water?" With an almost inaudible moan Quyen hunched over and
showered his brow with kisses. Outside, the evening was falling, the
last of the light sallow on his skin. After a while Truong gathered his
breath again.

"Ma will sing to Child?"

"Sing for the poor child," said the old woman.

Quyen nodded. She started singing: a Southern lullaby Mai hadn't heard for years, her voice more tender than Mai had imagined it could be.

Truong shook his head weakly. "No—not that one." He made an effort to swallow. "My favorite song."

"Your favorite song," repeated Quyen. She bit her lip, frowning, then swung around mutely, stricken, to Mai.

Mai reached out to stroke Truong's hair. She said, "But Child must sleep, *nha?*" She waited for him to completely shut his eyes. Quyen found her hand and held it. Mai cleared her throat, then, surprised to find her voice even lower, hoarser than Quyen's, she started singing:

> I am the vigil moon that sheds you light
> My soul abides within the Thousand Peaks;
> Where drunk with wine and Long-Tuyen sword you seek
> And slaughter all the leopards of the night.
>
> And in the steps of Gioi Tu, seize Lau-Lan
> And quash the Man-Khe rivers into one.
> You wear the scarlet shadow of the sun:
> And yet your steed is whiter than my palm . . .

Abruptly her voice broke off, then she swallowed, picked up the thread of melody again, and sang it through, her voice as hard as Quyen's face was tender, her voice resolute and unwavering, sang it through to the very end.

The old woman nodded to herself.

The next morning—the morning of their thirteenth day—a couple of the fishermen sighted land. A swell of excitement, like a weak current, ran through the boat. People looked at one another as though for the first time.

"We made it," someone quietly announced, returning from deck. He paused on the companionway, his head silhouetted against the sunlight. In the glare, Mai couldn't make out his face. He said, "We're safe now." The words deep in his throat.

Quyen and Truong were underneath the stairs. Mai had left them to themselves during the night. Now, with those others strong enough, Mai followed the man above deck. Outside, the dawn sun steeped through her as though her body were made of paper. Dizziness overwhelmed her when she saw the half-empty deck—had they

been so depleted? She thought, with an odd pang, of Truong, his incessant counting. Then she saw the prow, teeming with people, all
peering ahead, attitudes stalled in their necks and shoulders. She
made her way forward, then spotted, far ahead, the tiny breakers on
the reefs, and behind those, the white sand like a bared smile. Birds
hanging in midair over the water.

During the night she had come to her decision. Her thoughts starting always with Truong and ending always with her father, upright
in his hospital bed, staring at some invisible situation in front of
him. A street with its lights turned off. She came into morning feeling a bone-deep ache through her body. The boat would land—they
would all land—Mai would write to her family, and wait for them,
and then she would look after Truong as if he were her own child.
The decision dissolved within her, rose up with the force of joy. She
would tell Quyen. She would look after him, completely, uncondi-
tionally, and try not to think about the moment when Quyen might
ask her to stop.

Nearly weightless in her body, Mai descended the companionway.
When she reached the bottom she spun and searched behind the
stairs. There they were. The hold awash with low talk.

"Chi Quyen."

She was about to call out again when she sensed something amiss.
Quyen's back—folded over Truong's sleeping form—it was too stiff.
The posture too awkward.

Mai moved closer. "Chi?" she asked.

Quyen's crouched torso expanded, took in air. Without turning
around she said, "What will I do now?" Her voice brute, flat.

Mai squatted down. Her heart tripping faster and faster, up into her
throat.

Quyen said, "He didn't."

She said, "All night. He wouldn't wake up."

She was wrong, thought Mai. What did she know, thought Mai.
When she'd left last night, Truong had been recovering. He'd been
fine. He'd been asking Mai, over and over, to sing to him. What could
have happened?

Quyen shifted to one side. He was bundled up in a blanket. The
bundle tapered at one end—where his legs must have been. Mai
could see no part of him. How could this be the end of it? She wrung
the heels of her hands into her eyes, as if the fault lay with them.
Then she felt Quyen's face, cool with shock, next to her own, rough
and wet and cool against her knuckles, speaking into her ear. At first

she recoiled from Quyen's touch. What was she saying? She was asking Mai for help. She was asking Mai to help her carry him. It was time, she said. Time, which had distended every moment on the boat—until there had seemed to be no shape to it—seemed now to snap violently shut, crushing all things into this one task. They were standing—when had they gotten up?—then they were kneeling, facing each other over the length of him. Quyen circumspect in her movements, as though loath to take up any more space than her son now needed. She seemed not to see anything she looked at. Together, the two of them brought the bundle aft, through the shifting, silent crowd, past the derrick crane, where a group of the strongest men waited. There the wind turned a corner of the blanket over and revealed the small head, the ash beauty of his face, the new dark slickness of his skin. With a shudder Quyen fell to it and pressed and rubbed her lips against his cheek.

Anh Phuoc, standing with three other men, waited for Quyen to finish before touching her shoulder.

He said, to no one in particular, "We'll make land soon."

As though this were an order, Mai took Quyen's arm and led her the full span of the boat to the prow. Again, the crowd parted for them. They stood together in silence, the spray moistening their faces as they looked forward, focusing all their sight and thought on that blurry peninsula ahead, that impossible place, so that they would not be forced to behold the men at the back of the boat peeling the blanket off, swinging the small body once, twice, three times before letting go, tossing him as far behind the boat as possible so he would be out of sight when the sharks attacked.

The Rabbits
Donald Revell

I.

After the soul of the flood
Let go its dream,
I let go mine.

Outside, the rabbits lived and died
As before, deep in the knowledge
Of stillness safely resting inside
Everything that moves
And in the medieval carpeting of clover.

I've seen apparitions since forever,
Domains I knew I'd someday enter
And never did. As a mourning child,
I marveled. As a bicycle rider, I sped
Through turns that did not bring me home.
The flood let go its dream.
Rabbits lived and died in clover.

II.

How much would you give for one day's happiness?
I love the image of Christ's happiness when,
Still in his swaddling clothes, he reached
To lay his hand upon the pure white rabbit
Mary held in her white hand for him.
The image is Titian's. The day was ending.
What did Christ pay? Today in my garden,
I saw white feathers dangling in a spider's web
In bright sunlight. How much would you give
For one day's wings? My father changed a book
Into a house that flew. He died slow.
I think he wanted me to know that death

Was never mother to anything. Mary
Held a white rabbit in her white hand, knowing
Every child is born abandoned. All pay.

III.

I knew a domain, a bicycle, and Denver.
I knew an abandoned child who was my mother,
Dead now. And so I know that beauty is a foundling,
A bicycle leaned against a disappearing tree.
Never once did I enter that green domain in Denver.
Morning after morning I rode faster and faster;
Always the trees disappeared, and then the house,
In a wink of an eye of a garden, would be gone.
I do not dream about it. There's no need.

In Titian's picture, in the background, a shepherd
Tends to a cluster of lambs. Not one of them
Is half so white as Mary's rabbit. Nor does the Christ child
See them. His hand is a counterweight
To the shepherd's hand. His gaze is a foundling
Abandoned in a disappearing tree.

IV.

Mist white mountain fog and valley fog
Cool spaces
Like those between the letters of the names of stones
But no
I am not thinking of this earth nor seeking
Higher ground
I am watchful in these mists that quiet me
I am
A white gaze into a greater whiteness
Not seeking
Only waiting to see one face with eyes

The smaller of two islands
The smaller of two islands

Eyes of a foundling
Cloudbanks of white clover

V.

A man once wrote a book about a lemon skin,
But I say
Nothing gets written.
Joys are creatures.
There are no books in the soul, only eyes
Meeting at the kitchen window at sunrise.

I make the coffee, and the rabbit watches me.
I rattle cups in the little basin, and he watches.
Something has driven all the predators from the sky.

From two islands,
You could make a city.
I know mine.
In all his life, a man loves only one
And he does not choose it.
Mine is two islands, and I live on the smaller one.

"Make music," the rabbit says.
I cannot.
"Make the hawk's wings fold forever."
I cannot.
I can only tell you, although you are past hearing,
Christ's embrace of the woodlands hereabouts
Drove God out of the trees.

VI. THE VISION OF SAINT EUSTACE

In the antlers of a stag,
Christ on a cross-tree . . .
Have I one, if only one,
Conversion left in me?
My city is too far.
Islands are impossible
Because of empire, because of torturers,
Because not even drunkenness or prayer

Donald Revell

Takes me the very little way
From murder to white clover.
God was driven out of the trees,
Taking shelter in a stag.
Not far, in the parched grass, one rabbit fleeing one dog
Leaps.

Sally Werner

Joanna Scott

TOUCH YOUR FINGERTIP against a bubble. Feel the pop of cold. Cold, clear water squeezed from subterranean stone. Water seeping into the spring, filling the basin, spilling over the mossy slate ledge, flowing with a persistence peculiar to rivers, tumbling across a gentle series of plateaus, over a hillock, and down, down, down, for two hundred and sixty curving miles to the lake.

Here at the source of the Tuskee. Look around. Balance on your knees against the stone rim, cup the water in your hands, and drink.

Splish splash. Brrr. Drip, drip, drip. See the different paw prints pressed in rich mud. Fat muskrat scooting away and back again, wood sparrow bathing in the shallows, carcasses of yesterday's mayflies spinning with the flow. Slugs and worms, snakes and frogs hidden in the muck.

Gurgling source of life. Good, plain water bubbling up out of the earth, widening into a lazy meadow stream, gathering depth and momentum along its descent. Clear current stirring silt into a dusky brown, stirring brown into a frothy yellow, eroding stone, cascading over precipices, deepening glacial moraines, powering turbines and generators, filling irrigation ditches, flowing past fields and houses, picking up sewage and chemical waste and runoff from the roads, ripening with a thick luminescence before spilling out into the lake.

Help me!

What was that?

Roar of the falls. Splashing shoals. Raindrops piercing the surface on a cold autumn day. A single spot of foam traveling along the water's surface, disappearing between ripples, sliding forward, splitting and converging in serpentines.

There it goes, there and there.

Have you ever heard the story of the Tuskawali? They were little creatures said to have the faces and hair of humans and the spotted

335

bodies of tadpoles. Hatched deep inside the earth, they squirmed from the molten center, through cracks in the sediment, up into the aquifer, and finally, when they were full grown, they emerged with the fresh water into the spring and swam downriver in search of mates. The natives believed them to be the sacred incarnations of fate, begot in the underworld for the sole purpose of multiplying possibility in the world. Their goodwill could be cultivated simply by being left alone.

The early explorers at first dismissed the natives' accounts of the Tuskawali as superstition. Then they saw several of the minute creatures circling in the clear water of the spring, gliding just below the surface. They saw dappled clouds of Tuskawali swimming at the edge of the meadow, where the stream deepened before descending down the mountain. They even saw one stretched on a rock, soaking in the sun. The creatures were too swift to catch with bare hands, so the men used sieves and fine-woven nets, scooping up the Tuskawali by the dozens. They dumped the tiny captives into bottles filled with river water, packed them in crates, and carried them east, to be loaded onto ships and sent back to England.

Invariably, the Tuskawali died either during the journey to the coast or on board the ships. The men hoped to bring home the strange carcasses, if nothing else, as proof of their existence. But the bodies floating belly-up inside the bottles disintegrated into a silt that within minutes became transparent. And then, of the twelve ships that transported the bottles, two went down in North Atlantic storms, four were sunk by Spanish frigates off the Azores, four others lost their cargo to fire in Southampton harbor, and one sailed off course, disappearing into the frozen waters of the Arctic. Only a few bottles actually made it into the hands of scientists at the Royal Society, who tested the water with all the means available to them at the time and found no impurities beyond a slightly elevated level of phosphorus. And as for the handful of eyewitnesses who had returned to England alive, their reports were all dismissed as hoaxes.

The Tuskee River flows north across the state border, through the Southern Tier and up into Canton Lake. Its source is on the edge of a cornfield in the highlands of the Endless Mountains, the spring where the Tuskawali were said to have come out of the earth. After the natives were driven from the region and before the tractors made the high slopes accessible to farmers, the forest undergrowth grew so dense and the outflow so thick with swamp grass that the exact location of the spring was forgotten—until the night in 1947 when a sixteen-year-old girl left her newborn infant on the kitchen table of her parents' home and ran away.

Splish splash, halluah, halluah. Where was she? Oh buddy, weren't they in trouble now.

If only she had a buddy.

Or a blanket to keep her warm.

Or soap. She'd give her little toe for a bar of Liggett's perfumed soap. And for such a sacrifice she deserved a piece of milk chocolate as well, along with a guarantee that she'd never again go through what she'd just been through.

But with water, this good, fresh, pure spring water bubbling like happiness, she'd do all right. She didn't need nobody. Anybody, rather. She knew her grammar well enough to get by. *The cock's crow came with dawn.* Until she went to work for the Jensons, she'd had Miss Krumbaldorf for three-quarters of fifth grade. Miss Krumbaldorf with her narrow shoulders and string-blonde hair and freckled nose: she was perfect and devoted herself to teaching students everything they needed to know so that when the time came, they could decide how best to make use of their God-given talents.

Was it because of Miss Krumbaldorf that Sally made the irreversible decision to leave her newborn son for her family to raise and run away from the world? If only the world weren't so darn big. Everywhere you go, there it is.

And just when you think you've had enough, you find a quiet place where the clear, cold water comes bubbling out of the earth. That's nice. And look at all the wild strawberries peeking out from behind their leafy curtains—enough to fill two buckets!

The afternoon sun offering a healing warmth. A wood thrush piping its three-note trill. If she weren't so all alone at this, the second beginning of her life, she'd have to consider herself blessed.

The first documented reference to Sally Werner is her birth certificate issued by the Peterkin county clerk in August of 1930. Her name appears once more on a list of children who in their twelfth year were welcomed as full members of the Good Shepherd Calvary Church, having been successfully *baptized in the Spirit*. But there are no surviving photographs of Sally as a child. She's absent from the family albums. Of her siblings, only her sister Trudy would ever look for her after she left home.

Her parents, German immigrants from the village of Utilspur in the Black Forest, settled near the father's brother on the outskirts of Turnersville in the Peterkin Valley. Shortly after their arrival, they joined a Baptist church, and their devotion to their newfound faith quickly became the center of their lives. The father, Dietrich Werner, was appointed an elder, while the mother, Gertrude, led the Bible study group. Sally was their first daughter and their second child of seven. Somehow they managed to grow corn and winter wheat on their forty acres of stony land. They kept a small herd of dairy cows, and they sold Gertrude's homemade jam at a roadside stand.

An outbreak of polio in 1939 would take the life of their youngest daughter, Anna, and leave another daughter, Trudy, dependent upon a leg brace for the rest of her life. Dietrich and Gertrude Werner interpreted this loss as God's angry call for a show of stronger faith. And as anti-German sentiment spread with the escalation of the war abroad, they felt an increasing need to prove themselves patriotic Americans. They stopped speaking German even between themselves, and they spent less time running the farm and more time with their religious duties in town. They hardly noticed as their crop yield steadily decreased.

To help support the family, the oldest son, Loden, went to work for the local lumber company when he was fourteen. Thirty years later, he'd still be working for the same company, along with his two brothers. At the age of twelve, Sally was sent to the neighboring farm to help with housework and care for the young Jenson twins. For the next four years she was paid with room and board and a weekly allotment of sausages, which she brought home to her parents on Sunday mornings before church.

It was during a church picnic one August when her older cousin Daniel offered her a ride on his new motorcycle. He was twenty-three. He'd come back from the war blind in one eye. Though he'd been a timid boy, slight and pale, who had always kept out of the way at family gatherings, as a wounded veteran he'd gained a special status among his relatives, and he was allowed to follow his own set of rules. He'd started smoking hand-rolled cigarettes and drinking from bottles tucked in paper sacks. He worked only part-time as a clerk in a grocery store. No one knew how he came up with the money to buy a motorcycle. He was the type to keep his thoughts to himself, and Sally, who'd been watching him with interest from a distance, sizing him up and trying to get a better look at his damaged eye, was surprised when he offered her a ride.

She knew what her parents would have said if she'd asked them for permission to take a ride with Daniel. So she didn't ask them. She just snuck away from the picnic and met him on the dirt road behind the Jensons' barn. She hiked up her skirt, swinging her leg up and over the seat, mounting the bike as if she were mounting the Jensons' paint pony, and grabbed Daniel around the waist as he gunned the engine.

It was great fun riding back behind the reservoir and along the road that crossed a lower ridge of Thistle Mountain. Daniel made that bike go so fast that Sally's hat went flying, and when she screamed he just went faster.

Faster along the mountain's southern slope, faster along the zigzagging road, their bodies leaning together one way and then the other, down along the dirt road behind the junkyard, down through Stockhams Woods, careening into a field Sally had never seen before, bumping up and over a grassy mount so fast that the front wheel actually left the dirt road and they seemed to float suspended in the air, then dropped abruptly, slowed, and finally rattled to a halt in the middle of nowhere.

Crazy one-eyed Daniel—when did you get so wild? You who would only ever eat your potatoes mashed, never fried or boiled. And always adding sugar to lemonade that was already sweet. You were changed by the war, along with the rest of the world. Because of the war, people now knew what could happen. But as Father Ludwig of the Good Shepherd Calvary Church liked to say: *knoving eez nawt veezdom.*

Daniel, lacking in *veezdom*, urged, "Come on, Sally."

"Where to?"

"Let's just have a walk around."

They walked for a while along the path that grew narrower toward the end of the meadow, the brambles scratching Sally's legs, closing in, until the path faded to nothing, there was no dirt left to see, the sun was low in the sky, and it was time to get back home. But Daniel wasn't ready to go back home. Daniel had a confession to make: all this time—

"What time?"

"Forever."

For forever, he'd known that Sally had special feelings for him. The way she looked at him. Her smile. Gee, when she smiled at him, it was all he could do not to—

339

What was he trying to tell her?

Though she should have known better, she couldn't help but grin. That was her habit. Grinning Sally, who by then had a reputation for being able to charm all the youth of Turnersville. As it turned out, she'd unintentionally charmed her cousin Daniel.

What a silly boy he was!

Such a darling girl—why, he absolutely had to kiss her!

He pressed so hard against her that she tripped and fell beneath him. She instinctively grabbed him as she went down, which he seemed to take as proof that she wanted him just as much as he wanted her. And while he tickled her and made her shriek with laugher, she did want him enough to tickle him back. His good eye sparkled; his bad eye stared at a skewed angle and was veiled with a pearly film. What a strange and fascinating fellow! No matter that he was her cousin—that was part of the fun of it. It felt right and natural to be misbehaving. That's all they were doing. Misbehaving in the way that can't be helped when you're young and full of life and out of your parents' sight. Until Daniel went too far, and by the time Sally realized what was happening, she couldn't bring herself to try to stop him.

Doesn't it feel good, Sally? Doesn't it, doesn't it? He loved her and he couldn't help loving her.

It was over just like that—an action too quickly completed to be undone. And though she could see from the look in his good eye that her cousin really did love her, all Sally could think to say in the cool bitterness that came with an understanding of having failed to protect herself was, "Don't you ever do that to me again, Daniel Werner. Now take me home."

She worked for the Jensons six months more, until her pregnancy was showing too much to be hidden by sweaters. Daniel, desperate to claim his cousin as his wife, made it known that he was the father, but Sally refused to have anything to do with him. She must marry him, her parents told her. She'd rather die, she said. Daniel wrote to Sally, describing the joyful life ahead for them together in long, garbled letters, which she tore up without ever answering him. At home, she worked as hard as she could, shucking, lifting, hauling, boiling berries into jam, and hoping that exhaustion would put an early end to her trouble. She hissed at her mother's admonitions and invited her father's rage with her foul language, feeling with a secret satisfaction the sting of his powerful hand against her ear and then the ringing that she hoped signaled a deeper pain. They couldn't make her marry Daniel Werner against her will. Oh, yes they could. Oh, no they couldn't. Still her belly grew fatter as the snow turned to rain. And then the day came when there was nothing left to do but run away.

Running, running, running up the jagged slope behind the rows of new corn, over the stone wall, through the woods and meadows. Sting of nettles. Gray sky of dawn. Bark of a startled deer. *Don't be afraid, it's only me.* Running, running, running. Baby will have his bottle of warm milk by now and a clean soft diaper to replace the soiled one she'd left on him. *Goodbye, baby.* He'd been alive a whole forty-eight hours, and she hadn't bothered to give him a name yet. She would let her parents name him. They'd name him Moses. No, they wouldn't. They'd name him something shameful—Job or Ishmael or, worst of all, Sal—so he'd never forget his shameful mother.

Running, running, running, because that's what a girl does who has left her baby in a basket on top of the kitchen table, like a pile of fresh-baked biscuits. And all the while listening for the sound of voices filling the empty air, calling her to come back.

Sally!

O Lord our governor, whose glory is in all the world.

Where's Sally?

Has anyone seen our wretched Sally?

Look what she forgot to take along with her!

And who's surprised?

Almighty and everlasting God, from whom cometh every good and perfect gift.

Laura, check the attic. Loden, check the cellar. Clem, ride over to the Jenson place, see what they know. Tru, watch Willy. And the baby.

Sally isn't here.

Sally's gone away.

Bad Sally. Doomed Sally. The flesh lusteth against the Spirit, and the Spirit against the flesh.

Give unto us the increase of faith, despite—

A mouth of cursing, deceit, and fraud. Tush, she said with vanity, I shall never be cast down. And look what happened.

341

Where's Sally?
Sally's gone away.

Is that her name carried on the wind? *Shhh*, says the breeze moving through the meadow. Don't speak. The world will watch in silence as she runs, the sky empty of consolation. No one is calling. They've already given up on her.

But still she runs. Running, running, running. How many lives start over this way, by putting one foot in front of the other?

Bad Sally will come to a bad end—that's what they'd been saying ever since her cousin taught her about love. While other Turnersville girls her age were finishing their schooling and looking forward to marriage, she was—

—running, running, running.

Not from sin, not from judgment, not from responsibility, not from her brothers and sisters, her parents, her newborn son, or the judgment of the Lord.

Dear Cousin, I'm running, running, running away just to break your goddamn heart. Such is the letter Sally Werner would have written, if she'd had a pen and paper.

In this corner of the world hidden from prying eyes, in the grainy light of dusk, on a June evening in her sixteenth year, Sally knelt at the mossy edge of the spring, cupped her hand to hold the fresh water, and drank her fill. The water was as cold as ice. Colder. She ate those sour strawberries by the handful, and then, in the darkness, she made a soft bed from dry pine needles and slept. She slept for one hundred years. And she woke to a whole different life.

How was it different?
It was raining.
Oh.

A soft, soaking rain fell all day. It was the kind of rain that washed away caked mud from fingers, blood smears from a sanitary pad, and dirt from the soul. She sat beneath a rocky ledge beside the spring and waited for the rain to stop. Late in the afternoon, she was as bad a girl as ever.

Bad Sally.
That's her.

In ancient times the oracle would have predicted a bad end. But there are no oracles in the modern world. There are only fears and hopes.

And hunger. Dear Jesus, she was so damn hungry she was ready to eat her shoe.

But still she sat there below the dripping shale, feeling cold through to her bones and furious at everyone she could think of—God, her family, Miss Krumbaldorf, the Jensons, the men who started the war, the German soldier who threw the grenade that sent shrapnel into Daniel's eye, and of course Daniel Werner himself, who couldn't see straight enough to know that he would never convince the cousin he loved to love him back.

Dripping, bubbling water. It was early in the month, not yet summer, and with the rain the temperature was dropping steadily. There could be frost in the morning. She'd freeze to death if she didn't do something besides sit there watching raindrops disappear into the spring, the bubbles pop, the foam swirl, and—why, look at that sneaky little worm slipping out from beneath the lip of stone, sliding soundlessly into the water. Just a slimy gray newt with yellow spots. Yet in the tension of her loneliness, it was more than that.

She stared at the surface, trying to catch sight of the creature as it swam away. At first she didn't see it moving in the water. Then she saw the tiny snout sticking out above the surface, the black beads of its eyes locking with hers as though challenging her to imagine the potential for conversation.

What else was there to do but say hello?

At the sound of her voice, the newt pulled itself under water with a jerk, leaving only a single circle where its snout had been. As the faint ripple widened, Sally caught sight of thready brown hair trailing below the surface, hardly more than a shadowy blur in the water. And were those arms stretched out, along with the flickering motion of tiny hands paddling through water? There and gone, leaving enough of an impression for Sally to wonder about what she'd just seen.

But wonder doesn't last long when a belly is rumbling its complaints. Sally had never heard the legend of the magical Tuskawali and didn't want to have to figure out how to make sense of what she'd seen. Why, a newt was just a newt! Forget about it. More importantly, the spring was a vessel of stone and mud spilling water in a constant stream. The water moved through the narrow channel and toward the meadow as if on a single-minded mission, going on its way with a certainty that Sally envied. Where, she wondered, was it heading? Where would it lead?

She couldn't begin to guess the answer. Her parents' farm was at the bottom of the east side of Thistle Mountain. Here on a distant western plateau, the stream meandered through the meadow and then bent toward the slope. She'd never been on the west slope of the mountain before. She'd never been farther than the field behind the junkyard where one Sunday afternoon she'd lain with her cousin Daniel.

As soon as the drizzle had lightened to a warm mist and before the sun had sunk behind the far ridge of pines, Sally Werner set out walking, following the bank of the meadow stream, descending through the forest as the stream widened into a stony creek and fell over mossy granite shelves. The creek would lead her to her destiny, or at least that's what she wanted to believe. The flowing water was the next best thing to an arrow mounted on a sign with her name on it.

This way, Sally Werner.

A girl in a plaid sheath dress and saddle shoes just walking along, stepping over roots stretched across the ground like knobby fingers, squinting against clouds of black flies, hoping that she was heading in the right direction, with a destination that would include a hot turkey dinner, walking to the rhythm of the ballad she was making up to tell the story of her life.

Mother, daughter, sister, lover.
Wretched Sally Werner.
And then what?
Then she disappears down the mountainside.
Quick, come say goodbye to Sally.
Goodbye, Sally.
But she's already gone.

From Fire Exit
Robert Kelly

How could I miss you I've been right here with myself
and missing is a devious art
one that needs its Aeschylus

(frantic raptures of abandonment tu me manques
always too polite to specify)
whose poetry would be a vast forgetting

a machine forever waiting to be installed
is the sweetest morning dear Proust
what language does this day speak

let it be a cleaner lingo
hidden from the dynast who rules over us
but I am not permitted by my ragione

reason to doubt his right to do so
though I would unseat him if I can
to everyone a Rocinante of one's own

or change my name
I never liked me anyhow
get on a bus to Annapolis

plenty of hot water and Coke for breakfast
left-handed government
pallid sailboats stand out in mist

but not today, only sun sheen
only the glue that keeps us thinking
insert here from Coleridge

Robert Kelly

I suppose we would call that thinking
all by yourself in the dubious hotel
while waves crash unobserved on rocks

one morning she was gone
and all the rest was thinking
lots to think about in a white wood wall

and in disorder something more
an urgent Christian 'burn
only in your heart, leave

the stake to those who believe in the state,
banish martyrdom,' jihad
is a massacre within,

as if there were a way to do it
overtake the wind and freeze the rainbow
hold everything in mind

keep balance, halte Maaß
said Dürer, keep the measure,
understand divine proportion in your hand

Saturn in Libra, perspectiva
artificialis, a cherry bomb
goes off on Barrytown dock

thirty years back and it remembers
but who was the girl in the car with him
remember just the hum of the refrigerator car

left all night on the railroad siding
idling, but who was the woman
and the river and who is the moon.

*

We change the lines but it cannot change,
starbeam trapped forever in our amber
{star} put there as an easy sign

so the knowers know and the doers forget
and both be darkened by a random thought
the same pretty little cloud, nuvoletta,

star and heart must rhyme in some language
the mark on the wall that means
a movement in your soft mouth

a sound in the cave—
apposition they taught: to set
two or more words in balance

so each casts its glow and shadow on the other
arid though the space around the signs but not between,
the between of anything is the loveliest tune.

*

No action in the Achaean fleet assembled
even killing has to wait for night
uneasy shepherds grumbling at their sheep

this is no place for an animal
a man with eyes
something is about to begin to begin

the World Cup of Waiting with no referees
arms spread to catch
a living noise from the sky

old women wore veils when I grew up
matrons' eyes behind violet organdy
gauzy with little flecks of flowers

a line looped round the light
then they wore nylons to vanish and reveal the ordinary
always had to coat their presences

Robert Kelly

or else they'd overwhelm us
but not tonight
too many islands in this world

sometimes things are done and never know it
a court hand engrossing a charter
all good comes from the queen

to her I recommend this rubble
comely pebbles on a midnight ocean
lit only by the intelligence

the dark pain that can't help seeing—
and it is only that special pain that sees
only the pain that understands the door

and the little boy who watched the fire exit
all through the movie and understood
that led to the real mystery

the thing outside the theater
on the other side of all this art
but you could only get there through this confusion

there, waiting for him out there,
a thing in a world of things
a thing is patient,

often they told him about heaven
he guessed it was a place
where understanding was,

they knew the answers and they told you
and you saw the back side of the moon.
But what if the dead are as dull as the living

what if nobody knows?
What if there's nothing really there
and you have to make it up new every time

or bring it with you
knowledge squeezed through confusion
like a child being born into this world

and there it would be in the other
a gasping knowledge full of pain and relief
licked into shape by a weird (that is, fated) geology

where stones are soft again
and cool fire plays around your hips
and it turns out it isn't about knowing at all

it's about saying
and sound by sound making it so
into real place

a poem is a ouija board without the wood
it shows you where you want to go
the sea is no color but the sky

try it drink it all down
and see what colors are left
words are always looking for silence

a text always in love with the end of itself
gnomic palaver, meat on your plate
then forget theory, Nietzsche is just mustard now

changes the taste of what you think
just enough to make you think he thought it
the Crucified, the one with powerful ideas

until he sang, music
is no way to please the Muses
or only one way and watch the waiter move

and the hostess perched behind the reservation book
and TV crews devouring this same stew
we thought was our food our life our destiny

Robert Kelly

we have no destiny
we only have what we found in a book
the taste in someone else's mouth

when we say I love you and they say nothing
and what is there for music to say
the philosopher collapsed in the street

the philosopher endured a restriction in discourse
we do not know the words he said in that condition
sun and moon go hide and seek

you grow up part of a time machine
we're at the stage where only kindness helps
publish it not in the streets of Askelon

no one listens to the silence in the heart
whose sound is it, one thing can save us
us us always you're talking talking

there is no us, that's the problem
if there were us we would be living at this hour
not this rain of flies on Pershing Square.

Refugees
Matthew Hamity

MY MOTHER KEPT JARS OF moondust in the kitchen cabinet, replenishing the stock after each lunar mission. She would be gone for months at a time and my uncle, who was also an astronaut, would stay with my brother and me. When she returned, she would mumble hello and escape with a jar to her bedroom.

Hours later, when she finally emerged, the jar empty, her nails white with dust, she would say, 642, or she'd say, 998, or 1201, always with great sadness in her voice, the greater the number, the greater the sadness, counting the days that stood between her and the next encounter with the moon. On the rare occasion that she cooked, the dust would inevitably end up in our soup. If I complained, she would declare that moondust, like tofu, takes on the taste of whatever it's cooked with. Close your eyes and slurp, she'd say.

I came to anticipate my mother's moonward journeys as much as she did. The second she stepped out the door, I'd go into my room and open the window by my bed. I would stare out at the sky and wait for night. As the sky turned gray-black, I would place my thumb and forefinger at each of the lunar poles and bring them together, squashing the moon along with my mother and grinding them both into a fine dust. It didn't matter that she wasn't on the moon just yet, that she would still be busy conducting microgravity experiments on the forty-six-and-a-half-hour translunar flight, experiments like GRASS (Gravitational Rising Archetypal Semiconductors Special) and VICKS (Visuo-motor Independent Coordination Kinetics Special), which she said would someday lead to new treatments for sleep disorders, and the way she said it, you'd think sleep disorders were the gravest problem in the world. I couldn't wait for the next moon to appear so I could squash her again.

But just a few nights later, after another of my uncle's bawdy tales (all of them revolved around Yury Gagarin, the first astronaut to complete an orbital space flight mission, a minor feat, my uncle said, compared to Yury's organizing and participating in the first ever interplanetary orgy), my anger would yield to the moon's magnetic power, and I would go back to my room and tip my head out the window, opening my mouth as wide as I could, waiting for some of the fat white light to drip down on my tongue. I wanted to fill up on moonlight, and during those moments, I believed that I could. I believed I could love the moon and that it would love me back. I believed I could be happy. Who needs a mother? Who needs her?

My father had left when I was small and pink, when my brother was still fetal. We never saw him again. That made my mother one of two single parents in the entire National Manned Lunar Missions Agency. (A renegade group, the NMLMA was founded twenty-seven years ago in Dallas by eight astronauts, my mother and uncle among them, who were displeased with NASA's moratorium on lunar missions. They were also unhappy with the increasing number of unmanned robot space missions. At the beginning of each year, the NMLMA, now ninety-two strong, builds a robot only to explode it.) The other single mother was Rita Betts, but Rita had a billionaire ex-husband (the divorce settlement had gotten the NMLMA off the ground and the alimony helped keep it afloat) and a live-in who did all the housework and took care of her three kids. Rita used to brag that she had never changed a diaper, that she didn't even know what her kids' shit smelled like, so my mother said Rita didn't really count. But my mother only barely eclipsed Rita's maternal performance. I can still remember watching her change my brother's diaper, her hands quick and rough, like she was patching a leaky field joint. Of course there was no time for baby powder.

As if relations between the moon and me weren't complicated enough by a negligent astronaut mother, when I was eleven years old, my uncle died in the lunar plains. According to Darla Meltzer, one of my uncle's paramours, he'd begun to lose it after six hours and thirty-two minutes of moonwalking (this was corroborated in the official NMLMA antiliability report by Sal Creech and Nelly Fordoon). He'd blathered that, living much of their lives beyond the protective shield of the earth's atmosphere, they were all a hundred times more likely to get cancer than the Joe Earthbounds and Jenny Leadfoots. He said he was scared of dying, that no one fucks a dead man. He'd laid down in the smallest crater he could find, his head in the center, his feet at the lip, his body a perfect crateral radius, and demanded that someone bash his skull in with a phosphorous rock he'd been holding tight all morning (Fordoon and Creech claimed the rock was shaped like a woman's face). I can't live with this fear of death any longer, he'd said. He'd begun to cry and wouldn't stop until finally, Robert McKenzie, who had never liked my uncle because he suspected him of sexing his wife while Robert had been at the bottom of the ocean testing moonwalking techniques, obliged.

I was angry. First the moon had stolen my mother's affections; now it sat idly by while my uncle was destroyed. I needed my uncle around because he'd been a reliable source of the carnal knowledge my mother denied me. Since the second grade (because my mother was single, we didn't have the money for the tiny private NMLMA school the rest of the astronauts' children attended), I had been able to impress the other kids with his stories, substituting Yury Gagarin's name with that of Mr. Sellis, the principal, but now, with my uncle gone, I ran out of juicy details and soon became a favorite target of the middle-school bullies. They called me Astroglide, told me to suck their astronuts, broke my nose. My brother said I should stop wearing my waning gibbous moon sweatshirt. He had me try on some of his sports clothes, but, looking in the mirror, I felt like an impostor. Even in his Minnesota North Stars jersey.

After my uncle's death, I would not look at the moon directly. I treated it like the sun. If I went out at night, I wore a visor. I applied sunscreen after sunset. I complained of how the moonlight sapped all my energy. But when almost two years had passed and exactly 719 moons, I grew unbearably lonely, and on a particularly clear night, I caved, ogling the huge pockmarked face. I could almost feel the moon pulling me toward it, could almost feel its gravity. But the earth kept dragging me down with its own force. This was also the night that I noticed my first armpit hair.

Pubescing, I saw my uncle's demise in a whole new light. It now seemed a romantic idea, being murdered on the moon, erotic even. (I asked my mother whether she'd ever considered masturbating on the moon and she raged at me to mind my own business. She had been forced into early retirement the month before because her eyesight had declined below the 20/150 minimum for uncorrected vision. She'd tried and failed to get the rule repealed by the NMLCFQM, or National Manned Lunar Committee on Flight Qualifications and Manners. It was cruel of me to ask her about the moon, not to mention masturbation, given her emotional state. She would wander the house muttering that she could see 20/20 with her contacts so what the fuck did her uncorrected vision matter. She had run out of jars of moondust.) But I didn't want my skull bashed in like my uncle's. I wished to be choked, preferably by a lady astronaut, preferably by a lady astronaut with small palms and longish fingers, though not to death, of course. Just enough to scare me into loving life.

Sadly, I am not an astronaut. I have the low cholesterol, the hawkish vision, the degree in engineering, a thoroughly annotated copy of the NMLCFQM handbook (I can recite the following passages by heart: "Long Hair," "Group Prayer," "The Dangers of Nail Clippings in Microgravity," "Hogging the Window," "Fair Fights," "The Joys of Smoking in Microgravity almost Outweigh the Dangers," "NASA Jokes"), over three hundred hours of flight simulator experience, and inherited astronaut blood. It was my emotional volatility that kept me out (the psychiatric tests had gotten more thorough since my uncle's death). My mother said that it was not entirely my fault, arguing that the move toward diversity in space was partly to blame. (She'd been suffering occasional flashes of racism, and I must admit that her hatred of others made her indifference toward me more palatable by comparison. She still blames the sole black guy on the NMLCFQM for the rejection of her appeal, though the vote was unanimous.)

Now I would never fulfill my fantasy of near-suffocation on the moon, nor would I ever dip my bare feet in the Mare Spumans, as my mother and my uncle had done on their first lunar missions. My uncle used to say that love on the moon was bound by one-sixth the gravity and one-sixth the bullshit. And I knew that he was right. I could feel it in my cheerless earthly bones.

I was still living at home, watching my mother sulk. I began to wonder if perhaps I'd been too hard on her. After all, I knew better than anyone just how seductive the glow of the moon could be. Plus, she was letting me live at home free of charge, the two of us surviving on her modest severance package. I decided I would try to join our depressions (my mother insisted on calling it her decompression), but I found it impossible, since all she wanted to do was watch *Star Trek* and pretend to make fun of it, when, clearly, she liked the show, couldn't get enough.

I feared the weight of my body might overwhelm me, each heavy step a reminder of all that I would never know. Even Sal Creech, the fattest astronaut in the program, knew a lightness of being I never would.

If it hadn't been for my girlfriend, I don't know what I would have done.

She wasn't really my girlfriend. More like a girl who worked at the Save-Way Grocery as a butcher and made my loins stir. I liked the way she sliced the meats, how tender she was with the loins, how the violence came slow. She seemed to feel their pain. I half expected her to scream out in writhing animal hysterics, giving everyone gooseflesh, even the elderly customers, with their dying ears and skin. But she never made a sound.

Steadily changing were the beliefs that had previously propelled me through life: when my mother loves me, I will finally be happy, had become, When I am on the moon, I will finally be happy, had, for thirteen alcoholic hours, become, When I am dead, I will finally be happy, had become, When I know the love of a woman, I will finally be happy.

Several weeks after the official rejection notice arrived in the mail (Dear Mr. Moynahan, We are sorry to inform you that, after much deliberation, we have reached the conclusion that you are unfit for the NMLMA. We appreciate your interest in the agency and hope you find happiness here on earth where you belong. Sincerely, Doug Trebble, AdMISSIONS Board Chairman P.S. Enclosed are eight pack-ets of complimentary address labels, each with a different phase of the moon. If you derive some enjoyment from the labels, please feel free to send a donation.), I built up the courage to speak with the butcher.

She was weighing some venison when I said I could take her to the moon.

I don't get high, she said.

No, I mean the actual moon. On my rocket.

Yeah, right, she said.

I showed her the key.

Intuiting my imminent rejection from the agency, I'd had a copy made of the key to the simulator weeks earlier. It looked like any other key, except that the words SIMULATOR KEY were engraved on both sides. I paid the locksmith triple to keep his mouth shut.

It says simulator key, she said, turning the key over in one blood-stained glove. Not rocket key.

Well yes, I said, that's true, but the simulator has its advantages. No one has ever died on the simulator. Also, if you have to go to the bathroom, you don't have to strap yourself into a harness.

I don't know, she said.

Don't you ever get lonely? I asked.

How could I, she said, when I've got all this to keep me company? She motioned toward the meat in the display window, big red hunks splintered white with fat.

I didn't know what to say. Luckily, she began to laugh. Of course I get lonely, she said.

Then come with me.

You're with those moon people, the NALM or whatever?

No. I'm independent. My own man.

So you're not really an astronaut then.

I tried to hide my hurt. In a way, I said, aren't we all astronauts?

I'm a butcher, she said.

OK, maybe I'm not an astronaut—the NMLMA didn't want me, jettisoned me like a Food Stick wrapper—but maybe with you I could be.

How romantic.

Tease if you like, but I'm suffering here. I wake up with hope slipping away. It slips while I sleep. Do you know what that's like? Where you once saw the new moon, you now see nothing but blackness. That's the world I'm living in.

A world filled with only the dullest blades, she said, somber suddenly, gazing down at her cleaver.

So you sympathize.

No, she said, but I've never been in a simulator.

How's this Sunday morning sound?

I happened to know the astronauts would be sleeping in Sunday because they'd been calling my mother all week, trying to convince her to attend one of their parties that Saturday night in Singing Hills. There they'd stay up until sunrise, celebrating the full moon, serenading their Big Girl as they called her, and then they'd sleep it off the next day. I had never been invited, nor would I ever be.

I'll come, she said. But it'll have to be early. I've got to be back by nine for my shift.

I made a vroom sound, misleading her a bit, as the simulator has no engine (nothing moves, shakes, or jostles; the chair you sit upon doesn't even swivel).

A man cleared his throat behind me. Excuse me, he said. Miss? I'd like some corned beef. Excuse me?

Gimme a moment, said the butcher.

W decided on 6:00 a.m. Sunday at the Save-Way (she didn't give her address to strangers). Wear something that breathes well, I said. The simulator doesn't have air-conditioning.

*

The days between my asking her out and Sunday were some of the best I'd had in a long time, rivaling even the sixth day of astronaut training when Guy Jensen had said that my LAT score would make any mother beam.

Anticipation is one of my favorite things—one of the few things I really look forward to. I pictured her naked, of course, and on my lap, while I manned the controls whispering, Tonight's moon is full. Tomorrow's will be fuller.

I stayed away from the grocery. I even refused going to the Snuffer's across the street when my brother invited me there for lunch with his fiancée. (He's a teacher at Robert E. Lee Elementary, not an astronaut, and thus possesses a capacity for solicitude, unlike our mother. She always said he would have made a wonderful astronaut if he weren't so goddamned nice. She said my problem wasn't kindness but lust. She said this with moondust glinting in the hollow of her throat, but I knew better than to point out the hypocrisy.) I stayed away from the grocery because I feared I'd run into the butcher and ruin everything before anything. Already my heart swelled with thoughts of her. Her. I still didn't know her name.

I began to wonder what it might be like to spend the rest of my life with a pronoun. Maybe something like a one-night stand that lasts forever. I'd always felt more alive around strangers (at the movies, I insisted on sitting beside at least one stranger, and did so even when accompanied by my brother and his fiancée). Now here was my chance to keep that mystery pulsing for all my married life.

Then again, like everything else in the world, it would get old at some point, and eventually, chances were it would drive you crazy, the not knowing. One person goes behind the other's back and does some research, rifles through desk drawers, calls the other's parents. The other retaliates by changing his name. He brags that she will never guess it. On the first try, she guesses right. Isador, she says. Infuriated, he goes down to the courthouse to change it once more and when he comes home, she says, Maurice.

Many days and names later, one of them is dead.

I pulled up to the Save-Way three minutes before six in my mother's Mitsubishi, just as the sun was glancing over Singing Hills. I waited there, imagining all the astronauts belting out a final tune, probably that ridiculous "Moontide's Pulled Me Under and I Ain't Comin' Back" (my uncle would hum it in the bathroom, his farts the bass line).

At five after six, the butcher emerged from behind the building. I got out to open the door for her but she went and sat down on the mechanical horse that my mother used to ride while my brother and I did the shopping. She'd brought her cleaver. She wore a T-shirt tucked tight in her khaki shorts.

It only used to cost a dime, I said, sliding a quarter and a nickel through the slot.

That's what your mom said last night, she quipped, the horse beginning to move up and down beneath her in odd little jerks. The horse was turquoise. She slapped the horse's hard plastic behind.

I looked back at her. You can say whatever you want about my mother. My mother's but a black hole.

The horse was already starting to die, slowly. The ride had always been a rip-off. I stared into the horse's turquoise eyes.

Guess what, she said.

What?

You should be thanking your lucky stars for that black hole. You came out of that hole. Where would you be without that hole?

She dismounted the horse just before it died and got in my car. She tapped the cleaver on the window.

I was afraid and aroused.

I drove aggressively to the simulator because I wanted to impress her, making several unnecessary lane changes, but I don't think she noticed. She was busy playing with the radio, changing my preset stations to all the foreign language ones. I asked her if she spoke Russian and when she said that she didn't, I started translating what the disc jockey was saying. Tomorrow night, we'll be having a big party in Little Moscow. Bring your mothers and your brothers and no others. A good time will be had by all. We will not tell jokes but we will laugh anyway. We will laugh at the old man who is dying and the young woman who is crying and then they will laugh also and that is when the party will really begin.

She shook her head. You've got it all wrong. He said that he found the cure for his unhappiness today. He found it because he finally stopped looking for it.

You're a liar, I said, and she said, I am indeed.

I was ready to pull over and make love but when I suggested it, she just turned up the radio.

The simulator was on the twelfth floor of a white spherical building called the Surrogate that had taken eleven years to construct, the facade a supposedly perfect representation of the moon's surface with each of the craters visible from earth in the correct location and proportion. (Everybody knew it was just a lame copy of the Epcot Center but no one other than me had the nerve to say so. This is not the moon, I said, the moon is the moon. I should not have been so honest. Honesty is not encouraged in the NMLCFQM.) The simulator was old and not really a simulator as the NMLMA didn't have the funds for an actual simulator, using all of their money on the lone rocket and to pay the costs of the lunar missions, not to mention the mortgage on the Surrogate. The NMLMA spent over ten thousand dollars per mission on Food Sticks alone. So the simulator was more like a video game for astronauts, made difficult because you had a half dozen retirees with laptops controlling the action from behind you, their eager breath on your back, constantly staging malfunctions when you least expected them (e.g., loosey-goosey side hatch, congested nose cone, stubborn launch umbilical tube, angry Q-Ball, and good ole-fashioned pad fire). Most of the time, I panicked and then the retirees would start chanting, Haha. Haha. You will never leave this earth. You will never leave this earth. My mother was among them (she was the youngest retiree by thirteen years), and though she chanted louder than the rest, she never looked at me, not even when I said, Mother.

I tried to hold the butcher's hand as we walked up to the entrance. She brushed me off. I tried again and this time she pointed at the cleaver stowed in a leather sheath hanging from her belt.

There was a numeric code that you had to enter to get inside the building. It was supposed to be changed every day, but astronauts are lazy when they're not in space (they resent having to spend any time at all on this crummy planet with the rest of us and hate to be bothered with any sort of earthly toil. Among their own, astronauts do not even call themselves astronauts. They call themselves refugees), and so the code remains the same for weeks on end before someone finally gets around to switching it, and even then, there's a lot of grumbling about why they have to remember so many goddamn numbers when they've got more important things to worry about like planting retroreflectors and atomic beams on the lunar surface and discovering new ways of protecting themselves from sexually transmitted diseases (there's a lot of promiscuity that goes on during the missions due to the close quarters—not enough space in space—and yet condoms aren't allowed on board because of the fear that just having them around will encourage more sex). I punched in the code, 54321, and we were in.

The first floor was really just one room, and a small one at that, on account of the Surrogate being a sphere. I asked her if she wanted to see the stained-glass window that my mother and Nelly Fordoon and Gayle Blevins had painted but she said she didn't have time to dilly-dally. I said that I hoped she had at least a little bit of time and winked. She said I had better take her to the simulator right now or else.

The elevator was in the center of the room and though the stained glass was only ten feet away on the wall of the far side, she wouldn't so much as glance in its direction. She couldn't stand still. She was chewing her cheek and her bottom lip at the same time. Her lip was imprinted with tooth marks. Was she that excited about the simulator? If so, she was in for a letdown. Or maybe she'd seen the love inside me and gotten nervous. It was, after all, a gaping love. It had bored my mother to tears and reduced my brother to a pitying fool who couldn't spend more than a minute around me without asking, Are you sure you're feeling all right? Having had only one serious relationship and a long-distance one at that (a minimum of two hundred twenty-one thousand miles between the moon and me at all times), I had love to burn.

At the center of the stained-glass window was my uncle, in full spacesuit, with a ring-of-Saturn halo over his head. He looked fat, but that was due to the curvature of the window. There were still a couple panels of glass missing (they had never gotten around to completing the memorial though my mother claimed they'd left it that way on purpose to mirror the unfinished life of her brother). As we stood there waiting for the elevator, hot air and mosquitoes passing freely through the missing panels, I told the butcher about my mother and my uncle, how they had never been close, how my mother had said he was just like my father, fucking anything that moved, how it was not until after my uncle died that she began to feel differently. A little death went a long way in smoothing out all the blemishes and the bumps, I said, concealing in the way that only death could. She was finally able to see her brother exactly as she wished and he could no longer muck it all up by existing.

If I died, maybe then would my mother love me, I said.

The butcher muttered something under her breath.

What?

She wouldn't repeat it.

Feeling sorry for yourself is perfectly healthy, I said, guessing at what she might have said. Perfectly healthy.

She grunted and we stepped inside the elevator. I said, This is it. This is the simulator. Up, up, and away we go.

I started thinking that maybe I shouldn't have made that joke, since the simulator was about as entertaining as an elevator. Maybe I could impress her by docking the computerized rocket on the computerized moon station without a hitch now that the retired astronauts would finally be out of the picture. Then again, maybe I knew what I was doing. Maybe I wanted her mad at me.

The twelfth floor was almost halfway to the top of the building, thus making it one of the largest. We walked around and around in circles that got smaller and smaller (the corridors were structured like a flattened pig's tail), passing the ladies' restroom, the minister's quarters, the trampoline, the interrogation room, the cigar emporium, the handicapped bathroom (no one used it, but Texas state law required one), the mediation room, the meditation room, the grieving center, the gentlemen's restroom, until we reached the simulator. I slipped the key in like I was doing something sexual or at least I pictured something along those lines in my mind while I did it. I let her step inside first. Her hair blew upward in a perfect brunet band. She floated higher until her head hit the ceiling. I tried to act unsurprised, like this happened all the time, and casually took a seat by the centermost of the three computer monitors. I didn't bother to turn on the simulator. Instead, I watched her. The patterns on the bottoms of her sneakers were the most beautiful things I'd ever seen.

I was still rooted to the ground.

Take off your shoes, she said. Maybe they're too heavy.

She had a point. My vintage Gagarin boots weighed at least a couple pounds. I took them off and still, nothing.

What are all those switches for? she asked.

It doesn't matter anymore, I said, glancing at the hydroxyl terminated polybutadiene gauge, now that you're up there, so far away.

Stand up on the chair, she said. See if you can reach me.

I had come through on my promise and now she wanted to reward me with proximity. I could feel the love brimming inside me, strong as nausea and just as terrifying. My testicles were tingling, my little

361

planets, as I called them. I imagined us making love with her arms around my neck, choking me, our bodies quivering in the air like branches before a storm, her voice a whisper that slowly bloomed into a shriek: My poor little bird, my unfortunate little bird! Perhaps she'd even let me call her Luna.

I climbed onto the chair and swiped at her foot, grasping it easily. I could have had her knee if I'd tried. I don't want to pull you down, I said.

Don't worry, she said. You won't.

I started clambering up her body, and sure enough, she stayed right where she was, floating. When I reached her waist, I laid my face against her side while she played with my hair. I reached into her shorts.

Hey!

Her shirt came untucked and blew upward, hovering around her chin. There were Band-Aids patched over her side, stretching from her waist to her breast, overlapping, covering every inch.

What happened? I asked.

Nothing.

Come on. You can tell me.

I don't want to.

I pulled on her breasts to hoist myself upward. One of her nipples was hard in my palm, the other was not. Don't you trust me?

How bad do you wanna know? Real bad?

I was trying to get her other nipple hard.

How bad? she repeated.

Bad, I said.

OK then, since you wanna know bad: It was a boating accident. A terrible, horrendous boating accident. My father was drunk and lost control of the boat. It was a huge boat. They had to remove my spleen. How's that?

A boating accident? Is that the truth?

Maybe. Yeah, sure. Whatever floats your boat.

She started laughing.

I want to know the truth, I said.

Oh shut up. You're just horny.

Did your father hurt you?

Big-time. Ripped my spleen right out with his bare hands.

You can joke all you want, but mothers and fathers are serious business. They can ruin us.

You think so?

Our parents brought us into this world, I said, without our permission. That means they owe us. It means we deserve all the love and sanity they can muster.

She shook her head. Guess what.

What, I asked.

By now the soft nipple had hardened and the hard one had gone soft.

You've got it all wrong, she said. Your mother's not the problem. It's your spleen.

My spleen?

That's what's weighing you down.

She unsheathed her cleaver. Her face was full and pale. I stared hard, trying to imagine what her cheeks would look like cratered.

Fine, I said. Go ahead. I've been waiting my whole life for this.

You have, huh? She started rolling up the bottom of my shirt, her fingertips cold. She rolled it up to my armpits. Hold it right there, she said. I'm gonna lighten your load.

The blade shined like a nova. I closed my eyes and clenched my fists.

Five, four, three, two, one, she said, and then, a quick gust of air.

When I came to, I was lying on the floor of the handicapped bathroom. She was cupping water from the sink and splashing it on my face.

I felt lighter. I felt good. Maybe she was right.

Did I float?

Like a stone, she said.

I looked at my stomach. I was still encased in skin, no gaps or tears.

Where's my spleen? I asked.

Same place it's always been.

I felt all over my body like it was someone else's.

Guess I missed, she said, and helped me to my feet.

She had me drive her back to the Save-Way even though it didn't open for another hour and a half. She got out of the car, didn't say goodbye. I drove around the block, wishing my erection would go away, then wishing it wouldn't. When I came back, she was gone. I parked my car in the empty lot and walked the perimeter of the Save-Way looking for her, passing a wayward grocery cart. It might be fun for her to give me a ride, I thought. I could squeeze in with my arms and legs dangling out like a big boy and she could push me until she started to love me or one of the wheels broke.

I found her sitting with her back against a Dumpster, shirt off, head down, cleaver in hand. There were slashes of raised, uneven flesh on her stomach, beneath her heart, where the Band-Aids had been, a bright red webbing of scars.

I watched while she cut herself, drawing the blade across the skin under her ribs, biting down on her lip, the scream still getting through.

When I got home, I called my brother. I asked if he could help me find a job.

Hospice
Thalia Field

just as suddenly it was time to practice dying, a Buddha in slow wave
     sleep
bottomless, weak against the synchronous pull of the stream
(last offering: a meal, then pain
tasted—refused)
mind the mind
walking the last six miles to Kusinaga

She is the most important one, and now she's leaving
He's the most important one and he'll be leaving
          I won't let you!
and the Tathagata gave Ananda
the elephant's look

breathing

not breathing

a body following the eye around

FIRST WATCH OF THE NIGHT

Train for confusion and old age. A bed wired to the wall, and a wall-
mounted TV. Dirty floors and mauve curtains, and waking in another's
bed.

Confusion says reach up, and then bad for reaching up. Confusion says
wake up again.

The bending down and then bad for bending down.

The saying "stand up" and then yelling "no standing!" The saying "sit" and "why are you sitting?" The situation of being in the charge of order, the order for the direction, the overall authority, the otherwise inversion of orders. Write the letter and wait. Why did you write the letter and wait? Don't say anything. Why didn't you say anything? Try to unfold the map and step on it. Wait a few days. I told you to do it the next day. Why did you step on it?

To be host, guest, stranger, enemy, is to derive from the latin *hostis*. A hostile welcome in a house of illness. Hospitality.

543 BC flowers and birds gather in monk's robes. The pains from Cunda's generous meal grab from the gut, and the Tathagata's mind sees pain as pain.

The Tathagata reclines in the lion's posture on his right side, his mind a perfect mirror. Mara enters. Another old age might be less prepared. Mara would like to empty the trash.

Patience.

REM sleep waves turn short and frantic in this bardo's dream-mirror. Guard against views from every line of sight; every hearing already an echo—make the most of it? Is this still a life? Enough world to hang yourself.

Mara offers an open pen.
Books make me feel like it's OK to die, someone says.
But the child makes me afraid. To leave something that needs you? An unfinished book needs me, and makes me afraid. I haven't said what I was saying. Just look at autumn flames in the window. The teacher goes and the teachings go on. After an hour of having nothing to do, I could just blow away. This wind, even a few moments of it, says, "Pass on."

Mara looks around the room and says, "Pass on."
The Tathagata knows Mara's tricks. "No thanks, I'll take three more
   months."
He tells Ananda about his death.
"But how can you die, what will be left?"
The students make haste with truckloads and feasts.

SECOND WATCH

Three months ago she announced, "I'm dying" and birds chipped crumbs from the snow. I will let go at the timely hour, she said. Mara came but I made no claim on self-preservation, no final craving for life. Like an old cart, the body is fastened with weak string and makeshift parts. Be a refuge unto yourself. Eighty years make the body frail. Three months hence the Tathagata will utterly pass away. Mara comes to offer a room. Lunch. Ice water. To seduce the mind to taste the tasteless.

The Tathagata hung his bed in two trees and went for a last drink from the river. In silence, he refused any more food and all other things. His visitors' grief consumed their minds; they tangled their hair and withdrew to the side. Dying is active work. To be born is too. But one can practice being tired of working.

A great earthquake an hour later.

NEXT WATCH

The last characters in the dream are not necessarily significant, but minor characters without many names who wet the lips and adjust the pillow. They lean or stand where others step back, a warm place filled by cooler air, causing a breeze.

When visitors push open the room divider, clocks pause. Blossoms
    drop in winter.
Papers scatter, clearly disordered. Tissues ball up.
Ananda listens to the Tathagata's silence, and the only children sob,
    "We can't lose you."
The ones who have not gone far into the stream worry it's too late.
"How can you not lose me?" the patient asks. Ideas separate and change shape. Practice getting lost in sleep; practice not arguing with dreams.

Thalia Field

FOURTH WATCH OF THE NIGHT

breathing

not-breathing

Make the map from the beginning, from the first rehearsal, a blank
cloth spread from point to point and held in the running edge by the
wind on one side, flapping as we wrestle it to a surface. To paint
the map, the second rehearsal, to train for it, to start with "here" and
work our way outward, to find other references and jot them in, even
with small indicators, a color or house shape, something to remember
and locate it by. So this way we can begin at birth, just as we learn
where food comes from, and the breast, the smile, to map the face we
call family, not just "faces" but the one we remember and want, the
specific face that makes a map possible. From there we move to lines,
edges, the corner of a room. What's inside the room, and what's not,
or the doorway and the lines of the door, leading the eye beyond
the door to a space between lines, possibly a larger house, a small
hospital, or a large forest. Someday the map will tell us if it's small or
large, depending on its scale to the neighborhood and something like
a cultural average. Mapping toys, lunches, the way to school, the
storms—the path gains thick lines, the first to be followed, first lost.

To rehearse everyone as your only child, take a blurred photo. A sick
room. Faded flower patterns—and the bed, table, and wall TV. There
are machines and echoes of machines. Plastic ice bucket. Yellowish
gown. She turns eighty at the calendar's pace. There are waves of
activity, and brains torn off.

Patience; the clear light bardo in the deepest sleep.

The specialist reads the blood and you're not to move.
On the right side, death rests. On the left, blood flows toward birth.
And you become the puppet. And you submit by the throat.
When the signs of dying are full, there is no reason to force. Sit up,
    Madame.
Shaking the body does not return consciousness. Madame, swallow.
We will not lose you when you lose yourself. You give up your feet,
    your voice, your hands.
You give up your plans, your time, your year. And all the photos

which must be labeled. To finish the archive means sorting time.
Machines mediate conversation, you don't have to. Patience,
Madame, can you hear your body talking? Carefully try saying
   nothing.

Dying is diligence. For the elderly, the visitors' tears feel violent, if the
dying is not crying. She announces in English, "There is someone in
the bed and I want to get back in. Help me, I am not in my room, and
this is not my number." She means, can she have her map back?
Dying is not crying. All this hard pain feeds another wolf. The world-
wolf cries when it cannot find its pack.

FIFTH WATCH

The Tathagata's richest disciples cart feast-meats and fruits to the
double doors, but the hospital can't fit them. Stuff piles in the parking
lot and bushes. And the Tathagata remains silent and does not accept
the offerings. The visitors smash their heads and withdraw to sit at
the side. The tiny only child must start there. Babies, you may not
tear up maps. You offer and we, in our dreams, refuse your deaths.
The world-wolves groan. The moment has passed for spiced pastries
and flowers. Once born, fears clutch the babies to offer them. But the
Tathagata in silence refuses the gifts and the visitors flail their arms
and spit and withdraw to sit at the window. The Tathagata's only
children are having such a bad dream they are beside themselves.
Practice dying in sleep or you'll just keep waking up. Birth—he
reminds them—has lost memory too.

I observe the whole scene like a documentarian, she says. I am
curious about this experience and would like to continue to watch it.
How do you know where to turn, driving all these dark roads? Maybe
he lived here before? Yes, but how do you know where you live? A
diaspora of citizens without government or country. And in this I may
still ask questions, mostly of young nurses—their sex lives, and how
they feel about hospital work.

In her shaky hands the visitor sees pictures and letters, handed to
those who find their portraits shocking. I meant to return this to you,
she says, shoving envelopes to the side table where pills roll along
the bedpan. I'm done with the archive, now all I have to do is die.

Half-joking language cut with morphine, a slur. The torment of Dorian Gray, she mumbles, racing a passing thought, wasn't his precious portrait, but that by the end he didn't recognize his own   (story?)
                                                                —sleep

breathing

not-breathing

How long is left? the visitor grabs a doctor turning here and there.
The Sala trees drop their blossoms at the wrong moment.
A recent birth. What do you expect? How can a footprint hold an ocean?
Train in being helpless. Soft foods first. Soft food last. Good teeth in
    between.
Then a sudden feeling of recovery, of something taking place
    beforehand.
Each death a unique work of art; a face in water.

For the first few days she was everyone's favorite patient.

SIXTH WATCH

Then a sudden impression of recovery, talking and eyes and smiles and recovering talking. The visitors sweep the curtain open; a meal with an apple. Then eyes and hands animated, sitting up and swallowing, and even some bites and a few details and a name and a picture glued together. Look, a window beyond the curtains, and warm leaves, and a sky going on. This window that doesn't hold itself open. Speak gently to the window, let it know it's a window and you are some wind. Reassure the wind of the window. Resume training. She begins to falter at the sight of the flowers. Do not distract the dying from dying. Die harder, you might be thinking. Die faster. Hold hands with the dying as recovery vanishes.

breathing

not-breathing

SEVENTH WATCH OF THE NIGHT

Morpheus sleeps a baby's sleep while seas hover, the medicine takes time to work; a new pain across the gut. It's folding in again, nausea as a sudden absence of nausea that loads the room into focus. Relieve the bitter taste or just force more food. Eat against death. There's a food part to every object. Swallow, sit up. Medicine, Madame, one two three. Sit up. Eat the cloth, postpone the book until they change the word order and bring in the life part. In the control stomach, which is outside itself, sits the nausea or rather how patient you can be. A bitter swell, increasing the patient, wires and the rolling floor as she spills on it. Fat tongue in the throat.

Madame, what are you doing over there? The sight of other dead people won't shock. She shouldn't be standing up. Nurse calls in help. Morpheus always playing with shapes.

Do not try to reorient reality for the patient.

Mara has brought some friends.

Mostly, the increase in hospitalization removes the long line to names. Heaving. And adds careless smells of iodine and something in the toilets that never belonged to you. Wind says, "Which way?" An adjustment of medications remains likely. Bloody gums, the death diet and baby diet of mushed foods—the brain works in the dark. The suck reflex encourages a desperate mouth. Organs shut, don't shut up. All in the dark.

Watch your mind as Mara and Morpheus lean close.

breathing

breathing

The word for patient means be-the-baby, or the amorous part you cradled: a growing Narcissus in a forest beyond wits. Host of strangers—Ananda emerges to tell the story. Simple Echo wanders without a self to protect. Patently senseless. Even soft food, forced, hurts the jaw and chokes a "no" to stop everything and everyone from climbing into the bed.

Morpheus opens his archive, the son of sleep, restless in this mess. Mara brings more visitors, and they too become strangers. This is the whole family now, awake in her fitful room. Old and young, it's not easy to tell. We arrive at the scene, a wider river, the peace river through a continent divided by herds. Morphine river with mouth open and a terrible rattling from the relaxing of the larynx.

EIGHTH WATCH

And there is a moment when you are not the patient or near the patient and it is like sanity. And it is rhythm and murder. In the disguise of healing, in the disguise of the labor that is dying, giving birth to more birth, mewing—just do not say unnatural. Why didn't you say unnatural? Guard your mind, its rapid-eye movements. Watch what you can't possibly watch, and mumble greetings that sound like the opposite. Like hearing clinging to the world.

Then open the forest slowly, removing all tree limbs and trailheads. The echo gains strength and has no more to do with you. That's fine, Madame, you would like to know we'll think of your story, even as you push it away. Where will it go? In sleep we enter this vacant reverie—this *hospitium* with dirty floors.

Only to train in the fortress of reflections. Open a window? Peer
    into the stream.
Why did you open the window? It's in the book. It's written right here that there are a lot of pages offered for review. When the manuscript arrives for reading it has lost its voice. Narcissus, stream-crosser, kneeling in mud.

NINTH WATCH

Maybe I'll just be spontaneous, she says, and takes Mara's hand.

breathing

breathing—Oh well, it's too late for that. Do not distract. The hand a cold bone. More visitors come after breakfast and offer everything the patient liked: Magazines. Mints. Apricots. They hold themselves up: "Don't you love us?" The Tathagata refuses the offerings and the visitors cut themselves with knives and withdraw to sit at the side.

Don't scream at the dying. A new nurse comes close, impatient with medicine. Sit up now, *un, deux, trois,* Madame. She has long given up speaking, but responds to the voice like a baby. A voice is love and she responds. Pain is an echoing laughter, Monsieur, please step away. Step close, push down the tongue, finger the throat. Breathing will be a sign that death is close, when it runs wild and then collapses for a long time.

not breathing

not breathing

Accidents dense, as whole organs release and are lost, float off, and harden. Bring them back for a change of sheet, in these loose moments of shit and liquid, that last day's smell that is fuller than anything you've smelled in the past tense, brown and not right. She confesses she would like to die now. Telling it to the window. But now isn't the window and she suffers it.

The Tathagata's bed orients North-South. It's not personal. An earthquake is certain at an unknown moment. No reasonable doubt. The medication will change; the aides and orderlies come in shifts. A baby's monitor goes off and people go running. Fear is all in birth, the gurgling sounds of a newborn. But rattles and blankets—death has the exact same toys. Even sucking a wet cottonball to the lips.

When the outbreath becomes much longer than the inbreath, it won't be long now. Turn the body but not at the very end. Roll the sheet at the sides and lift if you must.

NEXT TO LAST WATCH OF THE NIGHT

Left-lying for the baby. Right-lying for dying. Block the right nostril, head on the right hand. The Tathagata died on his right side. Refused all offerings and a reading: I will not read this out loud and you won't stare at my absence. If you can't agree on my death, I haven't said anything.

There are periods of no breathing, even up to 45 seconds.

The pulse sensor, the beeping lights. Nurses rush over. The baby is startled and shaken awake. Nurses trained in holding and feeding babies do not work with the elderly. Doctors say nothing when asked how close death is. What will happen first? What will happen next? How will we prepare? What are you doing with all that sleep if not practicing not waking?

LAST WATCH OF THE NIGHT

The buildup of waste in the organs, the uncoughable pools. Don't panic now. The machines echo back quotes to the corpse. Characters by the bed see an uneaten lunch. Touch a bite, it won't be touched. The TV-talk makes a joke. I dreamed someone came in to ask how I died, and I asked them to go back out, saying, "I'm working on it."

The Venerable Ananda leans against the doorpost: "I am still a student and have to strive for perfection. But, alas, my teacher, who was so compassionate toward me, is about to pass away!"

Enough, Ananda.

Narcissus wears an old costume, enters the forest, fends off all clinging, all desire projected on him, on his beautiful body. He kneels to quench his thirst but becomes paralyzed in the view of his life, facing a reflection. Raise the head and unpool the mouth. When the body turns waxy and yellow, the blood is already moving away and puddling in bruises underneath. Pass through cold. High fevers. He thinks he hears his reflection speak, but can't understand. He wants so badly to hear himself he won't leave the scene, eventually forsaking food, and even trying to drink disturbs the image, so his lips and tongue itch with thirst. Earth, water, fire, and wind elements dissolve from gross to fine, in order of appearance at birth. At the very last, a tiny amount of blood and sexual fluid, red and white, leaves the body. The subtlest aspects of mind become light. As long as he stares, it's not in Echo's power to speak first. There is no way to be the audience to this performance.

She wants to be sure about the archive. The echoes are just machines. Stop saying the echoes are the world-wolves in pain. The visitors beat their heads and howl and refuse to move to the side. To laugh may be the last dignity, the last world we can share. Ananda enters the tent with the visitors. Manjushri and Ananda describe intense colored lights flowing from the Tathagata's facial orifices. A final display of one who, utterly awake, never wakes again.

TENTH WATCH OF THE NIGHT

And when they hear Ananda's news, the kings and goddesses with their sons, their wives, and the wives of their sons, grieve with their hair madly raised, pounding the ground they roll from side to side, lamenting: "Too soon!"

Hearing that hearing is the last sense to quit the body, the visitors rush to yell at the corpse. Sometimes the dying will wait to be alone to die. Do not confuse the mind. It takes a final permission to stop holding on, one last practice. Holding the breath means it rushes back in, the visitors and their offerings. Out the window starlings gather. Conjured, they fly off.

LAST WATCH OF THE NIGHT

Echo stumbles blindly through the woods, the surprise hallucination, empty open clatter. Narcissus reborn another minute, homeless, animal of a last "I love you." I love you, says the dream.

At a certain point, they're still taking blood samples. But not any more. Winds pass heavily through the head. The stock photo of floral curtains burns away. The props and costumes are sent for disinfecting. After the rush, a doctor takes the pen and slowly signs the paper.

Helplessly, she whispered, "I've lost my glasses"—and the visitors got up to scan beneath the bed, the blankets, even though she couldn't read or see. Chairs scraped the floor in a ritual of searching.

Can you hold an enemy up? Madame, a hand? Can you hold your tongue down, Madame, *allez-y.* Suddenly she's all in English and one two three, Monsieur, stand back. She's not breathing. Madame, sit up. Monsieur, we've got it. Please step back.

She becomes agitated in the lifting. More moaning.

not- breathing

not- breathing

No one finds the glasses that were taken accidentally.

Outside the private room, death stories are as boring as birth stories.

The clock has 12 hours marked around a circle; a tool for teaching.

Hours cause more hours, the minutes, more minutes.

Twelve o'clock is caused by 11 o'clock, and 11 by 10
even 1 o'clock is caused by 12 o'clock and 4 o'clock by 9 o'clock.

Looking away from the clock, at any minute a chance of earthquake. The Tathagata gives his last lesson: "All you know will change and be gone. Train to be lost now."

The little child you love; Paris, birds, food—what isn't finished in the book you want to finish? The moon is full and the month is May.

Rushing to the emergency room, you offer everything to buy a way home.

A mother gives all the only children the elephant's look.

Hearing is the last sense to go.

Day for night and night for day, the hospital rehearses its empty beds.

The Historic Voyage of the *Rosalind*
R*obert* A*ntoni*

ON THE EVENING OF November 2, 1844, the *Rosalind* was at last
ready to depart. Her passenger list included the first thirty-one officially designated "pioneers" of the Tropical Emigration Society, all
gathered at the forecastle rail beneath a clear and starry winter sky
to gaze, perhaps for the last time in their lives, upon the lights of
London flickering farther up the Thames. Suddenly a small, rodent-
like woman appeared, scurrying across the deck. She waved her
arms above her head, screeching hysterically, "*Anschlag! Anschlag!
Anschlag!*" Captain James Damphier, under whose austere command
the ship fell, had already sounded his charge to send the sailors
scrambling toward the bow, and begin the laborious process of weighing in the anchor. He had sung out his third "Heave-ho!" when, with
undisguised irritation, the captain issued a countercommand. He
turned his attention to the woman. But the only way he could get
her to say anything other than "*Anschlag!*" was to have one of the
sailors lower a bucket over the side, and douse her with cold harbor
water. Given that this woman's distinguishing feature was her prominently protruding front teeth, she now bore striking resemblance
to a drenched ship rat. She spit out a mouthful of water, raised her
skirts to her face to dry it off, and muttered, "*Mein Ehemann ist
verschwunden!*" Though a Scotsman by birth, Captain Damphier
could speak a rudimentary German. He countered, "En who, woman, is ye fuckin husband?" At this point it was revealed, with considerable alarm, that although his wife, daughter, and son-in-law
could all be accounted for, Mr. Etzler was not aboard.

This was peculiar, as a number of the passengers had seen him
arrive on the sloop earlier that afternoon with his family. They'd
heard him greet Captain Damphier (who was immediately put off at
being treated as a subordinate), and supervise the off-loading of his
luggage, which—despite all Mr. Etzler's previous claims of needing
nothing more for the tropics than the threads upon his back, and
these "strictly for reasons huff politesse"—was indeed excessive.
No doubt he fully intended to make the voyage with his followers;

377

where he might have disappeared to, at the final moment, and for what conceivable purpose, was a perfect mystery. It could only be surmised that somehow, during all the noise and commesse of making ready for the voyage, Mr. Etzler had slipped unnoticed back ashore.

"Less he's drowned," the captain suggested, producing several gasps from the women. "En aye good riddance, far as I'm concerned!"

Mr. Stollmeyer, who'd removed his coat to spread it around the shoulders of the shivering and still-dripping Mrs. Etzler, now stepped forward, his chest visibly inflated, long beard tousled by the breeze. He informed the captain, in no uncertain terms, that their departure must be suspended until such time as the whereabouts and safety of his comrade, Mr. Etzler, could be ascertained—

"He alone gives meaning to this monumental voyage!" Mr. Stollmeyer stated.

"En his strumpet's sauce-box!" the captain responded, resulting in further gasps from the women.

He turned his back and repeated his command for the sailors to hoist in the anchor.

Fortunately, Mr. Stollmeyer was able to persuade the captain to delay the ship's departure long enough for him to make a quick investigative trip ashore. A small rowboat was therefore lowered over the side, into which Mr. Stollmeyer descended by way of a rope ladder, the loop of a lit lantern clenched between his teeth.

"Ye've three wee hours," Captain Damphier shouted out behind him, already rowing away into dark. "Alterwise ye en *Shitesler* kin swim ye ruddy arses to Trineedad!"

At this pronouncement Mrs. Stollmeyer, with a frightful thump, dropped to the deck in a faint.

The two men returned in the nick of time. Mr. Etzler, at first, dangerously attempting to climb the rope ladder while simultaneously carrying an apparently heavy and obzockee suitcase. A rope net was lowered to the rowboat, into which Captain Damphier instructed him to place his piece of luggage, while Mr. Stollmeyer held high his lantern.

Instead, Mr. Etzler tucked the tail of his beard into his crimson vest, and he climbed into the net, carrying his suitcase. He shouted up to the sailors to hoist him aboard.

"A pestilence upon thy fayther's pestle!" the captain grumbled.

But when Mr. Etzler climbed out of the net, grinning like a bobo-lee and brushing himself off with his free hand, it became apparent that the suitcase was attached by chain and padlock to his left wrist.

378

Those members of the Tropical Emigration Society who'd hurried anxiously back up to the deck for their leader's return quickly identified this case as the one in which he carried his model (and generally *stood* upon during his lectures in order to reach the podium). Though they'd never seen the case chained to his wrist before, and they must have wondered why it had been so necessary for him to delay their departure and return ashore to collect it, since the real, life-sized machine—disassembled in its enormous crate—sat lashed to the deck directly behind them. (There was, of course, no possible way to get it into the hold.) Even those passengers aboard who knew nothing of the society, and were entirely ignorant of Mr. Etzler's inventions, could not have failed to notice this oversized crate with its mysterious markings—

SATELLITE
exclusive property of
J. A. Etzler
on loan to
TES
(all net profits 10%)

Now, still grinning like a bobolee, Mr. Etzler untucked his beard from his vest, and he approached the captain.

"How foolish huff me to leave him behind!" he nodded toward the case attached to his wrist.

And reaching into the breast pocket of his jacket, Mr. Etzler presented Captain Damphier with the following notice—

Finest English Silverware
Of the Highest Quality and Craftsmanship

IMPECCABLY SMITHED IN SHEFFIELD
(and generously donated to the TES)
by:

Charles M. Rake, Esq.
available aboard at special pre-landing prices!!!
(minus all transort fees + tax)

teaspoon—£1,3s.	tea pot—£17,5s.
tablespoon—£1,5s.	creamer—£5,3s.
soupspoon—£1,5s.	sugar bowl—£5,3s.
serving spoon—£1,7s.	tea tray—£7
fork (sm.)—£1,5s.	***tea set (4 pieces!)
fork (lg.)—£1,7s.	—£20
knife (sm.)—£1,5s.	soup tureen & ladle
knife (lg.)—£1,7s.	—£18
fish knife—£1,7s.	
***std. table setting	serving tray (sm.)
(6 pieces!)—£8	—£15,5s.
carving fork—£3	serving tray (lg.)
carving knife—£3	—£17
***carving set—£5,7s.	

(all inquiries see Mr. J. A. Etzler)

The *Rosalind* had been at sea for five days, and Willy had yet to catch a glimpse of Juliette. Even from a distance. Despite his uninterrupted, solitary wanderings of that portion of the deck allotted to the third-class passengers, in all weather and at all hours of the day and night. Despite Willy's untiring, though generally thwarted, attempts to gain access to other parts of the ship; once the voyage was under way, each of the three cabined classes was physically restricted to those areas that coincided with their rank and privilege. This included not only deck space and sleeping quarters, but the designated dining rooms with their attendant galleys, saloons, and parlors for recreation and relaxation, in addition to toilets and lavatory facilities. The third- and first-class passengers not only did not intermingle—socially or for any other reason—they were, for the most part, scarcely cognizant of each other's existence. Willy had begun to despair that even if Juliette *were* aboard, he would not encounter her before they disembarked in Trinidad.

The *Rosalind*, a three-masted, fully rigged schooner of 460 tons—capable of transporting 250 passengers, or nearly half that amount in tonnage as cargo—seemed a miniaturized, floating replica of the city they'd left behind: everybody had their place. With the wealthy congregating forward and nearest the main deck in their elegant cabins or dining halls, or reclining beneath a parasol on the lounges of their wind-shielded sundecks; and the farther astern and deeper into the ship's bowels one descended (like the basements and sewers of London), the more decrepit the environs and their inhabitants.

Willy's father seemed the sole passenger able to escape all of this carefully enforced segregation. Each morning, after a breakfast taken with his family of wretchedly prepared porridge and coffee, which consisted of used grinds stirred into lukewarm sugared water, he returned to the cabin he shared with Mrs. Tucker to change his outfit. Now he donned his new white linen shirt and embroidered vest, his silk cravat, new frock coat, and tall top hat. (Willy's own newly tailored attire, purchased prior to the voyage—at his parents' insistence, and to his great disappointment—lay packed away with the rest of his family's luggage in the hold, perfectly inaccessibly.) Mr. Tucker then made his way forward, past the deck steward posted behind the galley, to the first-class saloon. There he spent the rest of the morning and a good part of the afternoon drinking whiskey with Mr. Whitechurch and a handful of other gentlemen—though he had required Mr. Whitechurch's hand-written invitation to get past the pompous livery-clad butler. His father, Willy knew, also visited the Whitechurches in their first-class cabin, located just below the forecastle deck, adjacent to the first-class cabins of the Etzlers and the Stollmeyers. Those accommodations, his father had told him—with their private sitting rooms, four-poster beds, and luxurious bathrooms complete with full-length porcelain tubs and running hot water—were superior even to Captain Damphier's own!

To Willy, those parts of the *Rosalind* seemed as far away as Knightsbridge had from his old London borough, and just as out of reach.

Yesterday, their fourth afternoon at sea, Willy had spied for two long hours on the steward stationed behind the third-class galley, before he stepped away from his post for a moment to piss over the side. Seizing the opportunity, Willy hurried past the deck steward's turned back—leaping a low railing and descending a short flight of steps—and instantly found himself surrounded by a number of elegant couples, all dressed to the nines in full feather. He felt as though he'd stumbled into another world! These couples casually promenaded the first-class portion of the deck, one behind the other in circular fashion—as though the entire operation were orchestrated so that the women did not decapitate one another with the brims of their enormous hats—several of them holding glasses of champagne or toddies in their gloved hands. With an older couple even accompanied by their primped-up poodle, wearing a floppy black bow on top of its head and a red-sequined vest!

A few minutes later, his heart still racing, Willy chanced to glance through a window into one of the plush parlors; there sat Mrs. Whitechurch, together with a dozen other impeccably dressed ladies and young maidens. At one end of the room stood an upright piano, with two portly women sitting on the bench, playing a duet and laughing giddily. A large silver bowl of strawberries and cream sat on a table near Mrs. Whitechurch, together with an ample tray of biscuits, pastries, and finger sandwiches. With a steward in white tie and tails to pour their tea or coffee from shining silver pots, held in each of his white-gloved hands. (Willy's own lunch, a couple of hours earlier—no different from the other third-class passengers—had consisted of a single boiled potato and a piece of stewed beef so impregnated with salt he'd had to spit it back into his tin plate, and, of course, there would be no afternoon tea.)

Yet it was not the lavish victuals, adorning the lace-covered table behind which Mrs. Whitechurch sat so primly with the other dainty ladies, that so disheartened Willy. It was not even the idea that his mother and sisters were absolutely barred entrance to that particular parlor. It was the fact that Juliette was not sitting on the chesterfield couch beside her aunt.

He turned around and walked sullenly back to his own deck, in his own third-class portion of the ship—hopping the railing and stepping boldfaced past the deck steward—as though daring his reproach.

But on that fifth morning of the voyage, as Willy stood at the windward rail bracing himself against a stiff breeze, staring away at the gray, whitecap-littered, limitless sea, an idea occurred to him. He left the deck and the handful of other third-class passengers gathered there with their tattered coats and blankets wrapped around them. Willy descended the narrow, steep stairs, three levels below, to the cabin he shared with his sisters.

Willy knew that their family cabins would be unoccupied at that hour of the morning. Particularly now that everyone was over their initial bouts of seasickness. His mother would be in the third-class parlor, most likely with a circle of other women sitting on their blankets on the plank floor—possibly Georgina and Mary as well—each with a skein of yarn in her lap and a pair of knitting needles in her hands. What articles of clothing they could possibly be making, Willy hadn't a clue: sweaters for the tropics? Sometimes the women played draughts, gossiped with one another about Lady So-and-so or the French comte traveling in upper class, or they told stories and sang songs with the children—Amelia would be playing with a handful of other girls nearby.

His father would be up on deck with the other men, deep in discussion on some topic relevant to life in the West Indies or the TES—unless they were listening to a lecture given by Mr. Etzler himself or the comte—or he'd be with Mr. Whitechurch, drinking whiskey in the saloon. The other gentlemen aboard, Willy's father had told him, found it highly amusing that although Mr. Stollmeyer and Mr. Etzler had privileges in that facility, they entered it only occasionally—and not even to partake of an after-dinner cordial and cigar—but strictly chamomile tea or lemon bitters.

Willy shut himself into the cabin he shared with his sisters. He got down on his knees to rummage beneath Georgina's berth, until he located her lace brassiere. Tucked behind her parcel of clothing, Willy removed her only pair of high-heeled shoes. A pair of Mary's bloomers from the bundle beside it. He took out the small purse she shared with Georgina, containing a cake of cashmere powder and a lipstick.

Now Willy crossed over to his parents' adjacent cabin, closing the door behind him. He removed his clothes and dressed himself in his sisters' underclothing. He paused for a second: Willy ransacked the tall stack of his father's handkerchiefs, balling them up and stuffing two or three into each cup of Georgina's brassiere. Then he sat on the edge of a lower berth and rolled his mother's pair of wool stockings over his pointed toes, up along his stringy calves and knobby knees, clipping them into her "French" garters. From a package carefully wrapped in tissue paper, Willy removed his mother's red silk dress: practically shoulderless, with a daring V at the neckline and an extremely narrow waist, puffy mutton sleeves, and a quilted fringe along the hem of its wide skirt (she'd made it specially for herself before the voyage, and planned to wear it to the Captain's Ball when they arrived at the Azores). Willy stepped into the dress. He struggled for nearly fifteen minutes with his arms twisted and contorted behind his back—his breath held and his abdomen sucked in hard—before he managed to fasten the seven tiny hooks along the length of his spine.

Now, utilizing his mother's small hand mirror, Willy hurriedly painted his mouth a bright crimson with the lipstick. He drew small circles with the lipstick on each of his cheeks and rubbed them in, just as he'd seen his sisters do—somewhat dismayed by his mousy mustache and line of stubble along his jaw. Willy quickly applied the cashmere powder to his face. He removed a black lace scarf of his mother's, which he spread over the top of his head and tied in a large floppy bow beneath his chin. Willy took up her black lace shawl and spread it over his shoulders. Then he pulled on a pair of his mother's matching lace gloves, reaching to midforearm. He stepped into his sister's high-heeled shoes.

Willy realized that a couple of hours remained before the first-class ladies would assemble in their parlor for afternoon tea. He sat on the bunk again, waiting and listening. Before long he heard the clang of the steward's bell calling the third-class passengers to their lunch in the dining room two levels above his head. He listened to the scuff of their shoes as passengers entered the room, the clatter of tin plates and eating utensils being laid down upon the rough plank tables, even the scrapings of the steward's ladle against the sides of the stewpot.

Despite his hunger, Willy was happy enough to avoid this lunch!

He settled himself against the bulkhead, closed his eyes, and eventually dozed off.

He was awakened some time later by the sound of his younger sister, Amelia, bursting through the cabin door—which, in his haste, he'd neglected to latch shut.

"*Oh!*" She stared up at him, shocked.

Willy felt simultaneously embarrassed and panicked; his breath caught in his throat. But after a second Amelia's expression of alarm changed to one of gentle amusement—

"Nice to see you're in a better mood," she smiled. "Back to your old self!"

Amelia reached around him and began to search through the things under their mother's bunk.

"Seen Moffie?" she asked. "Mum said she packed her with the blankets under here. . . ."

Amelia grabbed up her rag doll and started out of the cabin. But she stopped short and turned around, still smiling—

"Better hurry. There's cocoa for the children this afternoon, left over from upper class!"

She closed the door behind her.

Now Willy became alarmed that he'd missed the ladies' teatime altogether. He waited for a minute, then slipped out of the cabin and up the narrow stairs, stepping as lightly as he could manage in Georgina's high-heeled shoes on the wood planking. Though wide at the bottom with its thickly quilted hem, the dress was several inches too short for Willy, exposing his thin, unsteady ankles, thick stockings bunched up around them. A handful of third-class passengers—most of whom Willy recognized as fellow members of the TES—were back up on deck, their tattered blankets wrapped around them against the breeze. Willy held his head up and clutched the shawl around his shoulders. He walked straight past them, clacking across the boards in his sister's shoes. Willy continued directly past the deck steward, stationed at his post behind the galley. But when he arrived at the low railing he'd hopped so easily the previous afternoon, he stopped short; there was no way he could negotiate the leap in his mother's dress and his sister's shoes. He began to panic.

A second later the steward was at his side, grinning peculiarly. He bent over and, to Willy's surprise, unhinged a portion of the rail, doubling it back on itself.

"Please, Miss," he winked in a manner Willy recognized as laden with meaning—though *what*, precisely, that meaning was, he hadn't a clue—presenting his arm.

Willy took hold of the deck steward's forearm in his lace-clad hand. He held his head up and stepped through the gap in the rail, raising his skirt with his other hand and proceeding, as gracefully as he could manage, down the short flight of steps, clacking across the boards.

As he entered the parlor reserved for the first-class ladies, the steward in charge—dressed again in white tie and tails—immediately took notice and put down his silver pots. He approached Willy from the other side of the room, much to his alarm. But the steward merely offered Willy his arm, ushering him to a seat—fortunately, at some distance from a small group of women sitting on the chesterfield couch, all chatting enthusiastically, cups of tea and little plates of pastries and finger sandwiches held daintily on their laps. The same pair of portly women sat before the upright piano, playing on the keys and giggling.

Willy looked around—Mrs. Whitechurch had not yet arrived.

This was, in fact, as far as he had proceeded with his plan: to get himself past the two stewards, and into the tea parlor. When Mrs. Whitechurch appeared he could attempt to communicate with her—in some secret manner he hadn't quite figured out—ascertaining first of all that Juliette was, indeed, aboard ship. He could then arrange for the two of them to meet.

But as he sat in his deeply cushioned lounge chair waiting for Mrs. Whitechurch—listening to the ladies tittering enthusiastically on the chesterfield couch, the women at the piano giggling away—he began to grow bored with himself; he also began to feel hungry. Now it dawned upon Willy that, in truth, he was famished. He'd scarcely eaten a thing since his family had boarded the ship six days before. Willy mustered up his courage, stood on unsteady ankles with his mother's thick stockings bunched up around them, and he approached the table spread lavishly with food. He took up the pair of silver tongs and, with some difficulty in the lace gloves, helped himself to a ham sandwich and one of cucumber, placed carefully side by side on a small porcelain plate.

But even before he could return to his seat, he'd consumed the sandwiches—practically inhaling each of them in a single bite—and unbeknownst to himself, doing a fine job of smudging the crimson lipstick he'd applied so neatly to his lips. Willy went back to the victuals at the table. Disregarding the tongs this time, he piled up a precariously tall stack of five more finger sandwiches—two of cucumber and three of Spanish ham—in addition to pouring himself a tall glass of iced lemon bitters from the pitcher.

Just as he went to turn around again, one of the portly little women who'd been playing on the piano approached the table from behind him. She looked up into Willy's face for a moment, smiling sweetly.

A second later the woman let loose a screech like a cat with its tail caught beneath a wagon wheel—causing Willy, in his state of shock, to toss his little plate and glass into the air—cucumber slices and ham slices and perfect little squares of thin white bread with the crust removed, in addition to chipped ice and lemon bitters, raining down upon the little woman's head.

Willy could think only to try to clean up the mess he'd made. Reaching quickly for the little plate, he attempted, with his lace-clad fingers, to pick up several squares of now-soggy bread; Willy slipped on a thin slice of ham in Georgina's high-heeled shoes and his mother's wide skirt, and he went sprawling across the plank floor, slick with spilled lemon bitters and ice chips and littered with disassembled finger sandwiches.

One lace cup of his sister's handkerchief-stuffed brassiere popped out of the dress's low neckline and the black lace scarf that Willy had tied beneath his chin somehow inverted itself—with the floppy bow now centered on the crown of his head—like the poodle in red sequins he'd seen promenading the deck on the previous afternoon.

By this time several other women had joined in for a chorus of screeching cats, and the tea parlor had dissolved into chaos. Willy struggled with considerable difficulty to regain his footing in his high heels and the wide, heavily fringed dress on the slippery floor. Aided by a small woman, her arm around his waist helping him up, whom he believed, in his state of alarm and utter confusion, to be the same portly one from the piano he had just flung his food over; she turned out to be Mrs. Whitechurch.

"Willy, my boy! What in *heavens!*" She reached up and tucked the cup of his brassiere back into place. "Juliette's been asking for you! Poor girl—she's been seasick since we started!"

For a split second Willy's heart burst with joy. He twisted the scarf around his smudged face, fixing the floppy bow beneath his chin again, breathing deeply, smiling with delight.

Then he felt a firm hand take hold of each of his elbows: at one side stood the steward in charge of the tea parlor. At the other—Willy now realized with sudden alarm—the deck steward stationed behind the third-class galley. And with the same indecipherable, queasy grin on his face.

"We'll give 'er some tea 'n' pastries!" the deck steward exclaimed.

"Directly!" said his companion.

The two men began to drag him off.

Willy looked backward over his shoulder, forlorn and frightened,

387

at Mrs. Whitechurch—still wearing her own expression of concerned bewilderment.

The stewards hurried Willy out of the tea parlor via a service door at the back. They lugged him along a hallway past the first-class galley, then down a series of dark, narrow stairs, lit solely by a hatch at deck level. With Willy stumbling along beside them in the high-heeled shoes—twisting his ankles again and again painfully—the two stewards dragged him brutishly down the stairs.

"In 'ere!" the deck steward shouted.

He indicated a rough plank door with a hole for a handle, latched shut with a short piece of wood nailed in the middle.

The deck steward turned the latch and flung the door open. They shoved Willy forward, into a dark hallway lined on both sides by other plank doors. In the dim light Willy saw that each had a dark hole for a handle, but these doors were locked with brass padlocks.

"Where's 'em clatty keys?" the deck steward demanded. "I'm risin for to the jab awready!"

"Hold yer hoses!" The parlor steward reached deeply into his pocket, feeling around.

"*Fuckin 'ell!*" The deck steward slammed the first door shut, enclosing the three of them in pitch darkness—

"We'll give 'er the jab right 'ere!"

"Better hope Cook don't come a-search of bacon!"

"We'll give 'im 'is fair share a bacon!"

Willy sat on the plank floor where the stewards had thrown him. Surrounded by darkness and scared out of his wits. He pressed backward, instinctively, to the far end of the hallway. Willy heard the two stewards pursuing him, feeling their way in the dark. Suddenly, in a burst, he shoved under and past them—regaining his feet in the high-heeled shoes—and somehow aware, simultaneously, of the dress's seven hooks along his spine, snapping open one by one. He moved in a rush toward the single spot of light in the darkened hallway: the small hole in the door at the end. He burst out and slammed the door shut.

Willy turned the latch, locking the two stewards inside.

He paused, leaning against the closed door, catching his breath; how he'd managed to escape, unscathed, and in a matter of a few seconds, Willy could not be sure himself.

He hurried away, the stewards pounding on the door and crying out behind him. On his way up the narrow stairs, he seemed to notice a flash of light coming from the corner of one of the steps. Willy thought to ignore it. Then he turned around and reached down quickly to pass his gloved hand across the floorboard—taking up what he realized a second later was a ring containing several iron keys.

Willy tucked them into his sister's brassiere.

Counted among those passengers traveling aboard the *Rosalind* were a handful of wealthy English and French estate owners. Some of them, including the notorious Comte César de Beauvoisin—as loud as he was large, with the somewhat disagreeable habit of animating his speech with one or the other of the half-eaten mutton legs held in his hands—even boasted claims to nobility. Having vacationed in Europe during the pleasanter autumn months, they were returning to the warmer climes and their properties in Trinidad. The conversation among these plantation owners centered, with little exception, upon the great hardships suffered in recent years: of the enormous monetary losses they had sustained since the emancipation of the African slaves.

Once the glittering jewels of the British crown—her veritable money machines!—the West Indies now lay bankrupt and in ruins. Not even the recent proposal of Sir Robert Peel and the conservatives, of imposing a duty on foreign sugar (e.g., Brazilian, Cuban, and American *slave*-produced sugar), offered any tangible hope. For even if West Indian sugar, exempt from such duties, could be bought cheaper in the mother country, who would work the fields at home here in the islands? The local population and the now-free Africans far preferred to toil a few leisurely hours tending their own small plots than to labor long, harsh hours beneath an unrelenting sun for the meager wages offered on the estates. At the end of the day their hard-earned wages bought them less food than they could grow in their own gardens—less goods than they could purchase if they bartered their excess produce at local markets—and with scarcely any effort a-tall.

But despite the unceasing litany of complaints coming from this group of plantation owners—of financial devastation, vast tracts of land that lay utterly abandoned, formerly fruitful fields overtaken by bush and returning to forest overnight—their conversation was animated. The estate owners had taken matters into their own hands. They had sought to solve their *own* problem (this problem created for them by the self-righteous, sanctimonious, bill-mongering MPs in London), and in a manner that seemed perfectly West Indian.

Hope was, indeed, on its way! It traveled upon the very same sea that they did. Bound, inexorably, for the same West Indies—for the very same island of Trinidad! This hope, however, arrived from a different direction. And although it was the same general direction in which Africa lay, it originated in another continent. For at that very moment, on another ship called the *Fatal Rozack,* a cargo of 217 indentured East Indian laborers was making its way from the city of Calcutta, bound also for the estates in Trinidad.

The comte claimed to have already purchased some forty-five of these coolies due to arrive on the *Rozack* itself. If the new labor scheme proved successful—and who could offer a viable reason as to why it should not?—he had already set aside funds to purchase hundreds more. Indeed, the comte estimated conservatively that his cane, cocoa, and copra cultivations in Trinidad, Tobago, Grenada, and the other islands were so extensive, they could employ a *thousand* coolies! Of all the estate owners aboard, he was the most vocal and enthusiastic advocate of this new strategy of importing indentured East Indian laborers.

According to the comte, these coolies were starving in their own country. Some of them—particularly the lower Sudra and pariah castes—lived loathsome, abominable lives; they were treated no better than dogs. These coolies were most eager—in truth, some of them even desperate—to sell themselves away on contracts of five or ten years, after which they would return home to India. At this time—when their contracts had expired and the coolies would more than likely no longer be useful, anyway—their owners would be absolved of all responsibility for them. (This had proved an expensive and tedious problem with the former African slaves, bound to their owners for life; in this regard *only* had emancipation served to the plantation owners' benefit.) The coolies would, by law, be provided their return passage, at which time the population of workers could be replenished by fresh, youthful, and unspent laborers, sent out on the same ships. For once this labor scheme was fully and permanently put into place, the ships would be sailing back and forth between Asia and the West Indies, virtually without interruption.* Even if the demand for these coolies grew to be so great that the

---

*The possibility of a choice for the indentured laborers to remain in Trinidad, or to be granted a small parcel of land in exchange for their return passage, would not be introduced until substantially later.

Indian population could not sustain it—an incredible notion indeed!—countless more indentured laborers were readily available in China.

During the period of indenture stipulated by their contracts, the estate owners would be responsible for the coolies' housing, care, and sustenance. For this reason new barracks of bamboo or mud huts were already under construction on the estates, or, if they had not already rotted and fallen to the ground, the quarters utilized by the former slaves were being renovated. Due to the Hindoo and Muslim religions that the East Indians adhered to with the utmost reverence (and, the comte pointed out, as a result of the "Indian hemp" and opium they habitually consumed), the coolies, unlike the former Africans, were extremely placid and agreeable by nature. Their Hindoo and Muslim religions also forbade them the consumption of animal food (another "fringe benefit" for their owners, according to the comte: *cheap fuel!*); the coolies maintained a strict diet of rice, channah,* and a few basic vegetables and roots. These staples could be grown easily and cheaply enough by the laborers themselves, on small plots located near the barracks set aside for that purpose. Or, alternatively, the staples might be imported for next to nothing on the same ships that brought the laborers: rice, dried channah, and "Indian hemp" traveled the sea without spoilage better than any other consumable commodities. Lastly, according to coolies' contracts of indenture, the estate owners would pay them a daily allowance of twenty-five cents.**

Comte César de Beauvoisin was also, as one can well imagine, the particular object of Mr. Etzler's seething and pent-up wrath. And not simply as a flesh eater. (Indeed, it was rumored that the comte's only luggage consisted of 106 cured Catalonian hams, and a flock of twenty-seven sheep from his farm in the Pyrenees, together with a collection of other live animals that made the *Rosalind* seem, in truth, like his personal Noah's ark!) For the first week at sea Mr. Etzler and the comte did not exchange a word together. Though the comte was present at all of Mr. Etzler's lectures, advertised and improvised, on the TES, his satellite, naval automaton, and his various other inventions. In fact, at each of these discussions and lectures

---

*Chickpeas or garbanzo beans.
**The local population and the former African slaves demanded wages in excess of eleven cents per hour.

the comte made a deliberate show of dedicating more attention to his pair of half-eaten mutton legs—reclining on a commodious chaise longue toted dutifully by the stewards from deck to parlor to saloon at his beck and call, with a large white napkin spread diamondwise over his enormous chest—shifting, quite audibly and voraciously, from one greasy fist to another. Likewise, each time the comte fell into an extended discourse on his indentured coolies, Mr. Etzler stood at a distance listening, without so much as opening his mouth. Until the experience had become so physically painful for Mr. Etzler he could no longer bear it, and he stormed off in a huff.

Not until the evening of their seventh day at sea was there any actual communication between the two headstrong men. On that evening there had been a particularly elaborate dinner for the first-class passengers, provided generously by the comte himself, the prize of his private menagerie: a recently born litter of eighteen slowly and delicately spit-roasted *petits porcelets,* each encrusted with a skin of the crispiest crackling. With Mr. Etzler and Mr. Stollmeyer making their standard demonstration of getting up indignantly from their seats as soon as the meat or fish course was served (on this occasion an entire piglet curled on their plates in the fetal position, adorned with a sprig of parsley in its snout), crossing the dining hall before the main table at which Captain Damphier and the comte sat, and whirling their full plates in the manner of Olympian strongmen tossing their disks, out the open window. Same as every meal taken aboard the *Rosalind* that Mr. Etzler and Mr. Stollmeyer attended— much to the scandal of the other diners—they did not touch a morsel that was placed before them until the final fare, when the stewards brought out the dessert tray of puddings, fruits, and nuts.

As usual, the majority of the gentlemen traveling in first class retired to the saloon after dinner for a brandy and cigar, the ladies to their tea parlor. But on this particular evening Mr. Stollmeyer and Mr. Etzler had joined them in the saloon for a lemon bitters. Mr. Etzler had launched, in one corner of the room, and in his heavily accented English, his case of silverware chained somewhat awkwardly to his wrist, into an impromptu lecture to several of the wealthy plantation owners present. As was his custom, he ascended a small coffee table to facilitate his delivery.

"West Indian plantachion owners"—Mr. Etzler spoke loudly enough for all to hear—"stuck in zee blind prejudices huff zair age-old practices unt customs, are dumb as donkeys! Belligerent unt boorish as billy goats!"

He cited, by way of example, the dangerous and particularly labor-intensive process utilized by the planters to crystallize sugar from extracted cane juice. This process could, he maintained, be accomplished virtually cost free (since there would be *no* labor involved) and danger free (since *neither* heat nor fuel would be required to boil the juice) by employing a procedure of his own invention; it had been thoroughly and rigorously tested in London by scientists and chemical engineers of the highest knowledge and experience.* Furthermore, his invention was now patented, due to the assistance of his faithful associate (here Mr. Etzler indicated Mr. Stollmeyer, who took a gracious bow), in Great Britain, France, Holland, and other countries as well. This process for crystallizing sugar, stated Mr. Etzler, like *all* of his inventions and discoveries—so praised by the world as advances of profound and extraordinary genius!—utilized only the most rudimentary and basic of scientific, chemical, and engineering principles.

"Zee problem wiz men since antiquity," stated Etzler, his voice growing still more voluminous, "is zat zey do not *reason!* Zey do not *sink!*" Stuck for centuries in their colossal state of mental sloth and barbaric ignorance, the generality of men do not even open their eyes to see what lies directly in front of their noses! In point of fact, Mr. Etzler boasted, his little chest expanded within the confines of his crimson vest, this invention for crystallizing sugar—which could easily earn him *millions* of pounds if we're only interested in offering it for purchase on the international market, and *not* for the general advancement of scientific knowledge and embetterment of life for all humanity—utilized the simplest chemical principle known to every "knuckleheaded schoolboy older zen zee age huff seffen!"

In the silence that followed Mr. Etzler's speech—a moment that felt, in truth, as though he'd sucked the air out of the entire room—the comte got up, with some difficulty, from his lounge chair at the other end of the saloon.

"*Écoutez ici,* Monsieur Etzler," he spoke in an even voice, holding

---

*See "The Sugar Question Made Easy," by C. F. Stollmeyer (London, John Wortham Publisher, 1844), "Everyone who is acquainted with the cultivation of sugar knows that the labors of the sugarhouse are most dreaded by the slaves, or free workmen, and also what waste and other casualties are attendant upon the process of boiling sugar. It is therefore with pleasure that I can announce that this very difficult point has at last been overcome by a gentleman of great talents, extensive learning, and extraordinary inventive powers—J. A. Etzler, who has succeeded in crystallizing sugar *without heating or boiling,* at one-fifth the cost of making sugar in the usual way. Experiments have proved this fact without a doubt," italics mine, pp. 16–17.

a fairly large and somewhat soiled canvas sack in his two hands.

All in the saloon turned to give the comte their attention.

"You crystallize sugar," he said, "without see use of fuel *ou le feu, oui!* for everyone here to witness, and I pay you see equivalent of ten thousand pounds in gold doubloons!"

With that he tossed his bag—in a resounding *shillink* and with a great exhalation of ancient dust—onto the coffee table before him.

"Fail," announced the comte, "*et avant le Christ avec sa Vierge Sainte,* Captain Damphier'll set you in a fuckin rowboat, adrift, *au milieu de la grande mer!*"

Another palpable silence followed the comte's pronouncement, during which every man in that saloon—not excluding Mr. Etzler himself, standing atop the coffee table with his silverware case chained awkwardly to his wrist, his mouth agape—watched the comte recline again in his chaise longue. He reached into his vest pocket, the livery-clad waiter stepping forward to light his cigar.

Now began the period of Willy's night prowling. His first objective was to recover his frock coat and the rest of his newly tailored clothing from his family's luggage in the hold, so that he might move with impunity between the third- and first-class sections of the ship. It took him four nights. He slept in his cabin during the day. Willy became a nocturnal animal: not long after the ten o'clock curfew— when the third-class passengers were required to be in their bunks and his three sisters had fallen asleep—he would slip out of his berth and take down the kerosene lantern from its hook on the bulkhead. (Though he wouldn't light it until he had securely relocked the plank door of one of the storerooms behind him.) Still wearing his nightshirt, in the dark, he'd tiptoe out of the cabin and up the stairs. Willy discovered that during the evening hours the deck steward was seldom at his station. If he happened to be there, he generally lay in the middle of a huge coil of rope, an unfinished flask of rum in his hand, snoring away.

Unless there was some special event for the upper-class passengers, they'd be sleeping soundly in their cabins by ten o'clock as well. Only the first mate and his watchman at the helm, or the cooks preparing meals for the following day, might be awake at that hour. But on his bare feet Willy moved silently across the boards. He ducked past the elevated, window-shielded station at midship that housed the helm. Willy proceeded forward, across the forecastle deck and down a flight of carpeted steps, past the deserted dining hall and saloon and the vacant ladies' tea parlor—past the open door of the first-class galley where the cooks tended their pots in a pungent cloud of smoke and steam—down several flights of narrow stairs to the hold. In pitch darkness, he knew by touch now which of the eight iron keys fit each of the eight brass padlocks, four doors on either side of the hallway.

Willy was always careful to lock the plank doors behind him again—squeezing the padlocks closed with his long, dexterous fingers shoved, conveniently enough, out through the holes that served as door handles. Still, there'd been a couple of close calls: the cook descending to the ship's pantry for some necessary ingredient for his pot, a steward sent to retrieve a bottle of whiskey from another of the storage rooms. But Willy had managed to out his lantern just in time. He grew accustomed—even in the midst of his wild rummagings through the veritable treasure trove of luggage and goods—to keeping a cautious ear cocked.

Willy *should* have been reunited with Juliette three days earlier. He now knew the ship's layout (at least that portion forward of the cabin he shared with his sisters) well enough to diagram and label each level: the purpose to which each room was dedicated, the contents stowed in every compartment. According to his calculations the Whitechurches' cabin—and the bed in which Juliette, at that same moment, lay peacefully asleep—was located two levels up, and only a short distance forward of the very compartment of the hold into which he had, presently, locked himself. For on that same night in which he discovered, finally, the whereabouts of the five brown leather trunks labeled—

TUCKER
TRINIDAD, W. I.

—and in the light of his kerosene lantern he'd shed his nightshirt, dressed himself at last in his newly tailored suit, including his boots and embroidered silk vest and frock coat; Willy *also* happened to find, in another storeroom entirely, the place in which the most valuable and luxurious articles aboard ship were stowed.

Waylaid by his findings, Willy did not let himself out of this particular storeroom for another three days and nights.

ATTENTION:

Saturday 9 Dec at 3:00 pm on the
forecastle deck J. A. Etzler to demonstrate
his patented invention for crystallizing sugar from
super-concentrated solution WITHOUT the use of
FLAME or FUEL for all those present & in exchange
of which the Comte César de Beauvoisin is pledged to
pay him the equivalent in Spanish Gold Doubloons of

£10,000

or, failing to accomplish said feat, the inventor has agreed
to place himself in the capable hands of Captain James Damphier
who shall set him, absolutely without remorse or any further recoil,
in a rowboat at mid-sea

HOPELESSLY & HELPLESSLY ADRIFT!!!

*** admittance fee ***

1st & 2nd class: 1£;   3rd class: 5s;   steerage class: 2s

Willy was not present on the forecastle deck for the demonstration
advertised by Mr. Etzler and Mr. Stollmeyer, though it was the first
event since the onset of the voyage at which practically all of the passengers aboard the *Rosalind* were in attendance, including the other
members of Willy's family, the Whitechurches, and Juliette herself.
That afternoon the sea was flat as a plate. As though to signal the approaching proximity of the tropics, it was colored a most luxurious
and glittering sapphire. In fact, the sun shone brighter and warmer on
that particular afternoon than it had since the *Rosalind* set sail fifteen days previously. Such splendid warm weather worked well in
Mr. Etzler's favor. At his specifications a small table was placed atop
the enormous crate that held the disassembled Satellite, lashed

down securely in the aftmost portion of the forecastle deck. Upon the table sat a fairly small and innocuous black box. No one could say when during the day the box had appeared there, or what might be its contents. Though it was the general speculation of all present that if the box did not contain Mr. Etzler's invention, then it must at least hold some ingredient or chemical substance necessary to his scientific demonstration.

Adding to the festivities Captain Damphier had ordered iced lemonade for the children, in addition to a special punch of his own recipe spiked with dark West Indian rum and Angostura bitters, to be served to all the adults. In truth, a considerable quantity of this punch had already been consumed when, accompanied by a resounding cheer, Mr. Etzler appeared at last at the bottom of the ladder installed by the sailors for him to ascend to his elevated platform atop the crate. He'd arrived a good hour and a half *after* the time stipulated on the announcement that Mr. Stollmeyer had written out by hand in multiple copies and posted throughout the ship.

But it was not the Comte César de Beauvoisin—as advertised in Mr. Stollmeyer's notice and sitting placidly enough in his chaise longue drinking a rum punch some distance away—who would be responsible for the mishap that ensued. And that very nearly resulted in Mr. Etzler's loss of life and limb. Neither would Captain Damphier be found guilty. Indeed, it would be due to the captain's own quick thinking and ready actions that his life would be spared! It would be the passengers themselves, not excluding two or three members of Mr. Etzler's society, who would find cause to respond in such an uproarious and unruly fashion. Particularly after offering up their very dear shillings for the privilege of witnessing this much-anticipated scientific experiment. Particularly after the rum punch began to run short.

Mr. Etzler tucked the tail of his long beard into his crimson vest. With obvious danger to himself and others as well—especially those spectators gathered directly beneath him—he began to climb the ladder while simultaneously carrying his case loaded down with silverware. Arriving safely to his elevated platform, he laid his case on the table and snapped it open. It was only then that the spectators realized that he had dispensed with the chain and padlock securing the case to his left wrist. Now he removed not knives and forks or a silver teapot, as some might have expected, but the model of his Satellite, in addition to a miniaturized version of one of its prescribed attachments. As was his custom, Mr. Etzler snapped his case closed again and placed it on the plank boards of the crate beneath his feet, stepping up on top of it.

Taking advantage of the crowd gathered before him—in English that became increasingly inflected with German, and less easy to interpret, as his excitement grew—Mr. Etzler launched into an impassioned lecture on the subject of his agrarian machine. The fact that he happened to be standing atop the crate containing the very mechanism that he now elucidated for his audience added a further poignancy to his delivery. Of course, a good number of those spectators present—members of the TES and others as well—had heard all of this verbatim on a number of occasions already. Other passengers, including a handful who knew absolutely nothing of Mr. Etzler or his machine, were similarly disinterested: they had offered up their shillings to see a "scientific demonstration" (which, in the minds of most, meant an experiment of extraordinary and arresting chemical magic). They had *not* paid to hear a lecture on some silly model that looked, to them, like the plaything of a mischievous boy—a rabbit-sized rack of medieval torture. And if they did not get the spectacle, in the very least, they had surrendered their hard-earned shillings for the somewhat perverse pleasure and privilege, as advertised, of seeing this peculiar little puffed-up man who thought so highly of himself, set adrift in a rowboat in the middle of the sea.

One way or another, they were going to get their money's worth.

In response to a handful of rather indignant shouts to "Get on with the bloody experiment!" or something similar, Mr. Etzler put down the model of his Satellite, and he took up the miniature attachment.

The purpose of this attachment, he explained, was to instantly crush sugarcanes of the greatest conceivable quantity with the highest possible rapidity and yield of pure juice—by the power of nature and his Satellite alone—without the use of any labor whatsoever. That is to say, *human* muscle and blood and bone and sinew. Including, Mr. Etzler stated loudly, his chest now visibly inflated, *EAST INDIAN INDENTURED LABORERS* who are, in point of fact, no different from the African slaves who preceded them! Human beings procured by a trade—now a capital crime in all *civilized* countries of the world, with the exception of the United States!—that abominable bartering of human souls that disgraces the history of mankind, is a stain and blot on the reputation of our ancestors, that disgraceful and abhorred practice of so-call *CHRISTIANS!*

Disregarding the angry shouts of his spectators—the majority of whom could care a jot about the Africans who had long been emancipated throughout the British Empire anyway, or these Hindoos who were so exotic they could scarcely be imagined—Mr. Etzler continued shouting in a similar vein. Seemingly oblivious to the growing danger of his own predicament.

Finally, when he could no longer be heard over the uproarious protests of his audience, he took up the small black box sitting on the table before him. With his free hand he took out a handkerchief to wipe away the beads of sweat that had gathered across his brow. Mr. Etzler waited patiently for the boisterous crowd to quiet itself.

"Now," he said at last, "zee reason for today's gathering: a demonstrachion huff zee prowcess for crystallization wizout zee use huff fire or fuel—a chemical principle utilized by my patented invenchion, soon to revoluchionize sugar production in zee West Indies, unt throughout zee worlt!"

Here, with the exaggerated flourish of a master magician, Mr. Etzler lifted off his bottomless black box. He revealed to the crowd a plate upon which sat a glass beaker half filled with a viscous-looking clear liquid, a pencil lying crosswise over the container's open mouth, from which there appeared to dangle a thickly encrusted piece of twine—

"Ladies unt gentlemen," Mr. Etzler said proudly, "I give you zee rock candy!"

There were bottles of the finest French champagne that Willy taught himself to uncork. To enjoy the pop and fizz of the foam surging forth from the bottles' narrow necks, then tingling along the back of his parched throat. Bottles of the most coveted twelve-year-old Irish whiskey, which he learned to drink with the foamy champagne as a chaser. Willy now utilized the blunt back edge of his penknife's blade to scrape away some salt crystals that remained—the sharp edge to hack off wedges of hard, semitransparent, desiccated skin with a few wayward tufts of coarse hair—then, finally, carving for himself paper-thin slivers of the finest acorn-fed Spanish ham, stamped PATA NEGRA. It melted on his tongue like curls of butter. There were globe-shaped cheeses the size of *ships' buoys* encased in their skins of bright red wax, labeled HOLLAND EDAM. Swiss cheeses and rounds of Italian PARMESANO big as wagon wheels. Smaller cheeses in flat, mold-splattered boxes of light wood labeled ENGLAND STILTON, FRANCE CAMEMBERT, ESPAÑA MANCHEGO.

In the shadowy light of his kerosene lantern, locked into the hold of the gently rolling ship, Willy ate patiently. He ate purposefully. Willy paused from his eating for a sup of whiskey, a long cool draught of foamy champagne. He ate until he could eat no longer. Until he was satiated. Engorged. Bloated. Willy drank until he could drink no more. Until he had filled five entire champagne bottles with his own piss, and carefully recorked them. His stools wrapped ritually in lady's negligees of the finest silk, the packets tucked into an enormous discarded glass bottle, its lid clamped-down tight, labeled ΕΛΛΗΝΙΚΗ ₣ΕΤΑ ΣΤΟ ΕΛΑΙΟΛΑΔΟ.

Willy outed his kerosene lantern and tumbled with a groan and a thud onto his back. Onto the rough plank flooring at the bottom of the ship with the pleasant sound of bilgewater sloshing back and forth someplace, the unceasing creak and jar of the ship all about him—those faintly nauseating yet delightful smells of mold on the cheeses and across the desiccated skins of the hams hanging from the ceiling and swaying gently back and forth in unison like another ocean floating above his head—Willy passed out and he dreamed of eating and drinking. He awoke again and lit his lantern and ate and drank with such studied, slow, precise, and celebratory enjoyment, such patient, purposeful pleasure, that he felt he must be asleep dreaming that he was awake drinking and eating. Or else he'd died in his sleep and woken up in heaven, dreaming and drinking and eating.

After three days and three nights locked into this particular storeroom of the hold—after a final, uninterrupted sleep of fourteen hours—Willy awoke clearheaded, despite a somewhat persistent throbbing at his temples. He felt mildly hungry. Most definitely he felt thirsty for a sup of whiskey or a long, deep drink of cool, foamy champagne. Willy did not eat. He did not drink. He lit his kerosene lantern and located his frock coat and embroidered vest where he had hung them on nails among the swaying hams three days before. His top hat where he had set it safely on a shelf beside the Stilton cheeses. Willy put them on. He made his way toward the plank door.

Willy outed the lantern again, reached into his pocket for the keys.

Like a pirate Captain Damphier swung on a rope of the rigging over the heads of the enraged passengers. They were all shouting, climbing onto each other's backs and shoulders in their attempts to reach the top of the tall crate where Mr. Etzler stood scared out of his wits, eager to tear the little man limb from limb. So many of them had tried to climb the ladder at the same time that it had tumbled backward, sending a dozen men sprawling across the deck and very nearly over the railing. Captain Damphier landed safely at the top of Satellite's crate beside Mr. Etzler. He swiftly tied a loop at the end of the same rope he had swung across on, bowline knotted and pulled tight around Mr. Etzler's waist. With the same smooth motion he reached behind to the thick post of the mast, and uncleated a halyard securing one of the enormous mainsails in position high overhead.

With an economy and efficiency of motion and countermotion that even Mr. Etzler must have appreciated, the huge mainsail with its thick heavy boom dropped down along the mast with its canvas flapping loose in the breeze, and hoisting Mr. Etzler, simultaneously and smoothly, up into the air almost to the top of the mainmast of the *Rosalind*, as though he were flying. He hung there, perfectly safe, high above the heads of the enraged and shouting passengers, swinging slowly side to side with his little arms and legs flailing, his crimson vest in the bright sun.

Mr. Etzler was still hanging from the top of the mainmast on the following morning, fourteen hours later, when Willy made his way up the stairs from the hold, dressed in his new boots and top hat and embroidered silk vest and frock coat. As he walked past the dining hall for the first-class passengers, he looked through a window and noted Mr. and Mrs. Whitechurch taking their breakfast. Willy made his way across the vacant forecastle deck, oblivious of the little man dangling high above his head (not before evening, under cover of darkness, would Mr. Stollmeyer dare climb the mast to cut his comrade down). Willy descended the short flight of carpeted stairs to the upper-class cabins. He recognized Mr. Whitechurch's walking stick, with the shiny silver panther standing on its hind legs for a handle, leaning against one of the door frames. He entered without knocking. Willy proceeded past the empty, enormous four-poster bed (big as the entire cabin he shared with his sisters; that cabin he now recalled as though from a distant dream, seemingly so long ago he had lain in his cramped berth). He walked directly and as if by instinct toward a smaller bedroom off to the side, where he found Juliette sleeping peacefully.

Willy sat gently on the bed beside her in his frock coat and embroidered vest and tall top hat. He watched her sleeping with her silken hair spread across the pillow, a faint rosette of the sheet's creases upon her cheek, the ribbon at the neck of her gown loosened to reveal the soft white skin covering her clavicle. Willy watched the slow rise and fall of her chest. He felt her warm, moist breath.

Eventually Juliette opened her eyes, still half asleep, staring up at him dreamily. After a moment she sat up against the pillows, smiling—

"Such a silly outfit, Willy! Wherever did you get it from?" Juliette shook her head. "You look like the boy who brings my breakfast—though considerably more handsome!"

"Never you mind," Willy said after a second, taking her hand. "I've a place for us finer than these clothes and even this cabin. Finer than the royal chambers of Buckingham Palace!"

The Translator
Mary Caponegro

WORDS ARE SLIPPERY—as treacherous on the tongue as ice under one's feet, and as wondrous as the latter's vitreous texture to the gazing eye. German is a solid language, all agree; Italian, French: more liquid. But what language would be flattered to be designated flatulent? Considering the coexistence of these varied states of language matter, one could hardly expect the Tower of Babel to be as charming as the Leaning Tower of Pisa. It is therefore a foregone conclusion that language is to blame for almost any complication one encounters in one's daily interactions. And when you spend your hours gallivanting among languages, I assure you, the likelihood of complication becomes exponential. For we rely so heavily on the fiction of translation.

Ironically enough, a translator, who strives so valiantly to be, as the expression goes, part of the solution, may inadvertently compound the problem. According to these less-than-subtle mathematics, I am intrinsically a prime offender. Please note my dutiful formation of a fist, its somber placement on my chest's left quadrant, the standard Latin recitation of the penitent: yes, I'll say it, mea culpa. And then, because I am a pedant to the core, I'll follow penance with a lesson.

When matter changes state, we learn in elementary chemistry, energy is neither gained nor lost. But in the case of verbal matter, the rule reverses; the rule itself perhaps evaporates. Call it perversity or unpredictability or merely instability—that an hour of haste, American style, transforms into a Mediterranean hour of punctuation; of stasis. *Ora:* hour/time; *punta:* full stop, period; *di* is obviously of. Thus the term *rush hour* is freeze-framed to *stop hour,* by the time it moves from US or British to Italian soil—or more precisely, asphalt.

It's a cliché, I realize, to say Americans are always in a rush or uniformly crude or fat! (Given their country's infamous obesity epidemic, some do rather saunter!) But in all earnestness, I've embraced Italian attitudes more than I'd care to admit, and haste is clearly sacrilegious in this nation, never mind counterproductive. Among the

English-speaking academics of my acquaintance (that vocation that I myself might have entered were I more enamored of stability, more practical, or more—all right, yes, Liza, even more—pretentious), the idiom favored in the analysis of complex ideas is to *unpack*. How glib this infelicitous expression sounds to one whose ears have been attuned to nuance.

Legend sees perniciousness in my profession. This cursed prejudice derives from an Italian (or Sicilian?) uttering the famous epigram: *traduttore traditore*, the translator is a traitor! But perhaps you could forgive *this* sort of traitor for a fancy prose style, as it *goes with*—that's the idiom, yes?—the territory. The deed accomplished by a translator is surely less piacular than murder. All right, here is a question less rhetorical: isn't it betrayal when some complex, carefully elaborated argument or thesis is greeted by the cavalier proposal "Let's unpack that." You know as well as I do that the mascot of our millennial era is that uniformed Cerberus, male or female, who stands at every airport security checkpoint, that stern, earnest individual who grills you to insure that you your*self* performed the act of packing your valise, without assistance or intrusion, thus insuring all personal effects therein to be your own, completely your responsibility. Unpacking thankfully remains uncensored. And I am fully guilty of collaboration regarding my American friend Liza's unpacking.

Who is Liza, you inquire, as if there could be some analogously simple three-word answer, in the manner of a grade-school catechism recitation. Who indeed is Liza? I formulate this strenuous equation daily. I'll start abstractly, as I often do. Consider Bernini's *Apollo and Daphne* at the Museo Borghese—a museum that, for the record, once did not require these elaborate advance reservations; so much for spontaneity. Is not Bernini's majestic sculpture the quintessential artistic embodiment of haste turned to stasis? And in my own subjective version of the myth, starring as the stopped-in-her-tracks sylvan nymph is in effect my Liza, passively enacting the hypostasis by which moment turns memory, flight, as it were, taking root. (Pedant that I am, I must here recite Ovid but I can't as yet produce translation in verse on the spot.) If it is the case that Daphne was ingeniously protecting her virginity, sensibly avoiding any congress that divested her of what my academic friends call (please insert inverted commas) *agency*, my Liza has inverted this scenario: she too has made stasis of haste, but in her own contemporary manner, by eschewing *agency*, though she wants so desperately to be unburdened of her version of—insert again inverted commas please—*virginity.*

If you'll excuse my mixing mythemes, let's return to Cerberus, and the layered repercussions of one's packing. I'd like you to consider whether customs officers and security personnel, as they forage for controlled substances or box cutters or over-quota measurements of liquid, or blighted foreign produce bearing vermin or bacteria, whether they censor the more nuanced, subtler—one might call it metaphysical—contraband that is the bread and butter, if you will, of cultural translation. I'd posit that only a security officer possessed of some exotic, paranormal, psychic X-ray vision would discern that Liza brought the rushing (and its paradoxical fruit, paralysis) with her, that she packed it unassisted and unconsciously, just as people say, colloquially, you brought the weather with you (as a compliment or an accusation, depending on whether what's been brought is rain or shine: *scuro* or *azzuro*), and she is thus either the casualty or the beneficiary (depending on one's view) of the capriciousness of cultural translation.

Standing in inverse relation, Italy, for its part, is either blighted or boosted (depending also on one's view), engaged as it has always been in this perpetual tourist sweepstakes—recipient of yet another awestruck, culture-shell-shocked tourist, in this case the winner of the Liza prize. Italy has cut a deal, one might say, and Italy itself might say the following: you ogle the Berninis, Caravaggios, and Michelangelos, and we in turn will ogle you, *bionda bella.* But my Liza doesn't realize she has already signed on the dotted line—with Italy, that is. With me she is not so much oblivious as tentative. Let me supply the background.

The bargain that we struck was this: if she was bold enough to remain in Rome indefinitely without the required *permesso di sojourno,* then in exchange for her temerity, she would acquire indefinite *permesso* to reside with me. This permission will, I've told her, have no expiration date. Do you think me perverse for putting Liza at risk? I do not think myself perverse (though as I mentioned earlier, my vocation is perceived as such). Would you like to hear a sampling of the risks that I take on a daily basis? For example, if one translates clumsily, one is accused of lacking nuance and not doing justice; if too elegantly, one gives undue credit, as in an inflated grade; in each case, one misrepresents the author. Meanwhile, if one tries to be, as they say, fair and square, one is accused of being pedestrian, middling, workaday, nothing more. When I goad Liza to be brazen, it is toward much milder risk taking than I have just enumerated. I merely want to teach her to express herself, *fully* express herself—directly. A so-called crash course in boldness, you might say.

She, on the other hand, thinks her insufficiencies will be cured through one or two so-called immersion courses in Italian language, taken locally at one of the innumerable Italian programs customized for foreigners. She yearns to fully comprehend Italian idioms; her battered brain swoons with confusion before the *conjunctivo*. But what she needs more fundamentally, in my opinion, is an entry-level course in taking chances. She thinks she can cut a *bella figura* in speech if she masters the subjunctive and its nuanced applications. She is *bella*, both in *viso* and *figura, molta bella*, but I have also made a bargain with myself that I will not exploit her unless I can equip her with the means to seduce me, i.e., any man or woman, anyone—of any nationality. Because I will not overpower; that's too easy, not a level playing field so to speak, so easy it's . . . immoral.

You're still not satisfied. You want to know how I arrived at Liza? (Patience, reader dear, answer in transit.) Why does she intrigue me? Were I a photographer, I could answer more expediently, more suc-cinctly: present her as a figure in the foreground of the landscape, that is, cityscape, of Roman rush hour, though she appears at first unfettered by this urban frenzy: a slender blonde, a striking one, at times seeming to float above the pavement in her romantic, empire-waisted, sweeping-skirted, linen sundress, its fabric tinted the most perfect shade of pale mint green. She is somewhat ill at ease with the inevitable attention paid her. It unnerves her; looking closer one can observe the line of her lovely mouth harden, her elegant jaw tense, the incipient panic in her intriguingly unstable aquamarine eyes (*les yeux bleu, die augen blauen, gli occhi azzuri*), whose own tint shifts as if a polarized lens, when she moves from inside to out-side, under saturated blue sky. Just wear the attention, I often advise her, just wear it like a cape thrown about your shoulders, casually yet elegantly. The secret, my dear, is this: do not let it trip you, drape it about you. At my elaborate extended metaphor, she rolls those gorgeous eyes, as if to say, how quaint you are, how useless is your silly simile. Does it not encapsulate contemporary culture: that the grandeur of a sweeping cape devolves into the coyness of a shrug?

You've likely seen that famous, almost clichéd, black-and-white Italian photograph, often found on postcards, depicting a gauntlet of idle Roman men on some *strada* or other, hamming it up for the camera (hamming, I suspect whether the camera is trained on them or not), admiring, i.e., harassing, an attractive brunette, whose disconcerted expression makes clear she had not expected the transaction of an errand to be quite so fraught with complication—that brunette's anxiousness as emblematic in Italian culture as the *Mona Lisa's* smile. God help her had she been a blonde! Or better still, you surely remember the analogously anxious faux blonde Monica Vitti in Antonioni's *L'Avventura*, surrounded by the mesmerized, vulture-like Sicilian men as she awaited her lover; the man through whose amorous "agency" she had metamorphosed into her friend, the non-blonde and mysteriously missing Anna. Blonde from brunette, stasis from haste. As my Liza would say, with a shrug, Go figure!

Yes, back to Liza, upon whose heart-shaped face we can reliably place the postcard brunette's anxious look, trading the olive skin of the latter for the peaches-and-cream complexion of the former; trading as well their not dissimilar figures, such that Liza's long-limbed, shapely svelteness is now thrust into the foreground of the picture. Let me begin again. Initially to me she was only a slender blonde woman in a stylish and yet modest summer dress walking briskly during rush hour to the *fermata* at Piazza Sonnino carrying a small satchel over her shoulder and a book clasped in her hand. (Although admittedly a woman in Italy is always a noteworthy commodity; yes; to respond to an attractive woman is compulsory: a national pastime if not a patriotic duty, for a male, and if a blonde attractive woman, up the ante, double the alacrity.)

I watched her walking thus on a number of occasions but only when we found ourselves haphazardly together, stationary, did I initiate a conversation. "What is that you're reading?" I inquired, not as a ploy, but with genuine interest, and I found it intriguing that in response she merely placed the book, faceup and open, in my lap. The expression spread-eagled came to mind at the time, perhaps because I knew my question could, alas, so easily be construed as a come-on line—but it was a descriptor unworthy of the combination of mysteriousness and directness in her gesture.

Although she was indeed, for all to see, an eagle spread, sublimely, one delicious August afternoon, during an outing to the Hotel Ergiffe's sumptuous pool, so many sweltering kilometers from Centro or Testaccio or Trastevere. It is an image I will retain for many years: how unself-consciously she stretched her limbs, wearing that simple, elegant black maillot while leaning against the cabana wall, neither proud nor ashamed of her long, Berniniesque legs or her broad majestic shoulders or her strong but seemingly elongated arms, which she raised and spread before her like some beautiful, vertical bird about to take unharried, one might even say balletic, flight.

Quite the inverse of the pesky swarms of importunate starlings that gathered afternoons and at twilight to blacken the skies over Termini, or individually suicide-bomb themselves against the thankfully closed windows of the numerous villas that line the contrastively verdant Gianicolo. (A bloody nuisance are those starlings, though some find them ominous as well, an evil omen. Ancient cities harbor ancient superstitions, I suppose.) Meanwhile Liza was as natural and regal, as at home in her body in that moment as an ambassador's daughter, and indeed there are a cluster of such families in these parts, residing in posh residences upon the aforementioned Edenic hill on streets such as the Via Garibaldi or Via Angelo Messina and the like. Was not Daphne King Peleus's daughter after all?

Who knows, perhaps the splendid verdant Doria Pamphilli Park is full of girls turned tree. Not laurels but umbrella pines and cypresses, of course, for even metamorphosis must honor the indigenous. And after dusk, *tremonto*, when the vast park is officially *chiuso*, imagine how transcendent it would be if that resplendent arboreal cathedral figuratively—no, literally—let down its/her/their sylvan hair and expelled a sweet collective girlish giggle at the effectiveness of their ruse, while all of the Gianicolo's citizens heard in the distance the delicate shivery timbre of silver bells. For even nature, even children of the gods, even magical creatures require some privacy: a bit of shelter from our prying eyes. Tell that to an Italian, though.

An Italian man, it is said, has fire in the blood; he is easily ignited, and to honor female beauty is as elemental as to cry out at the sight of conflagration "Fire!" That calls to mind my Liza's favorite line in one of her most cherished films: *The English Patient*. When Ralph Fiennes as the laconic Count Almásy, with such singular inflection, utters, "Fire," it makes his leading lady roll her eyes celestially, just as Liza often does with me. (The thrust of his anecdote was to prove himself comparatively verbose against a man who offered only one word during days of travel.) But Liza does not mimic Katharine's gesture of forbearance when the handsome count delivers this incendiary punch line. On the contrary, fire on *his* tongue would appear to make my Liza swoon. Whereas for me, it is Kristin Scott Thomas's recitation of Herodotus that (here inverted commas) *sends* me. And when, in order to chastise her leading man for slouching far too sluggishly toward adultery, Kristin, playing Katharine, slaps him, you bet your britches that my pickled pecker perked up straight away, even prior to the kissing and the bodice ripping. Why does the tight-lipped fellow always get the girl, eh?—though one should not discount Phoebus Apollo on fire for Daphne in *The Metamorphosis.*

Pardon me, I would be derelict of duty were I to withhold attribution, for I neglected to mention not only ancient author Ovid, modern author Ondaatje, and Minghella as director, but also an anonymous Roman sage—the one who offered Liza the aforementioned charming metaphor regarding that which circulates in Mediterranean male veins. Folk wisdom, might one categorize it? The culture that condemns the translator sees its own men fueled by hearts that pump not iron but fire!—transmuting physiology to alchemy.

She met him at the bustling Largo Argentina while they waited for some notoriously tardy autobus; he explained to her calmly and matter-of-factly (rather than lasciviously or condescendingly) why it was inevitable that she be pestered constantly in his country. She was attentive to this native; more so, I would wager, than she ever is to me, given that she reported the exchange verbatim. In one sense he merely stated the obvious, but in another he had uncanny prescience, for her adventure commenced the moment that they parted ways, and he became in retrospect her fortune-teller.

What more quintessential anthropological encounter for a non-Italian woman is there than that with the Italian masher, fixture on any Roman autobus—where one has no opportunity to be, despite the moving vehicle, a moving target, in the manner of our agile, mythic Daphne. Thinking herself resourceful, even pragmatic, Liza, to insure against unwanted admirers while standing pressed against so many other bodies, had rotated her body to face away from an unsavory Italian businessman, as a prophylactic gesture of rejection. (You know that physics divides motion into three broad categories: rotational, vibrational, translational; by story's end I promise all three will have been miscegenated.) Nonetheless the latter exploited the bus's sardine-like density to purge himself at her expense.

Only after the fact had it occurred to poor Liza that she had actually made matters worse by turning her back to him, thus denying him access to her frown, her wrinkled brow, that signature locked jaw, thereby allowing him to be even more surreptitious, while unwittingly providing—turned as she was about-face—an even cozier

409

harbor in which he could nest his unsanctioned erection, which was at this point furtively ensconced against the contours of her subtle, fetchingly proportioned derriere. Any warm-blooded male, Italian or not, could infer that beneath the lightweight linen fabric resided ripe flesh such as a finger might sumptuously indent in the manner of Bernini's miraculously tactile *Pluto and Persephone*. It is said that a man yearns all his life to return to the womb or to suck again at his mother's breast, but when all is said and done, is there any texture more *gemutlich* than the flesh of a woman's pliant backside?

You know, I'm glad the impudent Italian lech didn't make contact by hand, only importuned with his arrogant cock through two layers of cloth; for the press of fingers, once you see Bernini's masterpiece, becomes more intimate than that considerably thicker—and ultimately far more clumsy—digit.

Signore, she scolded at raised volume (which takes courage for the girl, she's shy), but the terminal vowel emerged from her lips with the inflection of a feminine ending and thus confounded matters even further, considerably diluting the force of censure, though perhaps it was the most effective insult possible despite its inadvertence—though it was at the same time an obtusely counterfactual interpretation of the craven aggressor's identity! That's my Liza— ever bollixed, ever inadvertently theatrical—her florid cheeks betraying her resistance to an attention she did not quite mean to engineer. The Italian custom of cramming into each day no less than four *ore di punta* presumably gave Signore Masher the chance to return to his *casa* for *pranzo* (prepared no doubt by his mother or wife) and change his trousers before resuming work, but Liza was already halfway to the Vatican (its only free-admission day), an excursion she had planned for weeks; thus she elected to retain the soon-enough sundried stain in lieu of forfeiting. The trip, I mean, not the dress, which she washed later, twice, I saw it hanging on the wooden rack inside my flat for several days! The coincidence of her parading semen at St. Peter's, she realized even then, was so patently paradoxical, so potently sociological, as to be absurd. Therein lie the contradictions of Italian culture in a nutshell.

Let us (inverted commas if you will again) rewind a moment, and then (*virgule, virgule*) zoom in, so as to scrutinize and analyze more deeply. Though she was a victim, she is mortified, and she has raised her arm more awkwardly than elegantly, near frantically, not like a soaring eagle this time but a caged canary, to press the oversized oval button for *uscita* and angle her way through the press of people to the middle doors so as to exit the bus. Heading toward the Eternal City she now walks. Observe, jury: this peripatetic exhibit A: a semen-stained dress; not blue hence not newsworthy, stained not by presidential but civilian semen, no saliva there commingled, not in Washington but Rome, here in the capital not of First World politics but of Old World Catholics, where nonetheless (paradoxically) such antics would not cause a citizen to bat an eye. Such circumstances are taken in stride, given that prostitutes and senators here can collide at times within a single Italianate identity. You can be sure that those colorful court jesters referred to as Vatican soldiers were not staring at the stain when Liza glided by to purchase several *franco-bolli* as colorful as their own preposterous costumes to affix to the postcard she would mail from Italy's only efficient, reliable postbox, but at her attributes in toto, shall we say. (Its destination will in a future passage be addressed—double entendre, reader!)

Roman buses—any tourist, any native, any worldly person knows—constitute ecosystems all their own. (*Un bel casino* is the most apposite Italian idiom for this phenomenon.) For if you could peer into the myriad covert activity masked by sheer human volume you would find a clearing house of petty crime: robbery and sexual harassment, pockets being ever so subtly picked, furtive cocks unloading against random hips, incoherent maledictions, heated political arguments, desperate inquiries, boisterous explanations of directions (their specificity and intensity often inversely proportionate to their accuracy), frenetic hugging and kissing (cheek one to cheek two), halfhearted translations, copious bustling and shoving, crowds leaning in like lemmings toward the red stamping machine with the same dogged yet mindless persistence with which they might dip their fingertips into a marble basin of officially designated holy water (that lackluster sequence of morphemes cannot ever match its musical translation: *acqua sacra*), all the while muttering the requisite *scusa* and *prego*. Heavens, once I swear I saw a man bowing toward Mecca even as the bus kept turning corners (a considerable directional challenge to one's internal compass, I should think)—or so I assume, some form of prostration in any case; uniformed officials boarding when least expected, albeit infrequently, so as to check for any scurrilous infidels riding black.

And long about half July, when the tourist volume has tripled and the heat itself is, from Liza's stubbornly nonmetric Fahrenheit perspective, triple digits, and both natives and tourists are discernibly sweat drenched and restless, one senses there is in Rome something

411

about to explode. Fire in the city's circulatory system, would that sagacious bus-stop fortune-teller say? What is it about Americans and their intransigence; they are so inexplicably resistant to conversion—unless the Holy Roller fundamentalist variety. But when it comes to the mundane, the elemental: kilometers or liters or Celsius and centigrade or military time, and for that matter syntax, parts of speech, moods, tenses, etc., the raw material of translation, they are bloody hopeless! Or helpless? They cannot do, as the expression goes, the math. And thus must have it performed for them.

Forgive my outburst. I am opposed to muddleheadedness and superstition. Liza feels the *tessera* to be some kind of talisman, thinks that the colorful paper rectangle equips her with an instantly Italianate identity, whereas were she to purchase daily tickets she would be perpetually and immutably a tourist. I must debunk this sort of nonsense. I have explained to her time and again that the advantage of the *tessera* is considerable but strictly practical: one is spared the tedium and annoyance of having to go through the requisite motions; one is allowed to cut certain corners, one avoids having to enter from the bus's front and fight (adopting as one's demeanor that specifically Italian mass transit fusion of polite and pugilistic) one's way to the thoughtlessly if not sadistically placed stamping machine at the back. The pricey monthly *tessera* is a bargain not only for the infinite number of rides it offers in any direction (that is, if one were certain to use public transport copiously rather than sparingly) but for its power to reduce wasted motion on the bus itself, as those who wield it earn the privilege of entering through the back doors—illogical as that is, given there is for them no stamping necessary.

Isn't it so often the way, the privileged are granted further privilege, such as the infamous disparity in her country, four percent of the population with a quarter of the wealth, isn't that the statistic? But please don't quote me, I'm a word man, not a number man. (Although in comparison to Liza's grasp of the latter, I'm a mathematical wizard.) In any case, she always purchases her *tessera* religiously, the day before the new month starts, striding resolutely up to the *tabaccheria*, looking with those otherworldly eyes past those ubiquitous magazines designed for neither word nor number men but so-called leg men, breast, etc., men, and also past the newspapers and allegedly news-bearing periodicals: *La Republica, Il Messegero, La Panorama*, and *L'Espresso*, even past *Mirabella* and *Italian Vogue*.

When I first explained to her there was of *tessere* a limited quantity available, given that once the month's initial days have expired they become each day another fraction (approximately one-thirtieth) less valuable, I did not offer any specific advice, for in truth I hoped she might experiment with boldness; try on for size the bright red outlaw cape, engage in that nefarious hoax the Germans label *schwarz fahren.* Admittedly there is a risk (though very low) in this uncitizenly gamble; on rare occasions one is apprehended. I should not have shared with Liza my anecdote about a certain savvy but unlucky couple who were half caught (half haste, half stasis); in other words, the wife evacuated, allowing her husband to take the rap, thus she turned him metaphorically to bark, if not to stone. A trans-gendered Daphne, as it were. (Declare the verdict, Liza, I demanded after finishing my anecdote; was she an admirably pragmatic spouse, seeing no point in extracting double fines from the conjugal coffers, or a fickle miscreant, who failed to stand by her man, or—let's mix mythemes once again—a modern-day Euridice, not looking back?) Liza only rolled her eyes, providing incentive for me to play the devil's advocate, to explain to her that riding black was after all less complicated on a Roman bus than on a German metro car, where men in uniforms might be accompanied by German shepherds, or an Italian gondola, from which one could hardly, without peril, jump off!

I made no progress; Liza was insulted that I would dare augment her jeopardy by urging her to forgo another bureaucratic document, even hypothetically. Besides, she said, she'd come to view the *tessera* with some affection. Displayed upon demand, it was as salient a symbol as an Italian flag. And the place it represented was, in Liza's view, insistently bureaucratic, exceptionally inefficient, erumpently erotic. Once I gave up fantasizing Liza as the Bonnie to some phantom Clyde, we were in harmony again, agreeing that in Italy convenience was ever rationed, charm ever abundant, and logic ever elusive. Just right for you, the logic part, I teased—call me incorrigible—and then I made a slogan just for her: in logic's badlands Liza thrives, continuing through the evening to exhibit the affectionate blend of playfulness and censoriousness that tends to drive her mad, yet keeps her—of her own volition, mind you—tethered.

Oh did I mention, when she actually got to the Vatican, she bought a postcard of St. Peter's Square, then several more cards of the Sistine Ceiling: God creating Adam, the expulsion from the Garden, Satan tempting Eve, as well as two let's call them secular images: Hadrian's Castle, and the Knight of Malta keyhole. (Do they sell generic

413

Mary Caponegro

Roman postcards at the Vatican post office?—I can't recall; perhaps she purchased those at one of the innumerable tourist kiosks adjacent to San Pietro.) In any case, when she completed her transactions and affixed one of her lovely, sumptuous papal stamps, then placed into the bright red box her chosen *cartolina*, she did not send it to the States, or any other country, for that matter, but right here, to Rome. To me. A local call, as you would say. All that supererogatory efficiency for what could easily have been hand delivered. She's my private little paradox is Liza. (Also my palindrome, as she tends to go around in circles when deciding anything, perpetually directionally challenged.) Always clinging, somewhat awkwardly, to an element of mystery or ambiguity.

How can I capture the inflection of her enigmatic, though ostensibly straightforward, explanation? *It isn't healthy doing nothing but translating day and night. Besides, my intuition told me you were craving lighter reading.*

Nothing to Declare
Jonathan Carroll

IT BEGAN BY ACCIDENT, as romances often do.

He'd had another rough night. A few days before, their new puppy broke its leg while playing. It was now encased in a tight bandage that covered a third of its lower body. This wrapping drove the young dog nuts. Obsessively it tried to tug the bandage off with its teeth.

Things were particularly bad at night when it would clomp from room to room, couch to chair to floor, trying to get comfortable, and when it found that impossible, pulling at the bandage. They'd bought one of those stiff plastic collars from the veterinarian that look like an inverted lampshade but are meant to keep an animal from getting at its wound. But the collar scared the dog and its panic at having to wear the large unwieldy thing made them fear the puppy would do something to make the broken leg worse, so they took it off.

The man discovered the only thing that calmed the dog down was if he sat next to it on the living-room couch with his hand resting on its head. Then the puppy would sleep a while, but he didn't. Head bent to one side, a blanket draped over him, three nights in a row he'd done this and it showed. His face was swollen and drawn from lack of sleep. At six in the morning he'd lurch up from the couch goggle-eyed and staggery and go out for coffee to buzz some kind of caffeine life back into his exhausted body.

He always went to the same café because it opened early. The women who worked there were all friendly and seemed glad to see him come in. The waitress he liked most was a dark thin woman named Joanna. He knew this only because of her name tag, not because she'd ever told him. She was nice looking but not special. She smiled a lot and seemed to have an authentically sunny personality. She greeted everyone who came in and was patient even during the hectic times when customers couldn't decide what they wanted. On the third morning of his dog vigil, Joanna served him and said, "You're looking *tired.*"

He nodded, smiled, and because he was so sleep deprived, said by accident, "New baby." Of course he'd meant to say "puppy" but his mind was so thick and confused by fatigue that the wrong word came out. Oh well, what difference did it make—puppies were babies too.

"Ahh, a sleepless daddy! Lucky you."

And then of course it was too late and awkward to correct himself and say, "No, I mean *puppy*. We have a new puppy that kept me up all night."

Anyway it wasn't important—they were only making superficial morning chitchat. She walked away but a few minutes later returned with a big glistening cinnamon bun and put it down in front of him. "This is on the house," she said. "All that sugar will give you extra energy."

The bun was delicious. But how could he tell her now that he'd said it wrong and . . . forget it—it wasn't worth the trouble.

When he got home he told his wife what had happened. Right away she asked why he'd lied to the waitress. He said he hadn't lied; he slipped up and made a mistake. Because he was tired he'd said it wrong. That was way different from a lie. But he noticed his voice at the end of the sentence rose to a plaintive, defensive whine.

"No, you *lied:* you let her believe we have a new baby. That's not very nice."

He loved his wife but didn't like her then. She should have been amused; maybe shaken her head at the goofy situations we get ourselves into by accident sometimes in life. Instead she was scolding and pissy about it. He felt like protesting but held his tongue.

She persisted, *"Are* you going to tell her?"

"What, you mean the waitress?"

"Yes. Are you going to tell her about the dog?"

"I don't know. Why is this important to you? Why not just leave it alone? Who cares?"

His wife looked at him for a few beats but he could not tell what was in her stare. In reaction he really wanted to do something absurd like reach over and squeeze her nose, or stick out his tongue to remind her that neither of them held the high moral ground when it came to matters like this. They'd both lied plenty over the years—to each other and to the world.

He purposely avoided the café for a few days. But one afternoon on his way home he stopped in and Joanna was working. He thought about telling her the truth then but why? She'd probably forgotten their earlier conversation and bringing it up again would only confuse or perhaps embarrass her. The phrase "let sleeping dogs lie" crossed his mind and he smirked. All this nonsense had happened because of a dog that wouldn't sleep.

"How's that naughty baby of yours?" Joanna asked while serving his coffee.

Taken off guard he stuttered, "Oh yeah. Uh—better, thanks. Thank you for asking."

"What's its name? Is it a boy or a girl?"

"Oh, a boy. His name is Harry." Which of course was the name of the puppy.

The waitress crossed her arms. "That's a nice old-fashioned name—Harry. Good one. Good for you. Say, listen, can I ask you a question? Do you mind?"

"No, not at all." Without realizing it, he moved slightly back in his seat away from her. Joanna didn't notice.

"Is it hard? I mean, is it hard having a baby? My husband and I talk about it all the time but we just can't decide. There are so many pros and cons both ways."

He answered immediately. "If you have a good marriage, think of it like this: you already live in a house that you love. But one day you suddenly discover another room in that house you've never seen before. It's wonderful and makes your home better in ways you never imagined. That's what it's like having a baby. But if your marriage is already good, then you're happy living in that house even without the room."

She was impressed. "Wow. That's a really different way of seeing it. *Thank* you."

He was too ashamed to say you're welcome. The words were his brother's from last year when he'd explained what it was like having a new baby. But what else was there to say? He did not have children and knew nothing about what it was like to live with them. His brother's explanation was the best he had ever heard. Now he'd lied twice to this nice woman—once about the baby and then pretending his brother's words were his own.

Fortunately she was called to another table and walked away without saying anything else. A few minutes later he glanced to his right and saw she was on the other side of the room staring at him. The look in her eye was a mixed bouquet of admiration, approval, and plain old you're my kind of guy. He glanced quickly away but sat up straighter and couldn't help grinning although his eyes were turned to the floor. He walked home thinking about her look and how long it had been since his wife had given him one anywhere near it.

By the time the dog's bandage was removed, the man and the waitress were on a first-name basis with each other. They never flirted; they didn't do the verbal dance one does when you're attracted to someone. It was much more interesting than that because both of them were falling for the same person.

Deeply impressed by his analogy between having a child and the house with the extra room, Joanna (being naturally curious) now wanted to hear what he had to say about other things. She loved her husband and they had a successful, fulfilling marriage. But this was altogether different. It happens so rarely that you meet someone who perceives life from a unique perspective and in sharing it, expands your vision. All of Joanna's friends saw things pretty much the same way she did. Her husband was devoted and hard working but he was a hundred percent pragmatist; metaphors or poetic analogies didn't have any place in his world.

The man in the café was different. No matter what they talked about, he almost always came at it from a different angle, frequently one she'd never considered. When she asked what his favorite fruit was he said watermelon because it's so funny. Who the hell ever thought of watermelon as *funny?* But playing the idea over and over in her mind, it made a kind of loopy lovely sense.

She told him about the morning she drove to work and, by some miracle, had made it through five green traffic lights in a row. He immediately nodded like he understood and said, "Smallicious." When she shook her head that she didn't know what he meant, he explained it was his made-up word for the small but delicious things that happen to us in life every so often—like catching five green traffic lights in a row. "To me delicious is a big word—whenever I think of something delicious it fills my mind. But small is . . . small. So you have those two words that mean opposite things and they meet somewhere in the middle."

He never knew it, but after their third chat she bought a cheap pocket notebook at the stationery store next to the café and began copying down things he said—lines she wanted to keep. It was a great pleasure to get that notebook out at work when there was downtime and write in her ugly script things like "extra room/baby" and "smallicious." One day her husband saw the notebook in her purse and asked about it. She told him it was for recording ideas that came to her now and then. What kind of ideas? he asked amiably. Pleased by his interest, Joanna said sometimes interesting things came into her mind that she wanted to remember. Then she explained smallicious as if it were her own. His face remained blank until she finished. After repeating the word with just the slightest tinge of derision, he smiled like she was weird but that was OK—he loved her anyway.

Smallicious, however, was not the man in the café's invention; it was his wife's. He'd said it to Joanna that day because it was the perfect word to describe her experience with the traffic lights. But why didn't he tell her that it was his wife's creation and not his own? Again because of the look in the waitress's eyes after he explained it. He loved her silent but obvious admiration and the way her smile grew slowly as she began to grasp what he was talking about. He'd read somewhere that the next best thing to having sex with a woman was making her laugh. Surely then the third best thing was to make her smile approvingly.

After that day he was almost never himself again with Joanna. Whenever they chatted he became a wiser, funnier, larger-than-life person. He became the kind of man he had always dreamed of being. Using other people's ideas and lines, he led her to believe everything he said was his own, although it rarely was. He had always read widely and had a good memory, so it was not difficult coming up with great insights or mots justes to fit any occasion or conversation. He grew to look forward to their meetings not only because he had such a receptive audience, but also because he was becoming, at least in this woman's eyes, the person he had always wanted to be.

That is where the romance in this story appears because soon afterward, both he and Joanna fell in love with the man he pretended to be. He didn't do it because he wanted to seduce her and saw the ruse as an effective method to that end. No, he did it for himself. He did it to show himself that, under different circumstances, this dazzling fellow could have been.

The best part of having an affair is your lover is always fresh from the bath and smelling wonderful, thrilled to see you, eager to hold you, hear about your day or anything else you want to tell them. To him or her your breath always smells fresh, the eau de toilette you've worn your whole life is delicious, your stories are new, your insights original and compelling. Your lover's eyes light up when he or she sees you with a look that says where have you been all these years? I've been waiting so long.

Now when he walked into the café and Joanna was there, something secret and sacred came awake in both of them. They rose to each other's occasion. Without her, he was only himself. In her presence he became the man of his dreams, which permitted this greater self to actually walk a short while on the earth. Like the rich oenophile who owns a basement full of great rare wines, he kept bringing up bottle after bottle of his favorites for her—stories and lines from poems or great piercing insights—and she appeared to love them all.

Joanna had never met such an exhilarating man. By every indication he was not interested in having sex with her, which made their relationship even more special. He was interested in her as a person, and the things he talked about made her world larger. She only wished they had more time together—not just the few minutes it took for him to drink his coffee and have a little chat. She wondered if he was this expansive with other people. She hoped not but hastily scolded herself for thinking that way. She should just be flattered that this special guy enjoyed talking to her.

She wondered what his wife was like. He never mentioned her, which usually meant it was a good solid marriage that was no one's business but their own. *Or* it meant the less said about the wife the better. Either way, the waitress wondered about the lucky woman. Only once did she ask about her. He told a hilarious embarrassing story about something that had happened to a friend but of course he said it was his experience. On impulse, Joanna asked what his wife thought about it. Instead of answering, he stared at her strangely. She couldn't decipher his look. Eventually he shrugged, didn't answer her question, and changed the subject. For the next half hour she thought about his shrug and got angry at herself for obsessing about something so trivial.

The reason he had stared at her was at that moment he had become certain she had finally seen through him. The story he'd just told was so far-fetched that even adoring, gullible Joanna had realized it could not possibly have happened to him. Which meant other things he'd told her were probably not true either. The jig was finally up. He assumed when she suddenly asked what his wife thought that she was challenging him, indirectly saying uh-uh to this newest whopper he'd whipped up.

But after the long assessing look he gave her, he realized it wasn't so. Joanna really only wanted to know what his wife thought about the incident. On realizing his mistake, he was embarrassed and couldn't think of anything else to do but shrug.

That night his wife returned from a business trip. As always, he brought her a glass of wine and they sat together at the dining-room table, where she told him about her trip and the things that had happened. It was a long-established ritual both of them liked that served as a nice way to connect again after a few days apart. He always enjoyed hearing her stories and insights. A number of them he had told to Joanna.

"When I was in the airport waiting for my bag to come through, I looked up and saw those signs above the exits. You know, one's red and says 'Goods to Declare.' The other's green and says 'Nothing to Declare.' I stood there thinking probably every single person here has something in their bags that they *should* declare at customs but won't. If we were honest, not one of us would walk through that 'Nothing to Declare' exit but most people will."

He poured her more wine and said, "Do you know what psychologists say about thieves? Most of them take stuff because they believe they deserve it, not because they're trying to get away with anything. Maybe the same applies in the airport—people really don't believe they *should* declare things."

She wiggled her finger at him in a mock scold. "But I know I should pay tax on that big bottle of vodka in my bag or the carton of cigarettes."

"Not necessarily. You truly believe it's not right that they're asking for more money when you've already paid for it once."

She nodded. "Yes, but you still know you're doing something wrong. Now I am going to take a bath and wash off the travel cooties."

While she bathed he took the dog out for a walk. Of course her "nothing to declare" anecdote resonated in what he had been doing with Joanna at the café. So much of what he'd told the waitress was either false or stolen from someone else. The man she liked so much did not exist. If she were a customs inspector at the airport he could have walked up to her and said, "Everything in my bag is illegal. You should tax it all."

Such a good woman didn't deserve lies, no matter how entertaining or amusing they were. Right there and then he resolved that from that moment on he would only be himself when they met. He had many good qualities. He knew interesting things, was sensitive and observant. Maybe he wasn't the superman he had been faking for her, but he had his strengths and high points. Maybe she would like them; maybe she would like the man he really was and not the one he pretended to be.

He never saw her again.

The next morning, full of new resolve, he went to the café but Joanna was not there. That was odd because he knew she always worked Tuesdays. After his third visit there without seeing her, he asked.

A waitress named Giselle was vaguely surprised that he wanted to know about her former colleague. "Oh, she's gone."

"*Gone?* You mean she's on vacation?"

"No, she quit. I don't know why. We were never like really friends. Anyway, what'll you have?"

None of the women who worked at the café knew where Joanna went. All he could get from them—and he asked every one—was that she had told the manager she was quitting one day and that was it—she finished her shift and none of them saw her again. Even the manager didn't know where she went because Joanna was very tight-lipped about the whole matter.

More than anyone else in the world, Joanna loved her mother. So when the woman called to say she'd been diagnosed with pancreatic cancer and had no more than half a year to live, her daughter immediately quit her job, told her husband she was going to her parents' house for as long as it took, and was on the road the next day in her old car.

As one would expect, the next six months were hideous. Her mother deteriorated very quickly and the woman's last days would haunt her daughter for the rest of her life. Every night Joanna called her husband and, usually crying, told him what had happened that day.

Squeezing the phone cord so hard in frustration that it left dents in his palms, he felt useless and way out of his depth listening to his beloved partner talk. Repeatedly he asked if she wanted him to come and keep her company. Joanna always said, "No, no, stay. It makes me happy thinking about you there in our life. Like in our living room watching TV. Any time I'm able to clear my mind a little bit and think about normal things it makes me happy. I don't want you to be here and caught up in all this . . . mess." And then she would begin to weep again. That sound of her crying was the only thing that bound them together then over the miles and sorrow that separated them.

But the saving grace when matters got really bad, what she took out and unwrapped one at a time like rare precious objects, was the stories the man in the café had told her. They were some of the only things that buoyed her over those agonizing days. Sitting next to her mother's hospital bed while the withered woman slept, Joanna would smile or close her eyes contentedly when she thought of the stories he had told her in the last weeks. Sometimes she got out her notebook and looked at what she had written down there to remind her of their specific talks.

She didn't know what it meant to drown in her own life but the sorrow she experienced during her mother's final days brought her very close at times. What helped Joanna was remembering and then concentrating hard on some of the funny, memorable, or beautiful things the man had described. They gave her back some balance; they reminded her that life can also be funny and splendid, not just pitiless and lead colored as it was now.

Three days before she died, her mother finally opened her mouth and took the slim section of tangerine her daughter offered. She had not eaten anything for a very long time. The joy that surged in Joanna's heart seeing the food go in was huge.

But huge was not the word that came to her then; it was smallicious. What her mother had just done was wonderful, not small. Joanna hoped that small bit of tangerine tasted delicious. So maybe that was why the funny nonword came to her, stuck in her brain, and wouldn't go away.

Only later did she realize why smallicious owned that last great moment shared between them: because in another time, her mother would have liked the word too. With her sensibilities she would have understood exactly what it meant. She and Joanna would have used it often when they talked to each other on the phone. Smallicious.

Watching her mother's mouth move slowly there at the very end, the man's word was so strong in Joanna's head that she almost said it out loud.

Draft 82: Hinge
Rachel Blau DuPlessis

I.

The book is a mine
of intersections. Margins.
Its inner edges pun on hinge.
The book subsists
by spurt and overlap,
link and lack,
subject and answer,
declaration and perversity.

Hinges are cunning, pegs allowing circulation through notches. A
book hinges; it holds the doors in place so they may open. Like the
page, a cool mist slides down the mountain.

*

The book is a mine
of intersections. Statements.
Thickness implies the combustible.
Sparks catch flame and burn out words.
The fire of the book can even scorch itself.

"We stand bewildered before our own destiny. . . ." Perhaps there
should be no more poems, only acts of writing. There would be no
more books, but transfer points; no finished pages, simply work
sites. There would be no more honors because these mainly police,
with all the force of convention, any useful blunder art might
make. There would be questions, and thereupon other questions.
There would be no illusion of instrumental uses and no rhetorics
dibbling in frill or decor. There would be no worship. O, it would
be austere and demanding; o, it would be infinitely interpretable!

II.

Here's a single tangled page that stakes a claim.
Its interplays of hole and hold, of dead and dread
Seem dialectical, yet operate in a structure
Whose tip-top, top-you term I can't supply.

I don't know what to do, how to articulate it.
My stepping stippled feet feel cold.
There are clots in my ear from ashen coals
       and eyes set deep
       as refugees
       in exile from illusions of another world
       as from illusions of transcendence.
       Let the head smolder in its grief.

       But they were only illusions!

     *

Here's another tangled page that stakes a claim:
The interplay between hole and hold, dead and dread
Doesn't even begin to represent the tangle—the exposition
Being so complex.
Are you that surprised?

I've jumped on a strange train without checking the schedule for return. For anything. Outside, darkness, and no one is calling out stations. The present is dismembered. Undecipherable. The future is paralyzing. Where are we? The covenant? I understand that it is broken. Look—we have just passed the scattered tabernacle!

III.

  Rubble is continually before me.
  Silence of the stalled train.

  It lies in its own shadow; the day circulates.
  Is this the destination?
  Deep in the gutter, my margin split.
  The little needle

The patch of gluey parchment
The intelligence of textual scholarship
Can neither mend nor bridge it.
The page falls away.

*

Rubble is continually before me.
Silence. The stalled train
blocks the grimy tunnel,
its catenary off the current.

Wet, my life, and spent in wonder—
was it important? Did it matter?
Who broke these hinges? Who profits
from such resistance to turning. Why block
sorties from side to side, for understanding.
"What's it to you?" Stories, I mean,
There are things for which I am very stony and sorry.

Is there something I need to do that I am not doing?

IV.

First, arrive at the spur-line train stop
long out of service, virtually nameless.
A blur of faded letters taxes vision:
sgraffito—scratchy opposite of the readable.

I've heard about ghost tracks
underneath train stations,
where ghost people stand
awaiting embarkation.

-ston -ville -tola
-ash. Half Word gaps
get released from storehouses
of half-effaced maps.

*

First, arrive at the spur-line train stop
long out of service,
yet expect someone, expect to be met, to get picked up.

> Came tacit greetings from soldiers, but
> I was totally unprepared to encounter this
> "metaphor," and therefore stumbled,
> vertiginous,
> tripping over switches and formidable
> overgrown tracks.
>
> Day and night, night and day
> ostinato continues stubbornness
> in another language.
> My heart was in a basket.
> Or maybe in a passport.
> I fantasized
> about carrying it carefully into the woods.

V.

Look, I have carvings here on my hands.
The flesh lines of my palm can be read as letters.

In our writing **H**
on my right hand—
Acca acca acca
Aitch and aitch—
two uprights plus a line of force
zygomatic,
a simple yoke
of satisfying aspirate—
air being expelled in a heave,
loud as a sigh but more ironic.

On my left hand π
something endless that disappears straight into the universe
infinitely, with comic (albeit numerical) glee.

"Eclipse" is related to the Greek word
for abandonment,

although we are not quite orphans
but dots of consciousness
pierced by points of pulsing light
as far away as that
but close as this.

*

Look, I have carvings here on my hands
that open as if opening a book.
        Considering the textures of need and the paralysis of motives,
        considering what could happen in modest fairness,
        the newspaper suddenly stops. But it did not whirl
        as in the movies; it pulled itself together with a sucking in of breath
        and caught itself stolidly against a barrier
        and would not blow away no matter what the wind's direction,
        no matter how battered, partial, and twisted.
        That pole was like the peg of a hinge.
        That paper like a book, unbound and bound together.
        It was closed, but it could, like the palm and psalm of the written
        be opened, be regarded.

The first sentence teaches you to read; the second sentence tracks the surface.
Third and you're gone; then you arrive nowhere, in order to explore what that
"nothing" will generate. Suppose you cannot turn back? Suppose there is no
return? Then it is the poem, claiming nonetheless the interlock and open
hope of hinge. For it will sometimes say that there is a pivot. Yet sometimes
there is not.

NOTE. "We stand bewildered . . ." is a citation of Rilke's argument, made just after the beginning
of World War I, that art and theater should have prevented that war. The Rilke material (in a letter
from June 1915) is discussed in George Rochberg, *The Aesthetics of Survival: A Composer's View
of Twentieth-century Music.* "See, I have inscribed you on the palms of my hands" is the actual
citation from Isaiah 49: 16, modified here.

Angel of Death
Brian Evenson

I.

TO BEGIN, THERE ARE eight of us, but only one of us can write. And so I am assigned to keep a record of all that passes and to each day make the count of our number, and when one of us is dead or missing to inscribe his name in the back of the record. I have been given the blank book and a thrust of pencils just for this purpose, and though the others would not know were I to inscribe something other than what I have been commissioned, I intend to take my task seriously.

The difficulty comes in knowing what is real and what is not. There is no agreement on this. What I am nearly sure is real is bursts and jolts and the smell of singed hair, but others recall none of these effects, recall other things entirely. And how we came to slip from one dim world and its dim deeds to the place where we are now none of us are in any position to say. And why we are together, this too I do not know.

But here we are, and we are together, even if we cannot say why or even how. As for me, it was as if my vision ran dark and when it went lucid again here I was, in this new place, tramping my way wetly forward. Soon I was conscious of other footsteps surrounding me. And shortly we began to think of ourselves as a company, moving forward as if one body, though we knew not where.

But I am already beginning to sway from my purpose, and my scribbling in the blank book slows me as I walk. I lag dangerously behind the others. They will not stop for me, but sometimes they do call out to hurry me along. Thrusting one finger between pages, I hurry to catch up with them, sloshing my way forward. But soon, writing, I am lagging behind again, and so it goes.

Perhaps it would be enough for me simply to record the world in notation, scattered bits, things like—

walked, gray light

429

one more dead
walked, darker gray light
—and so on as I fully record the full names of the dead when they die.

But having begun in another fashion, I find it hard to believe I could be satisfied with less.

Here is what I think I know about how things stand for us now:

There are, or rather were, eight of us, together.

We are walking, or rather slouching, forward.

There are no landmarks. Nor, for that matter, technically speaking, any land.

We are going somewhere, for surely one is always going somewhere, even if that somewhere is only in circles. But where? And why do we not feel the need to sleep?

I have indeed queried some of the others, but they speak only with great reticence, in short, clipped sentences, just as I did before I was given the book. But now something has changed for me. There has, I fear, developed the worst of needs, the need to know, coupled reluctantly with an awareness that I probably will, in fact, never know. And yet I write. And cling too to that past I know, or hope, to be real: smell of singed hair, slowly fading vision.

Recorded now in the back of this book: two names. There are six of us left. The other two simply slowed and then fell to their knees, the water lapping against their thighs. And then each of them lay down, facedown, and we left him there, the backs of their heads and the blades of their shoulders disturbing the otherwise smoothness of the water's surface.

I add the latest dead man to the list in the book and then the remaining others each give me a share of their food: not much, a portion hardly bigger than my thumb. They extend it toward me, pronouncing their own names, and I take it, repeating their names as I do, assuring them that I will remember them when they die, that I will record them.

At first I thought it was a sort of immortality they sought in this recording, a sense they would not be forgotten. But it has become clear this is the last thing they want. Through their few words in response, I have gleaned that instead they fear not knowing if they are alive or dead, that they want their death marked out and delineated so as to be sure that they will not have to come to life again. That this can be done with the recording of a name I sincerely doubt.

And yet, still, it makes me mildly anxious to think that there will be no one here to record my own name when I myself die. How will I remember I am dead?

One more dead, his name recorded, the five of us trudging dimly on. The landscape in all directions fog and water, feet clammy and wet. Horizon, at least for me, undifferentiated, the light varying from dull to dark gray. Behind us, the last body still visible, a small damp island. Soon that too will be lost from sight as, in company with the other four, scrawling in this book, I continue forward.

II.

I do not know which one of them starts, but one of them, one of the other four, shuffles into place beside me as I walk. He gets very close and—perhaps not in the first instance but certainly in many of the instances that follow—even encircles me with one arm, aligning his stride with my own. I do not care for such intimacy; it makes it difficult for me to write. But I tolerate it, take it as one of the duties of having the blank book and the privilege of filling it.

And then, much of the time, the fellow will move slowly away, not a word exchanged, leaving me to wonder how to record our interaction in the book. Which, in a manner of speaking, is what I am doing now.

And yet, at other times, it has gone farther than this. I do not know how much I

An unfinished sentence, left long solitary as my mind churned over what, if anything, it was expedient to record. Finally I will leave it as it is, its own little outcropping of words, alone.

I myself am not alone. I continue on in this company, walking through a landscape that seems at no variance with anything, even

431

itself. Sky and water welded together without joint or seam, no sound but the slow roil of our footsteps.

No more of us dead yet. I will record it, after all: sometimes as they fall in step beside me they also whisper softly into my ear:
    —You are the one who will record my name when I die.
    —Yes, I whisper back. I am the one.
    —You know my name.
    —Yes, I say, I know your name. And I repeat it. I would record it here, in this sentence, on this page, but it is not to be written in the book until they are dead.
    He nods.
    —Yes, he whispers, this is my name. You will not forget it?
    —No, I will not forget it.
    —This is a promise?
    I promise him and, somewhat dazed, he moves off.
    This is what my connection with others amounts to now. It was perhaps, once, different, but what it was before, I can no longer recall.

No more of us dead yet. Perhaps the rest of us will walk forever.

Questions have begun to plague me. About where I am, what I am doing here, where we are going.
    As I have not even the faintest, most tentative of answers to them, I find I have no idea how to entertain them. Instead I will write:
    sky dark gray
    water as slate
    sloshing forward
and cling still to that acrid smell of burning hair, the last outcropping of my lost past.

And then, suddenly, a different conversation. One of them, a pale, gaunt man, after asking the same questions, tacks this one on at the end:
    —When will I die?
    —I don't know, I say.
    But he does not believe me.

—Please, he says, please look into my face and tell me when I am going to die.

I stop for a moment and so does he. I turn finally toward him and he looks suddenly afraid. I make an honest effort to see something in his face. But I see nothing.

—I don't know, I say again.

—Please, he says. Please.

And the look he gives me is naked enough that I finally promise him,

—Soon.

He nods, and smiles a little, and we hurry to catch up with the others.

But giving him such assurance is a mistake, for soon I am giving it to all the others as well. *I don't know,* I say. *I don't know.* And then, finally, giving in, *Soon.*

And yet we are all of us still walking, my small book slowly filling up, even though no more of us as yet have died.

sky as slate
water dark gray
stumbling forward

—Soon, I tell him yet again. Soon. Eventually I will be telling all of them, I know. But for now he is ahead of them, the most insistent for death. My answer will not satisfy him, or them, forever.

III.

—When will I die, he asks of me again. A day of flat gray light, no difference between water and land. I am tired of hearing him ask; I am becoming impatient.

—Now, I can't stop myself from saying. You will die now.

The other three around me stop when I say this, the first time I have seen them all stop at once. Suddenly, it is oddly silent. They wait, looking at both of us.

—Now, the pale, gaunt man says, and smiles. He lies down in the water, on his back. I write his name in the back of the book as he watches me, and then the four of us who remain set off.

I cannot stop myself from casting glances over my shoulder. He is still there, still lying in the water, his knees and the tips of his boots and the swelling of his chest cresting the water's surface. He has raised his head a little and watches us go.

No point posing questions. The world is brutal and life, when it happens at all, short. I could, perhaps, make up a past for myself from the scattered viscera of images I still believe are real. But why bother? There is not enough blankness left in this blank book for me to waste it on such luxurious reflections.

And then there he is, a dark spot behind us, in pursuit. The other three are mumbling to themselves, and then they pick up the pace. But he keeps with us, gaining on us rather than growing smaller, somehow more powerful than us. He is, after all, as one of those left suggests, dead. One can never, so he reasons, outrun a dead man.

So he gains on us, slowly but inexorably, until finally we fall back into our normal pace and let him come.

—I'm not dead is the first thing he says when he catches up with us.

—You are, says one of the others.

—No, he says, shaking his head, a little desperately perhaps.

And so I show him his name in the back of the no longer so blank book.

—No, he says. You made a mistake.

But the others have already turned away and have started to walk on. He keeps pace with us, still talking. The others refuse to speak to a ghost. Soon, so do I.

After a time he accepts his lot. He falls into silent step with us. He walks forward, dim, lost, and, though with us, alone.

Soon one of the remaining three sidles into step with me, wraps an arm around me, whispers in my ear.

—What is it? I say.

—Am I on the list? he asks.

—Are you dead yet? I ask.

—Am I on the list?

I show him the list. His name is not on it. He looks at it for a long

434

time, stopping me when I try to turn the page.

Why is my name not on the list? he asks.

I open my mouth to answer and then realize I don't know what, if anything, to say to this.

We walk together for some time. He keeps lightly touching my hand that is holding a pencil until finally I allow the pencil to enroll his name on the list at the back of the book.

—Am I on the list? he asks.

—Yes, I say.

And so he releases me and, like a sleepwalker, moves slowly away, now dead. He never again says another word.

And so it goes. First one and then the other of the remaining two approach me, and are only satisfied when I strike them dead. And then there is only me, alone, the only one living among a silent company of seven ghosts. When I regard them I can see the way in which their skulls are struggling to be seen through their skin. We slosh slowly forward, I and the seven men I have killed.

What is the next step? It seems inevitable that after a few dozen, a few hundred, a few thousand more strides, I will reach a place inside my head where I will see no choice but to record my own name. And then we will proceed forward, all of us a company of ghosts, silent, dead.

But for now, the last man alive, I take a step forward. And then another. And then a third. I will inscribe everything that happens. Daily, I will make the count of my remaining number. When the time comes I will write myself dead and gone.

Secrets and Lies
Valerie Martin

NORA FOUND THE MARIJUANA pipe inside a sock in her son Sam's
dresser drawer. She wasn't looking for it; she wasn't invading her
son's privacy. She was just putting his clean socks away, there was a
clunk, something heavy, unsocklike, and then she was shaking out a
small wooden pipe from which rose the thick, unmistakable perfume of the sixties.

At that moment the pipe was a secret her son was keeping from
her, but it was not yet a lie.

She thought about Sam. He was fourteen, bright, winning, his
grades were good, his teachers praised him, girls called him. Most of
the time, he was polite. He was kind to their old dog, Zephyr, and he
could make Beth, his older sister, laugh even when she was in a bad
humor, which was most of the time. Sam was perfect, but if he got
caught with this pipe at his expensive private school he would be
automatically expelled.

Nora dropped the pipe into her sweater pocket. She closed the
drawer and took up the laundry basket. She could feel the weight of
the pipe in her pocket like a leaden heart. She stopped off in her
study and slipped it under a pile of unpaid bills in her desk drawer.

The pipe was now *her* secret, but it was not yet a lie.

When Sam came in from school, he grabbed a bag of chips and
went straight to his room, where he stayed until Nora called him to
dinner. At the table he was cheerful. Had he checked the sock drawer
for the pipe? Did his good humor mask his fear of the confrontation
to come? Nora pushed her peas around her place disconsolately. "So
how did the algebra test go?" she asked Beth.

"Don't ask," Beth said, the too-ready tears standing in her eyes.

"Pass the potatoes," Sam said.

Nora handed him the plate, uncomfortably conscious of how resolutely her eyes stayed focused upon the potatoes. Great, she thought.
Now I can't look at my own son.

The pipe had become a lie.

When the children were asleep, Nora made the mistake of calling

436

their father, Jeff. His young wife answered, sounding nervous. She and Jeff fought a lot, Beth had told Nora; the marriage was doomed. When Jeff got on he snapped, "What do you want?"

"I found a marijuana pipe in Sam's drawer," Nora said.

"What does it look like?"

"Like a marijuana pipe," she said.

"Is it wooden?"

"Yes."

"Is it small, black?"

"Yes."

"It's mine," Jeff said. "I've been looking for it for a week."

Nora closed her eyes. Sam had never intended to use the pipe. He had taken it to get at his father, with whom he was increasingly at odds, and now she had betrayed him right into the lion's jaws. After seven years, Jeff was still resentful of Nora for forcing him to leave his family to take up with a woman half his age, and he liked nothing better than characterizing her to their children as a manipulative harridan. He would turn the whole thing into a major battle, and Sam would end up blaming her. "How stupid can you be?" Nora said, and hung up.

That night Nora lay awake, going over her options. She could try to persuade Jeff not to tell Sam how he had found out about the theft, but even the thought of such a conversation felt demeaning. She could say nothing and let Jeff and Sam have it out, then try to pick up the pieces and regain her son's trust. She could tell Sam frankly what she had done and why. This was the obvious best choice, but Nora knew Sam would take it as an attack on his character; there would be harsh words, tears, misunderstanding; something would be permanently altered between them.

In the morning she was haggard, but she was at her post at the stove when her children came down for breakfast. It was cold out; she had chosen oatmeal for comfort. Beth came in and put her arm around her mother's waist, breathing in the steam from the cheerfully bubbling pot. "I thought I smelled oatmeal," she said approvingly. Sam put a bowl of milk and raisins into the microwave. "I love oatmeal," he said.

Everything was fine, Nora told herself. Her children were eating oatmeal. Then they were out the door, their young shoulders bent beneath the weight of their schoolbooks. No sooner were they gone than she dug out the pipe, took it upstairs, and dropped it inside a sock—was it the same sock?—in her son's drawer. Maybe he had

437

never looked and found it missing. As she stepped out of his room, the front door slammed and Sam came charging up the stairs. "Forgot my bio book," he said, rushing past her. In a few moments he passed her again, clutching the heavy textbook. Bio book? Nora thought, as the door slammed behind her son, or had he come back for the pipe? Should she look to see if it was still there?

So Nora stood paralyzed on the landing, pretending she didn't know her son, pretending she did, every moment becoming more and more tangled in a web of secrets and lies. She couldn't remember which came first, the lies or the secrets, the secrets or the lies.

Just calm down, she told herself. Just get used to it. Most people live like this all the time.

The Aquarium of the Dead: Chicago Stories

Peter Orner

EDGEWATER TERRACE APARTMENTS, CHICAGO (2007)

BORN AND RAISED IN Chicago, my grandmother, as she approached ninety-seven, began to remember the childhood in the old country she never had.

One scene in particular: she remembered standing in a puddle holding a cabbage to her chest.

They took cabbages, she says. She eyes me long and hard. You think I don't know they took a lot more than cabbages? But they also, she says, seizing my arm and pulling me closer, took cabbages.

BROOKS BROTHERS, MICHIGAN AVENUE, CHICAGO (2002)

My father roams Brooks Brothers like a leopard in his own jungle. This particular hue of blue all his. Today, though, he's not on prowl. He's come in for—

What has he come in for?

A suit salesman gradually approaches. Mustache, a pronounced limp that makes him sway from side to side as he moves soundlessly across the thick carpet. Longish face, eyes set forward in his head, not quite buggy, almost. Not a handsome man yet not without dignity in his homeliness, my father thinks. But where's Charlie?

"Can I help you?"

My father's not sure what to say. *I'm only here for refuge.* How would this sound? He stares at the unfamiliar salesman. The salesman looks for a moment at his cordovans, then back at my father as if he's begun to understand. His eyes wetten slightly. There is comfort in our blueality. I know it. You know it. Nothing to be ashamed of. Here the harshness of the world is lessened.

439

"Where'd you get the limp?" my father says.

"I was born with it," the salesman says.

"Oh," my father says. He'd like to lean up against the false mahogany and whistle. Just passing the time.

"So you weren't in the service?"

"No."

"I was," my father says. "In Biloxi. Mostly KP duty."

"Kitchen patrol," the salesman says.

"That's right," my father says. "Soap and bubbles. My hands have been clean ever since. Relatively."

The store is mostly empty. A couple of younger salesmen murmur to each other in the back. No sign of Charlie.

"So," my father says. "How's the fall line?" Again only as one Brooks man to another. He doesn't want the obsequious song and dance. He only wants to talk a little shop with someone on the inside.

"Seersucker's back."

"Again?"

"In yellow and pale blue."

"Hmmmmm," my father says. "Hmmmmm. Anything else?"

"They're bringing back the three button."

"The three button? When did they get rid of the three button?"

"Last year. It was foolish. Last year everything was two button with double vents."

Double vents. Awful. A kinsman.

"You haven't been here long."

"No. I was out in the suburbs. Transferred."

"Transferred? Like in the army."

"In a way," the salesman says. "We are, after all, on the front line of fashion."

The salesman and my father laugh together. When they stop, my father says quietly, "It's lonely, moving around like that?"

My father's feeling a little wobbly. Drunkish at 4:00 in the afternoon on a Monday?

The salesman nods and half smiles. He doesn't show his teeth unless he has to. Again, it's as if he understands what my father's getting at in spite of the fact that my father isn't sure himself what he's trying to say.

"You get attached to a place," the salesman says.

"I myself haven't done much moving around. Not since the army really. I was born here. Staying in one place can be lonely too. Of course."

"Of course."

"I've been in the same office on Wabash for—"

The salesman breaks in, he can't help himself. "I was in North-brook for seven years."

"In the mall?"

"Yes."

"Good God."

"And before that I sold shoes at Fields in Lake Forest for eighteen years. Now that took courage."

"A week in Lake Forest."

"So you know."

"Snoots," my father says. "When you're born up there the doctor shoves a polo stick up your ass."

"So you know!" the salesman practically yelps.

"Jews know."

"Catholic myself."

"You're no better. To them you're worse. There's more of you."

The salesman rolls back on his feet and laughs harder now, and again, he and my father—kinsmen—laugh together until neither of them is laughing anymore but they're still laughing.

"Not a religious man myself," my father says.

"Neither me," the salesman says. "Still you drag it along."

"That's right," my father says. "What are you going to do?"

"What are you going to do?"

My father reaches for a display of belts hanging nearby. They look like a set of lonely tongues. He reaches for one and fondles it. "Alligator?" he says wistfully.

"Cowhide," the salesman says.

No, true. Brooks has never been known for its leather. Even so, my father thinks, you can never have enough decent quality belts.

"Say," my father says, "what happened to dear old Charlie?"

"Charlie Hubbard?" the salesman says. "Oh, they put Charlie out to pasture."

My father grips the belt. Charlie. Stories about growing up on a dairy farm in Wisconsin. Always sucking a cough drop that made him slur his words when he talked. One about a boot getting lost in the muck. Having to hop back to the house on one foot. And in the spring of that year, a shoot of corn growing up out of that boot!

He thinks of Charlie in a seersucker suit on all fours in a field chewing cud. When this city's through with you it spits you back to Oshkosh. It'll happen to me.

"Oshkosh," my father burbles. Still wobbly.

"I'm sorry, I didn't hear you."

"Oshkosh," my father says. "Oshkosh, Wisconsin."

Again the salesman nods. Again, he gets it. He gets Oshkosh. *Who is this person?* My father thinks. My father wonders. My father. He tries to look into the salesman's eyes, but doesn't get very far. It's as if the man's eyes have been varnished over. He's hiding somewhere in there and my father can't find him. This is all very strange. Dizzier now. Brooks Brothers afternoon. Outside, the paling cement light. In here the sinkingness, the old muffled feeling. A kind of happy drowning. And you could, couldn't you? Right here? In this deep welcoming carpet?

TOUHY AVENUE, NILES (1997)

The architect who designed it used a postcard of the real one and he didn't do that bad a job. It leans. Except that this leaning tower is only three and half stories high and next door to a used car lot in Niles. On their way home from cards at Twin Orchard, Bernice Burman and Gert Zetland always stop at a coffee shop across the street. Just a stupid funny thing. A whim of Gert's. Always made her think of her honeymoon in Italy although they never made it to Pisa.

They are sitting at their table by the window and Bernice is listening to Gert yatter on about her nephew Jerry, the maverick tort lawyer. Cars whiz by on Touhy Avenue. Occasionally someone slows down, someone who hasn't seen the tower before, and there's all kinds of honking.

Gert's voice, after all these years, has become an almost pleasant background gurgle. Occasionally Bernice sighs over one of Jerry's triumphs. Hears none of it. She watches the busboy clear away the cups and crusty soup bowls, a young man with tapered black hair and invisible buttocks. She wonders what he sits on. If it hurts in the bones. Maybe he never sits. Maybe he never sleeps. Clears tables. Clears tables. Maybe there is no end to the clearing of our tables? Mexican, he probably came across the border in his underwear. Maybe he'll look at her. And what would he see if he did. An old biddy making eyes.

Gert reaches and pinches Bernice's forearm.

"And so they offered eighty thousand to settle and Jerry, my Jerry, says to them, 'Blow it out your nozzle.' Oh, I know he said

442

something far more disgusting, but that's what he told his delicate-eared aunt, always trying to protect me from anything untoward. He thinks I was born in the seventeenth century. Even people born in the seventeenth century weren't born in the seventeenth century. Anyway, blow your eighty thousand out your nozzle! Can you imagine?"

"Nozzle?"

"Nose, Bernice, nose. What's your problem?"

Bernice waves her off. She sighs appreciatively over Jerry. Gert's hair is frostier than usual today. It looks like if you touched it, you'd get snow on your fingers. She thinks of mountains. God knows where they were, somewhere north of here where there's mountains, Michigan maybe, and Seymour said, Look, Bernice, look what the wind did. Like somebody came up here with a paintbrush. He was right, Seymour, for once. The snow didn't even look cold. It looked like sugar. And she remembers being vaguely afraid of those trees, remembers thinking for some reason that the snow was cruel to be so deceptive. How long ago? Seymour insisting we go walking in the snow in the mountains of all the cockamamie things and us getting in the car and driving for hours. Were the children with us? I can't even remember.

"Why don't they tear that thing down already?" Bernice says.

Gert pauses her Jerry narrative and looks curiously at Bernice. "What thing?"

"The tower."

Oh, the tower, Gert thinks. The funny leaning tower. Who cares about the—Gert leans forward and stares more closely into Bernice's glossy eyes and nearly gasps. She's withering. When did this happen? Poor darling. Seymour. Dead more than a year now and here he is, right in her face.

"And you know I saw the real one," Bernice says. "And you know what?"

"What?"

"It's taller, but just as dull."

"Dear—"

Bernice ignores her, honks into her napkins, and says, "In fact, I hated Italy. All that self-congratulation. They say the French are bad. Seymour said it was impossible, that nobody in their right mind could possibly hate Italy, that nobody on the face of the earth had ever—"

"Dear—"

But this time nothing stops Gert short other than her own simply not knowing what to say. What do you say? About the loss of a man who didn't so much torment Bernice as mutter nasties in her direction for fifty odd years. *For Christ sake, Bernice, stop the idiot talking, always the idiot talking.* She considers her own Milt, as irrelevant as a pair of old garage shoes, but what if he wasn't around? Milt with his morning peeing and his farts to beat the band. A sort of bland horror overcomes her. Gert reaches for her own neck and gently rests her fingers on her own pulsing throat.

Bernice is staring at the busboy with eyes she could swear—

"Bernice, you're lusting the busboy."

"What if I am?"

What do you say to that? Nothing. You don't say anything to that. You let it go. You let a lot of things go. Gert calls for the check. She roots around in her purse for her wallet. At Seymour's funeral Bernice said at least now she wouldn't have to water down the Scotch. Because old Sy wanted to die soused, his ship gallantly jouncing through a gale in the South Seas, and it was a battle till the day he keeled over in the driveway. "Demasted," was his last word.

Bernice said it was a relief and Gert knows now that she was either lying then, or it's become a lie. Which is worse? Does it matter? We end up having coffee and gabbing. We think it's the same but it isn't. Is this the last cruelty? That we hold steady and still—

CHICAGO AND NORTHWESTERN TRACKS, HIGHLAND PARK (1988)

We're waiting for the trains. After midnight and me and Barkus stoned again and lying on our stomachs on that huge corrugated sewage pipe in the ditch between the tracks and the bike path. It was about the light, the green gloom of the late-night trains, and how there were always a few people, bobbing heads, asleep, their pale cheeks pressed flat against the glass. And I remember Barkus saying that those trains were the moving aquarium tombs of recently dead suburban commuters. This is what happens. It's limbo. God's still trying to decide where to put these assholes. In the meantime, in order to preserve the souls of their bodies intact, he floods these trains with water and sends the dead to Waukegan and back again. Barkus laughed quietly. He was wearing sunglasses and a pair of his mother's slippers.

"Why aren't they swimming?" I said. "Train full of water, I'd swim."

Barkus rubbed his chin. I never invented anything new. I only added to things he came up with. But this wasn't bad. The dead swimming to Waukegan. I could feel him seeing them in his head. *Exactly. The laps of the damned. Water torture by boredom. There's a guy with a lash and a whistle, the kind only dolphins can hear. But every once in a while they sneak a look out at the world they once disdained because now they know. If only they'd been out here sharing a joint with us.* Barkus sat up and hawked a loogie into the weeds. He shrugged. "No, the dead are feetless."

MY FAVORITE INN, HIGHWOOD (1984)

My grandfather still wears his white Barry Goldwater pants. He smiles now. He's gently rattling his drink. That always round face, those few strands of hair left scrawled across his head. He's out. He's at Willie's. My grandmother, her heavy droopy face, her huge chorus girl eyes, those eyes that always got her noticed. It was always a competition among cousins over who most inherited her eyes. They're alone in a booth toward the back.

They don't talk much. It doesn't matter. All that counts is they're at Willie's. They wait for their tortellini soup. My Favorite Inn, Highwood, Illinois. Anybody in the know calls it Willie's. It's not a club and Willie takes no reservations. Doesn't matter if you're a bum or Ron Santo. You wait for a table at Willie's.

That was always the beauty of the place. A true democracy. Thank almighty God for Highwood! Years ago, an oasis, the only place to get a goddamned drink on the parched North Shore. And my Favorite Inn, of all the places to be, was the *only* place to be. And Willie presided. There was order to the universe. You waited at the bar till Willie came and tapped you on the shoulder. Willie, a pudgy, bellowy man with a tall froth of hair and huge white teeth.

Seymour! Bernice! Where you been all my life? I haven't seen you since Tuesday. Whatayou? Eating slop at home?

All those laughs. Used to be you could measure your life in those roaring laughs.

The soup's still tops, and the steak in marsala's still thick as a radial tire. Willie had a simple notion. Make the food good and make a lot of it. Then charge up the wazoo for drinks. They used to come here with the Pearlmutters, with Mort and Happy Bernheimer, with Sammy and Doris Pinkert. And they'd hold court in one of the big semicircular booths up front and laugh, talk golf, business, children, vacations, politics.

But years pile up. Divorces. Businesses go bust, children fail, people fall out. Saturday nights now people stay home and watch the shows. They die. They move to Florida. And Willie's kind of swank isn't swank anymore.

Tonight, the place is mostly empty.

Seymour! Bernice! You two still kicking around. It's a miracle. Myself, I could have sworn I dropped dead last month.

And my grandfather raises his head and laughs at the ceiling. And my grandmother reaches for Willie's beringed hands and Willie squeezes and my grandmother squeezes and for a moment there's nothing like it. To be seen, to be known by Willie in front of a crowd even if the crowd is a decade back in your mind.

My grandmother thinks of the smoky reddish light, how it used to slowly drift.

And there they are, three of them, my grandparents and Willie like the last soldiers standing.

My grandfather says, "For crying out loud, Willie, why don't you cash out and move to Sarasota? You don't need to stick around just for us."

"Fuck Sarasota," Willie says.

But it's true. Willie's tired. The act has just about run its course. And he could have retired eight times over with what he's socked away. He always preferred cash. God knows it made things easier. Some nights in the seventies they'd roll the paper money out the back door in a wheelbarrow.

Now even the light's exhausted, my grandmother thinks. It sags, bloodless, across the walls.

You go out. You get in the Lincoln and you go out—

Because what's the alternative? The silence of the house?

CHARLIE BEINLICH'S, NORTHBROOK (1979)

I go to Charlie Beinlich's with my father. I order a cheeseburger and fries. The cheeseburger comes. I pick up a fry and try to eat exactly half of it, gnawing off the ridges but leaving the essence of the fry itself. It clings like a worm to my finger.

"Stop that, will you."

"What?"

I eat the fry.

"Tell me about yourself."

"What?"

I look at the mounted sturgeon above my father's head. Its bulgy glass eyes and fat scaly body. Beinlich's is supposed to look like a fishing lodge with the pine paneling and all the fish on the walls except that it's on Skokie Boulevard across from the movie theaters Edens I and Edens II.

I start working on another half a fry. The ridges are where the good grease gets trapped away from the actual potato part so you want to try to save that part for later. It isn't easy to do. It's a surgical operation.

My father watches me. He chews his fish slowly, searching for the bones with his tongue.

Friday night in 1979. Dad's night. The rollicking suburbs. Best damn burger on the North Shore!

"There's nothing you can tell?"

"What?"

"I see. Already you've seen all there is to see. You've seen peace, you've seen war. You've been on the fucking moon with Buzz Aldrin."

"What?"

"You think this is all a joke?"

Time for more ketchup. I whack the bottom of the bottle and get lucky on the first try. The ketchup throbs, pooling thickly on my plate, and the fries poke out like the heads of ferry passengers drowning in blood. Like when the Eastland tipped over in the sewage of the Chicago River. All those people drowning in shit. I rescue one, eat the fry whole.

"Look at me once in a while, will you."

"I've seen you."

My father laughs. He pulls a bone out of his mouth.

"All right. You win."

He turns to watch the skirt of a waitress fling by. I watch the side of my father's scrubbed, ruddy face. He is the cleanest, most scrubbed man on the face of the earth. Dogs would be in heaven shitting on the snowy white carpet of his bedroom. In fact, Rico once took that liberty and it almost led to capital punishment.

The wreckage on my plate, the half-eaten burger, flooded fries, avoided vegetables. I push it away and wait for my father to pay the check.

I think of Rico's real death a couple of years after that glorious shit. One day he was lying on the kitchen floor breathing but he couldn't stand up. For a week he was like that. Breathing on the kitchen floor and not standing up. Here was a dog who spent every hour of every day wanting milk bones but that last week he wouldn't have eaten a milk bone if you shoved it down his throat. I know. I tried to jam one in his panting mouth.

SYLVESTER PLACE, HIGHLAND PARK (1976)

My grandfather forever lamented the fact that he'd gone all the way to the South Pacific and the only combat he saw was the age-old battle between the big fishes and the little fishes. Occasionally, he said, birds got in on the action. He did, though, lose one man. A young sailor, felled not by enemy fire but some kind of tropical fever.

We buried the boy, my grandfather used to say, at sea.

That was the grand talk. The not-so-grand talk was how they slid him off the board into the ocean. He'd tell this quietly. How they zipped him up in a canvas bag and placed him on the board. His ship didn't sail with coffins like the larger ones. So they had to make do with a bag. They draped him with a flag. All hands bury the dead. After a few respectful words and the slow bugle and a prayer, they raised the board and the last thing that sailor did on earth was make a splash nobody heard because of the roar of the engines and the wind. Until he lost his memory completely, my grandfather remembered that sailor's coordinates. Latitude 12°29′26″ S, longitude 130°49′10″ E. He'd repeat the numbers under his breath. I think of him massive behind his desk, his anxious hands, his fingers twiddling a freshly sharpened pencil. My grandfather was a hard man to love and most days he understood this and accepted it quietly. Every once in a while, though, he'd implore you to look at him, to see his sorrows, and that boy, that dead sailor whose funeral he presided over, would be raised again out of the Pacific. All hands bury the dead. He didn't remember the sailor's name, only that he was from a place called Two Hills, Nebraska. "How about that," he'd say. "To not remember a person's name, but that they're from Two

448

Hills, Nebraska." And then, always, me looking at his fluttering hands, he'd repeat the coordinates. Latitude 12°29′26″S, longitude 130°49′10″E.

"Why are we saved when others, so many others, aren't?"

Red-Hot Ruby
Robert Coover

ON HIS WAY OVER to Lem Filbert's garage to hunt down some wheels after a fortuitous cheeseburger and beer at Mick's Bar & Grill, Georgie Lucci stops in at the corner drugstore to check out the centerfolds in the magazine rack. It is a glorious April day, first of its kind, the sun's popped at last, he has money in his pocket, the birds and flowers are doing their hot-ass spring thing—it is a day in short for draining the old coglioni, for having one's ashes hauled, as they say in the Land of Oz, and Georgie is many moons overdue. His last fuck wasn't even one, just a tired blow job in the front seat of his city taxi by an aging whore—*una troia,* as his long-gone old man used to call his mamma while belting her about—which he had to pay for. He'd even make a play for the scrawny titless snatch behind the soda fountain, but he'd probably have to order something and he hates anything with cow milk in it and has a philosophical objection to spending money for coffee. He loosens the staples and slips the centerfold out of the magazine (if he wins a pot someday, maybe he should buy a camera and take up photography), tucks it under his jacket, and with a wink at the little jugless kid, who has been watching him, strolls out into the sunshine.

It has been shitsville since his vomitous predawn return on Sunday, *un merdaio di merda,* as his dear *babbo* liked to put it when speaking of his beloved family, but things have at last turned around. For the past two days he has been mostly slopping around in the cold, wet weather looking for a job, getting nothing better from it than a sore throat. The post office, the lumberyard, the strip mines, the flour mill, the bars, the gravel pits. *Niente.* Main Street is like Death Valley. Shops boarded up, jobless guys hanging about in the pool hall and barber shop, trying to stay dry, the streets potholed and littered with garbage. No trains, few buses, newspaper now just a print shop, the old hotel looking like a war casualty. Even the bus station pinball machines have been permanently tilted. His old night mine manager, Dave Osborne, apparently got suckered into buying the shoe store from the new mayor when he got elected, and Dave,

450

gone gray, looked twenty years older. Georgie figured there were worse things to do than tickle young girls' feet and peer up their thigh-high skirts, but Dave just shrugged when he asked and gazed off into the wet gloom beyond the shop window. At the Piccolotti Italian Grocery Store, the kid now running the shop laughed in his face. "Fucking highway supermarket's killing us," he said. "Go try them." He did. Offered himself up as a stock boy, bagger, delivery boy, whatever. The manager wouldn't even talk to him. He stole some razor blades and a candy bar and left, wondering what the fuck had dragged him back here. He should have got back on the overnight bus the same day he arrived. Nothing has happened here for five years, nothing good anyway, and nothing ever will, that's what he was thinking.

His mother was startled to see him when he turned up back on Easter morning, as big a surprise as Christ crawling out of his tomb and about as fragrant. "Where have you been, Giorgio?" she asked. "I thought you were dead." She fixed him some breakfast while he rattled on about the high life in the big city, but then when she saw he was broke and jobless, she started putting everything back in the refrigerator and cupboards again and cursing him for being *un imbecille, un testone stupido, un cretino,* same way she used to curse his old man. Another hand-me-down of a sort, his life story. She had shrunk up some since he had last seen her and had retreated into widowy black, though when Georgie asked if the old fellow was dead, she just shrugged and curled her lip and said she had no fucking idea, or Italianisms to that effect. Georgie was just a teenager when the evil old bastard took off, heaving a few chairs around and giving his *mammina* a thorough walloping on his way out the door. Except for his kid sister, all his other brothers and sisters had by then vanished over the horizon, and his sister was soon to follow, running off with a stock-car driver, but Georgie, pulling on his old man's abandoned boots, went down in the mines and was still there a dozen years later when Deepwater blew up, convincing him it was time to change careers. The only brother Georgie knows anything about is the one who became a priest and who still sends his mother a little pocket money now and then. Georgie saw a lot of stag movies up in the city, his favorite being one about monks and nuns having an orgy on the altar in a monastery chapel, and watching it, he couldn't help thinking somewhat enviously about his brother, though as best he remembers him, he was never very interested in *ficas.* Georgie discovered that his mother, poor thing, still distrusted banks and hid her money under her mattress, which helped him get through the next couple of days while he beat the streets like a *puttana,* looking for work. The old lady makes him feel guilty all the time anyway, he figured he might as well give her cause. And it's just a loan, he'll put it all back with interest when he hits a lucky streak.

Which may have just begun. Making his rounds this morning, he dropped by the police station to see Dee Romano. Playing pinochle up at the Legion last night (not part of his lucky streak), he had learned that Old Willie had been losing what few wits he had (as Cheese Johnson said: "Old Willie has lost his marble. . . .") and had been retired from the force, and though everybody at the table and no doubt half the town were applying for the job, Georgie decided to throw his own tattered sweat-stained cap into the ring. As he had expected, Romano, who had locked him up a few times in the days of his dissolute youth, only snorted at this prospect, but agreed to put him on his list of volunteer deputies in case of future need and suggested he go visit Mort Whimple at the fire station, he might have something. This cheered him up. He had always wanted to be a fireman, ever since he asked for a fireman's helmet for Christmas when he was six years old (he didn't get it, only got a cuffing when he cried about it), but Whimple said no chance, he was facing probable layoffs as it was, all he could offer him was a cup of coffee. Never say no. They sat in the sun by the firehouse door and gabbed about the disaster and the crazy evangelical doings back when Whimple was the town mayor and just before Georgie left town, Whimple shaking his grizzled jowls and saying he couldn't wait to get his fat butt out of that goddamned job and back here to the fire station. He had eyes too close to his big nose, one a bit higher than the other, giving him a clownish look that made everything he said seem funny. The chief filled him in on the town's nightlife— "After the Dance Barn burned down, whaddaya got? A coupla sleazy roadhouses, the old Blue Moon, and the Waterton whorehouses"—and said that probably the worst thing he could do if the town was burning down was try to save it. Georgie spun him a line about the good times up in the city, hinting at important family connections and a debilitating sex life. Why didn't he stay? Well, you know, dear old *mammina,* all alone. . . . Whimple seemed interested in that and asked about other folks in the neighborhood, and then got up and announced it was time for his monthly visit to the crapper. "But stay in touch, Georgie," he said. "You never know. If something comes up, I'll let you know."

Empty as that was, it was the first time Georgie had been treated with something other than derision in his job hunt, so it and the delicious weather lifted his spirits enough to go treat himself to a sandwich and beer at Mick's Bar & Grill, the old barbecue joint he preferred having been turned into a take-out pizza parlor in his absence. He didn't even have to dip into what remained of his mother's pile to pay for it, having picked up a few bucks in the pool hall over the past couple of days, cleaning up on the young fry, so he ordered up, feeling virtuous. A man of means like other men. Mick, a heavy guy with a high squeaky voice, was full of stories too. Georgie sat at the bar and heard about what a sinkhole the town had become since he left and how Main Street was dying as if it had an intestinal cancer, about all the people who had left or had popped off, who'd married whom and split with whom and screwed whose wives, about Mick's troubles with his alcoholic Irish mother (they were trading bad mother stories), and about the decline of the high school football and basketball teams and how it all seemed part of the general decline of morals among the kids these days, not to mention the rest of the general population, which was going to hell in a hangbasket, whatever a hangbasket was. Georgie said he thought it was something they used to use down in the mines, back before they had mechanical cages. Mick had a good story about how the old guy who used to own the hotel died right here in this room, laughing so hard at a dirty joke about a priest, a preacher, and a rabbi that he fell backward out of his chair and broke his neck. Mick pointed at a big table in the corner where he said it happened: "He just tipped back, hoohahing, and went right on over and—*snap!*—he was gone." "Well, at least he died laughing, not the worst way to go." "That's what I always say. Even the guys with him couldn't wipe the grins off their faces." Georgie elaborated on the line he'd just given the fire chief about life in the big city, inventing a few cool jobs, furnishing himself a swank bachelor's pad, augmenting the bigwig connections, and throwing in a ceaseless parade of hot chicks. Mick, all agog, asked him what the hell he was doing back here then, and he began to wonder himself until he remembered he was making it all up. He shrugged and said he'd got in a little trouble and had to leave town for a while.

Mick was just telling him how, speaking of trouble, business was so bad a year or so ago he was at the point of having to close down, until the mayor stepped in and gave him a tax break, when who should walk in but Mayor Castle himself, along with Chief Whimple and a couple of others, including that snarling asshole Robbins who runs the Woolworths down the street. They took the same table where the old hotel keeper had keeled over. Georgie got a nod from the fire chief, who then leaned over and muttered something to the mayor, and pretty soon they were all looking him over. He grinned and raised his glass and they invited him over, bought him a beer, offered him a fag, while Mick retreated to his yard-square kitchen off the bar to fry up some hamburgers. Georgie had had dealings with Castle and Robbins in the past, which he hoped they had forgotten, though as it turned out later, they hadn't. It didn't appear to matter, maybe even gave him an in. It seemed they were worried about the general flaunting of the fire regulations in town and, to avoid a senseless tragedy, they needed someone to help enforce them. What they had to offer was a sort of unofficial job both with the fire department as a part-time inspector and also with the mayor's reelection campaign, helping with fund-raising. "He knows how to talk to his own people," Mort said on his behalf, and the mayor explained that they didn't have enough money in the budget to pay a salary, but they could cover him on a sort of contract basis: five dollars for each preliminary visit he makes for the fire department, fifteen for actual inspections, and two percent of all the money he collects personally for the campaign. He grinned and nodded, tossing back his lager, and he was told to report down at the fire station on Monday. They even picked up his lunch tab. On his way out the door, Robbins called out: "Oh earthling Ralphus!" and the mayor boomed: "The Destroyer cometh! Makest thee haste, our spaceship awaits thee!" Georgie, ball cap tipped down over his eyes, hunched his shoulders, waggled his arms as though shaking a sheet, and whooed like a ghost, which set them all off laughing so hard there was some risk of a sequel to the hotel keeper's demise.

When Georgie reaches Lem Filbert's garage, Lem is not in, but Georgie's old drinking pal and classmate Guido Mello is still working there, looking heavier and a lot soberer than he used to. Married now, couple of kids, as he says, he is showing the burden of that. Black grease on his fat nose where he's rubbed it, adding to his general down-in-the-dumps look. Guido tells him Lem is out test-driving a car whose shocks and wheel bearings they have just replaced, but if Georgie has come by looking for a job, forget it. Lem has plenty of business, these being hard times when people have to fix up their old cars instead of buying new, but he is not clearing much, people being reluctant to pay their bills, all that's keeping him afloat being loan money from the bank and the shitty wages he is paying Guido for too many fucking hours. But what can he do? Little as it is, his kids would starve without it. "He's one hardassed sonuvabitch to work for," Guido says, and smears the other side of his nose. "Maybe you should unionize," Georgie suggests, and Guido snorts and says, "Yeah, me and who else?" "Well at least you could be union president," Georgie says, but instead of laughing at that, Guido only shakes his round burry head and sighs. "Jesus, Georgie, we're halfway through our fucking lives and what have we got?"

Long tall Lem rolls in then in the battered green Ford he has been test-driving. Georgie greets his old mine buddy and baseball teammate and they shoot the shit for a while, Georgie filling Lem in on what little he knows about Wally Brevnik and other Deepwater refugees who fled town after the disaster and letting fly with his by-now well-rehearsed tales of the big city, which for the first time fail to impress, Lem meanwhile unloading all his sour gripes about the garage, the fucking irresponsible mining company, this pig's ass of a town, and the whole stupid fucking world in general. No, there's no baseball team, he hasn't swung a bat since Tiger Miller left town. Lem's brother Tuck was killed in the disaster and Tuck's wife, Bernice, is now living with him, doing the laundry and housekeeping and fixing him his lunchpail every day, just as if he were still working a mine shift. She has recently gotten involved with those evangelical nuts out at the church camp, which pisses Tuck off, and they have been having rows about it, but he knows Bernice was always close to Ely's widow and needs a connection, so he'll probably just have to live with it. Georgie asks him why he doesn't just marry Bernice, and Lem says, "Nah. Then I'd probably have to fuck her."

Georgie tells him he is back in town for a little while and needs an old junker to bum around in, what has he got? Lem looks skeptically down his nose at him, so Georgie, on the pretense of digging for a coin for the Coke machine, flashes his mother's roll and mentions that he's going to be working for city hall and might require wheels for that. Lem shrugs and takes him around to the back lot where a lot of old wrecks stand rusting in the sun. Lem recommends a little rebuilt Dodge coupe with about seventy thousand miles on it, allegedly, but Georgie's lustful eye falls on an old two-tone crimson-and-cream boat-sized Chrysler Imperial with Batmobile tail fins and gun-sight taillights, a fucking classic and perfect for his more urgent needs. Lem says it has had a rough life and he can't guarantee it will make it out of the lot without breaking down, but Georgie's heart is set ("Well, it's your money, go ahead and buy the goddamn thing," Lem says, "I could use the fucking repair business. . . ."), so they haggle for a while and agree on a price, and Georgie talks him into letting him give it a trial run, setting his half-finished Coke down as if planning to come right back to it.

Inspired by the baseball talk and the lush weather, Georgie takes a run out by the high school athletic fields, first closing the glove compartment door on the top of the centerfold so that it dangles there to cheer him on his journey. He has done a lot of driving up in the city, that being mostly what he did except jerk off, and it feels good to get back behind a wheel again, and on mostly empty streets and roads where he can open up. The old crate makes a lot of clunky noises, has no pickup at all, the gearshift is tricky, and the steering wheel is pretty loose, but what it has, he knows, is presence. In it, he is somebody, and, window down and arm out the window, he blows kisses and tips his ball cap to all he passes to let them know he knows it. He decides to name the fading beauty after one or another of his favorite blue-movie characters like "Nympho Nellie" or "Sally Sucker," but finally, given her colors, settles on "Red-Hot Ruby," who, as he recalls, also had a big thrusting creamy ass and lipsticked her anus.

He is in luck; the boys are having their first practice of the new season. He stops, keeping the motor running, to jaw with the coach for a minute and volunteer his services as a hitting coach, while the kids gather around to admire Ruby. Georgie could never field a ball for shit, but, a natural with any stick in his hand, he was always a good hitter, and the coach remembers that and says, sure, come along any time. Georgie, waving goodbye, feels like this day is turning into the best day of his life.

After that, he rolls around the periphery of town, the centerfold's raised *culo* flapping merrily in the breeze, checking out the motels and roadhouses that the fire chief mentioned for later on. "Big night coming, baby," he says, and raps the dash. He passes, chattering away to Ruby, or else to the centerfold—they're an agreeable blur in his mind—the Sir Loin steak house and old passion-pit drive-in movie, the driving range and country club, a few golfers already out enjoying the first real day of spring, the road to the gravel pits and the one to the Waterton whorehouses, the new shopping center, new when he left town, and the burned-out ruins of the old Dance Barn where the big bands used to come and where they served anyone who could see over the bar. First got his cork popped by the hand of another

under the table in a hard wooden booth in there, the hand belonging
to a girl just fourteen years old like his green young self. At the time,
he didn't really know what came next, or if he knew, didn't know
how to make it happen, so he lost out with that chick. Never mind.
Many more to follow. Georgie Porgie, pudding and pie, kissed the
girls and made them sigh.

He pulls into a filling station to add a few dollars of gas, patting
Ruby's provocative rear end while he's got the pump in her (a patch
of deep rust back there, he notes, like some kind of fatal crotch disease), and sees by the gauge it's just a drop in her bottomless bucket.
Ruby's the deep throat kind of girl; he could run through a pile pretty
fast just keeping her juiced up. He cruises the strip of car dealers,
many closed down, their vast lots vacated, but still flying their faded
flags and streamers; then Chestnut Hills, the cheap prefab developments built mostly for mining families at the edge of town where
there are no hills, no chestnuts, looking for who knows what. Some
broad from the past probably. A lot of scabby abandoned houses,
muddy yards, old cars, and trucks on blocks. Then it's the rich folks'
side of town with their big houses and flagpoles and fancy shrub-
bery—though even they are looking pretty seedy and uncared for,
and there are for sale signs on some of them—and finally, after a
clanking cap-waving spin down Main Street, on over the rusty un-
used rail tracks, overgrown with weeds, and into his own neighborhood. Dagotown, as the crackers call it. "Home, baby," he tells Ruby.
Mostly painted frame houses in various states of dilapidation, many
of them multifamily, overcrowded, and depressed, but comfortingly
familiar and welcoming in the warm afternoon sun. He tours all the
houses where former girlfriends once lived, letting Ruby show them
what they've been missing. Probably all married now, swarmed
round with brats and gone to fat or worse.

He spies Vince Bonali rocking on his sunny front porch with a beer
in his hand, and, as Ruby's been getting overheated ("Easy, girl!"), he
pulls over to the curb to let her cool off and invites himself up, thinking he might be able to hit his old faceboss up for a buck or two of
gas money. He is an understanding guy, they have been through a lot
together, had some great old times, he would do the same for Vince.
He'd heard from Cokie Duncan that Vince had sunk pretty low after
his wife kicked off, and he finds him so, a morose old *musone*, too
grumpy even to stand up and shake his hand, but after commisera-
tions and family talk and a few reminiscences about the old section,
Vince lightens up enough to offer Georgie a beer and pop another for

himself. Vince is wallowing a dead cigar in his mouth. "Want me to try to light that mess for you?" "Nah. If I smoked it, I'd have to buy another and I don't have the dough. Eating it, it last longer." He turns his empty pockets inside out in a demonstration before settling heavily back into the rocker. There went that idea. Vince nods toward the car. "Pick that piece of faggot junk up in the city?" "No. Here. Just shopping. Giving it a trial run. Gotta go turn it in soon." "Made a pile up there, did you?" "Well, hit it lucky a coupla times, but—" "You know, when I first seen you coming, Georgie, I had the funny idea you were looking for a handout. What a laugh that woulda been. All the spare cash in this town is at the bank. That's where this comes from," he says, holding up the beer. "That guy at the bank's supplying you?" "No, Angie. She works there. She buys the groceries now. She gives me an allowance, Georgie. A fucking beer allowance. You're drinking up part of my weekly allowance." That makes him feel just great. What is he supposed to do? Give it back? It doesn't even taste good anymore.

"You were smart to get your ass outa here, Georgie. Look at me. I haven't had a goddamn day's work since they shut the mine down five years ago. Five years ago this month, you realize that? It's been a long hard time. And it's gonna get worse. I don't know what the hell you're doing back here." He can't use his little *mammina* line, Vince knows better, and he doesn't want to suggest to his old face-boss (he's *still* the boss) that he has been in any kind of trouble (he hasn't really, other than the everyday). So instead he tells him about his new job as a fire inspector, thinking to earn a bit of respect. Vince snorts and shifts his wet cigar to the other side of his mouth. That thing really is disgusting. "They're using you, Georgie. It's a shakedown racket. You remember old man Baumgarten?" "The dry cleaner?" "Yeah. He was asked for a contribution to the mayor's so-called campaign fund, and when he didn't come across, he got a visit from the fire department. They found a lot of things wrong. So he fixed them. They found some more things wrong and he fixed them again. He was reminded that it was costing him more to comply with the regulations than to cough up the campaign fund donation. Still, he wouldn't go along, so one night his business burned down. The inspectors said it was faulty wiring and he'd been warned, he couldn't even collect on his insurance." "No shit." Georgie's good mood is sinking as the sun sinks. It was a mistake to come up here and let this sick old man bring him down. "Robbins is in on it too, right?" Georgie nods glumly. He really doesn't want to hear any of this. "It was those two guys who dropped us in the shit five years ago, you remember that?"

"How could I forget? That loony lawyer we spooked." A glorious night of masquerades and theatrical revelry (they were shitface spirits from another world), and then a would-be gangshag with an old buddy's widow and a drunken brawl, ending up in handcuffs down at the station with newsguys' flashbulbs popping. He, Vince, Cheese Johnson, and Sal Ferrero, though Sal had fallen away before the end. Georgie thought it was all hilarious, but Vince had big ambitions back then and that night fucked it for him. He turned bitter and weird after that, and it all ended in a daylight raid on the old lawyer's house while everyone else in town was out at the mine waiting for the end of the world and playing bingo. Their aim was looting, plain and simple, but the house was empty. Mostly empty. What Georgie remembers is all the dead cats. "I spun by Lee Cravens's old place a little while ago. Looked like nobody lived there. Whatever happened to old Wanda?"

"How the hell should I know?" It is clearly a touchy subject. Not much prospect of a second beer. Bonali has got his sulk back and is giving him a look like he wishes he were dead. Georgie glances at his wrist as if he had a watch there. "Well, shit, I better get the car back. I'll drop back and see you again soon, Vince."

"If you do, bring your own beer."

"Well, lookit what fell down the fuckin shaft," says Cheese Johnson when Georgie walks in.

Georgie has made the usual rounds, but it's midweek and raining, turning cold and windy again, it's doornail-dead all over town, and still too early for the roadhouses. He has never seen streets so empty. Like some kind of nightmare movie. Even the bowling alley and the Legion Hall, where he'd found two of these guys last night, were all but deserted. A few lonely old farts watching TV. Or more like the TV was watching them. The Eagles Social Club was his last shot. "I was wondering where all the action was."

"That you, Georgie? You musta forgot your hair somewheres. What drug you back to town?"

"Too much tail up in the city, Stevie, it was making an old man outa me. Had to come back for a rest cure."

"Well, y'come to the right place. Sure won't find no tail up here."

"I'm disappointed, Coke. I figured you'd be amenable."

"Listen at the nasty fella with his city ways!"

"You turned up just in time, Giorgio. I could use that five bucks I staked you Sunday."

"Lemme see if I can win it back, *cugino*. What's the game?"

"Dealer's choice, stud or draw, nothing wild. Cap's three raises, limited to a quarter each."

"A quarter!"

"If that's too high we can lower it."

"This ain't the big town, Georgie."

"OK, high rollers. Deal me in."

He's keeping up a brave front, but Georgie's earlier euphoria has drained away. Visiting Bonali was a real bummer, and the betrayed promise of spring weather hasn't helped. A new front has moved in like a kind of sudden sickness of the air and there's talk even of snow. April fool. What little he's eaten (there's an empty pizza delivery box on the next table, still giving off a spicy aroma, reminding him how hungry he probably is) hasn't set well, nor has the hip flask of cheap rye he has polished off; he should have picked up some antacids in the supermarket yesterday when he was in there. Worst of all, he has come to the sodden realization that he'll never get enough money together to pay for Ruby, cheap date as she is. Certainly not up here. Even if he took all these guys' money, there's probably not enough between them for a pair of windshield wipers. Which he has discovered is among the old girl's many urgent needs. Had to drive her with his head out the window in the worst of it. For all his bravura, he does wish he was back in the city. He misses the action, even if it's an action from which he is mostly excluded for lack of the wherewithal. All he has here that he didn't always have up there is a room to sleep in out of the weather, and the price for that is his old lady's ceaseless scorn and fury. Which can get worse. He can only hope she has not looked under the mattress yet.

"All I'm saying is that for the mine company fat cats the disaster wasn't nothing more than one bad hand," says Bert Martini. He only has one arm, having lost the other in the mine accident, so even in draw he leaves his cards facedown on the table, tipping up their edges briefly to read them, then tossing his quarters into the pot with the one hand he has left in life. These guys are all survivors of the explosion that blew out Number Nine's innards and closed it down, and they're still grousing about it five years later. And using the same lines. It's like time's stood still here. His life has been shit in the city, but not this bad. He borrows a fag from Bert and lights up with

Cokie's lighter. "They pocketed their winnings, quit the game, and went home, or wherever they go to get their fucking done, and left the workers holding an empty kitty."

"We're halfway through our fucking lives and whatta we got?" Georgie says, repeating Guido's line.

"Well, the clap," says Cokie Duncan. "Hemorrhoids. . . ."

"At least you got your disability pension, Bert," Steve Lawson says. Like Georgie's cousin Carlo Juliano, Steve lost a brother in the explosion. Steve sees Bert's quarter and raises.

"That makes me the lucky one, hunh?" says Bert, waving his stump.

"Put that thing back in your pants, Bert," says Cheese, meeting the bet and asking for a pair, "and stop showin off."

The best card in Georgie's rainbow hand is a ten of diamonds, but after Cokie Duncan drops his two bits in, he raises a quarter, pretending to want to throw in all he's showing, and it is not so much a bluff as an act of frustration, wanting desperately for something to happen, any goddamned thing, even a fight. Betwise, not smart. After drawing blanks, he tosses, and Carlo wins the little pile of coins with low triplets, Georgie's dwindling roadhouse reserve now diminished by his contribution to it.

When it's his deal, to do Bert a favor he calls seven-card stud. "I seen Guido today. He's not a happy man," he says, passing out the hole cards.

"Well, he up and married the Sicano girl, the one who was never quite right in the head, and one a their kids has a medical problem. Some sympdrome or other. So he's sorta lost his sense a humor."

"Sicano? The one we all banged in here on the pool table one night?"

"The same."

"Oh man. Well buttered buns. What'd he go and do that for?"

"Il Nasone never had many options amongst the ladies."

"He says Lem has turned out to be a hard man to work for."

"Who ain't? He should try that tightwad cocksucker Suggs for a spell."

Cokie and Steve, he learns, have got on part-time at one of the strip mines, but when he asks, he's told don't even bother, old man Suggs is not partial to Italians. "He only likes to abuse his own kind." Cheese got hired and fired out there and is now doing nonunion contract work in one of the last deep-shaft mines still operating in the area. Next thing to being a scab, but the strips are nonunion too, so no one is saying much. Cokie once had a wife, but she ran off during a stretch on the night shift so long ago no one around here remembers her anymore, Duncan included. Cokie was assistant faceboss in Bonali's crew and on the night of the disaster was left in charge when Bonali went looking for a phone. Georgie was sure Bonali was not planning to come back and they were all going to die if they just stood there in that smoky pitch-black furnace, so he and Wally Brevnik took off on their own. It was Georgie's intention to claw his way out by his fingernails if he had to. They went through some rough stuff, but Wally had a cool head and they eventually reached the top and already had a cup of spiked coffee in their hands by the time the rest of the section came up. All but Pooch and Lee.

Several of them have been out to the hospital to see Big Pete Chigi who has black lung and is breathing his last through respirator nose plugs, and he hears about Ezra Gray who was in Red Baxter's section and got out of Deepwater OK, but then went down in another mine a state over and got crippled in a fall that killed three other guys.

"Yeah, I seen him—broke his fuckin back. He's on rubber wheels for the duration. Ez was workin nonunion, so no comp or insurance. A hotshot lawyer talked him inta filin suit agin the owner, but the owner jist faded away like he never was. Like he disappeared inta the paperwork or sumthin."

"Same as what happened here. The ruthless dickheads. C'mon, Georgie, cheer me up. Goddamn make me sumthin. Send me down sixth street singin."

"Ez is completely off his nut now. Rantin about the end a the world'n all that. He travels some with Red Baxter, I heerd tell, out preachin that Brunist shit."

"How you hear all this, Steve?"

"From my sister-in-law. Tess keeps in touch with Ez's wife."

"Is old Ez here? Is he out there to the camp?"

"No," says Steve. "I never seen him and he'd be hard to miss."

At first Georgie thinks Steve might have got mixed up with those crackpots somehow, but it turns out Suggs has been helping the cult rebuild the camp, using his own workers for some of the heavy jobs, so both Steve and Cokie have been putting in time out there. It's not clear what Suggs is getting out of the deal, but they're pulling their normal wages, so no complaints. "So what's going on out there in the woods?" Georgie wants to know. "Are they wearing any clothes?"

"Oh yeah. Leastways by day. We don't stay past quittin time, so

462

I don't know whatall they git up to then, but it's purty fuckin chilly to go round bareass even if you're rollin round a lot. From what I could see, they're mostly jist workin their balls off, fixin the place up. Genrally I didn't reckanize no one nother than Ben—you remember ole Ben Wosznik—and Ely's widder. They kinda run things, y'know. And also Willie Hall's out there, Willie and big Mabel."

"That'd be a cute pair, butt-nekkid."

"And Lee Cravens's skinny little widder with all her brats, she's there too."

"Wanda?" Georgie glances up and catches Johnson's wink and gap-toothed grin.

"She's shacked up with some dumb bigass hulk. I mean, really big. They call him Hunk and he's carryin around a whole heap a excess mollycules. But he can move. I seen him dancin round on the open beams a the old lodge roof like a man who don't know what fear is."

"He ain't never been down a mine then."

"So what're you plannin on doin here, Georgie?" Cokie asks as he folds.

"Well, I just picked up a car. Supposed I might get into the taxi business."

The others laugh dryly at that as if he's just laid a joke, and he grins too, waiting to see what's funny. What's funny is the mayor's new licensing fee, and he gets an earful then about corruption in city hall and themes of like nature, so he decides not to mention his appointment next week at the fire station. "Besides, Georgie, they ain't no fares to be had anyhow. What kinda fuckin town you think this is?"

He knows what kind of town it is. He had forgotten, but now he remembers. He was feeling shitty when he walked in here, he's feeling shittier now. He has dealt himself a second king over a pair of eights, and he risks a couple more quarters, but Johnson beats him with a club flush, so even his luck is bad. He was about to propose a run to the roadhouses with whoever wanted to come along, but Johnson is cackling meanly as he hauls in the pot and the others are grousing in their tedious way and he really doesn't want to be around them any longer. Bert is back on the mine bosses again, so to change the subject and lighten things up, Georgie elaborates on some of the big city tales he has been inventing during his job hunt, including a new one about a high-price hooker named Ruby, red-hot Ruby, using anatomical details from the centerfold he's had hung in the car all day and personality quirks based on the old junker's clunky

463

behavior. "Well, we're just getting warmed up, you know, really shimmying down the road, burning rubber, when her fucking eyelashes fall off and she gets so hot she starts making these really nasty noises down below. . . ."

"Sounds like a real beaut, Georgie," Carlo says, laughing.

"No shit, she was. Even posed for one a them centerfolds. She invited me along for the photo session. She said me watching got her hot. Sure got me hot. She was a sight to see. An ass end to die for! I still have a copy somewhere, I'll show it to you someday."

"Hey, speakin a pitchers, show Georgie the ones you got, Cheese!"

Johnson shrugs, reaches into a paper sack, and tosses out a half dozen well-thumbed black-and-white photographs of two naked people doing a kind of sex manual thing on a leather couch. No hardcore shots, but the guy's well hung, they're both good-lookers, and the beaver shot with the guy standing over her like he's about to belt her one or else swat her with his dick is good enough to make you want to poke her. But they're a bit blurry and the light's bad. Could be stills from a cheap stag movie. Then he looks closer. "Wait a minute. Who is that? Is that Tiger Miller?" They're all grinning. All except Bert Martini, who says, "You shouldn't ought to be showin them photos around. She was a nice girl. And Tiger was a pal. When I was in the hospital he come by to see me near every day. I figure there's more here than what meets the eye." The others laugh at that.

"And that's the Bruno kid, right? Marcella. The one who got killed. She was in school with me. These are a little different from what's in the high school annual. Where'd you get them?"

"You remember Jonesy, useta work at the newspaper, back when we had a fuckin newspaper. We was playin cards's gittin blitzed together up to the Legion the night Jonesy split town. I walked him to his train and he give em to me as a see-ya-later present. I plumb forgot about em till them apocaleptics showed up agin."

"Sure you did," Carlo laughs. "You can tell by all the cum spots on them."

Something about the photos bothers Georgie. Not just the realization that something was happening back then and he'd missed out. He missed out on plenty. She always had a nice smile, but except for a few friends she kept to herself, he hardly knew her. Her brother was a complete psycho. Everybody avoided him and he supposes some of that rubbed off on Marcella. He doesn't remember anyone ever dating her. No, it's something about seeing her so exposed like that.

Not so much her naked snatch, he's seen his share of those, but all the rest of her, so laid open. Georgie has never seen that look on a girl's face before. Those looks. They change from photo to photo. But she is looking not just with her face but with all her body, her snatch as much a part of her looking as her eyes. Her navel or her toes. Her mouth, half open. So it's like something terrible is being bared that shouldn't be seen, something that, once bared, can never be covered up again, and he hates it that these cackling shits are ignorant witnesses to it. And she's so still. And silent. It's like she has been spread out to be carved up. Consumed. Well. She's dead. Must have died right after these pictures were taken. It's like getting the hots for a corpse. He wants to cover her up. Close her eyes. "Where's her brother now?" he asks, feeling soberer than he wants to be. "Is he out there at the camp?"

"Giovanni? Nah, they locked the loony away right after the world ended and he never come out."

"He's dead, I think," says Steve Lawson.

"Dead?"

"So I heerd."

So, Georgie decides, tossing in another losing hand, is this dump. He feels suffocated by the dead. He looks around the table. Even these guys are dead. The whole fucking town is a town of the walking dead, and he's going to be one of them unless he moves his ass. Besides, if he wants to score tonight, he should get on the road while he still has coin left to operate with. He glances at his wrist where his watch would be if he had one and announces he has a date waiting for him, gotta go. He had made the mistake of tossing some money on the table when he sat down and, as he gets up to leave, Carlo reaches over and snatches up a couple of loose skins. "Now you owe me three," he says.

"Ruby," he says, leaning his heavy head against her wheel, "Ruby . . . what I really feel like doing is shooting somebody." Georgie is sitting in the Blue Moon Motel parking lot waiting for the old girl to warm up. Soft wet snow is falling like a punch line for the stupid joke that is his life. He's cold, wearing only a shirt and jacket, feeling miserable. The only way morning's promise is going to be fulfilled is in a Waterton whorehouse, provided they still exist and he can find an old *puttana* who will take what little money he—he and his mother—have left. Ever hopeful even in deepest despair, he assumes that, on

465

a shit night like this, they'll take any trade they can get.

The motel was the last stop on his desperate but futile nightlong quest. For what? Cunt? More than that. Some kind of affirmation is what he was looking for. Some justification. Just a pleasant conversation with someone would have been nice. He is full of sorrow and could have used an arm around his shoulder. The roadhouses weren't completely empty. Worse. Those few out on the crummy night were all juveniles. Drunken teenage high school kids. Boys pissing themselves with their own confused excitement, a few girls going bad. Well, that was all right. Hey, let's rock. Georgie felt like one of them—he *was* one of them. But they didn't feel like one of him. They called him an old pervert. Baldy, they called him. Dildo. Gramps. One of them they were calling Moron even threatened to take him outside and beat the shit out of him if he didn't fuck off. He would have welcomed a brawl, but his own team had a membership of one and those red-eyed boys with erections bulging their jeans didn't look like they would know when to stop.

By the time he had reached the Blue Moon, he was no longer looking for women, he was happy only to sink into a drunken stupor and let his life end that way. Just as well, for there were no women to be had, unless one of the two couples in the room should have a blowup and leave a partner behind. He had hoped to catch the old girl who used to play a melancholic piano in here, but she had been replaced by one of those twangy hillbilly types, a long loose assembly of bones with some skin on them, wearing a sweaty cowboy hat and a plaid shirt. Boots that looked like they might not have been off his feet since he grew into them. When Georgie took his stool alone at the bar, the hick was singing about dead mommies and daddies, which was a real pickup. There were two older people in a booth back in a dark corner and a young couple on the dance floor sort of melted into each other, mouths together, the guy's big mitt on the girl's plump little ass, the other holding her hand and pressed against her boobs. The Georgie Porgie of old might have cut in on the young stud, he could still show the little cunt a trick or two, but he had taken enough knocks for the night. ". . . And each night as I wander through the graveyard, darkness hides me where I kneel to pray . . ." Holy shit. They're getting off on lines like that? When they parted mouths long enough to go into deep-gaze mode, Georgie recognized the girl: Bonali's hotpants daughter. The one at the bank. The boy, who was at least a foot taller, looked familiar, but he couldn't place him. Everybody around here looked familiar. It was a kind of curse.

Even the bartender turned out to be a brat from the neighborhood, a kid who was in grade school when Georgie was in high school. Only he wasn't a kid anymore either. Beardy. Already developing a gut. "White dove will mourn in sorrow," the hayseed whined, and Georgie, though suffering a deep grief of his own, decided if there was one more fucking chorus, he was going to trash the place. Gratefully, the song came to an end, though the lovers stayed in their swaying clinch on the dance floor, grinding away softly. The girl spotted Georgie past the boy's elbow (Georgie winked, she ducked) and whispered something to the boy and they left, and the older couple soon followed them out. The woman was either a whore or somebody's wife. If he'd come here earlier, he might have made out. It was when everyone was out of the place that, looking around, you realized how filthy it was.

The singer came over to the bar, to try to cadge a drink maybe, and Georgie told him flat out he hated hillbilly music. "Go fuck a horse," he said. The guy only grinned faintly out of the side of his mouth and shrugged and said he didn't like it much either but it was all he could do except drink and split the beaver. "Know a better way to make some bread?" "Well, I been looking. But no." That eased things, and though neither could afford to buy the other a drink, they ended up trading tales, leaning there on the bar, Georgie finding himself telling the truth for a change about his fucked-up family and fucked-up life, while the singer, who introduced himself as Duke (Georgie gave him his Italian name, just to let him know where he was coming from), told him about the shit life of the country music road circuit, and the even shittier life of the bush leagues. He said, when asked, he used to throw a little, and Georgie said he used to hit a little but could never stay sober enough to go pro. Maybe just being strangers helped. Georgie even got around to telling about the girl who had been killed, the girl who was, he only realized this just now, the true love of his life. "One thing bout country music," Duke said, "is they got a song for ever damn thing that ever went wrong. They ain't many different tunes, but some words is better'n others." "And some words are worse," Georgie said and asked him why he was singing that awful mommy and daddy graveyard *merda* when he came in. "The girl ast for it. It was the third time I'd done 'White Dove' for the moony little thing tonight. Probly has sumthin to do with the first night she got laid. Most usually does." Georgie felt warm enough toward Duke by then to ask him if he'd like to join him on a run to Waterton, go give the dog a bone, but Duke said it was still too early, he had to stay on until midnight in case anyone came in. "But I'll be around. Got no place to go. Drop in agin."

The fat unseasonal snow is still falling in thick clots as Georgie, hunched over the steering wheel, pulls out of the motel parking lot. After the warm day, it is melting as it falls, though it is a nuisance without windwhield wipers. Probably ought to forget it. Way he's feeling, he may not be able to get it up anyway. But it's his last chance while he still has wheels. Lem will be pissed off enough about him keeping the car overnight, especially since he won't be buying it, so no chance for seconds, it's tonight or who knows. Another thing he should have picked up on his rounds, he considers, was a pack of rubbers. Could have asked little Miss No-Tits in the drugstore this morning to go fetch them for him, telling her to be sure to get the right size. If she'd told him there was only one size, he'd have asked her what she was doing after work. But then she probably would have called her boss and had him thrown out. Would have ratted on him for stealing the centerfold.

"Goddamn it, Ruby," Georgie asks, "what's all this for? If life is such shit, why do we go on living it?" He answers himself: because you're scared not to, asshole. And because there's always hope for one more piece of tail. He pats the dashboard (he's glad he didn't turn her in, he'd be all alone without her), his nose at the windshield, trying to see through it, thinking about dying. Or rather, trying not to, but unable to keep it out. Where was Marcella Bruno killed? On this road? No, out by the mine. "What's it like, Ruby? What happens when you die?" The Waterton road is empty, almost spookily so. Nobody else fool enough to be out. No risk of hitting anybody, but it is easy to lose the road altogether. Maybe he should never let Ruby go. Just drive through Waterton and keep on rolling. Go somewhere warm, make some money, fix her up. Whitewall tires. Radio. Leopard-skin seat covers, soft to stroke. Then he sees it, a small dark thing scurrying across the snowy road out in front of him with glowing ruby dots where its eyes are. It startles him with its sudden challenging presence. Raccoon maybe. Cat. Squirrel. Whatever. It's dead meat. Georgie floors the accelerator. No pickup at all. If anything the old girl slows down. He knows if he can hit this thing, everything will be all right. "Come on, sweetheart, throw your hips into it! You can do it!" His fingers are snapping at the wheel as if working pinball flippers, his whole body twisting and pushing. The animal has frozen. He's got it! And then, just as he's about to score, Ruby starts to fishtail, he whips the wheel back and forth trying to straighten her out, everything is suddenly spinning around him, trees that weren't there wheeling about in front of his face, and he braces for the impact.

The whumping crumple of metal is not as loud as he'd expected, though in the silence that follows it echoes loudly in his mind. He has been thrown around a bit, but he's OK. He switches off the motor, leaves the lights on, crawls out. He has wrapped Ruby around a light pole on the passenger side, the old girl nearly cloven in half at the waist, her rear end at right angles to the rest of her. "Oh, baby. I'm sorry." He is. It is the saddest thing that has happened in a long sad day. He's even crying a little. For her. For himself. He walks around her in the falling snow, whispering his apologies. His farewells. He crawls back in on the driver's side to rescue the centerfold, looking a bit the worse for wear. He kisses the steering wheel, getting out. He has a long walk back to face. But first he clambers up on Ruby's hood and, kneeling there in pious homage, lowers his pants and, using the centerfold's taunting raised ass to arouse himself, jerks off on Ruby's cracked windshield, fantasizing a loving blow job ("Marcella! I love you!" he whispers as he comes). His final blessing. He wipes himself with the centerfold, no doubt inking his dick colorfully, and, a mile or so down the snowy road toward town, tosses it in the ditch.

Some Silly Thing
John Ashbery

It's so confusing these days,
what with the activity and the fuss, flurry,
fluster, what have you. I'm in sympathy more
with the elves and you, good, hospitable
demons we can cherish with. At least
in those times was the flour and salt of difference,
liquor of misunderstanding the baby's presence
withdrew. Some of us were born fooling around
to be captured later in life and classified.
More of us played the fingerboard. Then there were the oval tops
spinning away as though their lives depended on it.
What other streets made such an impression
and why? Why did some stand out or read
as darker while others registered as pale and correct?
The truth is nobody knows what is happening anymore.
I for one am not sure it's a mistake
to go crackling on like this, with parents in a tizzy
and royal figurines registering disapproval.
What if there never was an infinite series
bisecting one's own orchard? Would that help?
And if the silent reading and the listening coincided
in a bellicose fraction this side of miscellany, would
they be confiscated any sooner? To the contrary, I believe
we are just this side of an enormous breakthrough,
that the captain knows about us and is on his way over.

Similarly in the last century you would see feedback
degenerating into laissez-faire. It was nice for those who lived then,
but few would want to be part of the rival solution
even if it left them breathless and on the edge of a forest
in a gothic novel. And then there was all the turning out all right
to be commandeered and somehow exploited for one's own narrative
off of whose dregs we are still living today.

Wilde said that history is merely gossip.
To that add that portraiture is what a dressmaker's dummy feels
about today's hiatus or harvest, whenever bands of light
or shadow have taken over. Honestly, we're good with that.
It's like dawn in this globular attic room, one's inmost thoughts
to be breathed upon and revived like flowers, again and again.

Elegy: Or to Begin Again
Ann Lauterbach

—In memory of Katherine Mester Luzzi

1.

Way over in the particularities of evening
so many missing it seems we are alone at
last, you and whatever I am thinking about you,
not a happy thought, but not indifferent.
And that other world? The image
had receded under the angry
claims of the image, and in this redundancy
we stopped to buy apples, and to speak of the dead.
The face of the dead came into view
as a consolation, and the apples seemed
a magnitude of form, brightly gathered, a crowd.
These are impossible things to say clearly because
the proper name has less than accurate
attributes: so little had been copied from life.
But think now of Seurat. Think of *Child in White*
rendered as absent agitations of a crayon. The end.

2.

Or to begin again
gold touches the back of her neck. It spawns
a crest, a brief tattoo. She moves
into and beyond
shedding its improvisation, its effect.
The effect of gold is bright heat. She
seeks cover in a passing cloud, a passing leaf. Gold
moves off into the landscape, touching a wasp, a truck,
a stone. Down at the end of the path, a head
appears as that of a man, riveted to a wall.
Gold moves off and vanishes
as night ignites a halo
around the head at the end of the passage.
This is the assemblage of the nevertheless,
its sudden rupture. I thought of something else.
I thought of a stranger seated in a tent. The end.

3.

Or to begin again
I had wanted a location but had become embattled
in a zone of supposition and indirection.
The emergency is ink-stained.
A temporary orange blocks the view.
An ambulance is climbing slowly uphill.
Returning to the lost, a sound increased
over whatever exemption had been founded on passage.
Around and around they went, the metallic children,
carving an arena into the climate, an
erasure that would become a road, repeating the turn,
learning its rhythm in the denuded wood.
He began, *I sought, this time, to approach him.*
I thought then of the witness, of the body's carriage
moving downstream on a barge, and the small
red tug like a living toy, riveted to its mass. The end.

4.

Or to begin again
in the miraculous scale of the small nouns,
their mischief and potential.
Auden imagining the good at a sidewalk café.
Oppen staring into the face of a stranger,
into the face of his beloved Mary.
We want to be here.
I was thinking of table settings: folded napkins,
polished ware, sparkling glasses.
And the prayer? What was the prayer?
What if everything had slowed
and she had chosen to wait, to forget her chore?
There were, I recall, ripples of violence
that caught on twigs and snapped wires.
Words were spoken from too far away to be heard.
There was a blind spot, a stained cloth. The end.

5.

Or to begin again
suspended above the habitat, bees
dying in their boxes, salmon
desiccated in their nets, flight on flight,
origin marked by tracks in mud
and the river newly revealed
through naked bark
like a silver coin skipped across time
the migrations of time
the small noun time.
The world fallen from its skin
into the airy wild, abode of infinite
contractions, this in which it is, adhering.
A swarm and a nub, tumbleweed shadowed on ice.
The facts encroaching on intimate constraint.
These could be a hand, a voice. The end.

6.

Or to begin again
an accident disperses the law. Thrown there,
there. Less than forgotten
in the usual ditch of leaves, weeds, caps,
a massive gold afloat in the autumnal sky.
At whose approval? The call stuffed in a sock?
Faces of the war dead in a signature farewell:
boy, boy, boy, girl, boy, boy, girl
picturing evidence, picturing silence,
and the chorus ready to respond: *holy, holy, holy,*
to awaken the dead but not in the language of the dead.
Perhaps a finite contraction,
the child practicing to fly overhead, to drop the bag
on the dusty road below, to watch it spill into flames from on
high, from a mobile perch
cruising through its episodes of grief. The end.

7.

Or to begin again
some got lucky, came rushing
toward the giant appeasement of the given.
Singing along with the anthem
they distributed coupons to the rest
to redeem, solace for those who do not
begin but stay back in the infrastructure
of the singular: what you said, what I said, before
the fact. Were we to be among those to be counted
one by one, like days? Greeted by our host?
In which language? And what were we meant to
carry away, down the road a bit, into the rest?
Light strays across the dry grasses.
The arm lifts, the head turns.
A gathering, an image, a dispersal.
In whichever order. The end.

8.

Or to begin again: *now now*
birdlike, repeated,
the noise of nearness,
yet without either body or mouth.
In the mind's eye, a wall
painted robin's egg blue
behind Paul Klee's dirty yellow circus.
Nothing noticed, nothing gained.
A clown on his head, a dog, a ball.
And yet the acquiescent rain,
and yet the passage
of a massive chorus
through the fictive pilings of a cage.
Comest thou now? Comest thou now?
Repeated, birdlike, from over there.
Look up and then look away. The end.

9.

Or to begin again: virtuous moon
appears to be taking a star for a walk; I
cannot see a leash, but the star
is obedient. Together they traverse
the night sky. It is winter
and the ground below is a dull shell.
The secular ghost is chastised
in its moody camp; it fears ice
as it fears the dawn when the moon
will have vanished, star in tow.
It knows when things begin to melt
there will be a forgetting and, in the wan face
of the beloved, the stigma of desire.
Fuck desire, says the ghost, only
no one can hear and so no one can answer.
Fuck desire, it repeats, birdlike, at dawn. The end.

10.

Or to begin again: a gift is in the offing.
Something a sparrow might drop
on its way, something sent
across the boundaries of time.
Why is the deck at a tilt
so that the day and its objects
might slip off the edge? The boy
with the fiddle, his
dark brows flat, eyes recessed
into the harbor of play:
four strings, taut bow, the arc
of elaborations, note by note, his wrist
traversing their wake. Sound, what is sound?
The day has its spelling, the night also.
Tell me what she heard in the splashing instant.
Say the last kiss. The end.

11.

Or to begin again: still no sign
in the field of negation:
all appears to be ordinary.
Sea birds depicted above the sea,
the pretty couple dancing,
the buzzing saw,
evening clouds assembled, mountains dark.
Yes, but the page is not blank.
Yes, but the sun's pallor
consumes as it rolls
across the heavens, dragging
the head of the beheaded despot,
the embattled fishermen
combing the sea with nets,
the girl with a dove in her suitcase.
I had wanted to count the steps. The end.

12.

Or to begin again having quoted, inscribed,
having changed a few words
along the way, a gesture toward
the gaps between is not, is, is not.
Eve gives me a map traced on thin paper
with a red dot. The boys walk along the road,
their hoods up, their speech riddled.
The red dot is where they were headed
in the year of the snake. We decided
against perfection. We said
perfection is a morbid
judgment against the living.
The girl with red hair was imperfect.
They did not come with only a suitcase on a boat,
Eve said. The Dutch, I said, made paintings
of nature arranged as perfect death. The end.

13.

Or to begin again: thisness abbreviated:
margins, earshot. Have no herald, no scope
under such bearings, only an instruction
to carry on under the new doctrine's law.
A friend is known to speak
about the difficulty of understanding.
Could he climb higher to see better
as from a distant star
occluded beyond ever knowing?
Now obey this.
The steps lead nowhere, so only
the small bird, hiding under boughs, escapes
the mirage of escape.
Fidelity ruptures at the core.
Over there, where he hurls
his oath at the corpse of belonging. The end.

14.

Or to begin again: lavish permission,
ribbons placed back in their bag,
pulled through the sleeves
of the prisoner's coat, the suicide's
gun. The Arab men
are playing backgammon in the courtyard.
The preacher's voice fills the chapel
with iconographies of faith.
Our tears turn to ice
and the mourners stop along the path,
informal now, unretrieved, makeshift.
So that with nothing held back we sigh,
beyond time, for that green pasture where time
stands still. Does not. Does. Go back
before the beginning, before
a promise was made. The end.

15.

Or to begin again: chronicle of thaw
and the sitting hawk
and the tilting stones.
The place a
saturated edge
moving quickly along the road
up over the arc of bridge, flag, sun,
and the hanging man. Fact
dissolves into fact, proximate to
the slowest economy, the most forbidden dream.
The girl enters knowledge.
You can see her on the trail
of the smallest bug, the most inglorious weed.
We join her in the aftermath of promise
where she is studying the tides.
World without image dilates. The end.

16.

Way over in the particularities of evening
gold touches the back of her neck. It spawns
in a zone of supposition and indirection.
Auden imagining the good at a sidewalk café.
Origin marked by tracks in mud.
At whose approval? The call stuffed in a sock?
Begin but stay back in the infrastructure
nothing noticed, nothing gained
as it fears the dawn when the moon
recessed into the harbor of play:
the head of the beheaded despot
judgment against the living
the mirage of escape
stands still. Does not. Does. Go back
where she is studying the tides.
Go back to the beginning. The end.

NOTES ON CONTRIBUTORS

ROBERT ANTONI is the author of *Divina Trace* (Overlook), *Blessed Is the Fruit* (Henry Holt), *My Grandmother's Erotic Folktales* (Grove), and *Carnival* (Grove). His forthcoming book is a historical novel entitled *TES: The Tropical Emigration Society in England and Trinidad, W.I.*

RAE ARMANTROUT's recent book, *Next Life* (Wesleyan), was a *New York Times* Notable Book of 2007. She teaches at the University of California, San Diego.

JOHN ASHBERY's most recent books of poetry are *A Worldly Country* and *Notes from the Air: Selected Later Poems* (both Ecco/HarperCollins). His translation of Pierre Reverdy's *Haunted House* was recently published by Black Square/ Brooklyn Rail. The first volume of his *Collected Poems* will be released this fall by the Library of America. Since 1990 he has been Charles P. Stevenson Jr. Professor of Languages and Literature at Bard College.

MARTINE BELLEN is the author of several collections of poetry. Presently, she's collaborating with David Rosenbaum on an opera/nonopera entitled *AH!*

CHARLES BERNSTEIN's most recent books are *Girly Man* (University of Chicago), *Shadowtime* (Green Integer), and *Republics of Reality: 1975–1995*. *Content's Dream: Essays 1975–1984* (Northwestern) and *Controlling Interests* (Roof) have been reissued recently. He teaches at the University of Pennsylvania.

MEI-MEI BERSSENBRUGGE recently published *I Love Artists, New and Selected Poems* (University of California) and *Concordance* (Kelsey Street), a collaboration with artist Kiki Smith. She lives in New York City and New Mexico.

BRIAN BOOKER's stories have appeared in *The Antioch Review, Tin House,* and *TriQuarterly,* among other journals. His collection, *The Sleeping Sickness,* was a finalist in the 2005 Iowa Short Fiction Awards.

CAN XUE's novel *Five Spice Street,* translated by Chen Zeping and Karen Gernant, will be published by Yale University Press in the fall. A collection of her short fiction, *Blue Light in the Sky and Other Stories,* was published by New Directions in 2006.

MARY CAPONEGRO's new collection of stories and novellas will be published by Coffee House Press in 2009.

JONATHAN CARROLL is the author of fifteen novels. His latest, *The Ghost in Love,* the opening chapter of which first appeared in *Conjunctions,* will be published in October by Farrar, Straus and Giroux.

CHEN ZEPING, professor of linguistics at Fujian Teachers' University, has published numerous books and articles in the field of Chinese dialects.

SANDRA CISNEROS is a novelist, poet, short story writer, essayist, and founder of Macondo, an association of socially engaged writers. Among her many books are *My Wicked Wicked Ways* (Knopf), *The House on Mango Street*, and *Woman Hollering Creek* (both Vintage). She lives in San Antonio, Texas.

PETER COLE's new collection of poems, *Things on Which I've Stumbled*, is forthcoming this fall from New Directions. Recently named a MacArthur Fellow, he lives in Jerusalem.

ROBERT COOVER's newest work of fiction, *Noir*, will be published in Paris this spring. "Red-Hot Ruby" is a chapter from his current work in progress, a sequel to his first novel, *The Origin of the Brunists*.

EDWIDGE DANTICAT is the author of several books, including *Breath, Eyes, Memory*, which was an Oprah Book Club selection; *Krik! Krak!* (both Vintage), a National Book Award Finalist; *The Farming of Bones* (Penguin), an American Book Award winner; and, most recently, *Brother, I'm Dying* (Knopf), a memoir.

RIKKI DUCORNET's newest collection of fiction, *The One Marvelous Thing*, is forthcoming in October from Dalkey Archive Press. Many of these stories, including the one in this issue, first appeared in *Conjunctions*.

The long poem project of RACHEL BLAU DuPLESSIS is collected in *Torques: Drafts 58–76* (Salt Publishing) as well as in *Drafts 1–38, Toll* (Wesleyan) and *Drafts 39–57, Pledge, with Draft Unnumbered: Précis* (also from Salt). In 2006, she published *Blue Studios: Poetry and its Cultural Work* on gender and poetics, along with a reprint of the groundbreaking *The Pink Guitar: Writing as Feminist Practice* (both University of Alabama).

JULIA ELLIOTT's fiction has appeared in *Best American Fantasy, The Georgia Review, Puerto Del Sol, The Mississippi Review*, previous issues of *Conjunctions*, and other magazines. She lives in Columbia, South Carolina, where she sings and plays keyboards for the band Grey Egg.

BRIAN EVENSON is the author of seven books of fiction, most recently *The Open Curtain* (Coffee House). A new collection of stories, *Fugue State*, is forthcoming in 2009. He lives and works in Providence, Rhode Island, where he directs Brown University's Literary Arts Program.

THALIA FIELD has published *Point and Line, Incarnate: Story Material* (both New Directions), and *Ululu (Clown Shrapnel)* (Coffee House).

EDUARDO GALEANO is one of Latin America's foremost writers, as well as a distinguished journalist and historian. The winner of the first Lannan Foundation Cultural Freedom Prize in 1998, he is the author of *Voice of Time* and *Upside Down* (Metropolitan); *Walking Words, We Say No, The Book of Embraces*, and *The Memory of Fire* trilogy (Norton); *Soccer in Sun and Shadow* (Verso); and *Open Veins of Latin America* (Monthly Review Press). He lives in Montevideo, Uruguay.

WILLIAM H. GASS's most recent book is a collection of essays, *A Temple of Texts* (Knopf).

KAREN GERNANT is professor emerita of Chinese history and divides her time between homes in Oregon and China. Translations by Chen Zeping and Karen Gernant have also appeared in *Manoa, Words Without Borders, Black Warrior Review*, and *Ninth Letter*.

PETER GIZZI's recent books include *The Outernationale* and *Some Values of Landscape and Weather*, both from Wesleyan. He currently serves as the poetry editor for *The Nation*.

MATTHEW HAMITY is a recent graduate of Columbia University's MFA program.

LYN HEJINIAN's most recently published books of poetry are *The Fatalist* (Omnidawn), *A Border Comedy* (Granary Books), and *My Life in the Nineties* (Shark). Forthcoming in 2008 are a collection of poetry collaborations between her and Jack Collom titled *Situations, Sings* (Adventures in Poetry) and *Sage/Circus* (Omnidawn). She is also one of the ten authors of *The Grand Piano: An Experiment in Collective Autobiography* (Mode A), which, when finished, will run to ten volumes.

SHELLEY JACKSON is the author of *Half Life* (HarperCollins), *The Melancholy of Anatomy* (Anchor Books), hypertexts including the classic *Patchwork Girl* (Eastgate Systems), several children's books, and *Skin*, a story published in tattoos on the skin of 2,095 volunteers. With artist Christine Hill she is co-founder of the Interstitial Library, Circulating Collection. Her Web site can be found at www.ineradicablestain.com.

Among ROBERT KELLY's most recent books of poetry are *Threads* (First Intensity) and *May Day* (Parsifal). A novel, *The Book from the Sky*, is forthcoming from North Atlantic.

PAUL LA FARGE has published two novels: *The Artist of the Missing* and *Haussmann, or the Distinction* (both Farrar, Straus and Giroux). His third book, *The Facts of Winter*, was published by McSweeney's in 2005.

ANN LAUTERBACH's collection of essays, *The Night Sky*, has recently been published in paperback by Penguin. She is Schwab Professor of Literature at Bard College and co-chair of writing in the Milton Avery Graduate School of the Arts.

RICHARD "BROWN" LETHEM lives and paints in Berwick, Maine. Aucocisco Gallery in Portland shows his work, and he is on the faculty of the University of Southern Maine.

BEN MARCUS is the author of *The Age of Wire and String* (Dalkey Archive), *Notable American Women* (Vintage), and *The Father Costume* (Artspace). He has recently published stories, essays, and reviews in *Harper's, Bookforum*, and *The New York Times*.

VALERIE MARTIN's most recent novel is *Trespass*, from Doubleday (Nan A. Talese). A new novel, *My Emotions*, is scheduled for publication in 2009, also from Doubleday.

CAROLE MASO, author of nine books, is currently working on a novel, *The Bay of Angels*, and a collection of stories, *Mother & Child*. She teaches at Brown University.

CHARLES McLEOD's fiction has appeared in *CutBank*, *The Gettysburg Review*, *The Iowa Review*, and *Third Coast*. He was a writing fellow at the Fine Arts Work Center in Provincetown and a Steinbeck Fellow at San Jose State University.

EDIE MEIDAV is the author of *Crawl Space* (Farrar, Straus and Giroux), *The Far Field: A Novel of Ceylon* (Houghton Mifflin), and the forthcoming *The Beauty of Choice*. She is the recipient of a Bard Fiction Prize, a Kafka Award, and a *Village Voice* Writers on the Verge Award.

RICK MOODY is the author, most recently, of *Right Livelihoods: Three Novellas* (Little, Brown). He is currently at work on a new novel.

BRADFORD MORROW is the founding editor of *Conjunctions*. He is the author of *Come Sunday*, *Trinity Fields*, *Giovanni's Gift*, and *Ariel's Crossing* (all Penguin). The recipient of a 2007 Guggenheim Fellowship for fiction, he also received the 2007 PEN/Nora Magid Award for excellence in literary editing. He is currently at work on a new novel, *The Prague Sonatas*, and teaches at Bard College.

JAMES MORROW's most recent novel is *The Philosopher's Apprentice* (Morrow). He is also the author of the postmodern historical epic *The Last Witchfinder* (Harper Perennial) as well as the Godhead Trilogy (Harcourt). From the book *The Philosopher's Apprentice*, by James Morrow. Copyright © 2008 by James Morrow. Reprinted by permission of William Morrow, an Imprint of Harper-Collins Publishers.

ANDREW MOSSIN's new collection of poetry, *The Veil*, was published by Singing Horse Press, which also published his book *The Epochal Body*. He is currently revising a manuscript of critical prose, *New Americans: Readings in Masculine Subjectivity, Literary Partnering, and Poetic Form*, and is at work on a book of documentary poetry.

NAM LE's debut collection of short stories, *The Boat*, is newly published by Knopf. He is the fiction editor of the *Harvard Review*.

JOYCE CAROL OATES, a frequent contributor to *Conjunctions*, is the author, most recently, of the novel *The Gravedigger's Daughter* and the story collection *Wild Nights!* (both from Ecco).

STEPHEN O'CONNOR is the author of *Rescue* (Harmony Books), *Will My Name Be Shouted Out?* (Touchstone), and *Orphan Trains* (University of Chicago). He teaches at Columbia and Sarah Lawrence.

PETER ORNER is the author of *The Second Coming of Mavala Shikongo* (Little, Brown) and *Esther Stories* (Houghton Mifflin). Among his many awards are the Rome Prize, the Bard Fiction Prize, and a Guggenheim Fellowship. He recently completed editing a book of oral histories called *Underground America*, forthcoming this spring from McSweeney's.

RICHARD POWERS is the author of nine novels. His most recent book, *The Echo Maker* (Farrar, Straus and Giroux), won the National Book Award. A MacArthur Fellow, he currently teaches in the creative writing MFA program at the University of Illinois at Urbana-Champaign.

JOAN RETALLACK edited and wrote the introduction to *Gertrude Stein: Selections*, just out from the University of California, which also published *The Poethical Wager*. Her books of poetry include *Memnoir* (Post-Apollo), *How to Do Things with Words* (Sun & Moon), and *Afterrimages* (Wesleyan). She is John D. and Catherine T. MacArthur Professor of Humanities at Bard College.

DONALD REVELL is the author of ten collections of poetry, including, most recently, *A Thief of Strings* and *Pennyweight Windows: New & Selected Poems* (both from Alice James Books).

JOANNA SCOTT's most recent books are a novel, *Liberation*, and a collection of stories, *Everybody Loves Somebody* (both Little, Brown/Back Bay Books).

REGINALD SHEPHERD's most recent book of poems is *Fata Morgana* (University of Pittsburgh). He is also the author of *Orpheus in the Bronx: Essays on Identity, Politics, and the Freedom of Poetry* (University of Michigan) and editor of *Lyric Postmodernisms* (Counterpath).

CHRISTOPHER SORRENTINO's latest book is *American Tempura* (Nothing Moments Books), a collaboration with artist Derek Boshier and Counterspace, a Los Angeles design firm.

COLE SWENSEN is the author, most recently, of *Ours* (University of California). She is the recipient of a Guggenheim Fellowship, the San Francisco State Poetry Center Book Award, the National Poetry Series award, and the PEN USA Award in Translation. She is the co-editor of the anthology *American Hybrid*, due out from Norton in fall 2008, and this year's writer in residence at the Beinecke Library at Yale.

FREDERIC TUTEN has published five novels: *Tintin in the New World, Tallien: A Brief Romance, Van Gogh's Bad Café* (all reprinted by Black Classic Press), *The Adventures of Mao on the Long March* (New Directions Classics), and, most recently, *The Green Hour* (Norton).

DIANE WILLIAMS's most recent book is *It Was Like My Trying to Have a Tender-Hearted Nature* (FC_2). She is the founding editor of the literary annual *NOON*.

Jeffry DeShell

Alexandra Chasin

Diane Williams

Pamela Ryder

Steve Katz

Fiction Collective Two

Publishing some of the most
exciting writers working today
fc2.org

In the Footsteps of
Conjunctions:39
The New Wave Fabulists

PARASPHERES

EXTENDING BEYOND THE SPHERES
OF LITERARY AND GENRE FICTION

Fabulist and New Wave Fabulist Stories By

L. Timmel Duchamp, Rikki Ducornet, Brian Evenson,
Jeffrey Ford, Alasdair Gray, Karen Heuler, Laird Hunt,
Shelley Jackson, Tom La Farge, Janice Law, Ursula Le Guin,
Leena Krohn, William Luvaas, Mary Mackey,
Michael Moorcock, Bradford Morrow, Laura Mullen,
Kim Stanley Robinson, Rudy Rucker, Ira Sher,
Randall Silvis, Jeff VanderMeer, Mark Wallace, & More

And Coming Fall 2008
ParaSpheres 2
& ParaSpheres Online

www.paraspheres.com

Burning Deck Spring 2008

Cyrus Console:
BRIEF UNDER WATER

This first book is a sequence of 55 short passages that uses prose narrative as a design element in a larger lyric structure. The title refers to Kafka's 1919 *Brief an den Vater*, reflecting a struggle with the notion of literary inheritance.

"terrific....The sensory detail of the writing, not surrealistic, not plot-oriented, is not even with the sense of 'leading anywhere' but accumulating both detail and expansion at once, opening a floating, fascinating, sometimes apparently violent yet detached terrain, as if not the author's psyche...but the world itself... seen from at once extreme and mundane edges." —Leslie Scalapino

Poetry, 64 pages, offset, smyth-sewn, ISBN13: 978-1-886224-87-2, original pbk. $14

Heather C. Akerberg
DWELLING

The poems of *Dwelling* investigate, musically and with "bended" syntax, the issue of form—in body, home, and poem. They ask questions like: Is a "home" a series of spatial or cognitive experiences? Is it shape, architectural elements, the experiences and interactions transpired there, the objects contained in, or the language ascribed to it? Is a "home" just a backdrop for events or is it another body, inside which is found the stuff of self, a body to be read like a text?
Born and raised in the Midwest, Akerberg lives in Omaha, Neb. *Dwelling* is her first book.

Poetry, 64 pages, offset, smyth-sewn, ISBN13: 978-1-886224-89-6, original pbk. $14

Caroline Dubois
YOU ARE THE BUSINESS

[Série d'Ecriture, No.20; translated from the French by Cole Swensen]
C'est toi le business uses an eerie cadence to examine the construction of identity in a media-saturated world. Focusing on icons of cult films like *Blade Runner*, she develops a haunting collage of overlay and echo populated by unsettling twins (a "sister," a clone, a verbal stutter), which evokes the doubles with which a society based on representation invests us. The book is poetry in its linguistic freedom, film criticism in its thematic aspects, prose in its physical shape. But it always pushes language toward new sensual territory.

Poetry, 104 pages, offset, smyth-sewn, ISBN13: 978-1-886224-86-5, original pbk. $14

Lisa Jarnot
SOME OTHER KIND OF MISSION

again available

Jarnot's 1st book is a mock-epic of the everyday as it might be discovered through juxta-positions of public and private information.

"*Some Other Kind of Mission* suggests that Language Poetry may be mutating, back to the modernism of Stein and Joyce, having been permanently inflected (or deflected) by a late twentieth-century sharpness and exasperation.... These are haunting, perplexing narratives of the inenarrable." —John Ashbery, *TLS*

"a turbulence-model of language, context-laden and yet future." —Sherry Brennan, *American Book Review*

Poems & visual pieces, 112 pages, offset, smyth-sewn, ISBN13: 978-1-886224-12-4, pbk $14

Orders: Small Press Distribution: 1-800/869-7553, www.spdbooks.org. In Europe: www.hpress.no
www.burningdeck.com

Black Clock

Aimee Bender · Tom Carson · Samuel R. Delany · Don DeLillo
Brian Evenson · Janet Fitch · Rebecca Goldstein · Maureen Howard
Shelly Jackson · Heidi Julavits · Miranda July · Jonathan Lethem
Ben Marcus · Greil Marcus · Rick Moody · Geoffrey O'Brien
Richard Powers · Joanna Scott · Darcey Steinke · Susan Straight
LynneTillman · David L. Ulin · Michael Ventura
William T. Vollmann · David Foster Wallace · Carlos Ruiz Zafon

Edited by Steve Erickson

Coming Soon Issue 9

www.blackclock.org · subscribe online

Published by CalArts in association with the MFA Writing Program

Photo Credit: Christopher Alexander, momentaryexistence.com

NOON

A LITERARY ANNUAL

1324 LEXINGTON AVENUE   PMB 298   NEW YORK   NEW YORK   10128

EDITION PRICE $12 DOMESTIC $17 FOREIGN

The Jack Kerouac School of Disembodied Poetics

Summer Writing Program 2008

Weekly Workshops • June 16–July 13 • Boulder, CO

WEEK ONE: June 16–22
The Wall: Troubling of Race, Class, Economics, Gender and Imagination
Samuel R. Delany, Marcella Durand, Laird Hunt, Brenda Iijima, Bhanu Kapil, Miranda Mellis, Akilah Oliver, Maureen Owen, Margaret Randall, Max Regan, Joe Richey, Roberto Tejada and Julia Seko (printshop)

WEEK TWO: June 23–29
Elective Affinities: Against the Grain: Writerly Utopias
Will Alexander, Sinan Antoon, Jack Collom, Linh Dinh, Anselm Hollo, Daniel Kane, Douglas Martin, Harryette Mullen, Laura Mullen, Alice Notley, Elizabeth Robinson, Eleni Sikelianos, Orlando White and Charles Alexander (printshop)

WEEK THREE: June 30–July 6
Activism, Environmentalism: The Big Picture
Amiri Baraka, Lee Ann Brown, Junior Burke, George Evans, Bobbie Louise Hawkins, Lewis MacAdams, Eileen Myles, Kristin Prevallet, Selah Saterstrom, Stacy Szymaszek, Anne Waldman, Daisy Zamora and Karen Randall (printshop)

WEEK FOUR: July 7–13
Performance, Community: Policies of the USA in the Larger World
Dodie Bellamy, Rikki Ducornet, Brian Evenson, Raymond Federman, Forrest Gander, Bob Holman, Pierre Joris, Ilya Kaminsky, Kevin Killian, Anna Moschovakis, Sawako Nakayasu, Anne Tardos, Steven Taylor, Peter & Donna Thomas (printshop)

**Credit and noncredit programs available
Poetry • Fiction • Translation
Letterpress Printing**

Naropa
UNIVERSITY

For more information on workshops,
visit *www.naropa.edu/swp*. To request a catalog,
call **303-245-4600** or email *swpr@naropa.edu*.

Keeping the world safe for poetry since 1974

DELILLO FIEDLER GASS PYNCHON
University of Delaware Press
Collections on Contemporary Masters

UNDERWORDS
Perspectives on Don
DeLillo's *Underworld*

Edited by Joseph Dewey, Steven G. Kellman, and Irving Malin

Essays by Jackson R. Bryer, David Cowart, Kathleen Fitzpatrick, Joanne Gass, Paul Gleason, Donald J. Greiner, Robert McMinn, Thomas Myers, Ira Nadel, Carl Ostrowski, Timothy L. Parrish, Marc Singer, and David Yetter

$39.50

LESLIE FIEDLER
AND AMERICAN
CULTURE

Edited by Steven G. Kellman and Irving Malin

Essays by John Barth, Robert Boyers, James M. Cox, Joseph Dewey, R.H.W. Dillard, Geoffrey Green, Irving Feldman, Leslie Fiedler, Susan Gubar, Jay L. Halio, Brooke Horvath, David Ketterer, R.W.B. Lewis, Sanford Pinsker, Harold Schechter, Daniel Schwarz, David R. Slavitt, Daniel Walden, and Mark Royden Winchell

$36.50

INTO *THE TUNNEL*
Readings of Gass's
Novel

Edited by Steven G. Kellman and Irving Malin

Essays by Rebecca Goldstein, Donald J. Greiner, Brooke Horvath, Marcus Klein, Jerome Klinkowitz, Paul Maliszewski, James McCourt, Arthur Saltzman, Susan Stewart, and Heide Ziegler

$35.00

PYNCHON AND
MASON & DIXON

Edited by Brooke Horvath and Irving Malin

Essays by Jeff Baker, Joseph Dewey, Bernard Duyfhuizen, David Foreman, Donald J. Greiner, Brian McHale, Clifford S. Mead, Arthur Saltzman, Thomas H. Schaub, David Seed, and Victor Strandberg

$39.50

ORDER FROM ASSOCIATED UNIVERSITY PRESSES
2010 Eastpark Blvd., Cranbury, New Jersey 08512
PH 609-655-4770 FAX 609-655-8366 E-mail AUP440@ aol.com

Novel Pictorial Noise

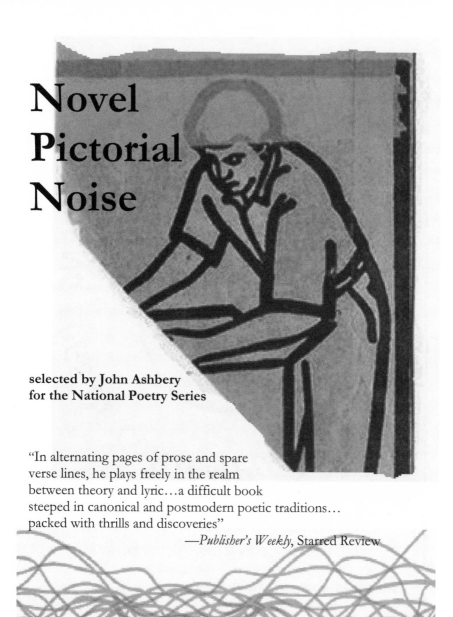

selected by John Ashbery
for the National Poetry Series

"In alternating pages of prose and spare
verse lines, he plays freely in the realm
between theory and lyric…a difficult book
steeped in canonical and postmodern poetic traditions…
packed with thrills and discoveries"
　　　　　　　　　—*Publisher's Weekly*, Starred Review

Noah Eli Gordon's new book * available in stores everywhere
Harper Perennial

ISBN-10: 0061257036 ISBN-13: 978-0061257032

Bard MFA

Since 1981 our summer MFA degree program has offered a non-traditional approach to the creative arts. Our emphasis on individual conferencing with faculty, school-wide interdisciplinary group conversation/critique, and a flexible schedule combine to both challenge the student and allow space for artistic growth.

Our Writing discipline emphasizes awareness of a variety of verbal, aural, and textual structures, and students develop an individual process of composition as well as a critical understanding of their field. Forms such as innovative poetry, short fiction, sound, and mixed-media writing are particularly well-suited to the structure and nature of the Bard MFA program.

2008 Writing faculty include:

Anselm Berrigan, co-chair	David Levi Strauss
Linh Dinh	Tracie Morris
Robert Fitterman	Leslie Scalapino
Paul La Farge	Fiona Templeton
Ann Lauterbach, co-chair	

Call or email us to schedule a summer visit, or check *www.bard.edu/mfa* for a schedule of upcoming information sessions.

Bard FICTION PRIZE

Bard College invites submissions for its annual Fiction Prize for young writers.

The Bard Fiction Prize is awarded annually to a promising, emerging writer who is a United States citizen aged 39 years or younger at the time of application. In addition to a monetary award of $30,000, the winner receives an appointment as writer-in-residence at Bard College for one semester without the expectation that he or she teach traditional courses. The recipient will give at least one public lecture and will meet informally with students.

To apply, candidates should write a cover letter describing the project they plan to work on while at Bard and submit a C.V., along with three copies of the published book they feel best represents their work. No manuscripts will be accepted.

Applications for the 2009 prize must be received by July 15, 2008. For further information about the Bard Fiction Prize, call 845-758-7087 or visit www.bard.edu/bfp. Applicants may also request information by writing to the Bard Fiction Prize, Bard College, Annandale-on-Hudson, NY 12504-5000.

Bard College PO Box 5000, Annandale-on-Hudson, NY 12504-5000

CONJUNCTIONS:46

SELECTED SUBVERSIONS

Essays on the
World at Large

Edited by
Rikki Ducornet,
Bradford Morrow,
and Robert Polito

Twenty-four essays that explore a cascade of human experi-
ence while rethinking the very nature of essay writing itself.
Features new work by John D'Agata, Joanna Scott, Geoffrey
O'Brien, Michael Logan, Diane Ackerman, Rick Moody,
Robin Hemley, Ned Rorem, Honor Moore, David Shields,
Forrest Gander, Rosamond Purcell, William H. Gass, Anne
Carson, John Crowley, Eliot Weinberger, Robert Harbison,
Sven Birkerts, Martine Bellen, Paul West, Fanny Howe,
Matthew Kirby, Kenneth Gross, and Shelley Jackson.
Includes a special portfolio, "Ten Unproduced Scenarios," by
The Quay Brothers.

CONJUNCTIONS
Edited by Bradford Morrow
Published by Bard College
Annandale-on-Hudson, NY 12504

To order, phone 845-758-1539
or visit www.conjunctions.com
$15.00

CONJUNCTIONS:47

TWENTY-FIFTH ANNIVERSARY ISSUE

Edited by
Bradford Morrow

This special Twenty-fifth Anniversary Issue celebrates a quarter century of innovative contemporary writing and features new work by some of the most distinguished voices of the day.

The issue presents new fiction, poetry, and essays by Jonathan Lethem, Ann Lauterbach, Jim Crace, Peter Gizzi, Joanna Scott, Valerie Martin, Robert Antoni, Lydia Davis, Robert Kelly, Howard Norman, Edie Meidav, Clark Coolidge, Marcella Durand, C. D. Wright, Christopher Sorrentino, Joyce Carol Oates, Reginald Shepherd, Rosmarie Waldrop, Elizabeth Robinson, Peter Dale Scott, William H. Gass, Micheline Aharonian Marcom, Can Xue, Martine Bellen, Marjorie Welish, Edmund White, Rikki Ducornet, Jonathan Carroll, Peter Straub, John Ashbery, Barbara Guest, Keith Waldrop, Maureen Howard, Lynne Tillman, Rick Moody, Julia Elliott, Rae Armantrout, Lyn Hejinian, Forrest Gander, Jessica Hagedorn, Brenda Coultas, Scott Geiger, Diane Williams, John Barth, and Will Self.

CONJUNCTIONS
Edited by Bradford Morrow
Published by Bard College
Annandale-on-Hudson, NY 12504

To order, phone 845-758-1539
or visit www.conjunctions.com
$15.00

CONJUNCTIONS:48

FACES OF DESIRE

Edited by
Bradford Morrow

Several dozen of contemporary literature's most provocative and adventurous writers explore the tricky terrain of desire in essays, fiction, poetry, and memoirs. Authors include Mary Gaitskill, H. G. Carrillo, Joyce Carol Oates, David Shields, Anne Tardos, Robert Kelly, Elizabeth Hand, Aimee Bender, Robert Olen Butler, Cole Swensen, Shena McAuliffe, Luc Sante, Kevin Magee, Mary Caponegro, Reginald Shepherd, John D'Agata, Siri Hustvedt, Jonathan Lethem, Chimamanda Ngozi Adichie, Will Self, Eleni Sikelianos, Lewis Warsh, Michael White, Rikki Ducornet, Andrew Mossin, Mei-mei Berssenbrugge, Paul West, Susan Steinberg, Donald Revell, Rebecca Seiferle, Tova Reich, Juliana Leslie, S. G. Miller, Brian Evenson, Carole Maso, and Frederic Tuten.

CONJUNCTIONS
Edited by Bradford Morrow
Published by Bard College
Annandale-on-Hudson, NY 12504

To order, phone 845-758-1539
or visit www.conjunctions.com
$15.00

CONJUNCTIONS:49

A WRITERS' AVIARY

SPECIAL FEATURE:
JOHN ASHBERY TRIBUTE

Edited by Bradford Morrow

A wide spectrum of new fiction, poetry, and essays about birds by writers from several continents, including Peter Orner, Howard Norman, Yannick Murphy, Anne Waldman, Tim Dee, Arthur Sze, Sylvia Legris, Merrill Gilfillan, Forrest Gander, Diane Ackerman, J'Lyn Chapman, D. E. Steward, Micaela Morrissette, Rick Moody, Eric Linsker, Nathaniel Tarn, Elizabeth Robinson, Maureen Howard, John Kinsella, C. D. Wright, David Shields, Melanie Rae Thon, Joseph Campana, William H. Gass, Martine Bellen, Catherine Imbriglio, and Sven Birkerts.

The issue also celebrates the distinguished half-century career of John Ashbery in a portfolio of essays co-edited by Peter Gizzi and Bradford Morrow addressing Ashbery's oeuvre, book by book. Contributors include Reginald Shepherd, Peter Straub, Charles Bernstein, Brian Evenson, Marjorie Welish, Ron Silliman, David Shapiro, Susan Stewart, Brenda Hillman, Kevin Killian, Ann Lauterbach, Rae Armantrout, Graham Foust, Eileen Myles, Jed Perl, Ben Lerner, Cole Swensen, Marcella Durand, Christian Hawkey, Anselm Berrigan, Joan Retallack, Richard Deming, Geoffrey O'Brien, Robert Kelly, James Longenbach, and Susan Wheeler. The portfolio also features rare early work by Ashbery as well as a portrait of the poet by Richard Avedon.

CONJUNCTIONS
Edited by Bradford Morrow
Published by Bard College
Annandale-on-Hudson, NY 12504

To order, phone 845-758-1539
or visit www.conjunctions.com
$15.00